Showing Signs of Violence

"A wonderful book, theoretically challenging, ethnographically rich, and exquisitely written. . . . At times it is lyrical and poignant; it is always a pleasure to read. Its brilliance lies in the way the author weaves together the aesthetics of ritual violence with the intrusions of history and the cultural politics of commemoration."

—Toby Alice Volkman, Ford Foundation

"At the very least, George shows us how productive language- and performance-centered ethnography can be. But there is much more to this study of disquieting human practices. Leaving behind 'explanations' that work when our rationalizations (evolutionary, functional, symbolic) are projected on them, this account convincingly argues that ritual violence needs to be understood as a historical phenomenon and 'problem.' Human history, though always distinctive, is, like freedom, indivisible; it is theirs as well as ours."

—Johannes Fabian, University of Amsterdam

"Fascinating and compelling. . . . Examines with great subtlety the cultural construction of violence, and in putting forward a notion of 'political affect' moves beyond prevailing ideas of emotion in ways that have great significance for anthropology and other fields as well."

—Benjamin Orlove, University of California, Davis

"A seductive analysis of headhunting and an arresting narrative as well. It places versions of 'local knowledge' on a wider stage of social and political forces, yet remains a well-focused and richly textured account of a single ritual."

—Janet Hoskins, University of Southern California

Showing Signs of Violence

The Cultural Politics
of a Twentieth-Century
Headhunting Ritual

Kenneth M. George

UNIVERSITY OF CALIFORNIA PRESS

Berkeley / Los Angeles / London

University of California Press
Berkeley and Los Angeles, California

University of California Press
London, England

Copyright © 1996 by The Regents of the University of California

Library of Congress Cataloging-in-Publication Data
George, Kenneth M., 1950–
    Showing signs of violence: the cultural politics of a twentieth-
century headhunting ritual / Kenneth M. George.
        p.   cm.
    Includes bibliographical references and index.
    ISBN 0–520–20041–1 (cloth: alk. paper).
    ISBN 0–520–20361–5 (pbk.: alk. paper)
    1. Rites and ceremonies—Indonesia—Bambang Region.
    2. Violence—Social aspects—Indonesia—Bambang Region.
    3. Head hunters—Indonesia—Bambang Region.   4. Discourse
analysis, Narrative—Indonesia—Bambang Region.   5. Oral tradition—Indonesia—Bambang Region.   6. Bambang Region
(Indonesia)—Social life and customs.   7. Sulawesi Selatan
(Indonesia)—Social life and customs.   I. Title.
GN635.I65G46   1996
394—dc20   95–36929
                                                            CIP

Printed in the United States of America

1 2 3 4 5 6 7 8 9

for the people of the headwaters

Contents

Maps and Figures

Preface

This book has to do with the language and cultural politics of ritual violence in a minority religious community in highland Sulawesi, Indonesia. More particularly, it is about headhunting ceremonies and their stubborn presence in the contemporary social life of a marginal, upland enclave, an enclave that has suffered the wounds of social and cultural dislocation just by staying in place. No longer so remotely situated from the centers of state and post-colonial order, this minority community has had to look for social terrain in which its legitimacy and autonomy can be asserted. In their search, they use what is at hand as well as that which has been brought from over the horizon. The discourse and violence of headhunting ritual have been tangled up in the social life and struggles of this enclave for a long time. Becoming familiar with the discursive construction of violence in the theater of head-hunting ritual is, for me, a way to acknowledge and make plain what this community has at stake as it tries to shape its history and its fate.

So as to be clear from the outset, this work is not a comparative study of headhunting traditions. Although I will refer to practices in other societies from time to time, I have no interest in putting forward here a general theory of headhunting. Neither am I interested in developing general theories of violence, ritual language, or social marginality. This is not a refusal of theory. Rather, it is a rejection of transcendant constructs and vantage points that would harness ethnography to the manufacture of a certain and fixed human universe. Gerald L. Bruns (1988) has encouraged us to think of philosophy as revisionary work, a means for keeping our ideas and accounts of the world plural, loose, and open to correction. Ethnography, I would argue, is a revisionary task as well. In taking ideas and theories and placing them in tension with a lived-in world, ethnography offers us a measure of our limits and our historicity. It is a means for acknowledging those who remain resistant to our sense of things, an entanglement with that recalcitrant other who demands nothing less—and perhaps nothing more—than recognition. It calls for readjustments to our moral and conceptual horizons.

Begun as a study of ritual speech and music, this work has led me to see violence as a crucial scene of textuality, a discursive bridge to other social, political, and experiential dimensions of human life—in this case, in an out-of-the-way community. To call attention to the textuality of ritual violence is not to undermine the seriousness of its consequences for that small community or for us. Rather, I see it as a way of throwing light on the complexity and power of violence and on its reach into other sites of symbolic exchange. Though there may always be slippage between violence and its representation in talk, song, and oratory, the language of violence always has pragmatic entailments. Dictating what the story of violence will be is fundamental to its exercise, and being in a position to do so puts someone or some group very close to the matrices of order and disorder.

Working with the discourse of headhunting ceremonies has obliged me to go poaching in other disciplines in an effort to relate music, literacy, Southeast Asian political history, gender hierarchy, topographies of grief and envy, and the dynamics of commemorative tradition to questions concerning ritual violence. I very much hope that readers in disciplines other than anthropology—in, say, ethnomusicology, Asian studies, religion and ritual studies, postcolonial history, folklore, psychology, and literary and cultural studies—will find something worthwhile in the following pages and forgive any shortcomings they may find. By the same token, I look forward to a multidisciplinary readership that can enlarge and revise the work undertaken here.

This book reflects the influence and assistance of many teachers and friends. My first words of thanks go to Jeff Titon, Daniel W. Patterson, James L. Peacock, Kenneth Irby, Jonathan Strong, and Dennis Tedlock for showing me some of the paths I might follow when going off to stalk poems, songs, and stories in other places. While at the University of Michigan, I had the good luck to study with Aram Yengoyan, Sherry Ortner, A. L. Becker, and Judith Becker; they have my warm and enduring thanks for their friendship, insight, and patient advice. Much in this book takes inspiration from the work of these ten scholars and writers, and I hope it measures up to their standards of care, creativity, and critical reflection.

Colleagues in the Departments of Anthropology at Tulane, the University of South Carolina, and Harvard have been a constant source of encouragement and intellectual challenge, and I hope they will take pleasure in reading this book. I am grateful in particular to Stanley Tambiah, Arthur Kleinman, and Byron Good for their critical response as I worked through ideas for Chapter 4.

Two other Harvard colleagues deserve special acknowledgment. First, I thank Michael Herzfeld for his endless puns and for his boundless critical energy and generosity. I joined his NEH Seminar on "Poetics and Social Life" at Indiana University during the summer of 1990, a time when I was brooding over how to turn a sprawling Ph.D. thesis into a book worth reading. Michael volunteered to read the thesis and gave me some enormously productive comments and suggestions. That kind, mad act was instrumental in giving me direction and resolve. He has my lasting gratitude.

Mary Steedly has been a steadfast colleague, friend, and confidante for many years. Circumstances have found us together in Chapel Hill, Ann Arbor, and Cambridge, and perhaps that is why it is difficult for me to imagine not being able to turn to her for personal and intellectual support. Her critical approach to ethnography and Karo social history has pushed me to reexamine my own work, and her being around has deepened my understanding of friendship and collegiality. Mary's interest and concern, not to mention her comments on several chapters, have made this a better book, and I thank her for that.

I am indebted to many others who have helped this book along by commenting on early versions of individual chapters or on the manuscript as a whole. I would like to mention in particular Donald Brenneis, Johannes Fabian, Douglas Hollan, Janet Hoskins, Webb Keane, Rita Kipp, Joel Kuipers, Toby Volkman, and Jane Wellenkamp. Susan Ferguson, Lindsay French, and Kate Hoshour also made comments that helped bring clarity or reason to the manuscript in some way. Last, but hardly least, Kirin Narayan and John and Karen Campbell-Nelson remained faithful listeners and eager readers, gently chiding me toward finer ethnographic work.

I want to express my very deep appreciation to Renato Rosaldo, Peter Metcalf, Bob McKinley, and Janet Hoskins (once more) for their encouraging letters or thoughtful remarks as I put this book together. I cannot imagine doing work on Southeast Asian headhunting traditions without building on their accomplishments. A number of friends and scholars also helped me fathom the music of headhunting ritual: particular thanks go to René Lysloff; his expertise and patient help were fundamental to my understanding of sumengo song structure and performance styles. I note, too, Greg Nagy,

Kay Kaufman Shelemay, and Deborah Wong; all offered key insights on choral singing.

Countless friends and acquaintances in Sulawesi made this a rewarding project. A. Makmur Makka helped in very crucial ways, as did Syamsul Arief, H. A. Oddang, S. Mengga, M. Saiyadi K., Mukhtar Saleh, and their respective families. The people of Mambi and Bambang showed me extraordinary kindness and hospitality for two and a half years. I cannot possibly name all of them here, but let me mention with heartfelt thanks the generosity and understanding of Abdul Rahman Enang, the late Johannes and Anton Puatipanna, and their families. I owe a special debt to the mappurondo communities in Bambang and Mambi, not only for their boundless hospitality, but for privileges seldom given to strangers. Their trust and patience, their kindness and knowledge, lie at the heart of this book. Finally, I can only hint at the immeasurable debt I owe Bombeng Boaz Rendeng (Papa Ati). He worked faithfully with me on this project, taking me to the farthest reaches of the Salu Mambi headwaters to teach me how to listen for the breathing of rivers and the felling of songs. His voice is in nearly all the lyrics that follow.

Vida Mazulis worked valiantly to keep the manuscript from smothering other kinds of intellectual interests in our home. Still, she took the time to go through portions of the book closely and critically, taking care to remind me of the need to historicize wherever possible, and making reasoned complaint whenever my prose got too clever or tangled up in itself. Her incisive ideas and patient companionship have helped me see my way through and beyond this work, and on to new projects.

Funding for the research that led to this book came from several sources. I gratefully acknowledge support from the Social Science Research Council; the Fulbright-Hays Doctoral Dissertation Abroad Program (Project No. G00-82-0543); the Wenner-Gren Foundation for Anthropological Research (Grant No. 4144); the University of Michigan Institute for the Humanities; and the National Endowment for the Humanities. My thanks go also to my Indonesian sponsors at *Lembaga Ilmu Pengetahuan Indonesia* (*LIPI*, the Indonesian Institute of Science) and *Pusat Latihan Penelitian Ilmu-Ilmu Sosial* (*PLPIIS*, the Center for Training in Social Science Research) at *Universitas Hasanuddin* (*UNHAS*).

Some passages and sections of this book have been published elsewhere. I thank the editors and publishers of the following journals for permission to reprint materials from:

Lyric, History and Allegory, or the End of Headhunting Ritual in Highland Sulawesi. *American Ethnologist* 20(4):697–717.

Dark Trembling: Ethnographic Remarks on Secrecy and Concealment in Highland Sulawesi. *Anthropological Quarterly* 66(4):230–239.

Violence, Solace, and Ritual: A Case Study from Island Southeast Asia. *Culture, Medicine, and Psychiatry* 19(2):225–260.

Music-Making, Ritual, and Gender in a Southeast Asian Hill Society. *Ethnomusicology* 37(1):1–26.

Felling a Song with a New Ax: Writing and the Reshaping of Ritual Song Performance in Upland Sulawesi. *Journal of American Folklore* 103(407):3–23.

Headhunting, History, and Exchange in Upland Sulawesi. *Journal of Asian Studies* 50(3):536–564.

All of the photographs are mine.

In preparing this book I had a good deal of technical assistance. I would like to mention Vivian Montgomery, who did a marvelous job transcribing the sumengo melodies into Western notation, and John P. Mallia, who carefully put the notations into computerized form. I also thank Daniel Glazer for redrawing my research maps and developing a simple sketch of Southeast Asia. Zack Whyte helped with the index.

Last, I want to thank Stan Holwitz, Rebecca Frazier, and others at the Los Angeles offices of the University of California Press, and the copy editor, Bill Carver, for taking interest in this book, and giving it their outstanding care. They managed to get the book reviewed, copyedited, and produced during the earthquake of 1994, the floods of 1995, and the several other trials that have come their way. I take that as a good sign.

K. M. G.

rel-ic (rel' ik), n. *1. a surviving memorial of something past.*
2. an object having interest by reason of its age or its association
with the past: a museum of historic relics. *3. a surviving trace*
of something: a custom that is a relic of paganism. *4. relics, a.*
remaining parts or fragments. b. the remains of a deceased per-
son. 5. something kept in remembrance; souvenir; memento.
6. Eccles. *(esp. in the Roman Catholic and Greek churches) the*
body, a part of the body, or some personal memorial of a saint,
martyr, or other sacred person, preserved as worthy of venera-
tion. 7. a once widespread linguistic form that survives in a
limited area but is otherwise obsolete.

—*The Random House Dictionary of the English Language,*
2nd Edition Unabridged, 1987

1

Relics from Alien Parts

An Introduction

It has been said that there are only two plots that really matter to stories and storytelling: "You go on a journey or a stranger comes to town."[1] If departures, returns, and unexpected arrivals make great material, then it may be that those we call headhunters have a real tale to tell. Not only do they go off on a journey, but they bring back a mute, disfigured stranger with them. And they tell stories about it. I know this because I have listened to them. I know, too, that there is something disquieting about finding wonder and grace in their songs of terror and blood and noise and death.[2] It is not a matter of surprise. After all, violence is no stranger to art: the bodies heaped or strewn across paintings, epics, and theater tell us that. I think the disquiet may have to do with finding oneself seduced by the spectacle and adventure of violence, by its clarity. It is the disquiet of thinking that you could be its victim or the one telling its tale. It is the disquiet that comes from assenting to a story of violence and acknowledging the passion and revulsion that quickened within you.

The force and seductiveness of headhunting stories remain real even when violence is left behind. In a sense, the headhunter's story always leaves violence behind—the bodies of the fallen are absent, elsewhere, just over the horizon of the senses. There is nothing "here" except the narrative and the dread trophy of the violent feats that happened "then and there." Consider, then, the oddness of a dumb, stolen head listening to the story that celebrates the death and dismemberment of its own person.[3] For many traditions of headhunting, though, it is a narrative of some kind that remains as the only presentable or recoverable trace of violence. Some headhunters—like the Ilongot men who have figured prominently in the work of Michelle and Renato Rosaldo—simply abandon the severed head of their victim, and return home to take up boasting and song. "We came home and sang and sang" goes an Ilongot headhunting story—a remark that prompted Michelle Rosaldo to say that celebratory song itself was the source of the "anger" that led men to kill (1980:56–57). Yet there are those, too, who have put the violence of headhunting behind them in a different way. Here I have in mind those headhunters who make their predatory raids in the past. Although they have long put away the headhunter's weapons, they conjure relics of violence from the past in order to animate the present. Their violence happens only in the commemorative work of ritual narrative and song. These are the kind of headhunters who people this book.

Where headhunters have put down their weapons and taken up song, the mimetic discourse of ritual offers an especially revealing look at violence. We see violence as a narrated form of symbolic exchange, something "figured" and "read," so to speak, through the discursive tensions linking dominant and oppositional social formations (Armstrong and Tennenhouse 1989; Chambers 1991; Feldman 1991; Medick 1987; White 1978), and shaped through the social poetics that frame experience (Herzfeld 1985; cf. Brenneis 1987; R. Rosaldo 1986). Nevertheless, the intrusions of history, along with the ambiguities of commemoration, complicate our readings of the headhunter's violence. Slippage, disjuncture, and irony begin to characterize the way in which a circumstanced and recalcitrant social world stands apart from the idealized vision of the headhunt. The edifice of ritual and all of its pragmatic concerns begin to tremble.

The problematic gaps between the discursive projects of ritual and the instabilities of the social world beg a story, too. What stories need to be told about headhunters who do not take heads, but who nonetheless stage rituals about headhunting? How should they be told? Consider the following narrative:

Long ago	*Now*
They took heads ⟶	They take effigy heads
	They take head-shaped surrogates
	They take coconuts
	They use coconuts bought in a market

This simple narrative sketch posits an originary violence that has been displaced over time. It gives the terrors of the past an illusory firmness and clarity. But each of the four "editions" or "versions" invites a different reading of the headhunters' story. If I close the tale with "They take effigy heads," a sense of violence lingers to haunt the present; the headhunter seems to be exercising choice. Closing the story with "They take head-shaped surrogates," I imply something else—perhaps that the headhunters' violence and capacity to act have been thwarted or contained. If I say, "Now they take coconuts," I am almost sure to raise a laugh, for the only sign of violence is a harmless, pathetic theft—one of the weapons of the weak. And last, should I close with "They use coconuts bought in a market," I risk giving the impression that contemporary headhunting is a masquerade or a relic amusement for those tamed or humiliated by historical change and the expansion of a commoditized world.

Other stories can be read in this narrative as well. It might be read as a fall from authenticity into fakery, a story in which "really real" violence and "really real" heads devolve into gesture and stage prop. Read from another prospect altogether, the narrative may look like the story of all simulacra, a story in which there is no distinction between originals and copies, between reality and representation. Yet still another reading may be the most common and troubling one: a story of progress, a story in which pagan violence is subdued and in which human characters ascend from a state of primitivism to one just shy of civility and modernity. This modernist story of progress has been a powerful one in the popular and intellectual traditions of the West. Those traditions have been instrumental in making a fetish of headhunters, headhunting, and the severed head: turned into extravagantly magical figures, trophy heads and headhunters have served a rhetoric of control in the West's encounter with "others" (cf. Fabian 1983; R. Rosaldo 1978; Trouillot 1991; White 1978). In short, these representations of other people's violence have played into the discursive violence emanating from colonial and postcolonial centers.

Among other things, this book is about the language, music, and violence of headhunting ritual, and about the cultural politics that have shaped them. Yet I hope it may help dislodge the cathected figure of the headhunter from that rhetoric which peoples our world with "savages," "pagans," and "monsters." My focus will be on the song and chant of a ritual headhunt called *pangngae,* a ceremony observed by a minority religious community on the island of Sulawesi, in Indonesia (see Maps 1 and 2). What makes this ritual so striking, these days, is its artifice. No one is killed, no actual head is taken. But its rhetoric of violence is unmistakable. By exploring the discourse of pangngae—especially its themes, its projects, and its situatedness—I hope to recognize what is at stake for the community when it convenes in the theater of ritual headhunting.

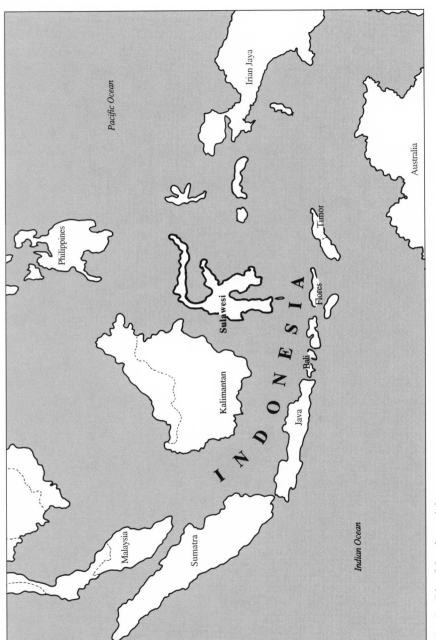

Map 1. *Island Southeast Asia*

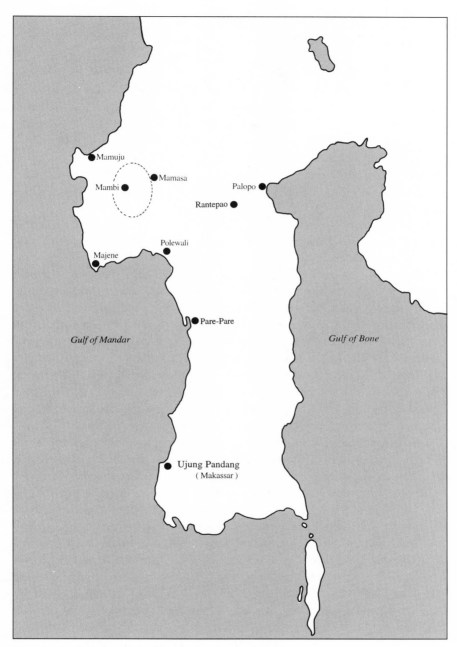

Mamuju

Mamasa

Palopo

Mambi

Rantepao

Polewali

Majene

Pare-Pare

Gulf of Mandar

Gulf of Bone

Ujung Pandang
(Makassar)

Map 2. *South Sulawesi, Indonesia, showing study area*

Objects and Encounters:
October 1982 and July 1983

"It's a kind of harvest festival." The *Kepala Desa*—the head of the village district—was leading me over the paths to the hamlet of Lasodehata, where he planned to show me something about local ritual tradition. Though his remark was quite clear, I didn't know what to listen for. I was a stranger to Bambang (the name of the village district). I didn't know the people, I didn't know the place, and I certainly didn't know a euphemism when I heard one. Guided by wonder and literality, I simply went along with him.

Some months later, when I began to get a hold on the local language, I learned that Lasodehata means "the phallus of the *debata* (or spirit)." The story goes that when some settlers sank the first hole for a housepost on that site sixteen or seventeen generations ago, they hit a large red rock. The moment they did, the angry bellowing voice of a mountain spirit complained of the wound. The settlers made amends to the spirit and named the hamlet in commemoration of the event. Years later, civil and military authorities objected to the hamlet's name and changed it to Rantepalado, "the field of jackfruit"—although no jackfruit trees grow there. About the same time, I also learned that the "harvest festival" was called pangngae, and that pangngae means "to take a head" in raid or ambush. But on that day in October 1982, walking with the Kepala Desa, my working premise was that I was about to see something that had to do with harvest ceremonies.

Lasodehata was very still when we arrived. People must have been away in their gardens and coffee groves. We stood below the shuttered door of a large house, the comb from a nest of wasps or bees hanging beside it, set out to thwart malevolent spirit-beings from intruding into the house.[4] No one was at home, so the Kepala Desa found a neighbor, stationed him at the foot of the house ladder, and then let himself in, beckoning me to follow. Fine shafts of sunlight reached down from the thatch roof into the dim, smokeless room. A large drum hung not far from the door, cinched up near a rafter. I took a picture of it, and a few weeks later carefully labeled the slide: *DRUM used in FERTILITY RITUAL, BAMBANG.* Moments after telling me about the drum, the Kepala Desa pointed up toward the loft, saying, "Those instruments (Indonesian, *alat-alat*) are blown to make a sound after prayers are made to the *dewi padi* (Ind. rice goddesses)."

I looked up, craning my neck to make out something I might recognize resting in the loft. I saw several large bamboo tubes—they looked like they might be flutes—and a snarl of plaited leaves. A small offering rack hung next to the instruments. I fussed with my camera trying to find the angle, the right light, a sharp focus, and I vaguely recall lying on the floor peering upward through the lens. I took another shot. That one is labeled: *RIT-UAL PARAPHERNALIA for Fertility Ritual, Bambang. Kept on rafters.*

That was my first look at the relics from a headhunt. They had been put away after the previous harvest (March 1982), and with the exception of the drum have since been replaced. I take out those two photographs from time to time, usually to wind up remembering how on that day I had hope-fully imagined sounds coming from a silent drum and sleeping flutes. I also remember Ambe Lusa, the Kepala Desa and a Christian of abundant good will and humor, who would die before I left the region with much-changed ideas about the harvest festivals he had described to me. His showing me that loft persuaded me to live and work in the area for the next three years, and I hold on to those photographs so that I can think back on the mo-ment. But to erase my ethnographic naïveté and mistakenness, I have recap-tioned them *"Violence: Still-Life I," "Violence: Still-Life II"* (see Figure 1).

Circumstances kept me out of the mountains for the next five months, and I would learn little about pangngae until the following October. Shortly after moving to the region, I found out that those who had turned to the church and the mosque had more or less forsaken the local ritual tradition that interested me, a tradition called *ada' mappurondo.* The mappurondo communities—that is, the groups of people who adhere to the traditional ritual order—were quiet and remote. During this time, it was largely Chris-tians and Muslims who interpreted local culture for me.

Two months or so after settling in the area, I joined Christian acquain-tances in wedding festivities at Salutabang, a village in Bambang with a sig-nificant number of mappurondo households. One of the mappurondo el-ders there, Ambe Teppu, confronted the host of the wedding. Mappurondo terraces had already been "wounded" by the till, putting into effect a village-wide tabu on noise, laughter, music, weddings, and other festive rit-uals. His anger went even deeper upon learning that my Christian friends had put on a surprise "culture-show" (Ind., *pameran budaya*) for me as light entertainment and education, a show that included some old headhunting songs, a chant invoking the spirits of women's household rites, and a staged version of a dance that in ritual circumstances would involve trance. Ambe Teppu saw it not only as poking fun at ada' mappurondo, but as sacred things out of place. Bitter about what had happened, he would later scold the newlywed husband:

I have coffee beans. I will give them to you and you can roast them up and make cof-fee. I have sheaves of rice. Go ahead and take them, and cook up some rice. But this is my religion. I will give you my religion. But don't, don't turn my religion into culture.

Fig. 1. *Violence: Still Life II. Bamboo flutes resting in the gable-end loft of a home. These large, decorated flutes—called* tambolâ—*are unique to local headhunting ceremonies. 1982.*

For me the words stung. This was a version of "the raw and the cooked" quite unlike the one I had digested in preparation for research.[5] Ambe Teppu was taking aim against the arrogation of local tradition by intruding ideologies and social groups. Powerful institutions were competing with the mappurondo communities for the ideological control and social production of words, meanings, and practice (cf. Vološinov 1973; Williams 1977). Resisting a civil discourse that denied him a religion and treated his sacred tradition as "culture" and "art"—matters I take up in this book—Ambe Teppu was also protesting conduct that abused and concealed the real nature of mappurondo practices.

Though they were aimed at his nephew, I took Ambe Teppu's words as an admonishment for me as well. After all, I was part of a "culture industry," albeit of a different sort. Although I had no intention of turning traditional sacred practices into ethnic song and dance (Ambe Teppu's most immediate fear), I wanted to be sure that I did not slight the mappurondo communities' authoritative claims to their own traditions. Ambe Teppu's words also reminded me that though he and I had been situated in unique ways by the varied histories and politics that worked through us, both of us were caught up inextricably in the same world. I met him at a time when the discipline of anthropology was subjecting itself to a critique of its representational authority and its complicity in the politics of domination.[6] Ambe Teppu's reprimand was forged in a similar spirit: the politics of culture do matter.

I had not gone to Sulawesi with the idea of working on the problem of headhunting or violence, but with plans to explore the biographical and autobiographical strains of ritual discourse. And indeed, ethnographic reports on Sulawesi had given me the impression that headhunting ritual was a thing of the past. As in other parts of Indonesia, headhunting rumors were common forms of terror, linked now, as in the colonial past, to the presence of police, military personnel, workers from large construction projects, and other alien figures (Drake 1989; Erb 1991; Pannell 1992; Tsing 1993, forth.). When I learned, some months after meeting Ambe Teppu, that mappurondo "harvest festivals" are headhunting rites, I was drawn to them, for several reasons. For one thing, it is very clear to me that pangngae is the central ritual apparatus within the mappurondo communities for asserting their cultural autonomy: the community that no longer holds pangngae is in effect moribund. Just as ritual theater was the basic cultural idiom for the nineteenth-century Balinese state (Geertz 1980), the ceremonial headhunt of pangngae forms a political drama through which the mappurondo communities try to control their past and their present. By the same token, the rituals are a means for these relatively egalitarian communities to display and read signs of spiritual and material potency (cf. Atkinson 1989; Errington 1989; M. Rosaldo 1980). But I do not of course mean to exorcise conflict from pangngae, for as Dirks (1994) reminds us, ritual can as easily exhibit or bring about conflict and instability, as put authority and order on display. For the moment I want to stress that the mappurondo communities' hold on autonomy, potency, continuity, and stability has been thrown into question by a civil order that contests or censures the very means for grasping them—the rhetoric of ritual violence. At stake is how pangngae will be claimed, reclaimed, or forgotten, and by whom. Conflict over ritual practice and representation is a fact of life for the mappurondo enclave in Bambang, and Ambe Teppu's protest was just one more skirmish in the ongoing struggle of a minority religious community to shape its own fate.

It would be misleading to describe this struggle as a struggle for identity. The conflict has to do with ritual practice and legitimacy, with authoritative claims to tradition, and with ways of coping with an uncertain world. For people who have remained faithful to ada' mappurondo, rituals are the events of time, memory, and tradition itself. Authoring and authorizing ritual "texts" are at issue in this rivalry with Christians, Muslims, and the civil administration. This brings me to another reason I was drawn to the ritual. The texts and textuality of pangngae not only were contested resources, but also promised a valuable point of entry into understanding the discursive construction of violence and ritual tradition. A study that dwells upon the discourse of pangngae, it seems to me, might take us far in coming to terms with ritual violence. At the same time, I think it will give us a glimpse of what the mappurondo communities have at stake as they negotiate their place in the world through a tradition of headhunting ritual.

Recent Commentaries on Regional Headhunting Traditions

Some of the more insightful commentaries on Southeast Asian headhunting traditions have shown a deep regard for local discourse and history. In particular, I have in mind here the work of the Rosaldos on Ilongot headhunting in the Northern Luzon region of the Philippines and, indeed, this book is in part an effort to resume the conversations they began. Let me sketch what I take to be their accomplishments, noting, too, the works of others that have shaped my interest in the discourse of head-hunting ritual.

Putting headhunting into historical perspective has been Renato Rosaldo's key contribution (1980). In very general terms, he was able to show how headhunting works as a central moving force in the improvisation of Ilongot social life and in the shaping of local memory and historical thought. For example, headhunting, as part of a broader pattern of feuding, often motivated marriages and residential moves in the Ilongot communities. At the same time, it served as a focal episode in personal and collaborative rec-ollections of the past. What is clear from Rosaldo's treatment of violence is that social improvisation and memory are mutually shaping: headhunting (as discourse and practice) was at once a way to apprehend the past and a way to respond to circumstances and contingencies of an ever-changing so-cial world.[7] The historical turn taken by Rosaldo also helped debunk the image of the timeless primitive. Not only did Ilongot headhunting cease many times in the last century or so, but it was fundamental to local history as process and thought—that is, it was fundamental to measuring change and the passage of time.

More recently, Janet Hoskins has pushed the analysis of history and head-hunting in another, fresh and illuminating, direction (1987). Hoskins ar-gues that *sejarah,* or "history," has become a new genre of authoritative dis-course at local and national levels in Indonesia. National history turns Wona Kaka, a Sumbanese headhunter of the early twentieth century, into a heroic figure in the national resistance to the Dutch colonial order. Yet in the his-torical view of some Sumbanese, he symbolizes local resistance to encroach-ment and absorption by *any* outsiders, whether Dutch or Indonesian. As a result, the two histories compete with one another, each trying to claim this headhunter as its own heroic figure by "reinventing" his past and his hero-ism. The history of local headhunting is thus a contested cultural resource, rather than a formative episode in the reproduction of the social order. It is the proving ground for heroic figures crucial to the ideological control of the past. In a subsequent study, Hoskins (1989) revisits the problem of Sumbanese headhunting, this time with an interest in the historical transfor-mation of "things." By examining the life history of a severed head, and tracing changes in its identity and value as it moves through eras of ex-change, alliance, and trade between rival groups, Hoskins shows how the relics of violence can be historied and reappropriated in the changing cur-rents of social life.

Michelle Rosaldo followed a different path in her work on Ilongot head-hunting (M. Rosaldo 1977, 1980, 1983). Unhappy with the shortcomings of structuralist approaches, she proposed an alternative framework based on explorations into the "tones of thought" through which particular cultures associate severed heads with passion, mourning, fertility, and envy. Ilongot headhunting, in her analysis, was caught up in local discourses on emotions, in age- and gender-based social hierarchies, and in notions of personhood. Her understanding of Ilongot emotions found tragic reprise in Renato Rosaldo's "Grief and a Headhunter's Rage" (1984), written after her unforeseeable death in 1981. An important statement on emotion, ritual analysis, and the positioned subject, this essay showed once more that an exploration of emotion and meaning could render headhunting as a plausible and compelling cultural practice.

I think I can distinguish my own interests in headhunting by quoting a brief passage from the final remarks in Michelle Rosaldo's monograph (1980:231): she wrote that she was "involved in showing how particular modes of speaking are illuminated by the social actions and relationships such speech describes." In this book, I want to show how ritual modes of speaking are themselves modes of social action and relationship and, as such, are practices that shape the social and historical world in which headhunters find themselves.[8] This approach has the virtue of making central to analysis a body of discourse that Clifford Geertz (1973:448) might call a "story people tell themselves about themselves" (see also Ortner 1978; R. Rosaldo 1986). Ritual songs, narratives, and liturgies do not merely reflect or represent social life, but are of practical consequence. The politics of representation consist not only of struggles over signifiers and signifieds, but also of efforts to control the pragmatic acts and social relationships emanating from representational practice.

Although Michelle Rosaldo was able to show the rich conceptual realm in which Ilongot headhunting made sense, she did lead our attention away from the kinds of discourse that stirred the hearts of Ilongot men and gave their violence purpose: the ritual songs called *buayat*. Interestingly, the buayat is prominent in an opening vignette in her book (M. Rosaldo 1980). She reports about how, on her return to Ilongot country in 1974, she pulled out an old tape of a headhunting ceremony she and her husband had attended during their first stay—a sacrifice and songfest that celebrated the murder of a lowlander by an Ilongot youth named Burur.[9] Hearing the buayat, her friends demanded that she stop the tape: it was too wrenching and painful for their hearts. "[T]he song itself . . . made their breath twist and turn inside them; it pained them because it made them want to kill" (M. Rosaldo 1980:34). It seems to me that this ritual song was a critical form of discourse that stirred men to hunt heads, one that rendered headhunting morally intelligible and valuable to the Ilongot themselves (cf. R. Rosaldo 1984:190). As Rosaldo herself notes, the song celebrated and renewed the angry passions of the headhunter (1980:56); and she reports that Burur had been sullen and withdrawn over the failure of his kin to celebrate his accomplishment promptly (1980:68). To be fair, the buayat probably thwart in-depth analysis: Michelle Rosaldo explains that the songs have "no linguistic 'sense' of which Ilongots are aware," adding indirectly that they are distinct from the boasts shouted out in them (1980:54–55). It was also the case that by 1974 the buayat had gone the way of Ilongot headhunting; they could not be retrieved for study. The same appears true of the boasting narrative song called *tarapandet*, which recounts a headhunter's journey (M. Rosaldo 1980:156–157).

For all of its ethnographic wealth and insight, the corpus of work by the Rosaldos does play down the significance of ritual in the analysis of headhunting. This has prompted complaint from Peter Metcalf (forth.), who has explored Berawan headhunting practices in Sarawak, Malaysia (Metcalf 1982). He remarks that the Ilongot case may be atypical when measured against the elaborate headhunting ceremonies commonly found elsewhere in the island region (cf. McKinley 1976; Hoskins forth. [a] and [b]). I share with Metcalf a fascination for the place of ritual in social life, but I am not inclined to worry over whether Ilongot headhunting is "typical." The Rosaldos may have had purpose in writing against the privileged position of ritual in symbolic anthropology (e.g. R. Rosaldo 1984)—indeed, I have a hunch that they felt it necessary to work around ritual in order to get at the complexities of experience and history—but their ethnographic work bears sufficient trace of ceremonial discourse to convince me that ritual speech and song may afford important insights into headhunting throughout island Southeast Asia.

Violence and Ritual Discourse: Themes, Projects, and Situations

There is no one way to get at ritual discourse. For example, explorations into the poetics and politics of ritual speech in island Southeast Asia have included detailed accounts of: canonical parallelism (J. Fox 1988); entextualization and authority (Kuipers 1990); the problems of voice and agency (Keane 1991); stylistic and thematic analyses of prayer (Metcalf 1989); the politics and history of genres (Bowen 1991); assertions of ethnicity and identity in a contested social terrain (Hefner 1985); oratory and political poetry (Atkinson 1984, M. Rosaldo 1984b); the efficacy of chant and its relation to local notions of power (Atkinson 1987, 1989); the eccentricities of trance accounts (Steedly 1993, Tsing 1993); the production of cultural coherence (Becker and Yengoyan, eds., 1979; Traube 1986); and the production of gender difference (Siegel 1978, Kuipers 1986, Rodgers 1990). Yet there is a common thread running through much of this literature: the authors recognize, albeit in different ways, that the history of society and the history of language are bound up with one another, and consequently that the study of ritual speech requires us to see how poetics and performance are situated in social life (cf. Fabian 1974; Bakhtin 1986; Bauman and Briggs 1990, 1992).

Much of the ethnographic literature prior to the historical turn in anthropology represented ritual not only as an instrument of tradition and traditional authority, but as a rigid, unchanging structure as well (cf. Kelly and Kaplan 1990). The same goes for ritual discourse, which commonly is portrayed as repetitive, formalized, conventionalized, and fixed (for example, see Bloch 1974, Rappaport 1979, and Tambiah 1985). In my experience, religious language is more supple and improvised than these descriptions would allow. Yet I would agree that ritual and ritual language show a certain stability through time. What troubles me is that we too easily forget that the fixity and formality we observe in ritual (and in tradition, for that matter) are not the properties of ritual language per se, but, rather, the outcome of a community trying to stabilize a body of discourse for continuous interpretive work. Whether that "stabilized" discourse serves the pragmatic interests of traditional authority or factors into the reformation of the social order depends largely on historical conditions, as Stanley Tambiah (1985) has pointed out. At issue for me is how communities produce, reproduce, and tactically alter ritual discourse in ever-changing social and historical contexts. In my view, there is no ur-text, no abstract cultural schema, no basically basic story or structure behind ritual.[10] There is instead an ongoing history of prior ritual events and texts being recalled and put in productive tension with the present.

As Jerome McGann has reminded us in his recent exploration of materialist hermeneutics (1991), texts are made and remade under specific social, historical, and institutional conditions, conditions that mark the horizon within which texts are interpreted and transformed (cf. Williams 1977). Discursive practices are always in service of one or more situated projects, and it is such projects that come to dominate (or set the grounds of struggle for) the pragmatic and hermeneutic dimensions of the textual acts in question (cf. Fish 1980, 1989). Different "versions" of a text, I would argue, trace its situatedness and throw light on the conflicts that determine its multiaccentuality. Indeed, remaking texts—in McGann's terms, "producing editions" (1991:33)—is a way to shape meaning (cf. Tedlock 1983, Fabian 1990). How this process took place in one specific Indonesian "situation" comes through clearly in the work of James L. Peacock (1968), who was able to show that differences and deformations of plot in performances by Surabaya's *ludruk* theater-troupes in the 1960s made sense with respect to the goals and ideological programs of opposed political camps. For traditional ceremonial discourse, I believe it is possible to demonstrate as well that rituals and their multiple stagings are made "for particular purposes by particular people and institutions, and [that] they may be used (and reused) in multiple ways, many of which run counter to uses otherwise or elsewhere imagined" (McGann 1991:47). Staging a ritual places it in historical relation to prior stagings and yet aligns it with immediate social goals, tensions, and anxieties.

For the mappurondo communities in Bambang, staging pangngae is part of a broader struggle to assert authority and control over their ritual tradition and their past. Yet there is no fixed way to do this. The communities instead bring out different "editions" of the headhunt in an effort to repeat the past and to respond to the contingencies of the present. Each performance narrativizes violence in keeping with living memory, and with the interests and problems of the moment. Because I have no record of ritual materials from the colonial or precolonial past except those recalled in the discourse of the present, my understanding of how the mappurondo communities fashion their headhunting ceremonies is limited largely to the horizons of a two-year period in the mid-1980s. I look, of course, to various liturgical genres in an effort to see what it is the communities are trying to accomplish. But central to my analysis is a genre of choral song called *sumengo*, which may be translated as "the singing." The songs are short: the typical sumengo consists of but three octosyllabic phrases sung by a song-leader and chorus. Yet the songs are so prominent in pangngae that it would not be off the mark to describe the ritual as a kind of sumengo-fest. In fact, the sumengo are the principle textual and performative vehicle for narrativizing the violence of pangngae, and in that sense they are analogues to the Ilongot buayat and tarapandet discussed by Michelle Rosaldo. For this reason, my exploration of different stagings or editions of pangngae rests largely on differences I noted in sumengo performances. That is, differences in sumengo performances suggested to me different ways to narrativize or aestheticize violence, and different ways to reproduce and make claims to ritual tradition in the theater of social life.

Much in this book is in keeping with text- and performance-centered ethnography (e.g. Becker 1979; Bauman 1977; Fabian 1990; Hymes 1981; Tedlock 1983), and with recent trends in practice theory (see: Ortner 1984, 1989; Dirks, Eley, and Ortner 1994). So as to elucidate a local narrative of violence and relate it to the flux of social history in the mappurondo communities, I will organize my exploration of pangngae largely in terms of its themes, its projects, and its situatedness. By "themes" I mean broadly and simply the subject matter of specific lyrics, liturgical texts, or canonical acts as they are generated in specific contexts of production and interpretation.[11] To give but a few examples, adornment, noise, and pity are themes that one commonly encounters in the representational and performative dimensions of pangngae. The challenge will be to relate them to the theme of ritual violence. By "projects" I mean the recurrent goals of the ritual. Although the search for prosperity might be considered the overriding point of pangngae, it is clear that the domination of an ethnic rival, the lifting of mourning prohibitions, the celebration of manhood, and the act of commemoration itself also factor into the ritual as purposive tasks. The themes and projects of ritual discourse, I should stress, are intertwined and lend each other intelligibility. It is through them that the mappurondo communities are able to conjure the headhunter's violence and give it significance. A look at the situatedness of pangngae can take us further still. In what kinds of communities do these rituals take place? What social conflicts and contingencies surround the headhunt? What events and forces lie behind and ahead of the ritual tradition we encounter today?

Let me outline, then, the structure of this book. Immediately after this introductory chapter, there follows a general social and historical sketch of the mappurondo enclave in Bambang. It should provide readers with a rough sense of the political culture and cultural politics surrounding pangngae. The next four chapters (Chapters 3 through 6) dwell largely on the themes and projects of mappurondo headhunting ritual, relating them very broadly to the social and cultural reproduction of the mappurondo communities. Chapter 3 explores the headhunting of the past and the way it is recalled in ritual discourse and oral history today. Here I try to make sense of headhunting and the polemics of ethnicity and highland-lowland exchange in the precolonial and colonial periods. I also use this discussion of history to critique the excesses of structuralist and other symbolic approaches to ritual headhunting, and to recuperate the political import of violence and the trophy head.

Chapters 4 and 5 trace the processual features of a contemporary headhunt from start to finish. Grief, violence, and solace are the key themes in Chapter 4; I relate them to the projects of mourning and making vows. As many readers will recognize, this chapter takes inspiration from and responds to Renato Rosaldo's "Grief and a Headhunter's Rage" (1984). Mappurondo practices suggest that the resolution of communal mourning is more significant than personal catharsis in motivating a headhunter's violence; that ritual refigures individual affect as "political affect" (consonant with the political import of violence); and that varied discursive forms such as vows, songs, and noise mediate the ways in which people (and the community as a whole) put grief behind them and resume their lives. I argue, then, that personal motives for taking part in contemporary headhunting spring not from powerful emotions but from obligations and acts made in discourse.

Chapter 4 follows pangngae from the time the headhunters leave their village to the time they return home. Chapter 5, by way of contrast, deals with the week of ceremonial activity that takes place after their triumphant return. Here I relate the politics of adornment and envy to the discourse of manhood, and to the local social hierarchies relating men to men and men to women. In this chapter we see males figured anew: they not only are valorous and violent as headhunters, but also show their virtuosity and authority as rhetoricians, as speechmakers. At the same time, the rivalry that linked the headhunter with his victim is now supplanted by a rivalry between husbands and wives.

Chapter 6 addresses the final project of pangngae: commemoration. In this chapter I try to locate the violence of pangngae in commemorative discourse itself, arguing that violence is both subject and generative force for its own reenactment in chant and lyric. I point out as well that commemoration is a mode of sociality. I look in particular at the social organization of choruses and relate such organization to everyday social hierarchy. But I also raise the issue of sociality to suggest that the politics of representation not only involve struggles for authority over signs, but also imply a struggle to inhabit distinct forms of social relationship.

Chapter 7 takes a look at differences in the commemorative work of four villages as they hold pangngae. Taking inspiration from McGann, I try to see how the discourse of pangngae has been situated and circumstanced—to scan, in other words, the performative and interpretive horizons for this ritual. Against a background of a tradition in crisis, I explore how agonistic play, irony, trance critiques, and written texts have become commonplace in the headhunt. The violence and memory of headhunting, and the interpretive work linked to them, are now inseparable from writing, reading, and the excited play of voice.

Chapter 8 extends further my concern for the situatedness of pangngae. I finally come around to the Christian and Muslim efforts to claim or forget local headhunting practices, efforts that are worked out largely in terms set down by the Indonesian state. My "texts" in this chapter are not sumengo, but a tourist pamphlet, analyses of local tradition by two theologians, and the quips and remarks of friends. Against these portraits of headhunting, I return to the figure of Ambe Teppu, the man who reminded me that the politics of culture do matter, most especially for minority communities too small to count in state and national orders. I close with a brief look at the mappurondo communities in 1994, and with some reflections on this work as a whole.

A Note on Research in Sulawesi

Most materials for this study come from roughly 30 months of ethnographic research in the mappurondo communities of Bambang between October 1982 and August 1985.[12] I have made no effort to disguise the places where I worked. Friends and hosts in the mappurondo communities, however, appear in these pages with their names changed. During the time I lived and worked in Bambang, I was able to witness and take part in pangngae eight times: twice in the village of Salutabang, three times in Minanga, twice in Rantepalado, and once in Saludengen. I recorded ritual songs and liturgical performances in each of those places, and all the lyrics that appear in this book are quoted from specific ritual performances. Day-to-day observations, casual conversation, household surveys, and village histories were the source of other materials that came to shape my understanding of ritual song and violence.

Much in this work hinges on the translation and interpretation of ritual speech and song, especially the sumengo. In an important sense, the project of translation and interpretation is an unfinished one. I keep going back to these songs, sometimes finding something I overlooked, other times finding new ways to connect the materials meaningfully to other features of mappurondo life and language. Readers will further extend and revise the project of interpretation. That said, it may be helpful if I provide a quick sketch of my encounter with these songs, and of my tactics and methods of translation.

As may already be clear, the genres of ritual song peculiar to the head-hunt are subject to a rigid set of local tabus. This holds for ethnographic dialogue as well. Villagers may not sing, rehearse, or even discuss these materials unless it is "headhunting season," so to speak—a period lasting between three days and two weeks. These tabus necessarily shaped my work with singers, lyrics, and performance. In particular, they framed the contexts in which performers and I could comfortably engage in a give-and-take with one another. By placing my inquiry within the sphere of traditional practices, I put a partial check to my impulse to control ethnographic dialogue. At the same time, the sanctioned period for ritual performance gave me a chance to raise questions about the sumengo and other genres and to ask villagers to reflect on the meaning and significance of the material.

Listening in and listening to mappurondo headhunting ritual is complicated work. Gatherings are exuberant; conversations, songs, and drumming all take place at the same time. Liturgical acts will silence the talk and instrumental music, but these acts are often whispered or muttered, or demand choral responses that are difficult to make out. My understanding of ritual emerges from being there, and listening to tapes and reading transcriptions prepared by my Christian language assistant from Salutabang, Bombeng Rendeng (Papa Ati).

During the postharvest season of 1984, I moved from one village to the next as the headhunting rituals closed in one and began in another. Papa Ati joined me in Salutabang and shortly afterward we repaired to the mountain market town of Mambi—downriver and out of the orbit of mappurondo social space—where we would be free to work on transcribing and translating materials into Indonesian and English. Once basic transcriptions were complete, we would together explore the songs' lyrics. We then took our understanding of the songs back to the different mappurondo communities for comment in 1985, when ritual conditions next allowed. Most of those to whom we turned were men, but at Salutabang and Minanga we were fortunate to have the help of women who were skilled sumengo soloists. Interviews with soloists, ritual specialists, and other villagers supplied me with information on singing, the origin and history of headhunting, and on people's impressions of sumengo performances and their encompassing tradition. We also gathered new materials in 1985, and rushed to bring them into our conversations about pangngae.

Translating the songs was hardly straightforward. Translations emerged from talk between a native speaker/singer (raised mappurondo but now professing to be Christian) and a stranger trying to become familiar with local tongues and with the life-worlds and political anxieties of the mappu-rondo communities. Talk was a mix of Indonesian and languages peculiar to Bambang and Mambi. Whole stories inform word glosses and the details of interlinear worksheets. The interpretive commentaries of villagers, too, were hardly straightforward, leading off, as they often did, into local history, personal memories, and other songs. But by and large the meaning of the songs and liturgies did not occasion much debate or disagreement. Interpreting the songs was not a pressing cultural problem; remembering them was. Sometimes people found songs enigmatic and beyond understanding. Other times singers and listeners acknowledged a plurality of meaning in the lyrics—and I have tried to capture some of that surplus of meaning in the chapters that follow.

The final months of fieldwork brought a fresh problem. Late in April 1985, I was able to attend pangngae at Saludengen, a village in which I yet had no friends or acquaintances. Aside from 45 new song texts, the ceremony yielded a performance style unlike those I had previously encountered. Further, it was in Saludengen that I discovered villagers who had begun to write down sumengo lyrics (though not the tune). Confronted with all of that, I had to rapidly reformulate my ideas regarding sumengo tradition and, indeed, headhunting tradition. I had opportunity to pursue some of my most important questions. Unfortunately, my visit was brief and many more questions had to go unasked.

Once again, I should stress that the work of translation and interpretation has not come to a halt. For example, working with ethnomusicologists after I returned home from Sulawesi gave me an opportunity to grapple with textual and melodic structures in ways I never imagined during my initial study (George 1989). Finally, in writing this book I have tried to place songs so as to help identify and make intelligible some of the key strains and themes in mappurondo headhunting ritual. That effort should not preclude further interpretive work—further "editions" in McGann's terms—by me or by others.

2

The Mappurondo
Enclave at Bambang

The Salu Mambi runs shallow and cold over a twisted, boulder-strewn course, its headwaters tangled in the forests of the Messila and Mambuliling massif. The name "Mambi" comes from the word *mambie,* meaning "hidden from view"—as by trees or tall grasses. A glimpse from the flanking trails is enough to confirm the name. The river winds into ravines and behind mountain spurs, and, like the hamlets nestled above its banks, can simply disappear beneath shrouds of mist and rain. With the exception of a few visits elsewhere in the mountain region, I lived and worked for roughly 30 months (between 1982 and 1985) along the part of the Salu Mambi watershed that stretches from the upper reaches in Bambang to the small but fertile basin at the town of Mambi.

Mambi is a full-fledged, if largely thatch-roofed, town, with market, schools, mosque and church, shops, *kecamatan* (Ind. regional subdistrict) offices, and a significant number of outsiders who work there as teachers, traders, or civil administrators. Most of those born and raised in Mambi are Muslim, and most nurture hopes of finding a place in a wider, more complex world—somewhat stalled beyond the horizon—be it through their religion, the Indonesian bureaucracy, the coffee trade, video cassettes and radio, or the promised roadway that in 1985 had yet to reach town. As one townsman remarked to me, their interests run with the river waters: to the coast, the sea, and Mecca.

East and upriver from Mambi, the settlements of Bambang form a rural precinct—or *desa* (Ind.)—of terraces, swiddens, and coffee gardens (see Map 3). When leaving town to walk the riverside trails up toward the

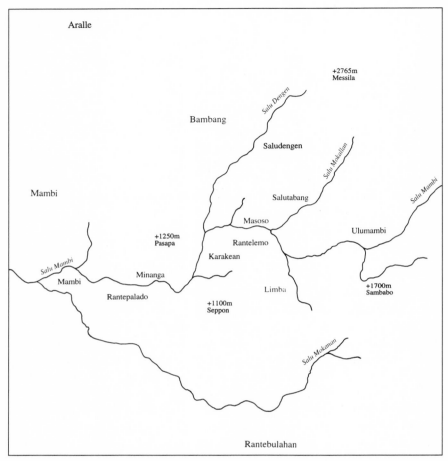

Map 3. *The Salu Mambi headwaters, the study area circled on Map 2*

headwaters, one speaks of "going inside Bambang" (*le'ba' illalam Bambang*) or even just "going inside." The phrase is apt in several senses. It suggests tracing the course of the river back behind the looming escarpment of Buntu Seppon into unseen places among the forests and folds of the mountain range. For the Muslim townsperson, Bambang is foreboding, *jinn*-ridden, and unclean, a place to be avoided and left to the imagination. Movement, real or imagined, into the terrain of Bambang captures something of a cultural outlook that associates upriver regions with ancestral tradition and authority. "Going inside" involves not only a journey into a remote and

Fig. 2. *A hamlet in Bambang, at the headwaters of the Salu Mambi. 1984.*

brooding terrain, but also an acquaintance with a past and some of its un-governable memories.

"It's like Texas up there," wisecracked Tapuli, a civil servant—and a Christian—always ready to beat me to the draw in a showdown over our knowledge of each other's cultural icons and images, "The people are cowboys." I don't think he meant to paint an image of lawlessness and violence so much as to hint that the people living in Bambang were a bunch of stubborn and occasionally hot-headed rubes who didn't have the sense to give up tradition for the civility and progress of the Indonesian order. Yet it is precisely the images of the violent, the lawless, and the pagan that come into use when the contemporary state wishes to define—and so oppose itself to—a suspect citizenry or a suspect era of history.[1]

For a century and more, Bambang has been a pocket for the ritual traditions once practiced throughout the Salu Mambi and Salu Hau watersheds. Although most of Bambang's residents have converted to Christianity since 1970, a significant minority has retreated deeply into ancestral tradition. Depending on time, place, and the persons to whom one is speaking, the ritual tradition can be called *alu'* (sacred knowledge and doings), *pemali appa' randanna* (literally, "tabus of the four strands"), or *ada' mappurondo* (the term that I favor and will explore below). Followers of this ancestral religion do not maintain or hold claim to an autonomous territory, nor have they joined together in formal political union. Considering the fracture of upland society along religious lines, and given the region's incorporation into the Indonesian state, I should emphasize that those who still adhere to this ritual order do not constitute an ethnic group, but, rather, a religious minority with a distinct ideological focus and identity as well as a distinct set of claims about headwater religious traditions. Although it is useful to think of them as forming a coherent religious enclave or collectivity, their communities and households are scattered throughout a dozen settlements along the upper reaches of the Salu Mambi. In a loose sense, these communities are autonomous, village-based, ritual polities. Living uneasily beside their Christian or Muslim neighbors and kin, and largely excluded from desa administration, members of each community oversee their own household and religious affairs, and usually convene as a village-wide ceremonial polity only during the annual headhunting rites of pangngae.

I took residence with a Muslim family in Mambi in April 1983, a few weeks prior to a spectacular solar eclipse that had everyone worrying about what prayers and ancestral observances would help ward off *sinar merah* (Ind. "red rays," i.e. infrared radiation). Two months would pass before I was to meet someone from the mappurondo communities upriver in Bambang. During that time, I stayed in Mambi and used the eclipse as a start-up topic in lengthy talks with Muslims, Christians, and members of the civil service about local ritual traditions. The last of these usually talked about the dangers of *animisme* (Ind. "animism"), of "praying to rocks and trees," giving proof once more that anthropological discourse can race ahead of ethnographers and greet them in the field. For these civil servants, the communities that adhered to local ritual tradition were *terbelakang* and *terasing* (Ind. "backward" and "estranged"), groups in exile that had yet to embrace a "true" religion (Ind. *belum beragama*).[2] Christians, and an occasional Muslim, had another way of naming those who followed such ritual practices: *tomalillin*, or "people of the dark," a term I took as a kind of slur on pagan belief, reckoning that it had roots in the scriptural and evangelical discourse of enlightenment that accompanies religions of "The Book." Most Muslims, meanwhile, spoke of these persons as *orang kafir* (Ind. "unbelievers") and called the pagan ritual order *ada' mappurondo*, "mappurondo *adat*."

The word *ada'* had clear roots in Malay and Arabic terminology for "custom" and "tradition"—*adat*. The word *mappurondo*, however, troubled me in my first months in Mambi. When I asked for glosses of the word in Indonesian, people usually responded with *sudah dipesankan*, roughly "already given [or passed on] as a message." But my early work with word roots in the Salu Mambi area suggested that this gloss was missing something. I tried a Torajan-Indonesian dictionary for clues. *Ma'parondo*, for the Sa'dan Toraja, means to shake with malarial chill or to tremble in fright ("like when you see a mad dog," someone was later to write me, quoting a Torajan acquaintance). After working later in the year with old manuscripts from Muslim lowland communities, I realized that *mappurondo* derived from the Bugis and Mandar word *ma-pura-onro*, meaning "already in place."[3]

From the vantage point of a social poetics—with its interest in the semantic and pragmatic history of signs and the contests waged over them— the term ada' mappurondo stands out as a response to the Muslim lowland cultures that had been extending their influence into the highlands for over three centuries. The term, I would argue, reflects the effort of highlanders to translate their ancestral practices into the interpretive and discursive framework of an intruding culture. As such, it captures something of the ambivalence that uplanders may have felt with respect to lowland culture. On one hand, it portrays (and thus constructs) ancestral ritual as prior autochthonous practice. All practices to which ada' mappurondo may be opposed thus appear as derived or alien. On the other hand, the term's derivation from non-autochthonous language suggests a concession—willing or forced—to a long history of engagement with coastal principalities.

Of the several terms that can be used to name local ritual tradition, I have chosen to use ada' mappurondo. When mentioned, *alu'* (sacred knowledge and doings) refers rather narrowly to liturgical acts and speech, most often in connection with women's household rites, rather than with men's head-hunting ceremonies. Alu' also smacks of the Sa'dan Toraja ritual tradition *aluk to dolo,* and, to be honest, I want to deflect the claims and opinions of those who too closely associate the Salu Mambi and Salu Sa'dan peoples, and who are apt to view Salu Mambi ritual practice as a derivative or marginal form of traditions born in a Sa'dan cultural hearth. *Pemali appa' randanna* designates much more effectively a unique, local order of ritual activity. Yet in the cultural politics of the headwater region, pemali appa' randanna is subject to the claims of Christians and Muslims, claims that would transform it from lived ritual order to past cultural heritage. For its general use among Muslims, Christians, and those faithful to ritual tradition, and for its social historical resonance, *mappurondo* strikes me as the more apt term.

In writing, then, about ada' mappurondo, mappurondo tradition, mappurondo ritual, mappurondo history, and the mappurondo enclave, I see myself caught up inextricably in the shifting cultural politics of upland tradition. At the very least, I want to acknowledge the authority of the mappurondo communities and the claims they make to local tradition through ritual performance. While recognizing the counterclaims of Christians and Muslims, and some of the more significant cultural ties to communities and societies elsewhere in Sulawesi, I think it critical that we listen for mappurondo voices beneath the din of a pejorative discourse that would define and then erase a contemporary minority religion. Ritual tradition—saying what it is and holding claim to it through practice—has become a cultural problem for the mappurondo enclave, for what is at stake is the making of social relations and social meanings, and the capacity of several small communities to shape their own fate.

The People of the Headwaters

Writing a patrol report in 1924, an anonymous military figure described villagers from Bambang as "coastal Toraja," an incongruous, if telling, remark meaning "coastal highlander" (anonymous [Militaire Nota] 1924). For most outsiders, the people of the Salu Mambi region are of marginal and ambiguous ethnic stock. Of course, the shifting ethnic affiliations and boundaries of the past may once have afforded them greater autonomy and visibility. But for the last 50 years or more, they have disappeared from the ethnic map of South Sulawesi, a map constructed, in part, through a colonial and national interest in identifying a governable plurality of societies and cultures. That map includes only four ethnic groups— Bugis, Makassar, Mandar, and Toraja—each presumed to have a distinct language, culture, and hearth territory. Depending on their social, political, and religious interests, most outsiders would recognize the remote area of the Salu Mambi as Mandar or Torajan. Still others—like the Indonesian Department of Social Affairs and my sponsors at LIPI (*Lembaga Ilmu Pengetahuan Indonesia,* the Indonesian Institute of Science)—would write off the Salu Mambi settlements as *suku terasing,* "estranged," "remote," "people in exile," thus placing them at the margins of the civil and cultural order of contemporary Indonesia (correspondence from LIPI 30 August, 1983).

For their part, the people of Bambang and Mambi call themselves *Todiulunnasalu,* "people of the headwaters." Although economic and religious factors can serve as points of contrast and comparison, the people of the headwaters usually distinguish their communities from the Mandar and Toraja on the basis of language, custom, and history. Though Christian villagers occasionally stress their linguistic and cultural affinities with the Sa'dan and Mamasa Toraja, the people of the headwaters more widely acknowledge a long history of involvement with the Mandar, the seafaring people who live on the neighboring coasts to the south and west. While recognizing such ties, uplanders are careful to point out the social and cultural differences that mark and shape their own ethnic order.

The speech communities of the mountain region are diverse, polylingual, and in flux (see Appendix I). Yet by and large these communities form dialect chains throughout the region, a pattern in which the languages of neighboring villages or territories share a significant level of lexical, grammatical, and pragmatic features. In a sense, then, the languages of the Salu Mambi form a linguistic bridge between Toraja and Mandar. The chaining of "dialects" (i.e. speech communities with real social, political, and cultural interests) has kept a single headwater language or linguistic standard from emerging. In fact, ambiguity, polylingualism, and the "marriage" of exogenous tongues are at the heart of Todiulunnasalu ethnic identity.

If linguistic differences have promoted highly localized identities associated with villages or territories, common adat tradition and political union have helped to construct a regional headwater identity. There are, of course, the shared ritual traditions of the pre-Islamic and pre-Christian past—an issue treated throughout this book. Here, it is worth noting headwater juridical tradition, called *ada' tuo,* or "adat of life." Under ada' tuo, no human life may be sacrificed in redress for a crime or offense. How well persons and communities abided by this tradition is open to question. Actual practices notwithstanding, adat tuo has served as an acknowledged ideal, one that was introduced, according to upland oral histories, to put a check to rebounding violence. The jural customs it replaced—*ada' mate,* or "adat of death"—linger, it is said, as the vengeful juridical tradition of the coastal communities in Mandar territory. For the people of the headwaters, then, ada' tuo stands out as an emblem of their ethnic differences vis-à-vis the Mandar coast. Note, too, that this way of declaring ethnic differences underscores the fearsome violence of lowland society and the need to manage upland feuding.

Contemporary headwater ethnicity relies particularly on recollections of a now-vanished upland political order.[4] Sometime in the sixteenth century, the scattered hill settlements in the Salu Mambi, Salu Hau, and Salu Maloso watersheds came together under covenant of mutual interests to form a relatively egalitarian political league called *Pitu Ulunna Salu,* the "Seven Headwaters." The members of the league were not individual villages (*lembâ*), but socially homogenous, multivillage territories (*pa'lembângan*) whose inhabitants acknowledged common ancestry and common adat traditions. The seven founding "adat territories" included Tabulahan, Aralle, Mambi, Matangnga, Tu'bi, Rantebulahan, and Bambang (see Map 4). A key factor that appears to have brought these adat territories together as Pitu Ulunna Salu was a common upland concern over trade and conflict with outsiders, and in particular with the Mandar coast. Indeed, oral accounts speak of the upland league as a response to Mandar political organization, wherein the territory of Balanipa assumed lordship over six other coastal communities by founding *Pitu Ba'bana Binanga,* roughly, the "Seven Rivermouths."

Over the course of the next three centuries, the league would experience turmoil and change as regional and islandwide power relations shifted.[5] But the rubric of Pitu Ulunna Salu endured into the late nineteenth century as means and metaphor for upland political cooperation. Along with ada' tuo, the covenant of Pitu Ulunna Salu no doubt promoted the ethnic affiliation of the highland territories. And less than 50 years later, the ethnic and political boundaries of Pitu Ulunna Salu would be resurrected under the Dutch colonial order to construct and legitimate a mountain administrative district (1917, Staatsblad No. 43). Yet with the coming of the Indonesian order,

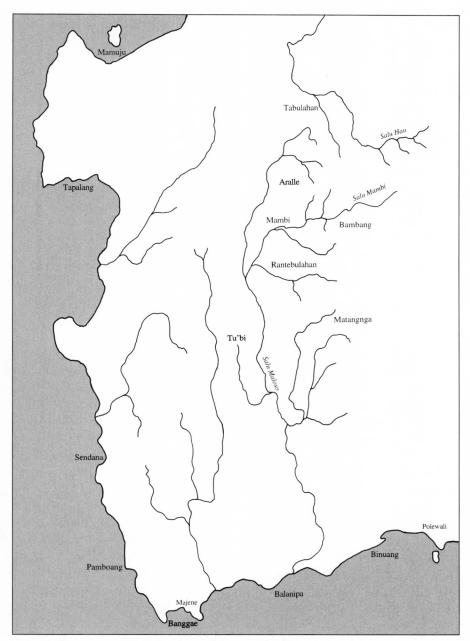

Map 4. *The regional* adat *territories: "The Seven Headwaters" and "The Seven Rivermouths"*

Pitu Ulunna Salu sank once more into obscurity, and with it faded the ethnic visibility of the headwater peoples.

The ethnic picture today is no less ambiguous than the one offered in the anonymous patrol report of 1924. Neither Mandar nor Toraja, but something in between: The coastal Toraja? The hinterland Mandar? As Pitu Ulunna Salu recedes further into the past, "Todiulunnasalu" grows more anachronistic as an ethnic designation. Some people have turned back to the mosaic of territorial identities—thus *ToMambi, ToAralle, ToBambang,* a person from Mambi, from Aralle, from Bambang. Others have already begun to adopt identities from contemporary Indonesian districts. For example, it would not be unusual to hear someone from the Salu Mambi area claim to be an *orang Polmas,* "a person from the regency (Ind. *Kabupaten*) of Polewali-Mamasa," and let it go at that. Still, a majority of people along the Salu Mambi consider themselves Todiulunnasalu, or people of the headwaters, and nowhere more so than in the mappurondo enclave in Bambang.

The History of Bambang in the Precolonial Era

Headwater political history begins with the marriage of Pongka Padang and Torije'ne' at Tabulahan sometime in the fifteenth century. Songs and narratives recall Pongka Padang as an elite Torajan son who wandered from the Sa'dan headwaters that lie in the mountains to the east.[6] Torije'ne', meanwhile, is something of a mystery to the uplanders. Her name is in the Makassan language and means "person from water" or "one from the sea." Who she was, why she carried a Makassan name, and why she was living at Tabulahan at the time of Pongka Padang's arrival is unknown, though written sources from the Mandar coast suggest she might have been I Sanre Bone, an elite daughter from the Makassar region. This "coastal-highlander" couple would give birth to four incestuous offspring (two brothers and two sisters) whose children would go on to settle Pitu Ulunna Salu and the Mandar coast. Accounts differ on the names, birth order, and settlements of Pongka Padang's descendants, yet all with which I am familiar agree that a son named Tammi' formed the adat territory of Bambang by opening hamlets at Lasodehata and Rantekaneei (which today make up part of the village of Rantepalado). His descendants subsequently settled both Bambang and the Salu Mokanan, the watershed that lies to the south in Rantebulahan.

The foundational discourse to which these stories of social and political origin belong consistently emphasizes themes of siblingship, seniority, and gender. For example, the stories of Pongka Padang and Torije'ne' assert a common parentage for the scattered mountain settlements, and thereby relate the upland adat territories to one another as siblings. As such, the mountain league used an idiom of siblingship as a basis of organization and cooperation. The same idiom, however, also captured some of the rivalry and divisiveness that periodically disturbed the upland alliance, throughout its history. In short, the stories of ancestral parents and siblings serve as a basis of cooperation and authority, even while masking or making intelligible the tensions implicit in upland politics.

Like many other Southeast Asian hill communities, the people of the headwaters reckon prestige and authority on the basis of age. Those more senior by and large wield more influence and authority, and enjoy higher status, than their juniors. But if ideas about seniority help order mountain social life, they also introduce the seeds of conflict. For instance, the most heated and feared disputes occur between a descendant's senior son and junior brother in their claims to be "next-in-line" with respect to inheritable wealth, office, and prestige. It is not surprising, then, that the clash and competition of oral histories and genealogies linking Pongka Padang, Torije'ne', and their son Tammi' to contemporary Bambang place a strong emphasis on seniority. The purpose is to weave stories that legitimize, clarify, or (in other contexts) challenge existing claims to political authority and status in the settlements. For example, the settlement at Rantepalado (and one of its male residents) has remained the only community that may hold claim to the title *Indona Bambang* ("The Mother of Bambang"), and with it, political leadership over Bambang, by tracing descent along senior lines to Tammi' and Tammi''s senior son. Other villages, meanwhile, carry other adat titles by virtue of descent from Tammi''s other children and grandchildren.

The stories of origin, descent, and authority have an unmistakably masculine character. They are plotted to foreground fathers, senior sons, and the political offices they hold. Mothers and daughters may figure in genealogical reckonings as "juniors," as "outsiders," or as convenient stepping-stones to more senior male lines. In these cases, women are bypassed as focal authorities. To take but one example, genealogical recitations and asides in the Bambang communities of Rantepalado and Minanga claim authority through Tammi''s sons while arguing that the settlements of the Salu Mokanan can trace relationship to the region's founder only through a daughter, said to be his youngest child. From the viewpoint of narrators in

Rantepalado and Minanga, feminized origins here undermine Salu Moka-nan claims to higher political authority.

It is worth mentioning, too, that uplanders use stories about Pongka Padang and Torije'ne' to situate differences in language and ritual practice in the mountain communities. Villagers in the western hill-country of Tabu-lahan, Aralle, and Mambi speak "language of the mother" (*basa indo*), while those living upriver and to the east in the rugged reaches of Bambang, Rantebulahan, and Matangnga speak "language of the father" (*basa ambe*). The distinction corresponds with contemporary linguistic patterns, for in-deed, communities with "paternal" dialects have more in common with the language spoken by the Sa'dan Toraja (Pongka Padang's ethnic back-ground, it will be recalled), whereas communities with "maternal" dialects show greater commonalities with the dialects of the Mandar coast. Father/mountain, mother/sea associations at one time held as well for differences in ritual practices. Prior to their embrace of Islam or Christianity, communi-ties at Tabulahan, Aralle, and Mambi staged postharvest household rituals known as *pa'todilopian*, "the time of the ones in the sailing vessel." Cor-responding rites for those speaking "father tongues" were called, collectively, *pa'bisuan*, "the time of quickening spirits," with individual ceremonies bear-ing names often applied to Sa'dan rituals. Commonalities in the regional ceremonial order, meanwhile, are understood as the wedding of different ritual traditions brought respectively by Torije'ne' and Pongka Padang.

From its beginnings in the sixteenth century to its final collapse around 1870, stability and cohesiveness always threatened to elude the upland league. Villages, for the most part, were free to run their own affairs under the leadership of the *tomatuatonda'*, or village head. Matters of interest to, or involving, neighboring settlements were resolved by convening village lead-ers under the authority of the *Indona Lita'* ("Mother of the Ground") of each adat territory. These adat communities, such as Bambang, were them-selves fairly autonomous polities, except when matters commanded the at-tention of the entire headwater league. In this hierarchic political structure, power and authority had no center. Rather, authority lodged throughout the hierarchy and rested on the consensus of male elders and those leaders selected from an elite to be first among equals. To sum up, then, the league could neither overcome internal dissension nor compel participation and compliance of its members, and so lacked cohesiveness.

As we have seen, a common concern over trade and conflict with the Man-dar coast helped bring the upland communities together as Pitu Ulunna Salu. Once again, the foundational idiom of siblingship structured the moun-tain people's understanding of regional political and economic relations. In their reckoning, it was the junior descendants of Pongka Padang and To-rije'ne' who settled the Mandar coast. So not only did this discourse bind mountain and coastal settlements together as siblings, but it also introduced a hierarchy of authority that encouraged the mountain settlements to look upon the coast as a dependent junior. This claim for greater authority and prestige also had a basis in the "natural facts" of mountain cosmography, in which the upstream world sits in an "elder" position vis-à-vis regions down-stream. I will have more to say about the political, economic, and ideologi-cal dimensions of this relationship in later chapters. For now, it is enough to mention that Pitu Ulunna Salu political organization had its roots in the in-terdependent and oppositional patterns linking mountain and coast. It arose in response to potentially hostile groups, and with the idea of stabilizing trade with the coast.

As I already have noted, the internal stability of Pitu Ulunna Salu was an-other matter. Remarks and remembered stories about the 300 years stretch-ing from the late sixteenth through the late nineteenth century paint an image of treachery and discord. Persistent rivalries and feuds between settle-ments suggest that "feud management" may have been a key issue for the upland league. The vigor of the slave trade further disrupted the highlands. Bands of warriors attacked other villages, seized captives, and then sold them to the Mandar for cloth, porcelain, and weapons. Uplanders, too, took some interest in building retinues of slaves for the purpose of expanding power and prestige, although slavery continued to be viewed as a coastal or lowland institution. Yet it was the arrival of Islam in the uplands during the mid-eighteenth century that seriously fractured the mountain league, as Muslim settlements moved closer culturally, socially, and politically to the Mandar, who had begun to embrace this religion over a century before.

The Enclave in the Headwaters

The coming of Islam to the mountains is remembered in dif-ferent ways. Contemporary narratives from the Muslim settlements that comprise Mambi and Aralle mention wandering teachers (Ind. *ulama*) and saints (Ind. *wali*) as the figures who first brought Islam to the headwaters more than 200 years ago. Such stories put emphasis on evangelical effort, sacrifice, and dedication, and on the growing understanding and enlighten-ment of the mountain converts. Mappurondo villagers in Bambang have a different story to tell, however.

The story takes place at Mambi. The coastal principality at Balanipa has sent a gift to Mambi—a copy of the Koran—igniting a quarrel with Mambi's upstream neighbor, Bambang. The recitation goes:

Says Indona Bambang to Indona Mambi:
Do not eat away at the house
by bringing a newcomer to the adat of Pitu Ulunna Salu.
Says Mambi:
Don't come to complain, Indona Bambang,
about the gift in my sarong from my lords at Balanipa.
Says Bambang:
Don't complain, then, about the smoke at the door of Salukona
who burns incense
and sacrifices a chicken at the border of the land.
I will mark the borders of the land at Bambang with thread
so that the newcomer does not eat away at the house.

The story, so far, tells of the heated words of political and ideological conflict over ritual practices. In headwater political tradition, neither territory may intrude into the affairs of the other, although Bambang, in its regionally acknowledged role as "watchpost of adat" (*su'buan ada'*), is obliged to sound alarm when it senses threat to the integrity of adat traditions. So as to contain the dangerous intrusion of Islam, here embodied in the Koran, Bambang secures its borders with thread; that is, it simply declares itself sealed off from Islamic discourse and its consequences.

Soon after, the *debata* (spirits) took offense at the alien text and abandoned the rice fields at Mambi, the ritual hub of upland agriculture. As a result, the harvest failed and famine set in. The recitation continues with the Indona Mambi pleading to the Indona Bambang for help:

Indona Mambi calls out, calls to Indona Bambang.
Says Indona Mambi:
Come here, Indona Bambang.
Pick up the fallen land and the fallen people
these your lands and your people.
Indona Bambang goes downriver saying:
Mambi, move it downriver to Panompa that Koran of yours.
Indona Mambi moves the Koran downriver to Panompa.

Once the offending Koran had been moved to a village downstream, the debata resumed their guardianship of the rice crop and prosperity returned to Mambi.

Although the immediate source of misfortune had been carried off to a

remote village where it would do no harm, Mambi nevertheless held to its
new faith. A dilemma remained: how could the moral and ritual tradition be
kept safe from the advance of Islam and the *ToSalam,* as the Muslims were
called? So as to prevent Islam from encroaching further on upland ritual
tradition, the league met and declared Bambang a retreat for mappurondo
tradition:

The newcomer eats away at the house.
The watchpost of adat
is a room covered by a dark shroud,
not to be seen
not to be heard.

With these words the highlanders concealed local ritual tradition from the
gaze of Islam, and placed it out of earshot in the upstream reaches of Bambang. At the same time, these words transformed ada' mappurondo into the
religion of a social enclave.

This version of upland political and religious history suggests that as
long as eight or nine generations ago the upland league was susceptible to
social and ideological fracture. It is also a defining and determining episode
in "local mappurondo history"—i.e. a vision of social time through which
the contemporary mappurondo communities at Bambang maintain ideological control of the past. This story acknowledges the religious plurality of
the mountain region, and so makes concession to the growing political and
cultural influence of the Mandar coast. I suspect, too, that the episode recounted here marks the time when "mappurondo"—the coastal term for
the already said and the already in place—began to slip into the discourse of
highland ritual tradition. If the story is one of concession and retreat, it also
gives foundation to the proud exclusionary discourse that distinguishes Bambang from neighboring territories. Villagers from Bambang have shouldered
the role of tradition-keeper as their peculiar historical task and destiny. That
moral and historical vision remains sharp among mappurondo and Christian
factions in present-day Bambang. For them, the history of Bambang has
been the history of guarding the living authenticity of adat for all of Pitu
Ulunna Salu.

The fervor and consistency of adat tradition beneath the "dark shroud"
was not enough, however, to put a check to social turmoil and discord.
Around 1870, raids from the Salu Mokanan watershed in Rantebulahan devastated Bambang.[7] Villagers fled north to find sanctuary in Aralle as warriors spilled into Bambang to take captives and raze hamlets. The intruders,

called *ToSalu* ("people of the river") began to settle Bambang. The original inhabitants of Bambang, the *ToIssilita'* (roughly, "people of the ground"), meanwhile opened settlements in the Buntumalangka' region of Aralle. During the course of the next 30 years, significant numbers of the ToIssilita' made their way back to Bambang to reclaim their abandoned hamlets and terraces. After resolving land disputes, the ToIssilita' rebuilt settlements at Lasodehata, Minanga, Saludengen, Masoso, and Ulumambi, leaving the ToSalu firmly lodged in Bambang's upriver region, having settled at Salubulo, Karakean, Limba, Rantelemo, Salukadi, Salutabang, and a different part of Ulumambi.

The ToSalu intruders powerfully altered the social, political, and cultural landscape of Bambang. Speaking a different dialect, practicing "irregularities" during ritual, and having usurped land and belongings, the ToSalu raised enduring suspicions among the ToIssilita'. Only the fact that the Salu Mokanan people, too, were able to trace descent from Tammi' allowed minimal political unity to be restored throughout Bambang. ToSalu recognition of the Indona Bambang at Lasodehata did little to overcome mutual suspicions or sore relations deriving from the raids. Nearly a third of the earliest Dutch commentary concerning Bambang (Smit 1937) deals with the ToSalu intrusion and the subsequent political calamity. More than 120 years after the fact, events are talked about still, smoldering in ToIssilita' minds, glowing in the ToSalu. Rarely do the ToSalu and ToIssilita' marry one another, and ToSalu representatives have asked the Indonesian civil administration for provisional status as a separate village-precinct, or desa, so as not to share authority with, or subject their interests to, the ToIssilita'.[8]

The Dutch and Indonesian Periods

Dutch patrols passed through Bambang for the first time during the 1906–7 mountain campaigns, and by 1912 civil administration was in place, the Dutch having set up small posts at Mambi and Aralle. The next twenty years brought many changes: the abrupt cessation of slavery, the introduction of taxes, the arrival of Bugis traders and the opening of the first upland marketplaces (at Mambi and Aralle, c. 1925), the considerable loss of life to famine in 1913 and to the epidemic of 1918, and the arrival of Christianity. Resistance to the Dutch was sporadic and of little consequence, showing none of the anti-colonial millenarianism noted in Central Sulawesi

(Adriani & Kruyt 1950 [1912]; Atkinson 1989; van der Kroef 1970). Indeed, Bambang remained something of an administrative backwater, never subject to the prolonged and intense colonial intrusion that occurred in Sa'dan or Bugis territory. After administrative reorganization of the region in 1924, the nearest civil and military posts of any importance were at Mamasa and Mamuju (40 and 60 kilometers distant, respectively), and colonial officers seldom interfered with the tomatuatonda' (village head) and indona lita' (territory leader) who were already in place, except to enforce collection of taxes and to make sure villagers adhered to Dutch policy and directives (cf. Smit 1937).

When the Dutch arrived in the highlands, the social and ideological enclave at Bambang was intact but still recovering from the ToSalu raids 30 years earlier. The upstream district was a hearth of mappurondo activity, whereas Mambi was fully Muslim, if nominally so.[9] It was no accident, then, that the Dutch missions ignored Mambi and devoted their efforts to converting the *tomalillin* ("people of the dark") in Bambang. In contrast to the social and historical forces that brought Islam to the mountains, Christianity arrived in the person of colonial and mission figures who were interested in direct administrative rule. There probably was little the mappurondo community could do to keep Christianity out of Bambang. A story is told about the Indona Bambang in the first years of Dutch rule. Faced with the dilemma of either forsaking local tradition or defying Dutch authority, he decided to subject Christianity to trial and curse:

They say he said, "If the adat of the ToSarani [Christians] is good, Bambang will prosper. If it brings ruin, it will be gored on the horns of this water buffalo."

The water buffalo—by tradition the grandest sacrificial animal—is an emblem of ada' mappurondo. Resonating within the declaration, then, was the threat that Christianity risked being gored on the horns of ada' mappurondo. Things did not turn out well. Before a year had passed, the Indona Bambang was dead—gored, it is said, by the very water buffalo to which he had pointed when making his declaration about Christianity.

The message was not lost on the mappurondo community. Yet there remained enormous flux and ambiguity in the reception of Christianity at Bambang. Impressive baptismal figures (Atlas 1925) and glowing reports about the conversion of the entire district (Veen 1933) at best reflect a transient and misunderstood engagement with the church. For example, initial mission work commenced in 1912 under the aegis of the *Indische Protestantsche Kerk* (the Indies Protestant Church) but amounted to little more than mass baptisms by an itinerant missionary (Krüger 1966; Rauws 1930; Veen 1933).[10] Schools were built with government assistance at Karakean and Rantelemo, and the Ambonese teachers installed there baptized nearly 2,500 persons (Atlas 1925:129; Krüger 1966:127). Yet elders today still remember these zealous Ambonese and insist that baptism was misconstrued at the time as a directive from the colonial administration. Indeed, a report on Bambang's local leadership written in the mid-1930s suggests that the church was yet to gain wide and lasting influence (Smit 1937).

The Protestantsche Kerk was unable to sustain its mission in the uplands, and so, in 1927, surrendered the evangelical field to the more conservative and pietistic *Christliche Gereformeerd Kerk* (Christian Reformed Church), the church that was to oversee the area until 1942 (Krüger 1966). The missionaries Bikker and Geleynse surveyed Bambang, and responsibility for Christian life there passed to Geleynse, who took brief residence at Lasodehata (Rantepalado) in 1930. His impact was comparatively modest, for later that year Geleynse opted to oversee this district from Mela'bo, a Mamasa Toraja village 30 kilometers from the settlements at Bambang. Few conversions took place, and many of those baptized earlier simply continued mappurondo practices without any pretense of being Christian. Locals mention that those who did convert often did so with the idea of winning Dutch support for their political ambitions; in other cases, sons or daughters of the elite were encouraged to convert in order to advance through the schools.

Missionary activity ceased with the Japanese occupation, and by 1950, the year Sulawesi joined the Republic of Indonesia, Christianity had only a limited foothold in Bambang, claiming but a few households in any village, save at Rantelemo and Karakean, where Christian missions and schools had succeeded in forming stable communities and a cadre of leaders. The fledgling *Gereja Toraja Mamasa* (the Mamasa Toraja Church) had by this time assumed control of the churches in Bambang and began to intensify its efforts in converting the district. Yet it was not until the early 1970s that large numbers abandoned ada' mappurondo for the GTM, a time when those supposedly lacking religion became suspect in the eyes of an Indonesian bureaucracy prone to associating lack of faith in God with subversive, procommunist leanings.

Mission figures were not without influence in cultural and ethnic politics. Throughout the colonial and early independence periods there were efforts to incorporate Bambang (and all of Pitu Ulunna Salu, for that matter) politically and ethnically within the Toraja sphere. Several civil officers who oversaw Pitu Ulunna Salu acknowledged the area's cultural and economic ties to the Mandar coast (e.g. Hoorweg 1911; Maurenbrecher 1947), however, and consistently argued against incorporation. The people of Bambang, for their part, viewed the Mamasa Toraja as political and cultural subordinates, and protested the political realignment of the mountain region, to little avail. Although Bambang and the rest of Pitu Ulunna Salu remained within *Afdeeling Mandar*, they were merged with the Mamasa Toraja to form a single administrative subdivision, or *onderafdeeling*, called *Boven Binoeang en Pitoe Oeloenna Saloe*—Upper Binuang and Pitu Ulunna Salu (1924, Staatsblad No. 467). Thereafter, Mamasa acted as a political, cultural, and economic center for the onderafdeeling, with the consequence of bringing about the political and cultural marginalization of Bambang and Pitu Ulunna Salu in the hinterland region.

From 1950 through 1965, banditry and rebellion troubled the area. The devoutly Muslim rebels led by Kahar Muzakkar took control of Mambi in 1958 and seemed poised to assault Bambang. Bambang organized rapidly under the ToIssilita' leaders of *OPR*, or *Organisasi Pertahanan Rakyat* (Ind. People's Defense Organization), who operated secretly from Saludengen. With aid from nationalist Battalion 710, Bambang attacked Mambi, driving the rebels and most of Mambi's townsfolk back to the coast near Mamuju. Not long after, treachery and rapacity on the part of the Bugis-led 710 caused the OPR to break off the alliance. OPR forced 710 to retreat to Mamasa, and then sealed off all trails into Bambang until civil order was restored fully in 1964.

The Political Stature of the Mappurondo Enclave at Bambang

Just as Bambang was an administrative backwater during the Dutch period, so it has been a backwater of development since 1965. Forming a part of *Kecamatan Mambi*, and organized and administered during the time of my work as a single *desa* from the ToIssilita' village of Rantepalado, it has no middle school, no health clinic, no electrification, no roads. Although a marketplace was successfully opened east and upriver, in the ToSalu village of Rantelemo, government-sponsored development programs usually falter at Bambang's door. Indeed, the desa required a visit by the *camat* (head of the subdistrict) and his entourage in 1984 to spur compliance on the issues of taxes and photo ID cards. The development picture in

Bambang was perhaps best summed up by a 1981 land-use map of Keca-matan Mambi prepared by the provincial offices of the Department of Ag-riculture and placed in the Kecamatan office. Desa Bambang was missing from the map, left undrawn. In its place were symbols indicating forest and mountains, and lines showing the land as part of other desas.

Since 1970, the mappurondo following at Bambang has suffered a rapid and continued erosion of its community. The heart of the problem is that local civil authorities do not view ada' mappurondo as a religion. Owing to a narrow interpretation of *Pancasila,* the creed of the Indonesian state, map-purondo practices go unsanctioned and fall under the rubric of adat (i.e. custom, *not* religion) or animism (i.e. a mistaken pagan enchantment with nature, also *not* religion). Thus putatively lacking religion (Ind. *agama*), mappurondo villagers are thus seen as lacking something in the way of good citizenship. The villagers became suspect in the eyes of civil and religious authorities, who from time to time have charged the mappurondo commu-nities with harboring pro-communist sentiments or anti-development atti-tudes. Clear efforts were made to pressure mappurondo children to convert to Christianity (or Islam) in order to advance scholastically, and, where pos-sible, to exclude mappurondo adults from holding office in desa or *lingkun-gan* (village) administration.

The result has been a sharp rise in conversions to Christianity since 1970, especially among the young, such that ada' mappurondo is increasingly the ritual tradition for elders and the disenfranchised. Today, it is impossible to find a village oriented wholly to ada' mappurondo. In fact, nearly three-fourths of Bambang's 5,000 residents have converted to Christianity, and look condescendingly upon their mappurondo neighbors and kin. Worse, their censorious attitudes have gained ideological and institutional support from the Indonesian government, whose state policies continue to cham-pion monotheistic religion as the keystone of solid, progress-oriented citi-zenship. In many cases, villages have seen bitter tensions drive Christian and mappurondo camps apart, perhaps nowhere so dramatically as in the ToIs-silita' village of Saludengen, where the sides actually exchanged rice terraces and moved houses so as to create an upstream mappurondo settlement and a downstream Christian settlement. And under strictures issued by Gereja Toraja Mamasa (the Mamasa Toraja Church), no marriages may take place between Christians and those who adhere to ada' mappurondo.

As should be clear, the mappurondo minority has little voice in modern desa political life. Although the Dutch at first drew from the mappurondo leadership to legitimate colonial directives (Hoorweg 1911; Smit 1937), subsequent administrations long ago supplanted Pitu Ulunna Salu and the Indona Lita', bringing an end to the character and scope of precolonial political authority. The mappurondo leadership of today rests with local groups of elders and "ritual specialists," whose authority extends no further than (village) lingkungan boundaries and revolves around the ritual and moral life of the mappurondo households located in a given settlement. Through 1985, efforts to forge a districtwide organization to shield mappurondo interests consistently met with failure, thwarted by the deep mistrust between ToIssilita' and ToSalu, lingering intervillage disputes, and a fear of relinquishing authority to persons belonging to other villages and other kin groups. Seeking recourse and state sanction through the auspices of Parisada Hindu Dharma—the Hindu leadership through whom the Sa'dan Toraja and the Dayak gained recognition for their minority religions (respectively, *aluk to dolo* and *kaharingan*)—has also met with failure, owing to the fears and disinterest of mappurondo elders and to the inability of Hindu representatives to work directly at desa levels without first establishing *kabupaten* (regional district) and *kecamatan* (regional subdistrict) offices.[11]

Mappurondo villagers see no way out of their predicament. Bewildered, marginalized, and made vulnerable by the changes that have swept through Bambang, they have lost ground in the struggle for control of social meanings and social relations. Still, they find ways to understand the new political order, to come to terms with its bureaucratic institutions and its concern for citizenship, through the vehicle of traditional cosmology. As one elder put it, voicing his complaint about the attitudes of schoolteachers and officials, "Animism? What is it? I don't know this animism. I only know that I am afraid, afraid of the spirits and afraid of the government."

The Contours of Mappurondo Social Life

What is social life like today in this minority religious enclave? As in the past, most mappurondo villagers are farmers and gardeners whose lives center on the household, the hamlet, and the relatives that make up a person's bilateral kindred. Owing to marriage patterns and ways of reckoning kinship, the mappurondo households in each village form a relatively close-knit group of kin with shared interests and anxieties. In my experience, these persons show a deep sense of belonging to their birthplace and homestead, of being tied not only to other people born in the village, but

Fig. 3. *A single-hearth house and rice barn in Bambang. A woman works in the yard between them. 1984.*

to its paths, the shadows of the surrounding hills, and to the sound of the rivers running along the valley floor. The village and its lands thus promote a comforting image through which people recall a common history and a common way of life. To offer but a glimpse of that life, let me here sketch a few basic "facts" about the mappurondo communities in Bambang.

SETTLEMENT PATTERN

Organization of the settlement begins with the house, or *ba-nua*. In contrast to the multiple-hearth houses of the past, present-day banua are usually single-hearth homes consisting of a front room, a partitioned sleeping area, and a smaller back room that encloses the kitchen area and hearth.[12] A married couple and their offspring commonly reside at each hearth and maintain their own rice barn in the yard. A cluster of houses—rarely more than 30—makes up a hamlet, or *tonda'* (also called *botto*), and the terraces and gardens resting on the slopes beneath a tonda' make up its *bamba*. All the hamlets, their respective bamba, and their outlying gardens and terraces together make up the *lembâ*, or village, which is administered by desa civil authorities as a *lingkungan*.

The villages in Bambang vary significantly with respect to the number of households and hamlets, and to the amount of land in cultivation (see Table 1, Appendix II). During the 1980s there were nine lingkungan in Desa Bambang, two of which incorporated settlements that at one time were organized as villages. They included Rantepalado (formerly Lasodehata, and incorporating Salubulo), Minanga, Saludengen, Masoso, Karakean, Limba, Rantelemo (incorporating Salukadi), Salutabang, and Ulumambi. As of 1984, these settlements together comprised 5,742 persons and 1,120 households.

It is worth mentioning once more that the ToIssilita' and the ToSalu make up distinct social and territorial groups in Bambang. Salutabang, Limba, Rantelemo, Salubulo, and the hamlet of Seppang at Ulumambi are the principal ToSalu communities. The ToSalu have also opened homesteads in Masoso, Karakean, and Rantepalado. The ToIssilita', meanwhile, have clustered in the settlements at Saludengen, Minanga, and Rantepalado, as well as in the older hamlets at Ulumambi. Although founded as ToIssilita' settlements, Masoso and Karakean are moving further within the orbit of the ToSalu.

The religious composition of the villages varies dramatically (see Table 2, Appendix II). As should be clear, there is a strong Christian presence throughout Bambang. Limba, Rantelemo, and Masoso, for example, have embraced the church. The mappurondo households remaining in those villages are so few that they can no longer stage rituals on their own.[13] Christians, of course, have power and influence in other settlements as well. But these same places also have significant mappurondo communities, albeit of varying size and activity. As for Islam, there is a single Muslim household in all of Bambang, located in Minanga, the village lying closest to Mambi.

ECONOMY

The local economy is largely one of subsistence farming, supplemented by income from cash crops, labor, and small-scale trading ventures. Hunting-and-gathering activities are in decline and contribute minimally to subsistence. Although the household is the basic unit of production and consumption, a great deal of cooperation takes place among kin with respect to labor and distribution. There are a few comparatively wealthy mappurondo households in each village, and a few very poor ones as well, but differences seem marginal in light of resource-sharing and the struggle of even the most prosperous households to carry on from one harvest to the next.

Hillside gardens are a mainstay of subsistence. The typical household, for example, maintains roughly half a hectare of land in garden crops. Emphasis is on semipermanent rather than shifting swidden gardens, with virtually no crop rotation and only brief fallows. Some plots, especially those planted with cassava, are kept in continuous cultivation until exhausted soils force a farmer to move on. Key garden staples are cassava, sweet potatoes, corn, and taro; these foodstuffs, rather than rice, make up the bulk of the diet. Gardeners also plant bananas, cane, beans, and different kinds of greens.

The prominence of the garden notwithstanding, locals say that rice is their most important crop and chief index to prosperity. Unlike garden cultigens, rice is a special, prestigious food, an absolute necessity for expressions of ritual hospitality. Mappurondo villagers consider it sacred and medicinal, believing that it grows under the supernatural guardianship of the girlish and easily startled *Debata Totibojongam*. The people of Bambang cultivate rice in flooded terraces, and make no use whatsoever of dry swiddens. Keeping with tradition, villagers generally plant one crop of rice annually. Without exception, mappurondo households are careful to plant and harvest in accordance with ritual practices and tabus, and tend to avoid new strains of rice introduced by the government (George 1989). Some families may own as much as 2 hectares of terrace land (see Table 3, Appendix II), but with rare exception, no household is able to raise a crop sufficient to make daily, year-round consumption of rice possible. Households report that they normally deplete their rice stores in anywhere from three to six months, and virtually all buy additional rice in the markets at Mambi and Rantelemo.

As a marker of prosperity and prestige, rice overshadows the contribution of garden crops to subsistence. At the same time, the importance attached to rice somewhat hides the crucial role of coffee in the local economy. Coffee cultivation antedates the arrival of the Dutch (Hoorweg 1911).[14] Colonial policy and market penetration of the highlands after 1920, however, did much to spur interest in this crop. Local farmers were at first ambivalent about coffee. Elders recall disputes over whether beans should be dried alongside of rice sheaves, some persons fearing that Debata Totibojongam would take offense and abandon her guardianship of the rice. Yet others prophesied that coffee would be a "tree of gold." At issue was whether a sacred or a mundane crop would dominate subsistence. The growth of markets and an encroaching cash economy ultimately worked in favor of coffee, although it has yet to dislodge rice as the basic measure of subsistence.

Since 1980, farmers have become more confident in committing land and labor to coffee (see Table 4, Appendix II), the value of which is subject to fluctuations in world prices and the strength of the Indonesian rupiah.

Growing coffee as a market crop has made it possible for households to buy their way out of subsistence shortfalls (as in the case of the 1983–84 rice harvest) and to gain the cash needed to pay taxes and school fees; to purchase clothing, kerosene, zinc roofing, and tools; and to buy rice terraces. Coffee has also allowed young, landless households to start up small trading ventures.

At the same time, villagers have grown dependent on this cash crop. For example, the 1985 coffee harvest was a striking failure, and despite an excellent rice harvest, farmers expressed worries and reservations about making it through the year. Mappurondo ritual activity during 1985 was a particularly revealing measure of the impact of the coffee failure. Ordinarily, an abundant rice harvest would presage a burst of prosperity rites. No such large-scale ceremonies were held, however, as villagers saw that they would have no coffee income to refill rice barns depleted by ritual.

Mappurondo villagers still play a subordinate role in the market network, in general lacking sufficient capital and social networks beyond the region to broaden or strengthen their ventures, and to challenge Bugis control of trade at Mambi and Melabo. Their attitudes toward debt, risk, and the social obligations that enter into trade take shape from a background of subsistence farming, a communalism informed by kinship, and a history of limited, if well-defined, exchange networks with the Muslim coast.

KINSHIP, FAMILY, AND HOUSEHOLD

Villagers reckon their kin relations bilaterally and can usually find persons whom they consider relatives settled throughout Bambang. Personal kindreds, for example, extend to third and fourth cousins. But in particular, people see themselves related through overlapping, ancestor-focused groups called *hapu*. Hapu organization is especially important to mappurondo society, for it permits the "networking" of persons, families, households, and territorial groupings. In principle, the hapu can be extended indefinitely, such that hundreds of persons, or in fact all of Bambang, may be considered *sahapu*, "of one cluster," that is, "of one origin." But genealogical reckoning remains shallow in most cases, going back no further than three or four generations, and even then in imperfect fashion. As ancestors fade from the memory of the living, so too does their hapu. Commonality of interest withers as memories blur or fade, and descendants take up their own special concerns. Thus, the hapu are fundamentally kaleidoscopic—shifting patterns of relationship that take shape as prior ones dissolve, overlap, or break apart.

The hapu offers a network of kin in which task groups take shape and lifelong friendships are born. Persons who are sahapu, and especially those who live in the same village, casually visit each other, help one another with labor or a loan of some sort, and often become inseparable companions. Relations within the hapu, then, are usually cooperative, harmonious, and reciprocal, and for hapu members to act otherwise amounts to a breach of proper conduct, causing serious offense and considerable social tension. Conflict between persons or households who are sahapu is hardly absent in daily life, to be sure, but rather than being torn apart by problems, the hapu membership attempts to soothe and settle tensions.

Though people necessarily look to ascendant generations in reckoning the bonds and obligations of kinship among peers and elders, they also look downward to descendants. The interest in and emphasis on descendants is clearly seen, for example, in the use of teknonyms, where persons assume names designating their relationship to firstborn children and grandchildren. Thus, the father and mother of a child named Ta'bu become Ambe Ta'bu and Indo Ta'bu, respectively, and all four grandparents (providing Ta'bu is their first grandchild) will take on the name Nene' Ta'bu. These teknonyms of course signal one's movement into different stages of adulthood, but they also imply a concern for descendants that runs beyond the matter of identity alone. That concern is for founding a prosperous hapu made up of all of one's descendants. As focal ancestor of an ever-growing hapu, a person gains prominence and respect, and at death is buried and honored by the hapu members.

Before moving on to other features of social organization, it is worth remarking that kinship in the mappurondo enclave is also predicated with respect to place of birth, or origin, in a manner akin to the Balinese concept of *kawitan,* as described by Geertz and Geertz (1975). For the villagers living along the Salu Mambi, the key term is *turunam* (and also, *katurunam*). The best, albeit unwieldy, gloss for the term might be "[the] place at which someone [or something] comes forth and descends to touch the earth." As such, turunam implies a "first appearance," and in its most common usage refers to one's village of birth. In other contexts it may refer to one's natal hamlet, house, or hearth.[15] What is clear is that persons experience a keen sense of belonging to their birthplace. Evidence for this strikingly deep attachment appears not only in song and poem, but comes across in the surprising energy and resolve shown by the gravely ill in their attempts to return to their place of birth before dying.

For the moment, the point to be made is that the villagers' own conceptualization of kinship rests not only on bilateral paths of descent, but upon a sense of place as well. In fact, the customary way of imagining kinship is to think of a hapu in the botanical sense: a cluster of bamboo, the jointed stalks of which represent lines of descent emerging from the common base of village or territory. Where one is born and to whom one is born together link a person not only to a specific set of relatives, but also to a whole community, its history, and its tradition.

The nuclear family, comprising husband, wife, and (unwed) offspring, is the most elementary social group in the villages, but it takes on a significant social, religious, and economic identity only when it tends a hearth and thereby acts as the core for a household. The importance of the hearth cannot go unmentioned. Until a family keeps a hearth of its own, it remains an adjunct to other families (generally that of the wife's parents), unable to conduct religious ceremonies, to have a voice in village deliberations, or to manage economic resources or exchanges autonomously. Once a family has its own hearth, it takes charge of its own religious, political, and economic interests, and effectively becomes a household of its own, even though it may share a dwelling with another hearth-owning group. Household membership, however, always stays somewhat fluid, as relatives are usually welcome to take up temporary or semipermanent residence with the hearth-owners and their children. In time, a household often encompasses an adjunct family, too, as a daughter and her in-marrying spouse begin a family of their own at the hearth of her parents. Or as parents become aged and infirm, the central or founding hearth is passed on to a son or daughter whose family becomes the core of the household. The new hearthkeepers will care for their elders and watch over their interests.

MARRIAGE AND INHERITANCE

Marriages, today, are monogamous. Historically, the case may have been otherwise, for people report that polygyny was a common and acceptable alternative for their elders. In fact, to judge from the way elder men spoke, polygyny appears to have been a marker of male prestige, connoting prosperity, sexual potency, charisma, and power.[16] On the other hand, accounts of the polygynous past link the practice to an era of wife-stealing, the passing of which men mention with a clear sense of relief. Divorce, meanwhile, is comparatively easy, though not without socioeconomic risk. It is something both men and women can and do initiate.

Incest tabus prohibit marriage with siblings, with parental siblings, with first cousins or their children, or with persons who are considered to have been raised at the same hearth.[17] A person may take a second or third cousin as a spouse, but marriages of either kind, called *sisahapuam* ("both of one hapu"), require that special fines, exchanges, and offerings be made. Villagers are ambivalent about sisahapuam marriages. For one thing, they frankly acknowledge that such marriages permit a consolidation of land and a restoration of office that once belonged to the hapu founder. For another, people observe that second and third cousins already feel a fondness for, and an obligation toward, one another, and thus make excellent husbands and wives. Yet villagers also feel that sisahapuam marriages can also introduce or exacerbate strains within a hapu, and many people would just as soon avoid such conflict. That ambivalence notwithstanding, roughly 50 to 60 percent of all marriages within the mappurondo communities are sisahapuam.

Uxorilocal residence strategies are prevalent and have promoted the formation of mother-sister-daughter "cores" within the household and hamlet. Indeed, a new husband is said to "live beneath the ends of the floorbeams" of his wife's natal home, a saying that captures his marginal status vis-à-vis his in-laws. Owing to hamlet (*tonda'*) exogamy, a preference for village (lembâ) endogamy (see Table 5, Appendix II), and the perceived advantages of sisahapuam marriages, the village settlement tends to be a strongly bounded, close-knit community.

Bridewealth, inheritance, prestige, and social realignments make preparations for marriage a tinderbox, especially in sisahapuam cases. Error and oversight can lead to serious affronts and bitter quarrels. In order to marry, a youth must give *somba* (roughly, "honor") to his prospective bride's kin. A form of bridewealth, somba customarily is made up of cloth and tools, goods of exogenous origin. But seldom does a youth collect these goods entirely on his own. He more often enlists the help of his kin in gathering enough materials for somba. During the wedding ceremony, representatives of the husband's side will make a gift of these valuables to the bride's kin, who divide the cloth and tools among themselves in proportion to the honor and respect due each kin member. Ostensibly flattered and honored by this bridewealth, the bride's kin give her to the groom.[18] They also reciprocate with meats and bundles of rice that are divided among the husband's kin so as to reflect the honor due each kinsperson and to acknowledge help in amassing the valuables used as somba.

Following their wedding, husband and wife each take their *mana'* inheritance from their elders: rice terraces are the customary form of mana', particularly for women, and are given in part with the idea of providing the couple with a base of subsistence. Secondary inheritance takes place after a parent or relative dies. The remaining inheritable possessions of the deceased, called *kambi'*, are distributed to relatives, who are required, in turn, to make a sacrifice to the soul of the deceased. Kambi' usually consists of household goods and small parcels of land, for more substantial holdings are normally transferred beforehand to descendants as mana'. Ideal distribution of kambi', according to villagers, should level out disparities in gifts of mana' to siblings.

Ritual titles and paraphernalia are not included in mana' or kambi'. It often happens that one of the ritual elite grows old and wishes to relinquish title and obligations. Unless village elders voice disapproval, ritual paraphernalia and duties are simply passed on to the handpicked successor in the family or hapu. The death of an officeholder creates a more problematic succession. Here, succession is entirely in the hands of village elders, who must pick one of the deceased's relatives for the vacant position. Fierce competition can break out among the deceased's siblings and children as they try to sway the elders in their choice.

Inheritance and somba figure critically into decisions about marriage. Never absent in the minds of husband, wife, and their respective kin is an interest in advancing their prosperity and status, the bases of which lie in inheritance. Meanwhile, somba exchange not only has the practical purpose of forging alliances, but also may reflect intra-hapu strategies and interests. Not surprisingly, the snare of village politics, too, is deeply planted in, and consumed with, matters of marriage, inheritance, and status.

PRESTIGE AND SOCIAL HIERARCHY

Prestige and social status in the mappurondo communities rest largely on age and seniority. Persons show deference to parents, grandparents, parents-in-law, and elder siblings, and expect the same from their juniors and offspring. Seniority in descent also plays a crucial part in making successful claims to inheritable and prestigious positions of ritual leadership. At the same time, significant terrace and coffee holdings, ritual displays of wealth and prosperity, and the ability to convene a retinue of followers bestow prestige on a person or household. For the community, then, age and seniority tend to create an unalterable set of status positions, while wealth and achievement offer a means for elevating prestige and influence. Given these two axes of prestige, a person's social status is inevitably and incessantly negotiated, contested, and kept in flux.

Disparity in wealth within the mappurondo community is not that great, and few households enjoy marked prosperity.[19] The villagers reckon wealth in terms of rice: those who grow and eat more rice are rich, and those who grow and eat little are poor. The more prosperous become *tomakaka'* ("one who is like an elder sibling"). The tomakaka' act as patrons to less prosperous relatives and villagers, permitting the latter to sharecrop or to borrow generously. Thus, relations of dependency and prestige find definition in idioms of siblingship and seniority.

Social hierarchy clearly has undergone change over the last century with the cessation of slavery and the erosion of mappurondo ritual life. Villagers gave several different descriptions of former ranking systems, but all accounts included mention of social dependents and inferiors who had been enslaved through capture or debt bondage. Yet idioms of siblingship and seniority once more entered the picture, here mitigating against the sharp demarcation of a slave class. Slaveowners incorporated slaves into their families as *adi'*, or junior siblings, such that relations of debt bondage and coerced dependency took definition from the reciprocal obligations that bound siblings to one another.

Villagers are emphatic that persons holding ritual or political titles form a social elite. Ritual cannot properly take place without the men and women who hold the appropriate ceremonial titles presiding. For their participation and the "burdens" they undertake, the ritual elite take home gifts of special meats. Thus, the ritual elite gain prestige through their specialized knowledge and their customary rights to sacrificial meats. The prestige of ritual titles remains strong, and claims to such positions continue to be a source of competition, conflict, and envy among mappurondo households. At the same time, the burdens of ritual office—living under special sets of tabu and hosting certain gatherings—make the titles less attractive to some villagers.

A GLIMPSE AT GENDER RELATIONS

Sexual politics and gender hierarchy make up an important dimension of social and ritual life in the mappurondo communities. Later chapters will treat the issue of gender in some depth. For now, a thumbnail sketch of gender relations will be helpful.

Generally speaking, the relations between mappurondo men (*muane*) and women (*baine*) steer toward balance and collaboration, and in many contexts appear to have the relatively egalitarian and complementary character one might expect in a society that uses age as the most basic criterion of prestige (Ortner 1981, 1990). Similarities aside, gender differences do exist and do order village life, especially in the division of labor and ritual practice. Yet most persons tend to view these differences as complementary in nature, and it is in part this perceived complementarity that keeps gender distinctions from becoming a problem in everyday life. It needs to be asked, of course, whether this complementarity has a basically egalitarian or hierarchical character. Indeed, the issue of control troubles and haunts the talk of equality, balance, sameness, and complementarity. But as a starting point for discussion, it is important to note that both men and women in the mappurondo communities use a discourse of complementarity to level gender differences and to portray them as fitting, natural, and reasonable.

This egalitarian discourse appears to be the common or predominant one. To my knowledge, no one claims men or women to be fundamentally superior to the other. Along with some basic ideas about human sameness, there exists a basic moral view about what makes a "good person" (*mapia penabanna,* literally, "with good breath"), irrespective of gender. Generosity, patience, and industriousness, for example, are valued in both men and women. Yet ideas about manhood and womanhood also need to be brought into the picture. In the mappurondo community, a man should have the valor and skills of a headhunter (cf. Atkinson 1990, and Rosaldo and Atkinson 1975). He has a reputation to keep and must learn to bluff or threaten others with a "don't mess with me" attitude. At the same time, a man should be able to persuade with high oratory and a sound knowledge of tradition. A woman, on the other hand, should be a skilled gardener and, when possessed by the debata in household ritual, a graceful dancer. Villagers do not stress a woman's ability to bear children but, rather, her domestic discipline. The favor shown a woman's capacity for domestic discipline does point to a troubling current in the seemingly egalitarian relations between men and women. Exalting women for their domestic discipline is perhaps a way to celebrate their controllability. In this sense, a good woman is one who monitors her own domestic behavior and thus spares another person—perhaps a husband or father—the need to rein her in.

Unlike the division of ritual activity, the sexual division of labor in the mappurondo community is flexible and relatively balanced. Women customarily plant, weed, harvest, and gather, while men till rice terraces, burn off garden plots, fish, and make homes, huts, and rice barns. Yet men and women are free to assist one another in these tasks. Childtending and cooking preoccupy women more often than men, but are quickly passed on as chores for children aged roughly seven and up. The division of labor is far more rigid, however, when it comes to hunting game or weaving: without exception, hunting falls to men and weaving to women. I have no evidence that villagers place differential value or worth on these various tasks.

It is marriage that brings men and women into complete adult status and binds them into a complementary relationship. As husband and wife, they become *bela,* a term unmarked for gender denoting a companion in a mutual task.[20] Through cooperation and companionship a couple aim at increasing the prosperity and status of the household, something usually measured by harvest surpluses, landholdings, sound health, number of children, and displays of hospitality and generosity. Although the bela relationship is a culturally acknowledged ideal, it is not unusual for it to be troubled with tension and asymmetry. First, and without exception, mappurondo men marry women several years their junior. Thus, a nongendered axis of prestige and authority based on age enters into the bela relationship, compelling junior wives to show deference to senior husbands. Owing to their seniority, husbands may be said to enjoy an edge of control over their wives. But it needs to be remembered, too, that uxorilocal residence strategies put a husband in a subordinate relationship vis-à-vis his wife's family. In fact, the most common cause of household discord during my time in Bambang had to do with soured status relations between sons-in-law and parents-in-law.

Traditionally, men have had a nearly exclusive hold on village political positions. The pattern continues today, at a time when the mappurondo community has to make concessions to the civil administration, and to those who have embraced Islam or Christianity. Still, women are not kept from bringing an issue before village men, nor are they prevented from holding village political office. That they seldom do so points rather directly to the asymmetries cloaked by the discourse of gender equality and complementarity.

Without question, village endogamy, hamlet exogamy, and uxorilocality are themselves political acts and constructions: they shape the way women and men participate in village politics. By virtue of their role in local social structure, married men have to become village politicians. Their interests and obligations span natal and affinal households as well as natal and affinal hamlets, and indeed, men show themselves to be consumed by local prestige politics. Women have more narrow political interests, ones that focus on their natal hamlet and that show deep commitment to the social bonds of mother-sister-daughter cohorts. It is not surprising, then, that locals think of the settlement as a male sphere, and the household as a female sphere. Positions of village leadership customarily fall to men, and the voices heard in gatherings to discuss village affairs are those of men. In principle, women may take part in these discussions or sit as village head. But for a woman

THE MAPPURONDO ENCLAVE AT BAMBANG

to do so would strike villagers as peculiar, and would certainly be a case of "beating the odds" (cf. Atkinson 1989, 1990, from whom I borrow the phrase). Beyond the rule that "village" rituals performed under the authority of men must take place before the household prosperity rites overseen by women, there is little evidence that the male-dominated village sphere is consistently valued above the female-dominated sphere of the household. I would suggest, then, that gender asymmetry in village-level political life may not be so much a matter of hierarchical value (male over female, public over domestic) as a matter of political scope. The village politics of men encompass the socially and residentially limited politics of women, but are not consistently accorded higher value.[21]

Both men and women take part in ritual life, and both have opportunities to become recognized specialists vested with the authority to perform certain ceremonial roles. More generally, men take center stage in *ukusam botto*, the rites of the settlement, while women assume authority during *ukusam banua*, the rites of the household (about which, more below). Although both husband and wife share a concern for the material prosperity of the hearth and family, it is the wife who is felt to be the guardian of household welfare. Her capacity to bring a providential presence into the home by being possessed or "taken by the debata" (*diala debata*) during ritual accords a wife and mother a significant degree of religious dominance, and places her at the threshold of the sacred. Men, meanwhile, play a more peripheral role in the religious management of household prosperity. Theirs is a world oriented to village welfare, prestige, and male peership.

To sum up, the gender differences and sexual politics of the mappurondo communities tend to resemble those described by Collier and Rosaldo (1981) in their study of hunter-gatherers and simple horticultural societies. Furthermore, they fit reasonably well with patterns described for other bilateral "hill tribes" in island Southeast Asia. Overall, there is in mappurondo culture a fairly egalitarian gender ideology that stresses the complementarity of women and men. If that ideological system posits differences between men and women, it nonetheless fails to organize the distinctions into a stable hierarchy of value wherein one gender could be said to be consistently subordinate to the other in terms of prestige.[22] With the exception of certain ritual practices, very little effort is expended on policing the boundaries of gender difference in daily activity. Asymmetries in authority do exist, but for the most part reflect a relational structure that puts emphasis on men in some contexts, and on women in others. Men emerge consistently as community leaders, while women assume privileged roles in the sacred business of the household. On the other hand, clear vectors of asymmetry appear in marriage, idealized as the egalitarian and complementary bela relationship. Here, a husband's anxieties about male prestige and peership lead him to find ways to control his wife and her domestic and sexual services.

MAPPURONDO RITUAL LIFE

I have saved for last a very simple sketch of traditional religious practices, the practices that define the mappurondo enclave as an ideological minority. The ritual tradition at Bambang, like that throughout the Pitu Ulunna Salu hinterlands, goes by the name *pemali appa' randanna,* the "tabus of the four strands." With this metaphoric term, villagers think of ritual life as a four-stranded necklace, the loops marking four kinds of ritual time, and the beads representing prohibitions and admonitions regarding practice and conduct. The looped strands of the necklace suggest that ritual life not only adorns the village—a theme articulated in headhunting ceremonies—but also assumes a circular, cyclical, and encompassing form. In a sense, the ritual order of pemali appa' randanna adorns both the village and time itself.

Briefly, pemali appa' randanna divides the harvest year into four periods, each with a characteristic focus, mood, and purpose. *Patomatean,* "the time of the dead," pertains to death and mortuary practices, and for that reason, lacks some of the seasonality of the other periods. *Patotibojongan* is in effect from the time the rice crop is planted to the time it is put into storage. The men's headhunting rite of pangngae then opens up *pealloan* ("the place of the sun"), a period that subsumes the remaining two "strands." The first of those strands is *pa'bisuan*; it concerns the exuberant rites centered on the village and the household, including pangngae. Once pa'bisuan comes to an end, *pa'bannetauan,* the season of marriages and divorces, takes place. After wedding festivities have come to a close, villagers await the return of patotibojongan.

A closer look at this ritual calendar, beginning with patotibojongan, should help frame a discussion of pangngae in later chapters. Patotibojongan refers to the timid and girlish rice spirits who descend from the sky-world to occupy each terrace. Upon the plowing of terraces and the casting of seed or the transplanting of seedlings, every mappurondo household will give offerings and prayer to these dabata. Subsequently, the community is absorbed in labor and enters into a somber tabu period that lasts until harvested rice is placed in the granaries—very roughly, an eight-month period stretching from July through February. All of that which might disturb the easily startled rice spirits—noisiness, laughter, storytelling, singing, drum-ming, and ceremony—is strictly prohibited. (Two important exceptions are funerary ritual and, as the rice matures and ripens, the manufacture of tops, swings, and windmills, the sounds of which delight the rice spirits.) At har-vest, final offerings are given to the rice spirits, who ascend to the skyworld. Sheaves of rice are then dried on vertical racks. When the last of the house-holds have collapsed their drying racks, patotibojongan comes to an end.

Not long after the drying racks have been put away, a group of men and youths will slip out of the village and go on the headhunting journey associ-ated with pangngae. Their boisterous return in the dead of night releases the mappurondo community as a whole from public mourning for the de-ceased and shifts ritual practices to pa'bisuan, "the time of the quickening spirit." Pa'bisuan divides in two: *pa'bisuam muane,* those village-level rituals held under the authority of men (also called *ukusam botto*) and the ensuing *pa'bisuam baine,* a series of sometimes elaborate rituals held under the au-thority of women for the benefit of individual households (also called *uku-sam banua*).

Men's ritual is limited to the annual, obligatory performances of pang-ngae and the prestigious and comparatively rare *morara* ("the bleeding" [i.e. of a sacrificial animal]), both of which are staged by entire villages.[23] It is in these rituals that the debata restore and enliven men's *sumanga'* (elan vital, or soul).[24] Both rituals exalt the valor and cunning of headhunters, and ex-tol the prosperity and prestige of the village and village tradition. But before morara may be staged, pangngae must be held. Pangngae involves as well, in most cases, only village residents, with occasional guests (most often kin or distinguished elders) from mappurondo communities in other settlements. Morara, on the other hand, requires a host village to invite guests from all corners of Pitu Ulunna Salu.[25]

Rituals belonging to women (pa'bisuam baine) commence once the rites of men have come to a close. Because morara is seldom run, pa'bisuam baine usually begins when the headhunting celebrations of pangngae end. Thus, the focus of ritual shifts from male to female, and from village to household. Run under the authority of women who hold ritual office, the ceremonies of pa'bisuam baine (five according to the ToIssilita' and six ac-cording to the ToSalu) aim at bringing prosperity and health to the presid-ing household and its hapu, by way of sacrifice and entrancing visitations from the spirits. The rituals of the female domain are sequential, moving from the small and simple to the grand and elaborate (called *parri',* "heavy," or "burdened"]).[26] Households must adhere to the set sequence and may not stage more than one rite per year. At the same time, a household is under no obligation to run one of these rituals unless husband and wife have made a vow to do so.

Following the season's final pa'bisuam baine ceremony, activity shifts to the fourth strand of ritual injunctions and admonitions—pa'bannetauan, "the time of human seed." Like the rituals associated with women, the weddings of pa'bannetauan could be called rice-sensitive, in the sense that they take place only when a household has enough rice to put on a marriage feast for a daughter. In practice, households will not stage an elaborate rite during pa'bisuam baine if they anticipate proposals from prospective sons-in-law, preferring instead to reserve the necessary rice supplies for a marriage feast. As might be expected, harvest failures dramatically limit the number of weddings staged in a given year. With the close of pa'bannetauan, the exuberance of pealloan subsides. Although no major ceremonies may be staged, villagers continue to labor or relax in relative freedom from tabus.

There exist a number of other rituals that are more contingent in nature, though some of them have a connection with pealloan. These stray beads, so to speak, have to do with epidemic, natural disaster, early stages of a person's life-cycle, and construction of a house. The crises of epidemic and natural disaster can befall a village at any time. Prolonged or serious illness is usually dealt with privately, after enlisting the aid of recognized curers (usually female) who possess knowledge of the incantations and offerings used to heal.[27] In the case of epidemic, however, village elders try to drive away the supernatural beings thought to bring illness upon the hamlets. A public sacrifice is held on a path downriver from the village (the cosmological direction of death and illness), and a frightening effigy is installed to ward off the beings' return. Similarly, disturbances within a hamlet—landslides, the toppling of trees, or the collapse of a house—are followed with calming sacrifices to the startled debata who may have unleashed the calamity.

Life-cycle rituals associated with pealloan include the now-defunct practices of male tooth-filing and superincision that were halted earlier in this century by Dutch and Indonesian authorities. Among extant practices, the ritualized presentation of clothes to children in their fourth year (peculiar to ToIssilita' communities) takes place during pealloan. Minor rites seeking a long life for a year-old infant, marking a child's contact with the ground (i.e. taking first steps), or beautifying an infant girl by ear-piercing happen by parents' preference and discretion during pealloan, too. But the earliest life-cycle rites—naming, and introduction of the child to the sleeping sling—happen within a month of birth and are not coordinated with pealloan. Finally, the very visible ritual event of installing a hearth in a newly constructed house (by taking ashes from the wife's mother's fireplace) happens without exception during pealloan.

This quick sketch hardly does justice to the complexity and texture of mappurondo ritual practice. Nonetheless, the basic character of the ritual order comes across in this outline of practice. At root, the ceremonial order—in its regulation of time, sociality, and discourse—establishes a powerful set of constraints on labor, consumption, and domestic and communal reproduction. Prosperity is perhaps its key theme—whether of person, household, hapu, or settlement. That discourse of prosperity, however, also includes, and makes intelligible, an anxious desire for prestige. Local religion thus sacralizes, and even fuels, the prestige politics that shape social life in the mappurondo communities. The rich symbolism of pemali appa' randanna also forms the context in which local gender differences reach their most radical formulation and display.[28] Such shifting asymmetries not only play a part in shaping human relationships but also inform the making of household and village as the key sites for the sacred politics of prosperity, authority, and power.

I should not leave the impression that the ritual order is free of pressure and change. Judging by the recollections of older men and women, pa'bisuam baine—in contrast to other portions of the ritual cycle—is in some communities on its way to becoming badly stalled with respect to the staging of parri' ceremonies. These elaborate rituals have always been difficult and costly to perform, and the current economy and the vast number of conversions to Christianity since 1970 have made them more burdensome and problematic for a household. As a result, the ritual cycle of today is one geared especially to weddings, funerals, and the headhunting rites of pangngae. The consequences for women should be clear—their place in ritual life has diminished somewhat and taken new focus.

Having sketched the basic social and historical outlines of the mappurondo enclave at Bambang, I can resume exploration of local headhunting practices. I should stress that Christians dominate the religious and political landscape in Bambang, just as Muslims do downriver in Mambi. Followers of these world religions have rejected pemali appa' randanna in everyday moral practice. The mappurondo enclave in Bambang persists, meanwhile, as a number of village-based ritual polities that have yet to coalesce into a territory-wide religious body. Living uneasily with their Christian neighbors and kin, reluctant to put aside the tensions that separate ToSalu and ToIssilita' camps, and often bewildered by the intrusions of the Indonesian state, mappurondo households seldom look beyond village boundaries and show little interest in joining a larger cooperative union. Nevertheless, all the map-purondo communities in this enclave have a consistent, historically informed vision of Bambang as repository and guardian of adat tradition. The tenac-ity of pangngae relative to other traditional ceremonies shows that the vil-lage remains the pivotal site for reproducing and giving institutional form to the broader ideological order of ada' mappurondo.

3

Defaced Images from the Past

On the Disfigured Histories and
Disfiguring Violence of Pangngae

At first glance, the mappurondo communities may seem an unlikely place for us to make sense of headhunting ritual. After all, during pangngae no enemy actually is felled, no human head is taken. What takes place is not a "real" headhunt, but something staged to look like one. The drums, songs, and loud cries, the feasting and speechmaking, the bloodless trophies come into play as villagers set loose their imagination in the ritualized mock-slaying of an outsider. It is easy—as it is reasonable—to suppose that the social, cultural, and political forces of the last 100 years have brought an end to "real" headhunting, leaving today's villagers with the ghost of former practices. From this vantage point, pangngae lingers as a troubling or perhaps amusing relic of more primitive and violent times. Yet I think what makes the annual headhunt of pangngae so striking and instructive is its artifice. The lack of actual violence, more broadly the frank recognition and exposure of incongruities between ideology, act, and circumstance, make explicit the desire of mappurondo villagers to recreate their ritual practices— and meanings for them—from the givens of the past and the contingencies of the present.

From the start, let me acknowledge that there are difficulties in writing about the headhunts of the past. The problem goes beyond knowing "what happened" along the banks of the Salu Mambi. In fact, it goes right to the issue of how ethnology has theorized and explained headhunting. I will

suppose—rightly, I believe, and with some evidence—that the upland villagers once upon a time took heads. At some later date, they stopped, or
almost stopped. Forsaking real victims and real heads, villagers began (or resumed) their traffic in surrogate skulls. Yet, there has been at least one instance in the last 50 years when a cohort of upland men have taken the head
of a human victim. The historical movements back and forth between actual
heads and surrogate heads, however, should not mislead us regarding the
ontological status of the latter.[1] We need not assume that the use of a surrogate head has to follow upon the use and abandonment of human heads.
To the contrary, a human head does not enjoy a privileged and prior position in the scheme of the real. A human head and a surrogate are equally
real, powerfully vested signs of violence. Seen from another angle, though,
the head and the surrogate are disparate versions of the "same" sign—each
with critically different entailments and consequences.[2] Whether a head or a
surrogate comes into use depends, of course, on social and historical conditions. The problem for analysis, then, is to write the biography of the sign—
here, the image of a severed head—noting its movement through time and
the way it falls subject to varying social and historical forces.

A second difficulty in writing about the past is to come to terms with the
"textuality of history" (Montrose 1989; cf. White 1978).[3] I can know about
the headhunting of the past only by way of the discordant traces, silences,
and erasures that make up local history. For their part, the mappurondo villagers of today claim that their tradition of headhunting ritual is unbroken,
stretching back sixteen generations or more. Two alien histories—that of a
colonial power and that of the headhunters' victims—are silent. Dutch administrative and missionary records, for example, are mute about headhunting in and around the Salu Mambi region, save for a remark about a supposed
"headbarn" to the north in Tabulahan (Kruyt 1942:550, citing correspondence with Bikker). That it goes unmentioned suggests that the ritual of
pangngae never seriously troubled the colonial authorities. Similarly, the ritual does not appear to have troubled the headhunters' usual victims—the
Mandar. They have no idea that they have lost heads, past or present, actual
and surrogate, to the uplanders. If the exuberant claims of the uplanders
are true, why do the victims and colonial authorities fail to mention Salu
Mambi headhunting practices? Coming to terms with the textuality of local
history means coming to terms with this mystery, and I will offer a reading
of the past that will reconcile these discordant, competing views.

Texts about the past have their own historical character, of course. Written or recited, remembered or forgotten, these texts owe their life to particular times and places and take shape in accord with the culturally specific

tensions and constraints of a lived-in social order. The same is true of the critical commentaries and ethnographic analyses heaped upon headhunting practices in island Southeast Asia. How anthropology has encountered and represented the headhunter is an issue that deserves the close scrutiny of a cultural or intellectual historian. Here I want to note only a few very general points about that literature.

Much of the early theorizing and "fact-finding" about Southeast Asian headhunting took place just after hill and island communities were "pacified" and brought within the orbit of colonial jurisdiction. I think it fair to say that headhunting ritual stands out in this early literature as a sign of an unruly and pagan otherness.[4] For some, the headhunter may have figured as a human grotesque, sparking curiosity, contemplation, and awe. More significant, however, was a desire on the part of the social order producing this literature to tame the headhunter's violence. That impulse or desire to tame demanded subjects that would acquiesce under threat, reprisal, and enticement. No surprise, then, that headhunting became warrant for reconnaissance and pacification campaigns, while its decline or cessation served as a measure of colonial and missionary success. The dark romanticism, the fear, and the will to control are all present, for example, in a brief passage from a report by J. F. W. L. Goslings (1933 [1924]), a Dutch civil officer assigned to the Galumpang region of western Sulawesi. He writes that, "Before 1905 Galumpang was 'terra incognita' where no European had ever set foot. The Galumpang people lived in a time of underlying feuds. . . . The hunting of heads until our regulation was in unbridled practice. . . ." (1933:57–58). As for curbing this entrenched ritual violence, Goslings showed little faith in the native tribunals and courts set up by the Dutch. Rather, he left it to "time, the Civil Administration, and the Mission" to bring about an end to headhunting (1933:68).

Seldom do these early accounts look at headhunting practices with respect to questions of domination and subordination.[5] Rather, the tendency is to fathom headhunting in terms of *belief,* an approach decidedly more theological than political or social. Once they had exacted control, colonial and mission authorities needed only to comprehend their pagan wards. With the collapse of precolonial political systems and relations of exchange, observers were less likely to witness the taking of human heads than to see a body of customs neutralized and distorted by the new social order. The violence of headhunting, in most cases, belonged to the past, where it could be interrogated safely for the intellectual projects of ethnology.

The early ethnographies and travel accounts that dealt with headhunting created a legacy for later work. The consuming question—"Why a head?"—

organized inquiry around problems of belief and causality (cf. Needham 1976). At the same time, it enshrined the trophy skull as a fetish for ethnographic analysis. Solving the mystery of the severed head, finding in it an intelligible form of native rationality—a belief that heads contained magical soul-stuff, for example—would surely solve the problem of headhunting. Subsequent eras of structuralism, Freudianism, and related modes of symbolic anthropology more or less revealed the same fascination with trophy skulls. The aim was to identify a perduring symbolic logic that necessitated the ritualized taking of heads. Contingencies of circumstance, purpose, and meaning, of course, had little place in this determinative and oftentimes univocal structural logic. Meanwhile, theories that emphasized the resonant multivocalism of ritual symbols did little to dampen the fascination with the head. To the contrary, theories that emphasized the semantic abundance of ritual objects, that trumpeted their rich polysemy, still construed the severed head as the locus of meaning. If ethnologists could no longer accept the view that the skull contained soul-stuff or potent seed, they nonetheless remained convinced that the head was full of meaning. The theoretical danger, here, was to overlook the intertextually contingent and constructed character of meaning, treating it instead as a decodable property of the symbolic object. In practical terms, this kept the severed head at the center of ethnographic interest, holding it in place as the proper object for interpretive work and play.

The mystery of the head lingers still, holding and being held by the anthropological imagination. Without question, it has shaped my work on pangngae and the mappurondo community. Yet I am interested less in finding an unequivocal answer to the problem, "Why a head?" What I hope to establish instead in the present work is a vantage point, or series of vantage points, from which the shifting ambiguities and ironies of the stolen head can be glimpsed.

Containers Contained, or Theory Turned on Its Head

A cohort of youthful headhunters came home to the village of Rantepalado on a moonless night in late April 1985. Let in on the secret of their approach, I had joined several mappurondo elders in their darkened homes, waiting for the shouts and flutes that would open the hamlets. Once the youths were back and the hamlet fires burned again, we sat up until dawn celebrating their return, gathered under a makeshift lean-to at the edge of the hamlet of Lasodehata. I talked a lot that night with Ambe Ka'du, one of the more brash and vocal young leaders of the mappurondo community in Rantepalado. Telling me about pangngae, he looked over at the boy-warriors and remarked, "The point is for the headhunters to bring back su-manga', got it?"

Sumanga' is a common term throughout southern Sulawesi for what might be called ardor, vitality, spiritedness, drive, potency, or soul (cf. Errington 1983, 1989). Sumanga' can rise, and it can be pulled by a woman's lips as she draws in her breath over the crown of someone's head during a ritual act known as *meala sumanga'*, "gathering sumanga'." In a sense, sumanga' is a kind of animating "soul-substance." Ambe Ka'du's remark seemed to echo support for the long-abandoned "soul-stuff" hypothesis of A. C. Kruyt (1906). Like other theories put forward around the turn of the century, the soul-stuff theory tended to be somewhat instrumental in its view, and wound up not only making conjectures about the mechanisms that made headtaking so efficacious, but confusing them for the principal cause or motivation behind the practice as well. In Kruyt's view, the head-hunter planned to make off with the beneficial soul-substance contained in enemy heads. Taken back to the warriors' village, the victim's skull would exude a life-energy that would restore health and replenish crops and live-stock. Although convincing enough to take in a skilled ethnographer like Raymond Kennedy (1942), the theory did not hold up very well on several counts, and was even abandoned by Kruyt himself (Downs 1955). For example, it fails to explain those cases, like that of the Ilongot, where the head was not taken home but was discarded instead (M. Rosaldo 1980; R. Rosaldo 1980, 1984). Second, headhunting practices vary with respect to the number of heads brought home. The majority of groups were like the Berawan, who sought just a single head (Hose & McDougall 1912; Metcalf 1982). Others trafficked only in bits of skull (Goslings 1933 [1924]; McKinley 1976). Even the Bare'e Toraja, whose headhunting practices provided the ethnographic context for Kruyt's formulation of soul-stuff theory, were content to take a single enemy head (Downs 1956:64). The number of heads customarily taken in a raid offered no uniform evidence, then, that headhunters were trying to amass or stockpile soul-stuff. More damagingly, few if any headhunters in the ethnographic literature made use of a soul-stuff concept in explaining the how and why of headhunting. In fact, head-hunters characteristically had little to say to ethnographers about why they took heads, except to remark that it was a matter of tradition.

Ambe Ka'du's words gave me eyebrow-raising pause. I pushed him: "The sumanga' is in the head that's carried back."

"No. It's like this, carrying back a head brings back sumanga'."

"So they carry sumanga' back from the coast."

"No. Bringing back something brings back sumanga'."

"Oh. Got it. So the head doesn't contain sumanga'."

"I don't know. Probably."

What I think Ambe Ka'du was trying to get across to me was that it is the *ritual adventure* of going headhunting that restores or "brings back" sumanga', not the traces of sumanga' substance that may rest in the trophy skull. His remarks suggest that by exercising and displaying their potency, the headhunters, like the ones who had just returned home in the middle of the night, do not lose their sumanga', but rather, add to it. I have no doubt that the young headhunters of Rantepalado were exhausted from their adventure. But their faces and laughter showed exuberant pride and lively humor. And they brought no trophy head with them.

As Needham makes clear in his critique of Kruyt and others (1976), soul-stuff theorists needed "a mysterious factor X" that enabled them to bring native thought on headhunting into line with their own sense of what causal logic must demand. Nonetheless, the line of inquiry that looks for the logic behind headtaking practices holds some appeal for Needham, inasmuch as he argues that an understanding of headhunting and its association with prosperity must involve an understanding of the "modes of causality as actually conceived in alien traditions" (1976:81). Others, like Derek Freeman (1979), place less faith in local discourse. But the familiar logic is presumed once more: taking heads leads to prosperity and promotes fertility and well-being.

Freeman's thinking is instructive, and typical. Sharply rejecting sociological approaches, he argues that the phallic and procreative symbolism of the head—a symbolism that he sees as psychologically grounded rather than culturally constructed—is the necessary basis for Iban headhunting. For him, the head equals the phallus and is a source of seed. Thus, it is "germinating heads" that provide the mysterious factor (se)x that causally links violence to fertility and prosperity. Enthralled with this kind of sexual symbolism, the poet-ethnographer Carol Rubenstein (1985:231) cannot contain what I read as a scatterbrained parody of Freeman's approach:

. . . the act of emptying out the brains of the taken head to nourish the earth of the group is the metaphor of the ancient practice. This creativity is the ultimate conclusion of the headhunting endeavor. The throwing of the brains onto the earth is the spermatic movement so that manhood may thrive. The warrior is seen in his godlike attribute of both taker and maker of life. Taking the head with its arcane powers and implanting the stuff of the head into the earth are the elements of a mythology for the creation of man and the world itself.

It is easy to poke fun at Freeman's and Rubenstein's fertile imagination as they work at understanding Bornean headhunting traditions. To their credit, they are making an effort to come to terms with the abundant reproductive imagery of Southeast Asian headhunting practices. But their work amounts to little more than a seed-and-sex version of soul-stuff theory. It still clings to the idea that there is something *in* human heads that brings about the prosperity of person, community, and field.[6] If the chants and songs of pangngae are any indication, it may be the discourse of disfiguring violence that in part connects heads and prosperity. A good example comes from the *ma'paisun,* the chant delivered by the *babalako* (or, in ToSalu villages, the *topuppu*)—the ritual specialist in charge of pangngae—when presenting the surrogate head to the debata. Facing east into the sun of midmorning, he calls to the debata met on the journey downriver, chanting their names with the steady rhythm and grammar of formulaic repetition. Once the chant "arrives" at the place of ambush, it begins to dismember the victim. But moments later the throng of people at the ceremony bursts with noise and keeps the babalako from chanting further:

debata mamunga'	debata landing the first blow
debata mamola	debata slashing open the neck
debata mamumbu'	debata wrestling over it
debata ma'tandean	debata lifting it up high
debata ma'peulu	debata taking the head
debata ma'pemata	debata taking the eyes
debata ma'peuta'	debata taking the brain
debata ma'petalinga	debata taking the ears
debata ma'pelila. . . .	debata taking the tongue. . . .

Here the gathering erupts with exuberant whoops and shouts as the chant disfigures the victim's head. At the same time that the crowd bursts with noise, girls and young women let loose a shower of areca nuts, being careful to pelt their favorite headhunters and lovers. Meanwhile, the babalako flings water from a small bamboo tube over his shoulder and onto the gathering. It is said that whoever and whatever is hit by the rain of water will meet with blessings from the debata.

Freeman or Rubenstein might argue that the shower of areca nuts and water symbolizes and makes palpable the fertile substance of the head. I think not. Rather, I am convinced that the words and performance of the ma'paisun form an imaginative context in which the disfigured human head and the ritual throng are made oppositional doubles. First, the chant brings the gathering along on the journey downstream, the approach into enemy lands, the ambush, and the murder. Suspense grows, and in the end the crowd lets loose a burst of noise, areca nuts, and water. *The throng cannot contain itself.* And they erupt just as the chant disfigures the severed head, taking its eyes, the brains, the ears—the moment when *the head cannot contain itself.* For a moment, then, the communal throng is like the disfigured head of an ambushed victim. With at least one important difference: the throng survives while the victim joins the dead. The doubling of throng and head requires a discursive context—here, the ma'paisun chant—that locates a "narrating" social body upstream and a "narrated" one downstream. The chanted discourse ends in a crescendo of violence and noise, and allows the narrating social body to unleash its will in murderous negation of the narrated double downstream.[7] The uplanders' sense and sensation of a violent, enlivening energy, and of their survivorhood, become signs of an enduring and unfaltering prosperity.

My critique, then, takes aim against a "causal logic" that puts the source (or cause) of social and material prosperity inside the head. There is nothing in a trophy skull that promotes well-being. Rather, it is *doing something* to a head, or with a head, that helps bring about prosperity.[8] But mappurondo headhunters complicate the picture with another telling consideration. More often than not, villagers at Bambang speak of headhunting as the *outcome* of prosperity, rather than its cause. Take, for example, the lyrics to one of the sumengo:

Ketuo-tuoi tau	Should the people come to prosper
taru' kasimpoi sali	runners wind from the slatted floor
malallengko toibirin	watch out you on the horizon

The lyrics paint an image of increase. The uplanders prosper and the floor to their house sprouts runners, showing signs of life and growth. It is then that the headhunters look for a victim in regions downstream. No one goes on the journey of pangngae when ill or burdened with grief for deceased kin, and, indeed, the scale and enthusiasm with which this ritual adventure is run suffer when a poor harvest or epidemic takes place.

In saying that headhunting is the outcome of prosperity, no claim is being made that prosperity *causes* this kind of violence. Rather, the mappurondo understanding of headhunting suggests that this kind of ritual violence comprises a part and a measure of what prosperity is all about. To put it somewhat differently, headtaking is a sign of prosperity, one that indexes and pragmatically shapes well-being. Like Michelle Rosaldo (1977: 169, 1980), then, I find it more fruitful to abandon the search for causal logics and to start looking, instead, for the forms of discourse and thought that connect headtaking and prosperity.

Having listened to the commentaries and explanations of villagers, and to the sacred speech and song of pangngae, I am inclined to think that a severed head and prosperity are brought together largely through a series of speech acts and discursive exchanges. I have already suggested that the ma'paisun counterposes the disfigured human head and the celebrating social body. Yet heads have a distinct and more significant place in the vows and entreaties that men make in discourse with or about the debata. In return for providential gifts—a good harvest, unflagging health, the resources to build a new home—men and youths make silent promise to the debata to join in the ritual ambush and beheading of an enemy. Related to the moral entailments of a speech act as such, the headhunt is a way to make good on a promise with the spirits.[9] I will underscore the significance of the headhunter's vow later in this book. For now, it is enough to recognize the trophy head as an object in the moral traffic of exchange between human and spirit worlds. After it has been obtained in fulfillment of sacred vows, the head is made to hear the desires and entreaties of the village:

Sapo lanapokende'i lamu-lamungan	Those [at the headwaters] want to make the plants rise
anna lanpobakka'i ma'rupatau. . . .	and they want to make the people flourish. . . .
Latinanda lako ongeam bulabammu	Soon you will arrive at your place of gold
anna lanapokende'i todiba' banaminanga	and [the debata] will make the ones at the rivermouth rise,
lanapobakka'i todiulunnasalu.	they will make the ones at the headwaters flourish.

Thus, the head is a reciprocating sign. With it, the headhunter fulfills a vow to the spirits. As such, the severed head is proof of the headhunter's piety and virtue. The presentation of the head to the debata not only frees the headhunter from the burden of the vow, but also marks the trophy as a gift in return for providential blessings, thereby earning the future favor and good will of the spirits.

In light of these discursive exchanges, we will do well to examine the transit and transformation of the head, bearing in mind, of course, that even if the mappurondo communities of today do not take real heads, they nonetheless talk and sing as if they do. Imagine, then, a world in which spirits dwell far beyond the horizon "upstream" and enemies live beside the horizon "downriver." The violent acts and discursive exchanges that take place in headhunting move the head from one horizon to another. Called *toibi-rin,* "ones on the horizon," before their ambush and dismemberment, the enemies in death become *sibirin debata,* "sharing one horizon with the spirits." This "cosmological move" along the river is also a journey that brings about changes in the social and phenomenological status of the head. Murdering, dismembering, and disfiguring a stranger in a remote land are willful acts to dehumanize a person-victim. In felling and beheading a victim, the headhunter turns a person into a lifeless object. The ritual discourse of pangngae, however, restores to the trophy skull its humanity. Brought back to an upland village, the head becomes a guest and friend, albeit one who must suffer humiliation along with the customary gestures of hospitality and honor.[10] What is significant here is that the language of hospitality, humor, and entreaty give back to the victim-head its subjectivity, its personhood. The head is once more a "you."

Robert McKinley's (1976) deft comparative account of Southeast Asian headtaking practices puts together a strong case that similar notions of cosmology and personhood not only are widespread in the region, but also play the key role in giving headhunting its rationale. Using a structuralist approach and a set of ideas that recall Georg Simmel's essay on "The Stranger" (1950), McKinley argues that the head is the preeminent sign of personhood, and that the taking of a head is a way to make enemy faces and names "friendly." Taking heads so as to incorporate enemies, in his view, traces back to a need to ritually (and logically) overcome existential contradictions (and threats) posed by the social categories and the cosmological or cosmographic notions that make up local ideology.

McKinley's insights are compelling, and he has gone further than any other commentator in unraveling the mystery of "Why heads?" Yet in claiming that headhunters are busy "winning souls for humanity" through the procurement of enemy names and faces, McKinley comes very close to building theory around sociological soul-stuff. Although sympathetic to any account that allows for the existential problems of others and that can tie headhunting to "reality maintenance," I think more has to be done to ground McKinley's work in the social and historical contingencies of a lived-in world, and in the practical effects of ritual discourse. For example, care needs to be taken to read, and thus theorize, "existential" predicaments so as not to overlook the political and social strains that give birth to them. In particular, those identified as strangers, enemies, or other outsiders never fall under those rubrics in a timeless or transparent way. Headhunting may be not only a response to the strange humanity of the outsider, but also a practical and historically contingent way to formulate (and perhaps control) outsiderhood. Similarly, a semiotic analysis of headhunting that ignores local discourse runs the risk of missing, or even suppressing, the ambiguities and strategized understandings of ritual violence.

Headhunting, History, and Exchange

Mappurondo cosmography fits very well with the topologies of violence and personhood described by McKinley. Recognizing, however, that cosmographic ideas can shape and take shape from a lived-in ethnic and political terrain, I want to examine how pangngae has related over time to the polemics, strains, and predicaments of regional order. I will put off for later treatment the problem of how contemporary headhunts (and a contemporary history of headhunts) mediate relations between the mappurondo community and the outside world. For now, my focus will be on the headhunting rituals and the highland-lowland ethnic relations of the precolonial and colonial eras. My purpose is to show that headhunting practices amounted to a violent declaration of social difference, a set of acts that not only fabricated the problem of outsiderhood, but also partially resolved it. In this connection, I will suggest—if only speculatively—how trade and labor exchanges of the past provided an important context for the headhunters' violent practices and thereby lent them shape, purpose, and intelligibility. At the very least, I hope to capture a sense of how headhunting mediated shifting patterns of dominance and subordination in regional politics.

In opening this chapter, I mentioned difficulties in writing confidently about the headhunts of the past. The problems have mostly to do with the textuality of history. On one hand, any account I give is mediated by and dependent upon textual sources, be they written or oral, local or alien, that already are deeply textualized and historicized. On the other, to tell the history of mappurondo headhunting requires a plot, a story of some kind. For the case at hand, I think I can draw the two problems together. To be more specific, the story of the surrogate head, of headhunting that is not headhunting, relates directly to the discordant claims and odd silences of competing histories.

Recall that villagers insist that their tradition of headhunting ritual is unbroken, dating back almost sixteen generations. Meanwhile, published records of the colonial administration and mission for the Salu Mambi backwater are sketchy and few, and make no mention of headhunting. The Mandar, too, are silent about headhunting raids from the uplands. Why do victims and colonial authorities fail to mention pangngae? Clearing up this mystery, it seems to me, should help clear up the dynamics of Salu Mambi headhunting, past and present.

Without wishing to exclude the possibility of colonial intervention in this headhunting tradition, I believe it useful and fitting to privilege local accounts in reconstructing the history of headhunting. Not to do so would be to deny the mappurondo community *their* history—yet another act of pacification. Judging from the chanted or sung discourse of pangngae itself, and from the informal commentaries of elders, the headhunts of the past played into exchange relations between this highland region and the coastal settlements of the Mandar and Bugis.[11] At the time, the highland and lowland communities were mutually interdependent, with the mountain settlements markedly subordinate in terms of prestige, material wealth, and political power. Pangngae momentarily reversed the hierarchical relations of interdependence: headhunters would ambush a person in a coastal hamlet, take the victim's head back to the mountains, and ritually present it to the debata so as to assure the prosperity of the upstream region. Headhunting practices thus served as a dramatic expression of upland resistance toward a powerful and oftentimes threatening coast. By the late nineteenth century, however, uplanders were already using a skull-shaped surrogate in place of a severed head. If the use of a surrogate marked a crucial shift in the politics and polemics of regional exchange, it also ushered in an era of bloodless resistance to forces that threatened the highlands.

DID THEY REALLY TAKE HEADS?

Ethnographic reports from Sulawesi make it clear that headhunting practices were common throughout the island's mountainous interior prior to Dutch administration.[12] In most cases, headtaking had its basis in ritual rather than in warfare or feuding as such, a pattern that suggests that claims linking headhunting to warfare and expansionism (e.g. Vayda 1969) are not applicable throughout all of insular Southeast Asia. To be sure, regional tensions and intercultural polemics played a part in shaping headhunting traditions. Yet the reports indicate that headhunters found more powerful motivations in ritual themes and obligations that linked such violence to grief, prosperity, and the reproduction of the social body.[13] In particular, the death of an important political figure appears to have been a key reason for holding a headtaking ceremony. In the context of ritual, these concerns made headhunting purposeful, intelligible, and right. They spelled out the headhunter's obligations and fueled a desire to kill. That headhunting was a form of sacred violence may also account for why the practice was so entrenched in the central mountain region. The post-suppression trade in skull fragments, for example, is good evidence that the rituals associated with headtaking remained crucial in local ceremonial life. Even then, actual headtaking occurred from time to time. De Jongh's report (1923) on the Karama River area, for instance, makes note of two headhunting cases adjudicated by the Native Tribunal at Mamuju in 1920.

Given what is known about the island as a whole, and about the central mountain region in particular, it would be exceptional if the territories making up Pitu Ulunna Salu did not have a tradition of ritualized headtaking. Headhunting customs were widespread and strikingly similar in character. Indeed, throughout the mountain region the term *mangae,* or a cognate form, meant "to go out in search of a head" (Kruyt 1942:544).[14] Insofar as the neighboring polities in Galumpang, Seko, Rongkong, Sa'dan, and Mamasa all practiced some form of headhunting, it is very difficult to imagine that Pitu Ulunna Salu did not traffic in heads, too.

The silence of the colonial record on Salu Mambi headhunting may simply reflect a lack of familiarity with the remote hinterland. Although a post was temporarily set up and occupied at Mambi within a few years of Dutch contact, civil and military authorities by 1920 had shifted their offices 40 kilometers away, to the larger posts of Mamuju and Mamasa. These officials were chiefly interested in security and economic development, and subsequently recorded events and conditions having a bearing on those issues. Pangngae goes unnoticed in their reports. I think it safe to argue, then, that the annual rituals did not disturb the enforced calm of the period or pose any special problems for the authorities. This comes as no surprise, for elders today insist that when peaceful conditions prevail, pangngae calls for surrogate heads.

We can be sure, however, that the missionaries were ready to seek out, confront, and subvert cultural practices that would impede the conversion of local peoples (cf. Bigalke 1981 and Volkman 1985). Given the mission program, it is difficult to imagine that Christians would have refrained from taking steps to halt headtaking activity, real or symbolic. Still, I think it important to ask whether the Dutch missions largely overlooked or ignored the annual rites of pangngae.

In contrast to efforts in the Sa'dan and northern mountain regions, missionary work in the Pitu Ulunna Salu communities was extremely shallow and uneven. As discussed in the preceding chapter, the initial mission work of the Indische Protestantsche Kerk amounted to little more than mass baptisms of uncomprehending villagers. A few Ambonese teachers later opened two Christian schools in the Salu Mambi district (Atlas 1925). Some ToSalu elders told me that in one village bordering on the Mamasa Toraja region these teachers gathered up and crushed trophy skulls kept from earlier times. Whether they did so with the idea of putting a halt to ongoing ritual practices or, more generally, of erasing "pagan signs" needs to be resolved. Yet no one recalls a mission or administrative campaign to end pangngae. It was perhaps enough for these Ambonese teachers to destroy the outward signs and traces of a violent local past, and leave ritual practice undisturbed. Whatever the case, the principal mission efforts were centered on the Toraja settlements around Mamasa, the site of the new administrative and military post, and left Pitu Ulunna Salu largely unshepherded.

The situation did not change dramatically when the Christliche Gereformeerd Kerk took over the evangelical field from the Indische Protestantsche Kerk in 1927. The first of the Christian Reformed missionaries, A. Bikker, worked primarily with the Mamasa Toraja. Save for a remark about a Tabulahan "headbarn" in a letter to A. C. Kruyt, I have found no references to headhunting in any of his published reports, including those that do touch upon ritual life at Pitu Ulunna Salu. Geleynse, assigned to Pitu Ulunna Salu in 1930, took very brief residence in the village of Lasodehata (currently Rantepalado), where pangngae is still performed today, but left no published reports. For these missionaries, then, pangngae does not seem to have been a critical or even noteworthy practice. Their silence is especially odd in light of the attention given to headhunting ceremonies in other regions.

It is worth mentioning once more that the headwater villages claim that pangngae has taken place annually and without disruption since the dawn of their own history, and that neither the mission nor the civil administration took direct steps to suppress the ritual. If this is the case, the failure of the Dutch to put a check to pangngae may seem especially strange, given their long-standing policy of eradicating headhunting. However, we need to bear in mind yet again the claims of today's villagers. They insist that Pitu Ulunna Salu had already stopped trafficking in real heads *before* the arrival of the Dutch, having reverted to a ritual search for surrogate skulls. Perhaps, then, a quieted and bloodless version of pangngae was already in place when the colonial powers began to administer the mountains.

There is thus little to guide us in determining whether "surrogate" head-hunting ever raised administrative or missionary alarm in the Salu Mambi region. But convinced that even surrogate headhunting would earn a re-mark or two, I think the silence of the colonial record tells us something very important: *looking for headhunting, the authorities did not see pangngae.* As to why, I want to suggest that pangngae masked itself, that to the few wit-nesses from the colonial and missionary order it did not, on the surface, ap-pear to be headhunting. In fact, it may have appeared to them as little more than "a kind of harvest ritual," the way contemporary Christians describe this particular mappurondo rite. The custom of using surrogate heads prob-ably did help cloak headhunting ritual from the view of the Dutch. Yet I be-lieve the disguise was more elaborate still.

Here it is helpful to remember that other alien history: not only is pangngae missing from the commentaries of local colonial authorities, but it also has no place in the historic memory of its traditional victims—the low-land Mandar. What disguise could have helped the upland headhunter hide his violence from his victim?

THE MOUNTAINS, THE COAST, AND REGIONAL EXCHANGE

The Mandar homeland stretches along the coast between Polewali and Mamuju. Devoutly Muslim, the Mandar are known as Sula-wesi's finest sailors and fishermen, and for turning out some strikingly fine silk fabrics. The Mandar devotion to the pursuit of status runs deep. In my experience, *siri'*, the keeping of dignity and face so often ascribed to the Bugis (Andi Zainal Abidin 1983a, 1983b; Errington 1989), reaches more radical expression among rivalrous and status-conscious Mandar men.[15] In any event, the Mandar cultural emphasis on a righteous defense of personal or family honor has impressed mountainfolk as a tripcord for violence.

According to oral and written histories, the mountain and coastal com-munities established regional polities in their respective areas during the late fifteenth or early sixteenth century, the period of Makassan expansion (Abd. Razak Daeng Patunru 1983; Reid 1983c; Samar and Mandadung 1979). As discussed in the preceding chapter, the upstream or "headwater" territories of Tabulahan, Aralle, Mambi, Bambang, Matangnga, Rantebulahan, and Tu'bi formed Pitu Ulunna Salu, while the downstream or "rivermouth" principalities of Balanipa, Binuang, Banggae, Pamboang, Sendana, Tapalang, and Mamuju took the name Pitu Ba'bana Binanga (see Map 4). Trade, armed incursions by the Bugis, and other regional concerns sometimes led these twin polities to act in concert. But more often than not the uplands and lowlands looked upon one another with suspicion. Above all, these polities were consumed with their own internal rivalries and power struggles (Sutherland 1983a; Yayasan n.d.). By 1872, both the upland league and the lowland federation had collapsed (see: Smit 1937; Sutherland 1983a).

Local and regional interests notwithstanding, the Mandar were very caught up in the political and mercantile dynamics of Sulawesi and the archipelago as a whole, helping Sultan Hasanuddin, for example, resist the Dutch and Arung Palakka at Makassar, and falling subject to the trade restrictions of the Bungaya Treaty of 1667 (Amin 1963; Andi Zainal Abidin 1982; ENI 1918; Abd. Razak Daeng Patunru 1983). Although a common ancestry linked the elite houses of the lowlands and the mountain region, the former were far more interested in gaining and consolidating prestige and power through marriage to Bugis, Makassan, and off-island nobility (see DepDikBud n.d. [a–d], 1981; Abd. Razak Daeng Patunru 1983; Sinrang n.d.; Sutherland 1983a; and Yayasan n.d.). Social networks of this kind not only bolstered the prestige and authority of the Mandar rulers, but also enmeshed them in the political and commercial intrigues of the island. The same networks also promoted social stratification, the proliferation of political offices, and the Islamization of the elite in the early seventeenth century.[16]

The Mandar economy hinged on the slave trade and on the export of upland or marine commodities. From the uplands came rattan, resin, corn, and fragrant woods, while the coast produced tortoise shell, tripang, dried and salted fish, copra, coconut, kapok, sago, oils, hides, and silk (Galestin 1936; Hoorweg 1911; Rijsdijk 1935; van Goor 1922; Veen 1933; Zeemansgijd, n.d.). Key imports were rice, salt, fabrics, weapons, opium, and ceramic goods. Although bound together as a political family under the leadership of Balanipa, the Mandar principalities were undoubtedly commercial rivals, each of which had access by rivers or mountain passes to hinterland areas that provided a flow of exportable goods.

When the Dutch patrols first entered the highlands in 1906, the communities of Pitu Ulunna Salu were economically interdependent with the Mandar coast (cf. Maurenbrecher 1947).[17] Although the uplands remained politically autonomous, the coast held far more power and prestige in regional relations. The Mandar states probably had little interest in placing Pitu Ulunna Salu under direct rule, especially if lowland politics and maritime trade were drawing most of their attention. Furthermore, in the latter half of the eighteenth century several communities in the upstream territories of

Tu'bi, Aralle, and Mambi had begun converting to Islam. The conversion of these communities strengthened their social ties to the coast and substantially weakened the mountain league. So long as the flow of upland goods and slaves passed into their ports, and so long as Pitu Ulunna Salu remained a fragmented political body unallied to other powers, the Mandar had little reason to exhaust material and human resources in subjugating the highlands.

For all the uplanders, salt, dried fish, weapons, ceramics, and cloth (which figured as a favorite article in the transfer of *somba* at marriage) were the key items to be brought back in return for the rattan, corn, and resin taken downstream. Oral accounts by uplanders indicate that the mountain communities kept up a long-standing trade in forest goods and labor with partner coastal settlements. Elders from the northern mountain districts, for example, say that their ancestors traded with partner communities along the northern Mandar coast: older men at Mambi, Aralle, and Tabulahan mention that their fathers made trade journeys to Mamuju, Tapalang, and Sendana. Similarly, settlements from southern mountain districts claim ties to Balanipa and Binuang on the southern Mandar coast.

Taken altogether, the reported pattern of historic trade is enough to suggest that pairings may have existed between the seven coastal polities and the seven upland territories, such that each Mandar realm had a reliable hinterland partner with whom to exchange goods. In reality, trade patterns were probably not always so neat: seasonality in the availability of goods, competition, and feuds, to name but a few factors, could have encouraged uplanders to switch partners on occasion. Still, to take one example, it was hardly a matter of accident that Rantebulahan, the nominal leader of the upland league, should act as hinterland to Balanipa, the dominant polity of the coastal federation. In fact, the elites of the two territories had convergent genealogies.

Slavery played a critical role in exchange throughout the upstream and downstream regions. For example, it is clear that the Mandar ports had a significant role in the export of slaves to Makassar, Pare-Pare, Kalimantan, and Batavia (see: Abeyasekere 1983; Bigalke 1981; Reid 1983a, 1983b; Sutherland 1983b). In addition, the Mandar were interested in obtaining slaves (and other dependents) in order to build substantial retinues of workers (cf. Macknight 1983). The mountain communities, meanwhile, had a different interest in the slave trade. Reciprocal labor exchanges between kin and limited opportunities for agricultural expansion meant that slaves could contribute little to the upland subsistence economy, but slaves were nonetheless of value, because of the price they could fetch on the coast. Captives, debtors, and even junior relatives were traded to the Mandar for weapons, cloth, or cash. The Mandar, like their Bugis neighbors, did raid their hinterlands for slaves, but Hoorweg (1911) and Goslings (1933 [1924]) indicate that sustained raiding rarely struck deeper than the mountain swidden communities lying just beyond the periphery of Mandar lands.

Nothing is known about the beginnings of migratory labor in the region, but by the late nineteenth century it had become an important factor in the economic interchange between uplands and coast. For example, Hoorweg (1911:103–105) reports large numbers of mountain folk making the trip to Mamuju in order to work as coolies, to assist coastal partners in "vandalism" (i.e. piracy), and to work dry-rice fields. The trek was annual and routine, and enough to provoke Hoorweg to complain that it resulted in the underdevelopment of agriculture in the mountain region (1911:104).[18] As he described it, these migrant laborers exchanged their labor for cloth, household effects, and small amounts of money. Yet given the food shortages and sociopolitical turmoil that troubled the mountain communities from time to time, migrant labor probably allowed uplanders to get supplies of food as well as prestige goods.[19]

Hoorweg does not indicate when the migrants usually arrived. The traditional upland agricultural calendar finds men at work on rice terraces from July through September, and October is devoted to clearing and planting gardens. Corn, another of the principal upland crops, usually goes into the ground in January, by which time the rice crop is almost ready for harvest. It would be unlikely, then, for men to journey down to the coast before late February, for to do so would run counter to their most effective subsistence strategy. (According to locals, women did not become migrant workers.) An exception, of course, would be the landless, but the local need for labor probably would be sufficient to keep them home in any case. Coastal fields, according to Hoorweg (1911:103), are planted in November. The next period in the cultivation of crops requiring intensive labor would be during harvest—about five months later, during March. It is in March, too, that the monsoon begins to swing to a westward direction and give favorable winds to Mandar sailors. In my reckoning, it seems likely that upland men would travel to the coast to find work at this time: the upland harvest would have been over, and the agricultural cycle required few labor inputs from males until July. At the same time, the coast could absorb the influx of manpower. March would also be a suitable time to carry forest products to the coast, especially if boats that had brought imported goods were readying to sail away with regional exports.

UPSTREAM, DOWNSTREAM, AND
PRACTICAL COSMOGRAPHY

If contemporary historical views are a reliable index to the past, ideas about siblingship, social reciprocity, and cosmography must have colored upland relations with the Mandar. Recall, first, that the cosmographic perspective begins with a reading of moral and historical facts from the natural fact of a river. In the local imagination, river waters flow from their sacred sources in the skyworld, down through earthly terrain, onward to the ocean, and then, finally, to the region of the dead beneath the sea. Whatever lies closer to the source is more sacred and more authoritative than that which lies below. By the same token, upstream regions are "before" and "elder" with respect to downstream areas. Sacred knowledge and tradition, too, have their birth in the headwaters, and flow "down" through time, person, and generation. The mountain settlements of Pitu Ulunna Salu, sitting as they did beside the headwaters that eventually empty into the sea along the Mandar coast, deemed themselves guardians to the prosperity of the region. Just as the rivers flowed from the headwaters to rivermouth, so, too, did authority, tradition, and well-being.

As detailed in the preceding chapter, the genealogies of both the coast and the hinterlands ran back to the children of Pongka Padang and Torije'ne'. According to upland recitations (and consonant with local cosmography), the junior siblings inhabited the lowlands while the senior siblings populated the highlands. Uplanders thus looked upon their coastal trading partners as siblings, but claimed higher status and authority for themselves by virtue of their descent and their place in the "natural facts" of cosmography.

Cosmography and siblingship, taken as metaphor and fact, set the basic terms for reciprocity and exchange between the mountains and coast. The uplanders' claim to higher status anticipated obedience and deference from their coastal kin. By the same token, the uplands—as senior sibling—carried an obligation to support and guard their coastal juniors, by sacrifice of their own interests if necessary. Though the perspective was decidedly hierarchic, it helped frame the complementarity between upstream and downstream siblings, and served as an ideological vehicle for rendering economic exchange as the sharing of gifts and services. Complementarity and hierarchy notwithstanding, the sense of siblingship between mountain and coast also suggested that ineradicable strains and rivalries existed between the two, that envy as much as sharing could propel the relationship.

In a sense, upland ideology contained certain truths regarding exchange relations with the Mandar. Forest and swidden goods, critical to the coast's maritime trade, flowed from the uplands. The relative prosperity of the uplands—measured by goods brought down from the hills—assured the prosperity of the coast. In short, the elder siblings *were* taking care of the younger siblings; the headwaters *were* replenishing the rivermouths. Bearing in mind that uplanders swapped their humble products for prestige goods, the "younger sibling" from the coast was bestowing respect and honor on the upstream "elder sibling." Taking a different tack, one could say that the Mandar probably were getting the better deal, and that the imbalances of economic exchange were in their favor. Yet, if upland ideology worked to mask distortions and asymmetries in exchange relations with the coast, it also served as a useful, if chiefly metaphoric, rendering of mutual interdependency.

Further still, the idiom of siblingship did not so much hide or mystify the realities of trade as act as their moral basis. If exchange is potentially dissociative and explosive in nature, then the imagined sibling bond between mountain and coast may have helped regulate the conflict engendered by trade (cf. Foster 1977). In other words, the mythically predicated idiom of siblingship, rather than the exchange of goods per se, made the trade relationship between upstream and downstream reliable. Without denying that economic interests and needs motivated regional trade, the idiom of siblingship became the moral context in which exchange could succeed (or, for that matter, fail).

There is little evidence that the Mandar viewed their exchange relations with the Pitu Ulunna Salu uplands in the same ideological terms; indeed, some claim that the coast is "senior" to the upstream regions (e.g. Syah 1980:18). But as long as regional trade patterns conformed to, or were amenable to, the upland interpretation, contradictory or divergent Mandar attitudes may have posed few challenges to upland thought. It appears that in their several centuries of exchange with an alien and potentially threatening coast, the mountain communities never scrapped the idiom of siblingship as their interpretive perspective on trade until the Bugis established upland markets in 1925.

GOING TO THE SEA

The highlanders all agree that their ancestors sought Mandar victims when hunting heads for pangngae. Indeed, the discourse of contemporary ritual continues to portray the headhunters' victim as Mandar. For example, the antiphonal singing called the *ma'denna* taunts the head to call to the Mandar nobility for help:

Denna le'	Denna le'
mattangko mattangko tau	quiet down people
le' ma'adendem ma'denna le'	le' ma'adendem ma'denna le'
Denna le'	Denna le'
anta tanantalingai	so that we can listen
le' ma'adendem ma'denna le'	le' ma'adendem ma'denna le'
Denna le'	Denna le'
buntu sirengke sitimba'	mountains banter, talk back and forth
le' ma'adendem ma'denna le'	le' ma'adendem ma'denna le'
Denna le'	Denna le'
tanete sipemannai	peaks taunt, lash out at each other
le' ma'adendem ma'denna le'	le' ma'adendem ma'denna le'
Denna le'	Denna le'
manu' marambai tondo	cockerels frighten the hamlets
le' ma'adendem ma'denna le'	le' ma'adendem ma'denna le'
Denna le'	Denna le'
aka to nakarambai	whom do they throw into a panic
le' ma'adendem ma'denna le'	le' ma'adendem ma'denna le'
Denna le'	Denna le'
ulu to nakarambai	it's the head that they throw into a panic
le' ma'adendem ma'denna le'	le' ma'adendem ma'denna le'
Denna le'	Denna le'
ulu petambako sau'	head, start calling downriver
le' ma'adendem ma'denna le'	le' ma'adendem ma'denna le'
Denna le'	Denna le'
tambai mara'diammu	call your *Mara'dia*
le' ma'adendem ma'denna le'	le' ma'adendem ma'denna le'
Denna le'	Denna le'
pasitammu babalako	have him meet the babalako
le' ma'adendem ma'denna le'	le' ma'adendem ma'denna le'
Denna le'	Denna le'
nakulle ai naeba	he is able and ready to fight
le' ma'adendem ma'denna le'	le' ma'adendem ma'denna le'

Denna le'   Denna le'
natendanni pa'pelalam   he bridges danger by the footholds [of truth]
le' ma'adendem ma'denna le'   le' ma'adendem ma'denna le'

Denna le'   Denna le'
ulu petambako sau'   head, start calling downriver
le' ma'adendem ma'denna le'   le' ma'adendem ma'denna le'

Denna le'   Denna le'
tambai baligau'mu   call your *Baligau'*
le' ma'adendem ma'denna le'   le' ma'adendem ma'denna le'

Denna le'   Denna le'
pasitammu ____   have him meet [name of the cohort leader]
le' ma'adendem ma'denna le'   le' ma'adendem ma'denna le'

Denna le'   Denna le'
nakulle ai naeba   he is able and ready to fight
le' ma'adendem ma'denna le'   le' ma'adendem ma'denna le'

Denna le'   Denna le'
natendanni pa'pelamba'   be bridges danger by rising steps [honor]
le' ma'adendem ma'denna le'   le' ma'adendem ma'denna le'

Denna le'   Denna le'
ulu petambako sau'   head, start calling downriver
le' ma'adendem ma'denna le'   le' ma'adendem ma'denna le'

Denna le'   Denna le'
tambai pa'bitarammu   call your *Pa'bitara*
le' ma'adendem ma'denna le'   le' ma'adendem ma'denna le'

Denna le'   Denna le'
pasitammu ia ____   have him meet [name of the younger leader]
le' ma'adendem ma'denna le'   le' ma'adendem ma'denna le'

Denna le'   Denna le'
nakulle ai naeba   he is able and ready to fight
le' ma'adendem ma'denna le'   le' ma'adendem ma'denna le'

Denna le'   Denna le'
natendanni kaloloam   he bridges danger by a true path [loyalty]
le' ma'adendem ma'denna le'   le' ma'adendem ma'denna le'

Denna le'   Denna le'
ulu petambako sau'   head, start calling downriver
le' ma'adendem ma'denna le'   le' ma'adendem ma'denna le'

Denna le'
tambai pangngulu tau
le' ma'adendem ma'denna le'

Denna le'
call your *Pangngulu tau*
le' ma'adendem ma'denna le'

Denna le'
pasitammu i ____
le' ma'adendem ma'denna le'

Denna le'
have him meet [name of headhunter]
le' ma'adendem ma'denna le'

Denna le'
nakulle ai naeba
le' ma'adendem ma'denna le'

Denna le'
he is able and ready to fight
le' ma'adendem ma'denna le'

Denna le'
natendanni piso lambe'
le' ma'adendem ma'denna le'

Denna le'
he bridges danger by the long blade [valor]
le' ma'adendem ma'denna le'

Denna le'
ulu petambako sau'
le' ma'adendem ma'denna le'

Denna le'
head, start calling downriver
le' ma'adendem ma'denna le'

Denna le'
tambai pangngulu bassi
le' ma'adendem ma'denna le'

Denna le'
call your *Pangngulu bassi*
le' ma'adendem ma'denna le'

Denna le'
pasitammu ia ____
le' ma'adendem ma'denna le'

Denna le'
have him meet [name of headhunter]
le' ma'adendem ma'denna le'

Denna le'
nakulle ai naeba
le' ma'adendem ma'denna le'

Denna le'
he is able and ready to fight
le' ma'adendem ma'denna le'

Denna le'
natendanni tandonggigi
le' ma'adendem ma'denna le'

Denna le'
he bridges danger by the ivory handle [skill]
le' ma'adendem ma'denna le'

Denna le'
ulu petambako sau
le' ma'adendem ma'denna le'

Denna le'
head, start calling downriver
le' ma'adendem ma'denna le'

Denna le'
tambai pappuangammu
le' ma'adendem ma'denna le'

Denna le'
call your lords
le' ma'adendem ma'denna le'

Denna le'
pasitammu i angganna
le' ma'adendem ma'denna le'

Denna le'
have them meet them all
le' ma'adendem ma'denna le'

Denna le'	Denna le'
nakulle eai naeba	they are able and ready to fight
le' ma'adendem ma'denna le'	le' ma'adendem ma'denna le'
Denna le'	Denna le'
natendanni bassi kambam	they bridge danger by thick iron [endurance]
le' ma'adendem ma'denna le'	le' ma'adendem ma'denna le'
Denna le'	Denna le'
ulu petambako sau'	head, start calling downriver
le' ma'adendem ma'denna le'	le' ma'adendem ma'denna le'
Denna le'	Denna le'
tambai tau kambammu	call your crowds of people
le' ma'adendem ma'denna le'	le' ma'adendem ma'denna le'

Other songs tell of the panic among Mandar hamlets, the churning of their rivers, and the spilling of their seawater. And the *babalako,* as presiding specialist, honors the head as a "grandchild" of the Mandar lord, Daeng Maressa. I will come back to these songs and look at them in more detail later on. For now, I want to point out that pangngae is a time for the uplanders to prey upon their coastal trading partners.

Songs and chants of this kind, of course, do not literally kill. But the images of violence that they call forth are direct and unmistakable. The ambush of a trading partner—actual or imagined—also tips us off to the way in which headhunting was disguised. The masking of pangngae at the time of Dutch contact had not only to do with the fact that headhunters sought heads that were not heads, but also with the fact that the quest was concealed in the ideology and practice of trade. Trade and ritual violence happened within one another's shadow, and headhunting thus dissolved before the eyes of colonial observer and coastal "victim" alike. The masking of pangngae is now deeply entrenched in local ritual tradition, even if the Mandar are no longer the principal trading partners for the uplanders. But contemporary evidence still affords a chance to understand why headhunting may have become concealed in this way.

Some telling data lies in the way villagers mention trade and headhunting. *Le'ba' le'bo',* literally, "going to the sea," is the term used for trade journeys and seeking adventure in other lands, and villagers still use the phrase as the most popular euphemism for the headtaking journey of pangngae. In a sense, the term collapses distinctions between headhunting and trade, subsuming them under a broader conceptual category having to do with journeys. Yet, following James Scott (1990), it is worthwhile, too, to recognize that the euphemism is a discursive tactic intended to obscure, to disguise. The pragmatic ambiguity of the term lets the headhunter make a threat or disavow violence.

Equally significant is the ma'paisun chant of the babalako discussed earlier. Calling out the dwelling places of the debata who live along the headhunters' trail, the specialist is in effect marking a route to the sea. These chants trace but one trail and name only one coastal settlement where a victim may be killed. Thus, the warriors from the ToSalu communities of Rantebulahan and Bambang travel (in chant) to Tenggelan in the Mandar principality of Balanipa; those from Mambi head off to Tanisi below Tapalang; the ToIssilita' villages of Bambang go to Abo in Sendana; and those from Tabulahan trek to Mamuju. In addition, the returning warriors typically identify the home of their victim when, arriving at the edge of the hamlet lands, they respond to the ritualized greeting of a village elder:

Elder:	*Cohort:*
Oe toakakoa'?	*Oe To Tenggelan!*
Oe toakakoa'?	*Oe To Tenggelan!*
Oe toakakoa' itim?	*Oe To Tenggelan!*
Oe what are you?	Oe ones from Tenggelan!
Oe what are you?	Oe ones from Tenggelan!
Oe what are you there?	Oe ones from Tenggelan!

These invocations and greetings bear out the claims of today's elders that cohorts of upland men returned year after year to the same Mandar settlement to take a head. Indeed, these ritual genres imply that the mountain communities tacitly coordinated their raids in such a way as to make sure that headhunters from Rantebulahan, for example, would not strike at Mamuju, the trading partner of Tabulahan.

Contemporary practices also suggest that headhunting "season" may have coincided with the uplanders' annual trade journeys to the coast.[20] Pangngae takes place once the harvest rice has been put away in the barns, usually between late February and early April. For warriors to leave their villages at this time on the 40–90-kilometer journey to Mandar territories means that they would appear on the coast right when agriculture and commerce (marked respectively by the March harvest and the shifting monsoon) could absorb manpower. Returning from a headhunt, warriors invariably carried what they claimed to be stolen cloth, weapons, and porcelain. Even today, theft has a place in headhunting ritual: along with the surrogate head, a small pile of goods—said to be stolen from the victim—is presented to the spirits.

Coinciding with a critical moment in the labor and trade calendar on the coast, terminologically fused with trade journeys, and targeted at reliable coastal partners and patrons, pangngae must have figured importantly in regional exchange networks. Claiming to be out on a headhunt, upland men were actually bartering and laboring on the coast. Or perhaps more accurately, while men were headhunting, they were also trading goods and labor.

It should be kept in mind that the uplanders of today insist that there were points in history when Mandar victims were indeed slain for their heads, just as they insist that current tradition prohibits the taking of real heads for the purposes of pangngae. Nearly all claim that the reason for taking heads from the Mandar had to do with feuding and retribution. As one ToIssilita' elder explained it: "It was to strike back. Our grandfathers would go to the sea [to trade or work] and someone would be killed or made slave."

A youth from a different village had a different story: "At first, no one took a head. Then slavery and war appeared. Then people killed one another and taking heads became custom."

However true explanations such as these may be, they divorce head-taking from its customary ritual frame, and link it to patterns of reciprocal violence. In other words, the accounts shift the moral perspective on head-hunting from the vantage point of ritual obligations to the desire for revenge in the endless back-and-forth of rebounding violence.

Papa Ati, my language assistant, gave me a broader historical account of headhunting practices. As he had heard it from his father, pangngae at first called for a surrogate head and stolen goods to be offered up to the spirits. The custom then underwent change in the time of *kende' tata asu* ("crazy dog rises"), when slavery, wars, and feuding took place; hunting for real heads became the rule. Once peaceful relations were restored between the coast and the uplands, headhunters sought out a kind of tuber, *tullu bulam* ("egg of the moon"), as a surrogate head. More recently, the coconut, a product associated with the coast, has become the customary surrogate. This account keeps headhunting within the moral frame of ritual, but also indicates that regional strife was a trip mechanism whereby symbolic dramatizations of headtaking were "rescripted" to include very real killings.

I pressed several elders about the matter of actual killings and how the Mandar would respond. According to most, the Mandar knew full well when the raids and ambushes were to take place—more than 80 mountain settlements would be sending out cohorts of headhunters during a six- to eight-week period—but did not want to disturb a practice upon which regional prosperity depended. The Mandar elite were even said to have designated specific settlements where the uplanders could take heads.[21] A Christian commentator of upland birth provides a similar explanation (Makatonan 1985:105), saying that the Mandar helped the uplanders seek a head because they, too, needed a human victim for their own ritual sacrifices. According to these upland formulations, the taking of real heads did not disrupt trade, especially in a time of violence, vendetta, and enslavement. In fact, such explanations presume that headhunting was in the interest of the victim's survivors, a viewpoint expressed in the ritual entreaties to the head (see the chant above, p. 67).

It is hard to imagine the Mandar going along with this. In my acquaintance with the coastal dwellers, I saw only a few signs that the Mandar associate upstream regions with greater prestige and authority and with sources of prosperity. In fact, the Mandar of my acquaintance had difficulty imagining their ancestors surrendering a head to the people of the headwaters under any circumstances. One acquaintance, for example, listened to my speculations about the uplanders' headhunting raids with some amusement. "That must have been long ago," he snorted, "and if they had tried that, we would have just cut them dead."

Still, actual headhunting may not have significantly disrupted regional order, an order that by its nature was probably given over more to turmoil than to calm. Judging by the upland accounts that found "reasonable cause" for taking real heads in regional patterns of vengeance and slavery, headhunting was merely symptomatic of intercultural tension. Still, the same accounts—ignoring as they do, the ritual framework of pangngae—do not at the start provide "reasonable cause" for surrogate headtaking.

If headhunting rites gained purposefulness and intelligibility in light of ideas about fertility, grief, masculinity, and village political life, they nonetheless put down roots in the volatile and ambivalent social relations of exchange between upstream and downstream. It follows, then, that the idioms that gave regional trade its moral context may also be the terms that provided a moral basis for headhunting. In other words, ideas about siblingship, reciprocity, and cosmography may offer important clues about why uplanders wanted to take the heads of Mandar victims.

Here, a story about the origins of headhunting told to me by Ambe Teppu may throw light upon the moral dynamics of the pangngae. As he told it, there were two brothers, the younger of which went to live on the coast. Some time later, the younger brother on the coast beckoned to his elder brother to come down from the headwaters. The younger one asked for help because everything had ceased growing in the lowlands. The elder brother pledged to help by appealing to the spirits at the headwaters, but told his sibling that he needed gifts that could make an appropriate offering. Thinking the matter over that night, the younger brother told his wife to clear out the house, leaving only tattered cloth and other damaged goods. When his brother came again the next day, the younger one told him to take everything that was in the house. The elder one carried the meager effects back to the headwaters and offered the prizes up to the spirits. In the meantime, the younger brother made offerings downstream. The spirits were pleased and restored prosperity to the coast. Thereafter, the elder came back yearly, took something from his younger sibling, and in this way guaranteed the prosperity of the coast. But the younger brother remained greedy and hoarded fine belongings to himself. Unwilling to share the fruits of prosperity, he continued to leave coarse or damaged goods for the elder brother. In time, descendants of the younger brother began to enslave the people of the headwaters. Slaves died in sacrifices to the spirits, and people began to kill one another upriver and downriver. It was then that Mandar heads were taken and presented to the spirits at the headwaters.

The narrative no doubt collapses myth and history. Yet it is not so important to separate the elements of myth and history as it is to grasp the moral drama that fuses them together. The key to the story is a violation of the moral relationship that binds siblings to one another. The elder sibling is obliged to help his junior brother and does so. The younger one, meanwhile, owes his senior brother respect and honor. Yet the junior brother deceives his elder sibling, hoarding valuable goods to himself, and thus withholds the signs (and currency) of honor and prestige. Later on, descendants of the junior sibling enslave their "senior brothers" at the headwaters. Duped, humiliated, and subordinated by his junior, the enraged senior brother begins to take heads in reprisal.

Although the story shows how the exchange of goods (and, later, of slaves and heads) promotes prosperity and cosmological balance, the scenario is one of ambivalent, inverted brotherhood. Trade is the correct and desired expression of exchange, but with the inversion of the brothers-partners relationship upsetting the moral order, reciprocity must become manifest as the ritualized killing and looting of pangngae. In this sense, pangngae is a special variation on patterns noted by McKinley in his analysis of Southeast Asian headhunting (1976). He finds headhunting to be the means for making distant enemies friendly within the exchange of souls critical to cosmological balance. Though headhunters in the Pitu Ulunna Salu highlands also seek cosmological balance, they do so through the exchange of goods and by taking a distant junior "brother-gone-bad" and turning him into a proper junior sibling again by resubordinating him through fatal ambush and placating ceremony.

Two sumengo from the ritual headhunt shed further light on the inverted moral order of the upstream-downstream exchange system. They concern prosperity, labor, and patronage. The first is one I have already mentioned in discussing heads and fertility. It is sung in warning to the Mandar:

Ketuo-tuoi tau	Should the people come to prosper
taru' kasimpoi sali	runners wind from the slatted floor
malallengko toibirin	watch out you on the horizon

The lyrics warn of the headhunters' prosperity and power. But the following sumengo may be sung in reply:

Naposarokam Bugi'	Made workers for the Bugis
natenakan ToMinanga	we're fed handouts by the Mandar
loe tama ri uai	it falls off into the waters

For the uplanders, one works for another under the terms of *saro*: within the context of saro, a person works for the sake of a relative or friend at the request of the latter, generally receiving a meal and a token share of the harvest (or wage) in the course of the task. The friends or relatives are obliged in turn to come work for the person who lent them a hand, and they, too, will receive a meal and shares. Failure to reciprocate does not indebt the friend or relative, but amounts to the arrogant claim that one's status is too great to permit one to work for another. In certain situations, this would offend the person who once lent aid. But to work for another person without being able to call for labor in return marks a person as a social inferior. When this happens—because of meager landholdings, for example—one is not affronted, but humiliated by one's own circumstances.

The song of reply presents the latter case. The uplanders are made laborers for the coastal powers without hope of calling them to the hills to reciprocate under saro arrangements. The uplanders get handouts of food (*tena*) for their work, but have no opportunity to give food to the Mandar in their fields back home in the mountains. These humiliating conditions provoke the stereotypic expression of futility heard in the last line of the song. The uplanders' chance to regain prestige and honor "falls off into the (river) waters" and is washed away. With it goes any real chance of restoring the relationship between senior and junior brothers to the moral ideal.

If the upland villagers resigned themselves to the fact that the Mandar had the greater means of power and prestige, they remained certain of their own place along the moral terrain that stretched across ideas about cosmography, siblingship, and reciprocity. Pangngae was less a facade for trading ventures than a complex moral statement or declaration that temporarily negated a more persistent skewing of correct relations between mountain and coast. The uplanders were willing, perhaps compelled, to deliver their gifts of labor and forest products to the coast, but the humbling realities of regional power and commerce gave them little in return. The symbolic killing and looting of pangngae, then, countered trade and labor exchange, and momentarily righted the conditions of upland interdependency with the Mandar. The people of the headwaters could thus recover their virtue and slake their envy by turning their partner-brothers into victims. Pangngae gave the uplanders a sense of survivorhood, and with it a taste of power and control not ordinarily theirs. The irony is that the uplanders' survival, in a material sense, did not depend on ritualized headtaking, but upon their acquiescence in regional trade and labor.

Seen from the vantage point of some of the contemporary mappurondo narratives and ritual practices, pangngae grapples with the incongruity between ideology and circumstance, much in the way that Jonathan Smith (1978, 1982) claims is characteristic of all ritual. In a sense, pangngae was— and to a degree still is—a way to enact or present an ideal vision of exchange relations that could be recalled and put into conscious tension against the real order of things. If the facts of regional exchange humbled the uplanders, pangngae was a counterfact that momentarily restored their virtue, authority, and status as seniors. The ritualized theft of heads and goods from the coast tilted the social relations of exchange in a direction most favorable to the mountain communities. The seizure of goods was a way to "make them ours"—incorporating the valuables without giving anything in return. At the same time, taking a head was a way to make the victim "ours"—a way to subjugate and incorporate the rival junior who was at once trading partner, sibling, and enemy.

POSTSCRIPT, 1906–1985

Surrogate headhunting is not the postscript to "the real thing" and to the related terrors of the precolonial past. Listening to elders from the mappurondo communities of today, "taking something else"—a surrogate skull, tattered cloth, coins, porcelain, salt, or goods to be used in somba wedding exchanges—has been at the heart of pangngae since its origin. When the Dutch stepped into mountain history in 1906, pangngae was already euphemized as *le'ba' le'bo'* ("going to the sea"), and thus tied to the ongoing regional exchange of gifts, labor, commodities, and slaves. Cloaked by various kinds of exchange between upland and coast, momentarily "scripted" for tuber or coconut surrogates, and staged in a language unknown to Europeans, pangngae showed few or no signs of violence to the small number of Dutch figures posted in the headwater region. Let me mention once more, then, two paths that the colonial response may have taken: first, the Dutch simply had not seen pangngae, or at least had failed to recognize the rites as headhunting ceremonies; or second, they recognized pangngae as a form of headhunting but were untroubled because of its lack of explicit violence.

The facts remain in doubt, of course. But I think a strong case can be made that the colonial order, for all its power and intrusiveness in exercising dominion over the mountain region, did not bring an end to pangngae. It is worth further underscoring that the colonial and missionary presence did not bring about the use of surrogate heads. Rather, surrogacy was already included as an originary feature of pangngae, and its currency at the time of colonial contact came as the result of *regional* politics, economics, and social relations. The interdependence of mountain and coast—an interdependence, it will be remembered, that led an observer to call the uplanders "Coastal Toraja"—was one in which the Mandar dominated. Considering that the taking of real heads might invite reprisal from a powerful adversary and partner, it seems reasonable that the uplanders would resort to effigies in order to practice their ritualized arts of resistance.

What the Dutch and subsequent Indonesian administrations did do was eliminate the conditions and circumstances under which villagers might "rescript" pangngae once again for the taking of human heads. Since 1925, the building of mountain roads, the spread of upland markets, the expansion of cash cropping, and the growth of a Bugis-dominated trading class have changed the patterns of regional exchange and, with them, the context for headhunting journeys. By 1975, mappurondo villagers from Bambang had more or less ceased making trade journeys to the coast, relying instead on the markets of Mambi and Mamasa. Today pangngae takes place only among the mappurondo communities at Bambang, along the upper reaches of the Salu Mokanan in Rantebulahan, and in the more northerly district of Buntumalangka'. In Mambi proper, the ritual is well within the memory of elders, having come to a halt several years before the Japanese occupation

(1942–45). In the meantime, it lingered until 1970 in Mambi's outlying settlements, usually as a ceremonial meal and (since about 1950) without the effigies and reenactments.

The mappurondo communities continue to face dilemmas posed by the recontextualization of ritual life. The headhunting that belonged to the violence, adventure, and politics of the past cannot be the headhunting of a censorious and socially fragmented present. As the patterns of precolonial upland-lowland exchange recede further into the past—patterns in which headhunting made sense and upon which headhunting made comment—I cannot help thinking of pangngae as a ceremony troubled with contradictions and incongruities, a reflexive metacommentary, a ritual about headhunting ritual. Men and youths no longer undertake an actual foray to the sea when off on the headhunt of pangngae. In fact, the journeys out of the village, once measured in months,[22] now take place within a few days' or few hours' time. Meanwhile, an increasing number of young boys have joined the cohorts of warriors over the years as the dangers associated with travel have become less threatening. No one carries any weapons save a work machete. In the modern order of things, these journeys bear little resemblance to those depicted in song and dramatic dance. Not surprisingly, the contradictions and incongruities between what is said to take place and what actually does take place in pangngae have grown, promoting a sense of loss and irony among villagers.

Yet ritualized representations of headtaking are still the crucial and lasting idiom of pangngae. Two years into my work I turned to my language assistant, Papa Ati, and told him of some doubts, "Maybe I am wrong in thinking that taking heads is the important part of pangngae. Maybe it is something else."

He held up his hand and signaled me to stop. "No, you're not wrong. It's like this. If you discuss pangngae, you discuss taking heads. That is the point—taking heads."

Perhaps talking about headhunting is a way to talk about a small community's efforts in resisting social and cultural threats from without. While there is some truth to that, I have to note that as a ritual of resistance, pangngae remains significantly lodged in the volatile and ambivalent relations of the past. An explicitly anti-Dutch, anti-Indonesian, anti-Muslim, or anti-Christian counterposture is next to absent in the discourse of contemporary rites. The ritual still pits the headwaters against the rivermouth, and in so doing makes a violent and local formulation of social differences. But those differences, forged in ritual ambush and murder, already see the "victim-stranger" as someone *belonging* to the headhunters' community, yet whose membership involves a *being outside and against* the group (cf. Simmel 1950:402–403). In this sense, the headhunter's "other" is always a partner, a sibling, a person just downriver. Within the discourse of pangngae, the Dutch and the Indonesian, the Muslim and the Christian, barely exist at all, except, perhaps, as shadowy figures of an allegorized headhunt. Yet in a more complicated and indeterminable way, the absence of these figures may mark either a very strong political challenge or a profound mystification of the world, namely, a (ceremonial) refusal to acknowledge the relations of interdependency that tie the mappurondo community to powerful social and historical formations.

The "making of an other" in pangngae, meanwhile, calls for a ritual object capable of holding the imagination and mooring the ceremonial practices of the community. The traffic of goods in regional trade offered a variety of objects that found their way into ceremonial discourse. But the prize, of course, came by way of murder and theft—a stolen, disfigured head.

Terror, Laughter, and the Grotesque

Myriad themes and issues come together in pangngae: grief and mourning, envy, eroticism, fertility, and ideas about masculinity, for example, routinely surface and intermingle in the discourse of the ritual headhunt. And they do so in complex ways. In the tangle of ritual discourse, the existential and sociohistorical problem of "making an other"—one of the principal and formative strains in pangngae—links with these other themes by way of the imagery of the severed head. For this to happen, the head must possess the character (and do the work) of the grotesque.[23] Like other kinds of grotesque images, the severed head can wed awe, terror, and violence to a ludic fascination with bodies, fertility, and ways of transcending death.[24]

First, the making of the other. Treating the problem of the other as a structural and existential feature of social life, McKinley (1976) argues that the trophy head is the most apt symbol for ceremonies like pangngae because it contains the face, the most concrete image of social personhood. The ritual incorporates the face of the stranger into the headhunters' community, and thus "restores the stranger's misplaced humanity" (McKinley 1976:124). I would add that such a "face-to-face" encounter restores the possibility of speaking to others, thus acknowledging "strangers" and making them accessible within the social give-and-take of dialogue (cf. Gusdorf 1965; Natanson 1970:34–36). At the same time, bringing this alien other within the headhunters' community becomes evidence for the stability and rightness of local power and tradition.

As helpful as these arguments may be, they gloss over or ignore the terrifying violence of the headhunter. Not only does the headhunter kill, but he dismembers. The headhunter's violence, in an important sense, ends in the objectification of "the other." But that violence also involves the mortification and debasement of the fallen. The ritualized project of violence that requires the taking of a life and a head is thus one that produces a demonized and degraded other. Further, it surrounds the degradation of the fallen in an atmosphere of festivity and laughter.

Here is where a discussion of the grotesque may shed light on headhunting ritual. By "the grotesque" I mean kinds of imagery and discourse that foreground the monstrous, the fantastic and bizarre, the exaggerated, the incongruous, and the terrifying or awe-provoking. The aesthetic and political aspects of the grotesque are by no means stable and uniform, but appear as particularized cultural and historical modes of discourse (cf. Bakhtin 1984, Stallybrass and White 1986). Nonetheless, the interplay of terror and laughter seems central to any notion of the grotesque, no matter whether it is an alien or comic world that is imagined. And to twist and disfigure a statement by Flannery O'Connor, it is in the language and imagery of grotesque that "man is forced to meet the extremes of his own nature."[25]

Taking a head in ambush is a marked, rather than unmarked, form of violence.[26] In the Salu Mambi region, it is recalled not as a feature of warfare and feud, but as a ritual act only. The ritual of pangngae serves, then, to mark the taking of the head as an extraordinary kind of terror, constrained with respect to time, place, purpose, and person. Already marked in this way, the violence takes a grotesque turn with the dismemberment and deformation of the victim. As such, the violence of pangngae is marked not only by its ritual dimensions but also by an anatomizing fascination with the body.

How grotesque violence figured into the ritual discourse of the past is uncertain. The contemporary language of pangngae, however, shows a recurrent interest in the grotesque and lurid. For example, the theme of dismemberment figures importantly in the ma'paisun discussed earlier in this chapter. The babalako chants out the protocol of mutilation—slashing the neck, taking the head, removing the eyes, removing the brain, removing the ears, and (in a 1985 recitation) removing the tongue. The dismembering and debasing of the victim's body also appear in the sumengo, but often are euphemized as the felling of a tree. In contrast to the precise mutilations enunciated in the ma'paisun, sumengo lyrics are more likely to deflect the imagination toward the "scene" of dismemberment. For instance,

Salunna Manamba	Where the Salu Manamba
sitappana Mangngolia	and Mangngolia mix waters
napambaratoi london	cockerels make it the cutting place
Mallulu' paku randangan	Trampled ferns on the river bank
naola londom maningo	stepped on by the cockerels at play
untandeam pamunga'na	lifting it up to show first cut

Both songs make a topographic move, placing the scene of dismemberment along a river. The lyrics in the first counterpose place and action through the image of branching. The confluence of two rivers, or, rather, where a river branches into two lesser ones, serves as the spot for dismembering and beheading a victim. The verb *baratoi* means to cut off limbs, ribs, or branches, things that protrude in number from a vertical "spine." Thus, the spot where the river branches ironically serves as the place for the "de-branching" of the victim. As for the lyrics that follow in the next song, the trampled ferns connote the excited rush to deliver the first slash. The lyrics direct the gaze of the listeners' imagination first to the ground, then upward to the wounded neck, held aloft as a gesture of exuberant dominance.

The discourse of the headhunt reveals, too, fascination or disgust with rot and decay. One song, for example, depicts the body of the victim as a fallen palm left to be consumed by a swarm of maggots and grubs:

Umbai' kabumbuannam	The humming noise is probably
banga disamboi solem	the banga palm covered with leaves
sumamberrem watinna	swarming grubs gnawing it up

Slain and abandoned to rot in a makeshift grave, the headhunter's adversary lies abused and debased. The most explicit gesture of revulsion often occurs, however, when the trophy head first is brought into the village. As the prize is raised up for all to see, the crowd of villagers turn their heads and shout *Bossi'! Bossi'!* "It stinks! It stinks!"

The grotesque imagery of dismemberment and rot renders the humiliation of the fallen in ways that stir curiosity, awe, and revulsion. The violent deformation of the victim's body also should be read as the disintegration and debasement of an oppositional or adversarial community. The blows delivered to the body of the fallen are blows to the Mandar community. Themes of noise and panic only underscore the disintegration of the rivermouth communities. Recall the opening lines of the *ma'denna*:

mountains banter, talk back and forth
peaks taunt, lash out at each other
cockerels frighten the hamlets
whom do they throw into a panic
it's the head that they throw into a panic

Terror and anguish over the destruction of home and settlement echo in the lyrics of many sumengo, too. For example,

Totiane'-ane'	Those who shake in panic
murangngi arrena tau	hear the yells of the warriors
pebalinna tarakolo'	the echoing of the muskets
Mui totadamba	Let them be the weak ones
bangom malim-malim mandi	getting up but still dazed with sleep
murangngi arrena tau	hearing the yells of the warriors
Anna maesora betten	And why is the fort in ruins
anna rondom bala kala'	and the fence collapsed into piles
pangngilanna bonga sure'	the scraping of carabao horns

Finally, the highland throngs who sing of this terror abuse their fallen adversaries with laughter. *Umpaningoi ulunna*, "playing with the head," is the penultimate ceremony of pangngae, staged the night before the feast of the cohort and the presentation of the head to the debata. During this ceremony, the community has the chance to heap honor and humiliating abuse on the enemy head. As is typical of headhunting rituals elsewhere in island Southeast Asia, the head sits as an honored guest in the home of the tomatuatonda' (the village head), or in the home of the cohort leader, and is presented with gifts of tobacco and betel quid. The babalako or topuppu will chant soothingly to the head, mixing pity and hospitality (see Figure 4):

For you this grandchild of Daeng Maressa
the one who is seated below at the rivermouth
. . . don't be red of face
. . . don't ooze blood from your throat . . .
savor your betel with a relaxed look
smoke your tobacco with contented breath
soon you will arrive there at your place of gold

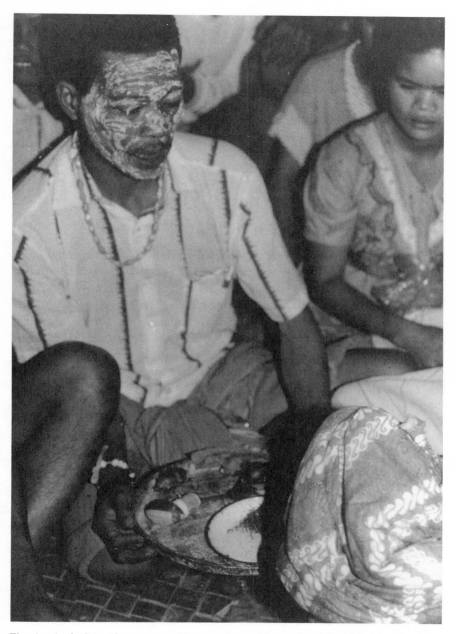

Fig. 4. *Ambe Sope, the* topuppu *(the one who presides at ritual festivities) in one of the* mappurondo *communities, offers areca, betel, lime, and tobacco to the surrogate head, here perched on a makeshift centerpost and swathed in a headcloth. After honoring their victim as a guest, villagers will taunt the head with song. Ambe Sope's face is caked with rice paste, intended to lighten and refine his complexion for the final ceremonies of pangngae. 1984.*

But as the evening wears on, the crowd will taunt the head with the caustic verses of the ma'denna. And from time to time someone will still shout out *Bossi! Bossi'!* and thereby provoke laughter from the gathering. Some ToSalu remarked to me that in the past, village women would occasionally dance in bawdy fashion with the head.[27] Things are tamer now, and the laughter of pangngae appears to have lost some of the derisiveness it may have had in the past. Yet laughter endures as a mark of survivorhood, power, and the capacity to surmount and control terror.[28]

As in medieval carnival (Bakhtin 1984) or the feasts of Saturnalia (Nagy 1990), the grotesque imagery of pangngae serves a discourse of regeneration and fertility. The dismemberment and rot of the headhunter's other becomes the source of renewal and rejuvenation for the upland communities. Put somewhat differently, grotesque imagery renders the political reversal of a dominant adversarial community as the earth from which the upland villages prosper. At the same time, the exaggerated and anatomizing violence of the headhunt evokes astonishment and awe among the uplanders. Taking a head is an extreme and marked act of terror, intended not only to frighten and humiliate an adversarial community, but also to stir dread and awe among those in the hills, and thereby allow them troubled recognition of their own violence. In the theater of pangngae, it is not enough to show stolen cloth and weapons as a sign of domination over the coast. It takes a disfigured head. For in gazing at the head, the uplander does face the extremes of his own nature: that alien other downstream and his own terrifying violence.

Coconut Relics

The language and imagery of the grotesque in Bakhtin's (1984) formulation is emphatically political, a form of undominated discourse that resists all regimes in their official exercise of talk and power.[29] Is this the case in pangngae? On one hand, yes; it presents counterfacts to the regional exercise of Bugis and Mandar hegemony. On the other hand, it is a mistake to forget that the grotesque imagery of pangngae lies at the heart of traditional upland "official" discourse and power. "Played straight," pangngae is not a festive or carnivalesque critique of mappurondo society.

The movement back and forth between human heads and surrogate skulls marked crucial shifts in the political relations between the mountain and coastal communities. Judging from the remarks of mappurondo elders, using a surrogate skull was already common practice by the time the colonial administration set out to eradicate headhunting in Sulawesi, and has remained so up to the present. As to the specific events and conditions that led uplanders to resume what is now a century-long traffic in surrogate heads, virtually nothing is known or remembered. Still, it is reasonable to assume that the idea of taking tubers or coconuts in place of severed heads was but part of a new, bloodless resistance to forces that threatened to dominate the highlands.

It is no accident that a coconut has become the favored surrogate. The formal similarities between a coconut and a skull—something obvious to both headhunter and ethnographer—speak for themselves. More significant, I think, is the fact that the coconut is a product associated with the coast. The palms do not thrive in the highlands, and as a result the coconut is considered a prestige food. It seldom appears in daily cuisine (save among Muslims—persons, it should be noted, who practice a "downstream" religion), but finds key use as a gift to a household hosting a wedding or prosperity rite. In the context of pangngae, however, the trophy coconut is never consumed or later given away. It remains a trophy-offering from the coast. As such, the coconut continues to do the work of the severed head, signifying and restoring the ideal political and cosmological relations linking upstream and downstream.

No one mistakes the surrogate for anything other than what it is—a stage prop—just as no one misreads its blatant symbolism. Forsaking the ambush of a coastal victim for the purchase of a coconut in an upland market, headhunters have made concession to political realities that have brought them powerlessness and despair. Part of that concession probably involved reformulating their historical understanding of regional exchange. In this context, the stories that portray real beheadings as an unwelcome, but nonetheless just, transformation of innocent surrogacy give the uplanders the moral high ground in the region's past.[30] Still, many of today's villagers show a considerable uneasiness when it comes to the violent representations of pangngae. On one hand, the ritual lets them discover and reflect upon the heroic virtues and sentiments necessary for the preservation of village polity and tradition. On the other hand, a real beheading would fill most villagers with dread. The sacred obligations of tradition, as presently interpreted, leave them trapped. Headhunting is terribly right and terribly wrong: it is good to think and bad to do.

It is worth mentioning that contemporary ritual practice suggests a symbolic avoidance or masking of this dilemma. When the warriors return to the village, they jubilantly hold aloft the trophy bag that contains the coconut.

Fig. 5. *Ambe Sope in the upstream, gable-end loft of a house, preparing to present the head to the* debata *(spirits). The head hangs enclosed in a dark woven pouch (center). Beside it hangs a rack for offerings, and above it rest the* tambolâ *flutes from a prior headhunting ritual. 1984.*

From the time the trophy is brought back to the village to the time it is placed as an offering to the spirits, out of view, in the eastern (or upstream) loft of an elder's house, it never comes out of the bag. The bag affords no glimpse of the prize within. It conceals what the trophy is—a coconut obtained through purchase or barter—as well as what it is not—a disfigured face stolen in ambush. In this way, no one can gaze upon the awful truth of the headhunters' violence *or* their humiliation in reciprocal relations with distant lands.

The violent and grotesque imagery of ritual headhunting is, among other things, caught up in the problem of outsiderhood and the historical shifts in regional patterns of dominance and subordination. Showing signs of violence has been the headhunter's way of making a practical cultural response to the threatening power of the outsider and the disorderly circumstances of exchange. As rites of reversal, current stagings of pangngae symbolically invert the social order of the region's past. Whether the predatory journey into the past evidences a displacement of contemporary tensions is difficult to confirm. The headhunt could arguably be a commemorative eruption of a sublimated history. These questions notwithstanding, the effort to disguise violent intent—journeying in the past, carrying no weapons, displaying no trophy heads—suggests the infrapolitics typical of subordinate groups (Scott 1990). In this sense, pangngae is a form of undominated discourse—contributing to, rather than substituting for, a practical program of resistance. But as subsequent chapters will show, headhunting celebrations *are also* very much a form of official discourse, a key to legitimizing mappurondo social order in each mountain settlement.

As Stallybrass and White (1986:26) remind us, "transgressions and the attempt to control them obsessively return to somatic symbols." Dialectical polarities—inside:outside, high:low, life:death, pure:polluting, us:others—are familiar markers on the social and symbolic terrain of pangngae. As the ritual's dominant somatic symbol—begging both reverence and disgust—the severed head works as an icon of the taxonomic or categorical violence done to the enemy's "body politic." In this light, the grotesque image of the severed head serves the social and political purpose of demonizing an adversarial community. Even in its momentary return from the status of "object" to re-humanized subject, the head suffers the humiliating "blows" of hospitality and laughter. Although the head elicits expressions of disgust, it also stirs awe. The relic of a marked and unusual violence, the head has the capacity to astonish, to exalt. In this sense, the severed head is a grotesque guise for the sublime.

The ambiguities of taking a head—real or imagined—have, I suspect, the potential to trouble the headhunter. After all, pangngae calls for the head-hunter to meet the extremes of his own nature. In face-to-face encounter with his alien double, he must confront his own capacity for terror, vio-lence, and laughter. Yet it must remind him of his subordinate place in the world as well. Since no later than the close of the nineteenth century, the trophy head has been masked and withheld from public gaze. The masking of the stolen head paradoxically announces and suppresses its own history. Surrogation, euphemism, and head-bag declare the humiliation of the up-land communities under Mandar and Bugis hegemony. But they also hide a history of "real" headhunting from view, leaving the past uncertain.[31]

Ironically, the social changes of the twentieth century have brought the mappurondo communities to a point where they recognize that the head is now a sign of their own outsiderhood, their own oppositional stance vis-à-vis Indonesian and global orders. In the current social and ideological cli-mate, headhunting does not resolve the problem of the outsider but inverts and exacerbates it. Yet local moral tradition requires this ritualized gesture of violence from them.

As for a century of ethnographic speculation on the logic and meaning of a severed head, it appears to be based on a misrecognition of the social and political dimensions of ritual violence. Commentators have been hypnotized by the grotesque, forgetting that it is a mode of political discourse, and have enshrined the head as a fetishized product of pagan depravity and primitive thought. If the mappurondo case provides a corrective lesson, the connec-tion between severed heads and fertility had nothing to do with a logic of seed and soul-stuff, but, rather, with the mortification of the rival, an act that served as the very measure of the headhunters' prosperity. The political turnabout envisioned in pangngae underscored the providential favor shown the headhunters' communities when the world is restored to the cosmo-graphic ideal. As one song puts it:

Illau' mandalal lisu	Down there deep in the whirlpool's eye
tountunnu tagarinna	the one who burns the incense grass
inderi rambu apinna	here the fragrant smoke of its fire

However fleeting or illusory the turnabout may have been as a political ideal, the headhunter's violence compelled those downriver to subserve up-land prosperity.

4

Violence, Solace, Vows, Noise, and Song

Ritual Headhunting and the Community in Mourning

Common to nearly all Southeast Asian headhunting traditions is a practical discourse that ties the remorseless felling of a victim to the cessation of personal and collective mourning. In most cases, taking a life in raid or ambush becomes an act through which a headhunter can put aside the emblems of grief carried by himself and others. Pangngae is not very different from these other traditions, for it, too, connects bereavement and violence. Although the scale and enthusiasm with which the ritual is run may vary, villagers conduct the headhunt with the idea of bringing public mourning to an end. For example, a term used throughout Bambang to describe the tenor of pangngae is *maringngangi'*. The word means to "ease," "lighten a burden," or "relieve," and conveys the way in which headhunting ceremonies dispel grief (*kabarataan*). In fact, the ToIssilita' of Minanga, Saludengen, and Rantepalado use *maringngangi'* as a common name for their headhunting practices. No less telling are two ToSalu terms for the headhunt, *untungka'i botto,* "opening the hamlet" (i.e. from prohibitions of mourning) and *untauam bahata,* "being persons who mourn."[1]

From my vantage point as an outsider, killing another human being for the purpose of bringing mourning to an end raised complex and disturbing questions about what people in headhunting communities think and feel about death, violence, and loss. Mappurondo villagers, by contrast, seemed less troubled by the moral and interpretive dilemmas that the violence of headhunting posed for me. Those I knew well showed great conscience and sympathy in everyday affairs, and saw murder as wrongful and alarming. For them, any murder within the headwater communities was a sign of treachery and discord, and threatened rebounding violence. Fortunately, the lessons and constraints of *ada' tuo* (the "adat of life" discussed in Chapter 2) have worked to keep violence subdued and comparatively rare. In fact, the uplanders in my acquaintance regard violence and murderousness as attributes of the very lowland communities from which they claim to take trophy skulls. The ethos of pacifism that guides upland life also draws strength from a curse said to have been placed upon the mountain territory of Rantebulahan over 250 years ago for the sacrifice of a relative or dependent during *malangngi'*, a household prosperity rite run by women. This frightening negation of the sacrificial order sparked a social and moral crisis, and is said to have brought an era of poverty and misfortune upon Rantebulahan that has yet to be brought to a close.[2] Some elders even attribute the collapse of Pitu Ulunna Salu to this ritual murder.

The violence of pangngae did not provoke the same kind of dread among my friends. I did make some of them uneasy by speaking as if the headhunters, past and present, were culpable of real and imagined murders. In doing so I conjured a world in which the headhunters' victims lived not as strangers and enemies, but as distant partners and persons worthy of human concern. My remarks also forced upon my friends a critical and demonized portrait of mappurondo practice. It was in the context of such conversations that mappurondo acquaintances would retreat into the past to find a moral basis for their headhunting practices. Stories about retribution in a time of feuds and enslavement were a way to make mappurondo ancestors and headhunting practices appear just.

The discomfort my remarks and questions aroused from time to time confirms for me the predicament of the mappurondo communities in the Indonesian national order, and the ambivalence villagers can feel when discussing or holding traditional rites. In the discourse of Indonesian citizenship, the mappurondo headhunter cannot find an appropriate victim, for citizenship insists on a sense of mutual belonging that encompasses and transcends regional and ethnic distinctions.[3] The social horizons of the past have been widened, shifting the boundaries of the human beyond those called for in pangngae.[4] In the terrain of state citizenship, taking the head of a lowlander is murder. Yet the state also denies the mappurondo community ideological and institutional support. Local ancestral practices go unrecognized: they have not been accepted as religion nor have they been canonized as *kebudayaan,* (Ind.) "culture." Given the pressures of the contemporary order, it is hardly surprising that this minority religious community would seek legitimacy in the past. The ceremonies and effigy heads of the present are reminders that call forth tradition and history. Looking back into the past in ritual performance, mappurondo villagers can see their practices as virtuous, intelligible, and right.

Stalking a victim in the past requires, in some sense, a forgetting of the present. But caution and concessionary gestures to the here-and-now are called for. The warriors of today carry no weapons except for their work machetes (used to fashion a *tambolá*—a flute made from bamboo and palm), and all are careful not to be seen near mountain settlements in daylight hours. As recently as 1974, some warriors would travel to the coastal markets at Polewali and spend a week or more in and on the town. During my time in Bambang, however, cohorts would journey no more than a dozen kilometers from their home, and then linger in the forest for a short time— a day, three days, a week at most. Certain settlements, like the one at Minanga, have begun to limit their warriors' expeditions to Saturdays, so that the young boys who take part will not be missed in school. And in what may be the most telling concession to the present, some cohorts, like those in Rantepalado, do not even bother to find a head trophy, but simply return to their hamlets with tambolâ flutes.

I wondered aloud to Ambe Sope, the topuppu of Salutabang, whether pangngae made sense in the current scheme of things. As the authority charged with directing pangngae, Ambe Sope could appreciate the purposefulness and contingency of ritual practice. Accepting of the concessions the community might have to make in conducting the ritual, he nonetheless regarded pangngae as an obligation of tradition. Sense or no sense, ancestral teachings demand the songs and liturgies of pangngae. But Ambe Sope also mentioned obligation fostered by need. Something had to be done, for it would be unimaginable to leave a village in mourning.

Ambe Sope's remarks, along with the common formulation of pangngae as an "opening," an "unburdening," or a "relieving," call attention to bereavement as a crisis or force to be put to rest in mappurondo headhunting ritual. Let me be careful to explain, then, that pangngae brings an end to *communal mourning.* People put away *public* emblems of their grief, and the community, as a collective, declares itself free from the burdens of mourning. In an important sense, pangngae occasions a discursive space in which individuals can work through personal feelings of grief or loss and get on with life. Taking advantage of the ritual to work through feelings of loss, however, does not always lead villagers to put grief and anguish irrevocably behind them. The end of communal mourning is hardly coincident with the passing of personal grief, nor should it be confused with the latter. The sentiments of specific participants are diverse, complex, ongoing, and largely indeterminate. Nevertheless, the celebratory mood and performative (or pragmatic) work of pangngae highlight a collective effort at overcoming loss. At the very least, the ritual tries to bring the scope of bereavement within measure. In this way, the headhunt plays an important role in patterning the rhythms of mourning and solace in the mappurondo communities.

Put in broad terms, it may be asked why the problems or crises of mourning have to be worked upon in the precinct of demonizing an other. In tackling this mystery, some ethnographers have suggested that grief or other turbulent emotions motivate and find catharsis in a headhunter's violence. I will discuss their work in the pages that follow. For the moment, I will just note that I see things somewhat differently: my understanding of pangngae convinces me that the resolution of communal mourning is more significant than personal catharsis in motivating the violent act of headhunting. I also place an emphasis on discourse as the generative site of both violence and solace. A variety of discursive forms—such as vows, songs, or noise—mediate the ways in which people and a community put grief behind them. Above all, the discourse of headhunting ritual refigures individual affect in collective terms as political affect, as a resource emanating from and giving meaning to shifting political situations and asymmetries.

Further questions may be framed around the "problem" of bereavement and ritual violence in the mappurondo community. Consider the ironic absence of bereavement in stories about the ritual's past. Although Ambe Sope and many others made it clear the pangngae was run for the purpose of bringing mourning to a close, not once did anyone suggest that a need to dispel grief motivated ancestral practice: the genealogy of pangngae was always recounted and justified in light of intercultural tensions and polemics. I cannot offer much on this point except speculation. Perhaps the crisis of loss and anguish "goes without saying," buried deep in the moral foundations of the headhunt. Perhaps it is dangerous for this minority religious community to structure history around grief.[5] In any case, *bereavement was never mentioned in a way to confer virtue or intelligibility upon the headhunts of the past.*

Given this tradition that attaches ritual violence to the human project of mourning, I am led to wonder, too, about what has happened within pangngae as the mappurondo communities have adjusted to an unstable

and sometimes menacing world. Their dilemma is not unlike the one encountered by the Ilongot: what can be done about mourning, how can one
live with suffering, when headhunting is out of the question (R. Rosaldo
1984:181–182)? Shifting social and political orders have put the violence of
the headhunt into flux, sometimes fueling it, other times dampening it. The
current suppression of ritual violence implies profound changes in the discourse of anguish and mourning for both the mappurondo and the Ilongot
headhunter.[6] The Ilongot response appears to be pain and despondency.
The long-standing "mappurondo solution" is to work with effigy heads so
as to bring mourning to a close. But are "effigy emotions" brought into
play? If the mappurondo headhunter of today cannot carry a weapon on his
journey, can we expect him to carry his anguish and rage? I suggest that he
does not, relying instead on "effigy emotions"—that is, representations of
emotions made in ritual discourse—to characterize the sentiments that become entangled in violence.

Topographies of Anguish and Pity, and the Problem of Catharsis

Earlier in this book I made mention of the riparian cosmography in which the mappurondo headhunter situates himself and his victim. It
will be recalled that regions downstream from the mountain territories lie in
the path of souls who follow riverwaters to the sea, where they sink in a
lightless whirlpool to the realm of the dead. The warrior cohorts of pangngae always journey in a downstream direction to find their trophies. Their
movement downriver and back could be read, following Downs (1955) and
McKinley (1976), as an effort to restore social and cosmological balance
to a world disturbed by the loss of life and the crisis of mourning. In this
structuralist scheme, the headhunter tries to subjugate death; the precise
identity or social origins of the stolen head seem beside the point—anyone
outside and downstream should do as a victim.[7] The life lost downriver bal-
ances the life lost upriver; the soul that traveled downstream is countered
by the trophy head brought upstream.
    The problem of cosmological balance does not inform every headhunt-
ing tradition in island Southeast Asia. Discussing the Berawan of northern
Borneo, Metcalf finds that headhunting is intended to "deflect the malice
of hovering souls" (1982:127), to "export" the resentment and jealousy of

the recently deceased (Metcalf forth.). Within Berawan eschatology, "death has a chain quality to it," and until deflected outside the community, "death will follow upon death" within the group (Metcalf 1982:127). The point of Berawan headhunting, then, is to make death someone else's problem, not to even the score of souls lost. Yet Metcalf's findings, like those of de Josselin de Jong, Downs, and McKinley, remain loyal to exchange theory: the latter three describe the direct, symmetrical exchange of the dead, whereas Metcalf sketches something akin to the indirect and asymmetrical exchange of unquiet souls.

Judging from my experience, mappurondo villagers do not link pangngae in any explicit way to the problem of restoring cosmological balance. Neither do they speak about hovering souls whose anger and jealousy might bring about further deaths.[8] Yet a rhetoric of "here and there" persists in the management of mourning. In shedding the burden of mourning, the community imagines an act of ritual violence taking place in the home of a rival subaltern from the past. Looking upon this violent scene through the ritual imagination has the potential to distract, dislodge, or possibly negate the anguish of those in mourning. If I am correct, then topography, the emotions, and social hierarchy work as transcodings of one another. In the discourse of pangngae, the journey downriver to fell and dismember a victim also marks a crossing into an emotion-scape of pity, remorselessness, and disgust. As I see it, these emotions are the expressive "masks" of political attitudes. Though they are not to be confused for one another, pity, remorselessness, and disgust do have something in common: they are felt in encounter with the subordinate and the debased, and always involve a "looking down" upon another, however fleetingly. They are political affects felt in the terrain of social hierarchy.[9] One of the key tasks of mappurondo headhunting, then, is to shift momentarily the look of the community away from "egalitarian" feelings of anguish and empathy that link villagers together toward the "superordinate" feelings of pity and remorselessness that position uplanders with respect to their historical rivals on the coast.

My views derive from listening to the songs and liturgies of pangngae, but also follow upon long consideration of work by Michelle and Renato Rosaldo on the emotional discourse of Ilongot headhunting (M. Rosaldo 1977, 1980, 1983; R. Rosaldo 1980, 1984, 1987, 1988). Though I risk conflating and oversimplifying their respective studies of the Ilongot, their understanding runs as follows: the violent ambush and beheading of a victim affords a cathartic release of *liget,* a term the Ilongot use to describe feeling stirred up by grief, anger, envy, or desire.[10] Comments from Renato Rosaldo's work are illustrative and emphatic:

Regarded as ritual, headhunting resembles a piacular sacrifice: it involves the taking of a human life with a view toward cleansing the participants of the contaminating burdens of their own lives. (1980:140)[11]

Perhaps we should begin by viewing headhunting as the ritual enactment of a piacular sacrifice. . . . This ritual process involves cleansing and catharsis. (1984:189–190)

[The Ilongot] saw headhunting as a way of venting their anger. . . . [It's] the ultimate place to carry one's rage. . . . They feel it is the ultimate act of violence and anger. Their sense is that it is cathartic. (1987:252)

Entangled with unfocused liget and burdened with the weight of insults, pain, and grief, the Ilongot headhunter discovers that he can cast off his disturbing emotions by tossing a severed head to the ground.

This portrait of the Ilongot fits rather well with most of the literature on the ethnopsychology of highland societies in island Southeast Asia. By and large, the island cultures favor emotional restraint and balance in everyday life. The effort to rein in the emotions, to place constraints on intense feeling, to avoid upset, and to keep dramatic emotional display offstage presumably causes certain emotions to smolder or to diffuse over time (cf. Hollan 1988). In the view of some writers, ritual events offer a context in which everyday constraints on emotion are suspended or relaxed. As a result, rituals become focal occasions for displays of aggressiveness, anger, grief, or exuberant feeling. If this is the case, it would appear that rituals are doubly marked off from the everyday: first by their formalized practices, and second by their cathartic potential. There are considerable theoretical difficulties in characterizing ritual in this way, and, for that matter, in so characterizing the realm of the everyday. Emphasis on the formality of ritual downplays its improvisatory character, and draws analytic attention away from uncertainty and contingency in ceremonial practice. Privileging ritual as the site of catharsis inclines one to treat ceremony as therapeutic practice or safety valve, and to ignore the capacity of ritual to provoke anxiety and trauma. It also runs the risk of skewing our understanding of catharsis by putting emphasis on those contexts in which the release of intense emotions is most subject to explicit ideological and aesthetic mediation. Similarly, an emphasis on the formality and cathartic potential of ritual makes everyday practice and experience appear unmediated and insignificant. Although I will not pursue the issue in the present work, I think the challenge for ethnographers will be to find ways to avoid pitting the ritual vs. the everyday, or the cathartic vs. the constrained, and instead capture them in the indeterminate and contested arenas of human practice.

Despite these reservations about the way the literature has characterized the ceremonial, the everyday, and the cathartic, I do agree that something that might be called catharsis commonly takes place in a wide range of ritual contexts, and that it informs more than a few traditions of ritual violence. The Ilongot, for example, made very clear statements to the Rosaldos about venting and managing strong emotions in the heat of violence and in the celebratory song-and-boast fests that followed a beheading. Striking emotional discharge also figures prominently in a number of Sa'dan Toraja rituals, leading Jane Wellenkamp (1988a) to argue that the Toraja possess a "cathartic" theory of emotion. Looking at expressions of intense grief in funerals, and at the violence of trance possession and ritualized kickfighting, Wellenkamp argues that the Toraja see personal emotional discharge as socially disruptive and necessary, and thus demanding of ceremonial release and containment. Somewhat surprisingly, her own analysis of headhunting ritual leads her away from connecting this form of ritual violence to bereavement (Wellenkamp 1988b). But her more general point about the ritual management of intense emotion in Toraja society would seem to apply to other cases as well, including the Ilongot.

Saying that headhunting is "cathartic," however, raises a number of problems. Citing a lively debate about the work of Thomas Scheff (1977) on emotional distancing in ritual, Wellenkamp (1988a:494) points out that "there is little consensus in the literature concerning precisely how 'catharsis' should be defined and identified, and under what circumstances it occurs for which specific emotions."[12] Nor, as Bruce Kapferer (1979a, 1979b, 1979c) seems to suggest, is it at all clear how and why ritual modulates the display and transformation of feeling. On a different note, our views toward catharsis need to be kept flexible. For example, efforts to portray catharsis as a force that threatens to disrupt community stability leads us to forget that the powerful and perhaps violent release of emotion may be in some contexts the very measure and image of social stability. And given that human experience is not so much a conditional state as an unfolding in time, one does well to inquire into the rhythms of pain and catharsis in the theater of ritual.

Renato Rosaldo's very moving essay "Grief and a Headhunter's Rage" (1984) has had an enormous impact on discussions of emotion, ritual violence, and the particulars of Ilongot society. But the essay, along with some misreadings of it, has obscured the far-reaching explorations that characterized the Rosaldos' earlier monographs on Ilongot headhunting.[13] For example, in trying to shed light on Ilongot violence, it calls attention to rage and bereavement without sufficiently reminding readers that the distress carried into the kill has heterogeneous sources: not only the enraged anguish of mourning, but the fires of envy, the sting of insult, the heart-piercing lyrics of a song. A close reading of the text shows that Rosaldo *has* mentioned some of these as the burdens that lead Ilongot men to take a life (1984: 190–191), but the theme of grief overshadows them. The essay also makes a signal contribution about the positioned subject, taking care to distinguish the driving burdens of older men from the volatile desires of Ilongot youths. Unmentioned, nonetheless, are the dilemmas of women (who cannot carry their grief on a headhunting journey), and the terrible turmoil of an adolescent who not only has lost a parent but is yet to wear the hornbill earrings that signal a headhunter's entry into manhood. And in the end, a reader is left wondering, too, about the political dimensions of a headhunter's catharsis. Although anguish or envy may make an Ilongot man want to take a head, there remains the political question, "Whose head?" An unpoliticized notion of catharsis does not, cannot, offer justification or rationale for the choice of a victim.

If I fault the essay for what it leaves unsaid, I do so in order to underscore the complexity and uncertainty of the cathartic act. The felling of a victim is the work of a swarm, some burdened with rage, some entangled with envy, some perhaps stricken with fright at the "smell of blood" (M. Rosaldo 1983:137). The suffering, yearning, and doubt carried into the raid have their origin in a tangle of lives brought together in a collective task. If there is a striking release of emotion in stalking and killing, it is witnessed in the context of comradeship, adventure, suspense, and the taming knowledge of elders. Then, too, there are the raids that fail, that get put off for a more auspicious time, or that wind up forestalled altogether by changing historical conditions. Indeed, one of the key arguments in Renato Rosaldo's *Ilongot Headhunting, 1883–1974* (1980), is that Ilongot raiding has been intermittent for the past 100 years. Cathartic violence is susceptible to the currents of political history. As Michelle Rosaldo (1980:34) relates, "even in the old days, grief rarely led to killing. In the past as in the present, intense and disturbing feelings only occasionally knew a headhunter's catharsis; more often they were lost in the distracting claims of daily life." And in those instances where an Ilongot did find a way to vent his rage in tossing the head of the fallen, did the "cathartic act" effectively end his mourning or his envy? In fact, as Renato Rosaldo (1984, 1988:432) himself has been at pains to point out, this ritual moment, for all its violence and drama, may be but one step in an enduring process of bereavement—a momentary respite from the grieving that will linger beyond the headhunt to reawaken in dreams, memories, and conversations.

To return to the mappurondo case, I find the relationship between ritual

violence, catharsis, and the modulation of grief and mourning just as complicated. Under threat of the law and the moral force of their elders' teachings, the mappurondo headhunters of today may not take a life during
pangngae. Where, then, do the headhunters carry their anguish? The ritual
largely denies them the acts of violence that (from an Ilongot perspective)
might help purge their hearts of troubling emotions. One instead encounters songs of violence and the hostile gestures occasionally directed toward
the effigy head. In principle, these songs and gestures of violence may be
enough to elicit or constitute a cathartic release for some participants.[14] My
own sense is that they do not. They do more to distract one from feelings
of anguish and sorrow than they do to lead to a cleansing purge of turbulent emotion. With the potential for cathartic violence so limited, is catharsis itself in question? If violent catharsis does not put the yoke to the tabus
of mourning, what does? As I have suggested, mappurondo headhunting
may call forth political affect in such a way as to "move" the community
out of mourning. The summoning of this particular form of political affect
does not tell the whole story, however. Rather, this summons is just one feature of the transformative project in which the ritual practices of pangngae
"rework" social experience and social situation.[15] In this light, the release
from mourning that is said to take place in the violence of the headhunt
may appear not so much as a purging of troublesome emotions, but as a
process in which people suddenly rid themselves of a burdensome situation.

The Journey Downriver

Having raised a complex set of questions about mourning and
the violence of mappurondo headhunting ritual, I turn to pangngae celebrations of the mid-1980s. The long, somber period that begins with the
plowing of terraces and the casting of seed lingers on after harvest. For eight
months, *pemali*—prohibitions on noisiness, laughter, storytelling, singing,
drumming, and exuberant gatherings—silence the mappurondo households
and hamlets. The tabus do not bring about soundlessness, but enforce a
quiet that allows farmers and spirits to coax forth the rice crop undisturbed.
When the last sheaf of the new crop has gone into the barn, and the last
drying rack is collapsed, harvest comes to a close. But the quiet continues.

Thought and concern turn toward the deceased for several days. No one
leaves the village and no one may do any work. Called *palitomate*, "back
to the dead ones," or *bulan anitu*, the "moon of ghosts," this three-day

period is marked by the sacrifice of water buffalos and pigs, whose souls will be of benefit to deceased relatives in the afterworld. Bulan anitu is, in a sense, a resumption of the ritual practices concerned with mourning that make up *patomatean*, "the time of the dead ones." Deaths, of course, happen throughout the year, and bring temporary halt to other activities as burial ceremonies and their concomitant restrictions on labor and the consumption of rice are observed for as long as four days. During the rites of patomatean, women retreat to the center of the homestead, where they keep watch over the deceased and begin to keen for the lost. It falls to men to bury the deceased away from the hamlet, and to coordinate the accompanying sacrifices. From this time forward, the immediate household of the deceased, and especially its female members, wears emblems of grief—ribbons of white cloth and, for wives, shifts blackened with ash and mud.

In effect, bulan anitu contemporizes all deaths that happened throughout the year—those who died during April, for example, are recalled along with those who passed away in November. Thus, the three days of sacrificial ceremonies renew the public representation of loss and mourning. Immediately after the rites of bulan anitu, time is reckoned as *panda pealloan*, "the edge before day," a period of uncertain duration and lacking ceremony. Although people resume labor in their gardens, an air of sadness and solemnity continues to hang over the hamlets. It is during panda pealloan that men and youths secretly slip out of the village in pre-dawn darkness to journey off on a headhunt.

The solemnity of panda pealloan is tempered with a sense of anxious, unarticulated waiting. People know or suspect that some of the village men have gone to take a head, but the blanket tabu against any mention of pangngae muffles their anxiousness and anticipation. Specifically, villagers believe that mentioning the headhunt may imperil those who "went to the sea." Not surprisingly, the same tabu complicated my knowing when pangngae was to take place in a village. Resorting to euphemism to bring up the issue seldom succeeded, except to amuse and annoy. With time, I became better at reading the "signs" of the headhunters' likely return. Even so, my efforts to know when ceremonies were to commence were at odds with the secrecy and uncertainty that shrouded the headhunters' journey. Like everyone else, I just had to wait for events I could not control or fully foresee. Looking back on it, the term *panda pealloan*, "the edge before day," captured these moods and tensions, likening them to the way one might look into pre-dawn darkness for a sign of daybreak—straining, expectant, and unsure. From the vantage point of this metaphor, solemnity and mourning are heavy nocturnal moods—the darkest hours that come before dawn.

As for the cohort of headhunters, some critical social exclusions constrain and mark its membership. Foremost among them is the one that closes the headhunt to women, an exclusion that institutes a lasting difference in gender ideology. In the context of the present discussion, however, another exclusionary demand is more striking: men and youths in mourning may not take part. This strict ban applies to any male within the household or immediate family of the deceased, and typically is reckoned to extend to first cousins. The effect of the tabu is to sequester and immobilize grief; the bereaved can do nothing about their anguish. In contrast to the Ilongot, then, mappurondo villagers cannot unburden their anguished rage by taking a head. Solace is not discovered in one's own violence, but is received as a gift from others.[16]

At first glance, mappurondo headhunting would seem to run counter to the findings of the Rosaldos. Yet if mappurondo tabus sever anguish and cathartic violence in practice, they conjoin them in theory. Sequestering bitterness and rage, in my view, is a way to avoid violence. In my reading, the tabu implies that anguish is dangerous and disturbing and can lead one to kill. Put somewhat differently, the tabu suggests that violence does offer catharsis and solace for the bereaved. Remembering that in the current order of things mappurondo headhunters do not want to fell a real victim, and should not fell a real victim, the tabu makes great sense. Because grief is so volatile and threatening to civil order, ways must be found to keep it off the trails leading to the sea.

Here, then, I want to suggest that the social and historical forces that have led the mappurondo headhunters to forsake human heads and to take up effigies of some kind have also brought about change in the discourse of mourning. The villagers have shelved ritual violence and the cathartic release it might bring to an anguished heart. If I am not wrong, this is not a matter of discarding violence and its cathartic potential, but rather, an effort to put them away. Just as villagers put headbags, tambolâ flutes, waterbuffalo horns and pig jaws from sacrifices, and other ritual objects up into the loft when they are through with them, so, too, have they put violence away in a place where it can hang as a keepsake. That anguish finds solace in violence is not forgotten. It is recalled in the negative sanctions of tabu and in ritual song.

A few examples from the sumengo tradition may help bring my point across more convincingly. Although the headhunters who depart from the village do not carry with them turbulent feelings of grief, the songs portray them as if they did. The following lyrics picture the headhunter as a predatory hawk, "blackened" with anguish, that is, darkened with the same soot and stain used to prepare mourning shirts:

Malallengko toibirin	Watch out you on the horizon
tomatilampe bambana	you low on the foot of our land
lembum matil langkam borin	the blackened hawk is heading there
Langkam borim panuntungan	The hawk blackened with mortar stain
lao menkaroi bonde'	goes to scratch circles on the coast
malepom pengkaroanna	the talon marks spiral and coil

Another striking song is one performed by women. In it, women respond with alarm as the hawk hovers over the village, darkening the sky with grief-blackened wings. They remind the headhunter not to turn his anguish toward the village and the women, but to carry it downriver:[17]

Samboaki' tole	Do not shroud us like that
langkam borim panuntungan	the hawk blackened with mortar stain
lao mengkaroi bonde'	goes to scratch circles on the coast

The image of the black hawk, a bird that locals regard as an omen of death, renders grief as undomesticated, predatory rage.

Felling the Victim

The transfiguration of the headhunter as a threatening bird of prey is a way to make visible to the imagination the burdensome rage of a community in mourning. The same image also renders a sense of journey, of a "going there," of the tremendous distances to be crossed by the headhunter. The imagination is about to go to another place in order to witness the scene of violence. From the vantage point of the community, the headhunters must move out of sight and out of hearing to find their victim. Moving beyond the horizons of sight and hearing takes the headhunters beyond the social reach of the group, beyond the territory of its senses. The community cannot look upon the ambush and murder that is said to take place. The only violence the community will witness will be that which is described, euphemized, and idealized in ritual song and celebration.

Even though the cohorts of today no longer venture into other ethnic regions, their departure from the hamlets is shrouded by secrecy and marked by ritual efforts to safeguard the group. Organizing the cohort falls to the *babalako* (as ToIssilita' call him) or the *topuppu* (the ToSalu term). Men and youths who want to go off on a headhunt, or who have made pledges to that effect, quietly talk among themselves in search of companions for the venture. Then one by one or in small groups, they secretly confer with the topuppu or babalako, who arranges for the time and place of their departure.

During my two-year stay in Bambang, the number of cohort members ranged from just a few men and youths to nearly 50. On more than one occasion, the pack consisted of two or three married adults, several unmarried youths, and a few novices below the age of ten. Of the married men, the person who vowed to lead the cohort took the role of *too'na* ("the [tree] trunk"). Another married adult, meanwhile, assumed the role of *lolona* ("the [tree] top"), the cohort's junior leader. Whatever importance these two roles may have had in the past, they serve today only to mark the higher status of adult males who journey under the obligation of a vow to lead. As for the male elders who oversee pangngae, ToIssilita' custom dictates that the babalako accompany the cohort on their expedition,[18] while among the ToSalu, the topuppu stays behind in the village.[19]

As the time to leave nears, those who have decided to join in the foray begin to distance themselves from women by observing certain tabus on foods, sex, and talk.[20] Then, by prearrangement with the babalako or topuppu, the headhunters meet together at the edge of a hamlet under the cover of pre-dawn darkness. Here, omens and sacrifices become especially important. A chicken is sacrificed, and its blood and entrails read. Bubbly blood, a hard heart, and a gall that protrudes well out from under the liver portend a successful raid. If the cohort happens to get a bad reading, or has, as the saying goes, *sala mane* ("the wrong chicken"), further birds are sacrificed until good signs are obtained.[21] When the topuppu or babalako finishes muttering the final words of supplication, the cohort lunges at the offering of food and grabs wildly for its contents. In former times, it was believed that the warrior who got the chicken's head would also take the victim's. Nowadays, the person to snatch the chicken head will be named as the beheading warrior on the return of the cohort.

Before the rising sun begins to lighten the sky, the cohort steals out of the village in a downstream direction.[22] The headhunters remain out of the village anywhere from one to ten days. During this time, some of the cohort members get the coconut that will serve as a surrogate head.[23] While still out of the village, the headhunters also gather the bamboo, rattan, and palm fronds needed to make their tambolâ flutes, flutes that when blown

produce an eerie, low-pitched bellow.[24] Most materials needed for the tambolâ grow on or next to settled land, and are obtained before the cohort
makes its trip home. In keeping with the secret nature of their journey, the
warriors must be careful not to reveal their identity as headhunters to other
villages lest news of their whereabouts be carried back to their home settlement. Above all, the headhunters must not allow themselves to be seen or
heard by women as they make their flutes.[25]

Back in the village, the sudden absence of husbands, brothers, and sons
may lead women to become anxious—or to put on a show of anxiety. Be-
wilderment at the disappearance of their menfolk recedes as the women realize that they are quite likely off on pangngae. To be sure, wives and mothers know that the men do not risk the dangers of real headhunting. Yet any
journey poses the danger of accident or violent encounter and can therefore
stir deep concern over a traveler's safety.[26] Gestures of worry and concern
are common. While the headhunters are away, wives and mothers will set
out special dishes of rice in the loft of the house as a ritual gesture intended
to ease the warriors' hunger. A wife is careful not to let anyone touch her
husband's betel and lime holder, and no belongings may be taken from the
house, an injunction that applies to fire and coals, as well.[27] Women also
take care not to goad, tease, or scold the men and youths who remain in the
village during this time.

Later, during the exuberant ceremonies of pangngae, choruses of singers—usually, but not always women—will describe the anxiety and concern
of women. For example, one sumengo depicts a wife who wanders about,
unsure if her husband—who left without telling her—is away on a headhunt
or off somewhere else:

Ma'lembe-lembe belanna	His wed companion has her doubts
ma'saleo bainena	his wife is walking here and there
nasanga tangkam maleso	she's thinking it's not really clear

Another chorus frets that those who undertook the adventure in order to
adorn themselves with warrior's bracelets have been gone too long:

Masae allomi lao	The day when they left is long past
pesuana lado-lado	ones called by the basket of beads
pa'palussu'na bandola	ones set loose by the bamboo chest

If the poetics of anxiety heard here provide some mirror of the distress and
concern of contemporary villagers, they show women as the ones who endure worry and the threat of loss. Fear of abandonment, in the discourse of

song lyrics, scars the experience of married women. Given the prominence
of women in keeping vigil and wailing over the deceased, the lyrics perhaps
reflect a thoroughgoing cultural and ideological understanding in which a
married woman's experience includes deep strains of brooding, worry, and
loss. At the same time, the fact that headhunters do return home suggests
that ritual discourse uses women as the foil for showing that loss and abandonment are not certainties.

The poetics and rhetoric of women's anxiety are partner to a broader discourse that idealizes the imagined violence of the headhunters as an agonistic encounter with a distant foe. Just as sumengo lyrics portray the de-
parting headhunters as predatory hawks, the journey's end downriver finds
them transfigured as cockerels. By way of contrast to the wild, predatory
hawk of anguish, the cockerel offers the image of an aggressive but domes-
ticated fighter, associated with struggles for dominance.

Mapianna mane' londong	Fine and daring that cockerel bird
lembun tama pangngabungan	hiding in a place of ambush
tisoja' ula-ulanna	his tail feathers cascading down
Malepom pengkaroanna	The talon marks spiral and coil
londom buri'na Mokallam	a speckled Mokallan cockerel
lao untolloam le'bo'	goes to spill waters of the sea

In depicting the headhunters' attack, some songs show only an oblique fascination with blood and violence. For example, many singings portray the
victim as a banyan tree or as a black sugar palm. A banyan is a common
metaphor for political strength and tradition, and the sugar palm connotes
that which is cared for and nurtured. The felling of the banyan and the
palm thus symbolizes the fallen body politic and the severed bonds of human care.

Barane' rumape	Wide and low-boughed banyan
umbalumbunni minanga	whose shade darkens the rivermouth
sau' natotoi london	felled down there by the cockerel
Naparandukkomi london	The cockerel springs forth again
taumpakentaru' tallem	keeping bamboo from sprouting up
taumpakellolo' indu'	sugar palms from growing new fronds

But other sumengo, like those quoted in the preceding chapter, reveal fascination or disgust with rot and decay:

Umbai' kabumbuannam	The humming noise is probably
banga disamboi solem	the banga palm covered with leaves
sumamberrem watinna	swarming grubs gnawing it up

The theme of disgust, I should point out, is not limited to song but also figures prominently in the presentation of the trophy head to the community (as we shall see).

Other lyrics call attention to loss, disorder, and anguish in the home of the victim. Above all, the songs do not so much describe a moment of cathartic violence as draw attention to the pitiable figure of the orphan or widow:

Nakua kadanna Bugi'	It is said that the Bugis say
sae omo palo'bangam	"They come again to empty homes
umbiunni ana'-ana'	to make orphans of the children"
Mennara keane'-ane'	Who are the ones that have children
mennara kepangngassean	who are the ones that look after
natiampanni balida	those who were struck by the batten
Umbai' ane'na mandas	It is probably just his child
sola ambembainena	along with his wed companion
kasapu-sapu di rindim	groping at the walls of the house
Mennamo tanabiunni	Who has not been made an orphan
tanasissimbaratai	not been given a ring of grief
londom malapa limanna	by the cockerel with gnarled talons
Sambanuami tobalu	One homestead the place of widows
satondo'mi ana' bium	one hamlet the place of orphans
santanetemi u'bu'na	one mountain the place of the graves

The strain of pity in these songs belongs chiefly to women. Men seldom know, or join in singing, these lyrics, and their "silence," it seems to me, is good measure of the remorselessness thought to accompany the slaying of their lowland rivals. In the discourse of song, it falls to women to extend pity to orphans and widows. Casting women this way contributes further to the cultural and ideological patterning of emotion and gender, a pattern in which women figure as the agents of sympathy and longing.

The lyrics of the sumengo, so far, evade mention of anything like cathartic violence. The songs suggest a displacement of anguish—its being carried over the horizon—even though pemali tabus immobilize it in the head-hunters' home village. Even then, singers say nothing about headhunters feeling "light" or "unburdened" in their deadly ambush of another. Rather, the lyrics mask the terrible horror of killing. On one hand, the songs play up the awesome power of the headhunter-cockerel as he knocks over trees, spills seawater, and tears up sand. On the other hand, they conceal the facts of violent ambush. In short, this poetry of domination euphemizes violence, both obscuring and exalting it. Similarly, expressions of pity or remorselessness seem to me but elements in a poetics of humiliation, especially if we recall the lyrics that voiced revulsion at the rotting, mutilated body of the ambushed, or those that conjured images of the panic and disorder amid the community of the slain.

That the ritual songs of pangngae fail to acknowledge ties between violence and catharsis should not surprise us, especially as we keep in mind that this lyric discourse barely mentions the anguish and rage of bereavement. Yet the silence about rage and catharsis does not mean that they are without consequence in shaping mappurondo headhunting tradition (cf. R. Rosaldo 1984:192). Their volatility and force have the potential to reawaken a threatening social order, and in recognition of that threat, they are "put away" rather than celebrated or unleashed by song lyrics. Seen in this light, the lyrics of the sumengo, like the tabus that keep grief-stricken villagers off the trails to the sea, do not suspend or relax restraints on turbulent emotions, but keep them in place. But as for the history behind this body of lyric, I can venture little. Perhaps the songs of the past did more to voice the pain of anguished hearts and to celebrate cathartic violence. Whatever the case, today's lyrics seem fitting in an era when the ambush of an innocent would bring reprisal from the civil order.

If the poetics of catharsis have been shelved in current discourse, the poetics of domination and humiliation have not. The lyrics of many of the sumengo discussed thus far summon pity and disgust, feelings appropriate to a subject who looks down upon another. The terrain that stretches between the mappurondo headhunter and his coastal rival thus includes vantage points for seeing and feeling. That is, local ideology reckons mountain and coastal political bodies in terms of place (inside:outside, upstream: downstream), siblingship (elder:younger), and violence (headhunter:victim), and, in so doing, locates the coastal rival in a lowered or subordinant sphere. Expressing pity for the anguish of the coastal victim serves as yet another transcoding of the idealized social hierarchy that allows the mappurondo community to look down upon a rival polity.

Expressing pity for the fallen is also turnabout for those mappurondo hamlets that have endured the weeks and months of mourning. If an anguished person was ever led to find solace in taking a head, his move from grief to catharsis was never simply a personal project for purging himself of troubling emotions but was also a political act consonant with communal ideology and interests. And by the same token, the communal political project of subordinating a rival in ambush no doubt created paths for individuals to cope with their feelings.

Signs and Songs of a Return

Within the discourse of ritual lyric, the headhunter begins his journey as a predatory hawk and slays his rival as a strikingly feathered cockerel. Not surprisingly, the headhunter's journey home finds him transfigured once more, this time as the *kulu-kulu*, or *sarese*, nocturnal birds whose calls are read as omens of prosperity:

Indu' ajangan di rante	Black sugar palm on the wide plain
lao natotoi london	its fronds hewn by the cockerel
nababa ma'kulu-kulu	carried by the kulu-kulu
Kulu-kulu sae bongi	The kulu-kulu come at night
sarese sae nannari	sarese come in blinding dark
sae umbungka' bambaki	come surprise and enter our lands

For those who had been left behind in the village, the fate of the headhunters is a matter of uncertainty and anticipation. Banking their fires at night, the villagers listen for omens of the warrior's victorious return.

But what about the headhunters? After getting the coconut that will fill their leader's head-bag (usually a worn rice pouch), the men and youths of the cohort begin making the other objects always carried home from the journey—the tambolâ. The songs of pangngae celebrate the slashing blows of the headhunters in making the instruments:

Kuluam mane rumandu'	The streamers beginning to sprout
tallem mane metotiam	the bamboo starting to show leaves
ladibatta sulim bulo	will be cut for the golden flute
Battangki' tallan	We hack at the bamboo
timpanangki' daun ube	we lop off all the rattan leaves
tapobungas sumarendu	we make sumarendu flowers

Each headhunter will prepare his own tambolâ from bamboo, decorating it with palm-leaf streamers, perhaps inscribing his name on the shaft, or etching it with geometric designs.

By custom, the headhunters are always said to be away from the village for *tallu bulam,* "three moons," regardless of whether they have been away for three weeks, three days, or three hours. With nightfall, the cohort moves out of its hiding place in the forest. Tambolâ flutes strapped to their backs, the returning headhunters approach their village in the dark. The leader carries the head and brings the cohort to the edge of the village lands. Above them the hamlets sleep in darkness, night-long fires having been forbidden by pemali tradition.

It is now time to awaken the village. As they move closer to the hamlets, the headhunters take their tambolâ and let loose a long howling note, and then shout "*jelelelele yuhuhu*" three times in a ritual gesture called *mua'da'.* Twice more the cohort members sound the tambolâ and let out the cry of *mua'da'.*[28] With that the group moves up the paths and deeper into the village, pausing twice more to deliver blasts on their instruments and shouts of "*lelelele.*" The suddenness of the bellowing and crying startles the villagers out of sleep and marks the beginning of *a'dasan* ("the shouting"), the night-long rite welcoming the return of the *topangngae,* as the headhunters are now called.

The topuppu or tomatuatonda' appears at the edge of his hamlet brandishing a torch of blazing kindling, while other villagers remain inside their darkened homes. Arriving at the foot of his hamlet, the headhunters once more let loose a clamor of flutes and shouts. The elder up above calls out into the darkness, hailing the "strangers." A greeting is given in return, and the topangngae let out another series of jubilant cries, while a company of male elders comes down from the hamlet. Soon men and women, bearing torches and singing somengo, stream down from the hamlets to greet the headhunters, bring with them gifts of tobacco, betel, and food. As the crowd prepares to honor the topangngae, the cohort leader holds aloft the pouch containing the head. People turn their heads or make faces, crying "*Bossi, bossi!*"—"It stinks! It stinks!" and then break into gales of laughter.

The song and feasting of a'dasan last until just before dawn. Songs celebrate not only the feat of the topangngae but the occasion of a'dasan itself:

Ia tole anna guntu	That moment when there is thunder
anna bumbu kaliane	and the rumble of dread places
pa'kuritannamo london	the sign of the cockerel's deed
Kusanga london toapa	I thought whose cockerels are they
sae umbungka' bambaki	come surprise and enter our lands
anna londongkira kami	and all along they're our cockerels

Fig. 6. *The* tomatuatonda' *("the elder of the village") comes out to greet the return-*
ing cohort of topangngae *(headhunters). He carries two torches: the one blazing in*
his right hand is the first fire to be rekindled in the village following the return of the
topangngae. *1985.*

Kisangangkami' maleso	We ourselves think it's very clear
karua ulu nababa	they're carrying along eight heads
pitu lente' nasoeam	as their seven limbs go swinging
Tanete a'dasam	Mountain of the shouting
paneteanna salombe'	the crossing place for the white tail
pangngilangam bonga sura'	the scraping horns of the spot back

Throughout the night, the headhunters are obliged to remain just beyond the edge of the hamlets. With first light, the topuppu or babalako puts
aside a single tambolâ in the brush near the place of a'dasan; the flute will
be retrieved at another time if another village, unable to run pangngae because of epidemic or an unusual number of deaths, calls for someone to release it from mourning. Taking up their tambolâ, the topangngae then follow the babalako or topuppu to the homes of the villagers who mourn for
those who have died during the past year. At each home, the headhunters
let loose a prolonged roar from their tambolâ and shout out "lelelele" three

Fig. 7. *While away on his journey, each headhunter prepares a* tambolâ *flute and decorates it with plaited areca or sugar-palm leaves. The "voice" of the flute releases the* mappurondo *community from mourning. 1984.*

times. With that, each home and each hamlet visited is free of the signs and prohibitions of mourning, and a week of unbridled festivity begins.

In the discourse of song, grief is "figured" as impenetrable haze or darkness. No one can see "beyond" or "through" the enveloping cloud of mourning. The headhunters, however, usher home the arriving sun of peal-loan (rituals of light) that will clear the atmosphere of bereavement:

Kabalarribao	The same here up above
katiro rambu rojana	looking everywhere into haze
tengka talataolai	as if we'd never pass through it
Malillimmi buntu	Dark indeed the mountains
saleburammi tanete	the peaks are lost beneath a cloud
allo pambukkai boko'	the sun opens from behind them

Coming out from mourning, in the local imagination, involves a restoration of sight. It also requires the help of others. The burden of mourning is not something that can be shaken off through personal effort, but must be endured until it is removed by the topangngae:

Leba'mi pote bolongki	Gone at last our blackened necklace
pota sissim baratangki	broken our ring of bitter grief
aka kilalami london	since the cockerel woke to act

Kept from finding cathartic relief in taking a head, the bereaved endure the signs of grief until the shouts of the headhunter and the sounds of the tambolâ mark an end to the darkness of mourning.

Ritual and the Rhythm of Bereavement

The emotions that villagers carry into headhunting ritual are complex, heterogeneous, uncertain, and shifting. The commemorative practices of *bulan anitu* (the "moon of ghosts") that take place just before pangngae no doubt intensify a sense of loss among at least some mappu-rondo villagers, but in my experience, people suffer their hurt with silence and restraint, and seldom show flashes of the anger that may come from grief. Whether a person's sense of loss beforehand has been given greater pitch, or continues to be diminished by the demands of everyday life, the discourse of pangngae offers the bereaved a moment of solace and distraction. A purge of bitterness through physical violence is out of the question, however, leaving the festivities to "lighten" the burdens of the villagers. Indeed, the idea of being "lightened" is fundamental to their understanding of what takes place in headhunting ceremonies (cf. M. Rosaldo 1980:27). Although from time to time I did spot someone unable to put away his or her sorrow during the festivities of pangngae, villagers usually threw themselves into the music, song, and mirth of the ritual.

What should be underscored is that pangngae *enacts* a change in the discourse of mourning. The measure of the ritual's efficaciousness has less to do with soothing private hurt and suffering than with changing the social and discursive situations into which villagers bear their grief. The return of the topangngae does not just *mark the end* of public mourning, it *brings it about.* Once the shouts of the headhunters and the voice of the tambolâ are heard (and a "voice" [*oninna*] is precisely what tambolâ are said to possess), all mourning prohibitions on foods, conduct, and dress are lifted, along with the pemali tabus that kept the village in silence during the planting and harvesting of rice. Removing the burdensome weight of these prohibitions through a declaration of sound is an effort to lighten grief by stripping it of its outward trappings. Here, then, a vocal cry and a droning instrumental voice have illocutionary (or performative) force.[29] Lacking the semiotic structure and content of the linguistic sign, and so, lacking a locutionary or message-bearing dimension in the strict sense, the shout and the drone nonetheless *announce* and *index* (point to) the headhunters' presence. They also announce and index the return of sound and noise to a long silent hamlet, and thereby *thwart* and *negate* the set of tabus that prohibited festivity. As constitutive ritual acts, the shout and the drone, timed to coincide with the rising sun, together bring about the exuberant ritual period of pealloan. In this sense, the sound of the shout and the tambolâ measure ritual time and give it shape.

Once this ritual moment takes place, the burdensome tabus and obligations of mourning are removed. Irrespective of their moods and feelings, the bereaved no longer need subject themselves to collectively imposed constraints on conduct, talk, and consumption. As I have already hinted, local discourse uses the natural fact of the rising sun to capture the social fact of this situational "move." Yet the suddenness of the shouting and the tambolâ's drone seem especially significant in effecting the change of discursive situations. Although the villagers wait anxiously for the headhunters to come home, the precise moment of their return and, indeed, whether they are fated to return home, are uncertain matters, shrouded by secrecy. Thus, the shouting and the blowing of the tambolâ come as a sudden (if welcome) surprise, erupting from below the somnolent quiet of the hamlets. In everyday contexts, a startling noise might raise a panicked response.[30] Here, ritual makes productive use of surprise, a "rhythm" and "tactic" commonly avoided in day-to-day conduct.

Yet the significance of surprise, of being overtaken by sound, goes beyond being a convenient way to mark time. Let me elaborate. Of the terms used to name rituals, none but pangngae may be rendered with the circumfix, *ka- -an* (a grammatical construction similar to *ke- -an* in Indonesian). For a speaker to say *"kapangngaean"* implies that pangngae happened without the speaker's intent, control, or deliberation (that is, it was unforeseeable, much like *kabarataan,* experiencing grief over the death of another). Other rituals always take the *pa'- -an* circumfix, implying a sense of doing something or bringing about something consciously and willfully (e.g., *melambe* may be rendered as *pa'pelambean*). Though too much can be made of terminological constructions, I think "kapangngaean" captures the sense in which it is the sudden and unforeseeable fate of the village to celebrate pangngae.

Furthermore, surprise is basic to the kinds of violence that take place or are said to take place in pangngae. Having encountered so many symbolic reversals and inversions in the discourse of pangngae, is it wrong to think of a'dasan as an event that mirrors and upends the headhunters' ambush of the coastal rival? In both events, the headhunters take the "other" by surprise. And in both cases, noise plays a prominent role. In the ambush that brings death to the unsuspecting, cries of anguish mix with the terrifying noise of attack. In the ambush that "lightens" the burdens of the bereaved, the shouts and the drone of the flutes emanate from an enlivening exuberance. (In fact, the *mua'da'* shout of *lelelele* is said to be both the name and the sound of a man's *sumanga',* or "soul.")

Two ToIssilita' terms I heard in Minanga can throw further light on the relationship between the ambush and a'dasan. Although *maringngangi',* "relieving a burden," is the most common way to refer to pangngae there, other key terms include *dia'da'i barata,* "shouting at grief," or, alternatively, *dirondongi barata,* "taking apart [or felling] grief." The latter term goes a long way in establishing parallels between these noisy events. Just as the headhunters fell and dismember a victim downriver, so, too, do they fell and dismember grief in their home upstream; mourning is an abject "other" to be slain with noise. The former term, meanwhile, suggests that the voice itself is a slashing weapon. Vocal noise and the war knife both cut. Yet in the poetics of violence, a movement is implied: the blows of the knife on the dumb body of the fallen give way to the vocal blows that will slash away at the grief holding the warriors' community mute. The knife will make its victim silent; the shout will give back to the bereaved a voice. Paradoxically, today's headhunters carry no weapons, and so it falls upon the "voice" given to the headhunters' community in a'dasan to enact violence against the rival downstream. That is, language and the imagination deliver blows to the enemy. In this sense, the poetics of violence actually reverse the temporal movement mentioned above: the vocal blows of a'dasan unleash the headhunter in celebratory song and allow the imagination to conjure a scene of originary violence where the war knife can fell a victim.

The sudden violence of a'dasan bespeaks both the unforeseeable and the inevitable destruction of mourning. Later in the ritual, during a period of impassioned speechmaking, men will allude to the unforeseen and inevitable acts of violence. For now, it is enough to note that local discourse places the situational move into pealloan, and thus the end of mourning, outside of willful human action. Equally important, the sudden and inevitable blows of a'dasan impose a rhythm onto grief and suffering. In saying so, I do not mean to imply that the conventional acts and presented ideas of a'dasan bring about a full release from anguish. In keeping with the views of R. Rosaldo (1984), Tambiah (1985), and Suzanne Langer (1951), I would assert that a'dasan is but a gesture—albeit a dramatic one—related to the ongoing and uncertain experience of loss and suffering. Nevertheless, a'dasan makes such a powerful eruption into the experiential terrain of mourning that I cannot help thinking that it serves as a landmark of some kind. In my view, a'dasan momentarily draws the bereaved together such that they are "shouted" at once, and offered solace in solidarity. That is to say, the inner phenomenal time of the tambolâ's drone and the headhunters shout, and the manner in which they form a single heterophonous voice, permit both headhunter and listener to share the vivid immediacy of sound (cf. Schutz 1977 [1951]). It offers communion as antidote to the memory and feelings of loss and separation that characterize bereavement. Furthermore, a'dasan may serve as a measure of experiential "inner" time, of feeling, promoting a sense of before and after (e.g. blinded by the haze of grief and seeing through it and beyond). Whether feelings of loss linger beyond the headhunt is not the point. But it takes a'dasan for a villager to be able to say that he or she has been grieving too long or just long enough. A'dasan makes it clear that enough time has gone by for mourning to be put away. Without a'dasan, no one knows the proper rhythms of experience; without a'dasan, grief would have no measure.

If pangngae affords someone a sudden release from grief, it does not happen in the violent ambush imagined to take place downstream, but rather in the "ambush" upstream. It is not the violence of the blade that offers solace, but the violence of noise and music. It may be that the unfolding ritual process directs grief to the shout and the tambolâ's drone, where it becomes focused, condensed, and brought to a climax in sound. But quite apart from their potential to purge someone of their inner anguish, the shouts of the topangngae and the sound of their flutes bring about an overwhelming situational move. Thus, the shout and the sound of the tambolâ may supplant or dislodge feelings of grief with a mixture of joy and longing. Laden with familiar memories and meanings, the cries of the headhunter and the deep resonant tones of the tambolâ promise relief and festive communion. After months of silence, song and laughter break loose again. Singing, laughing, and feasting can go a long way toward taking people's minds off their anguish. More pointedly, the ceremonies to follow a'dasan extol vitality, good fortune, eroticism, the pleasure of song, and the splendor of men—in short, themes and topics that run counter to the moods, sentiments, and conceptions associated with death and grief.

Though it is wrongheaded to think that a villager's personal sentiments will always be in accord with the moods and pragmatic workings of pangngae, we should not discount the political force of the ritual in convening a "feeling polity." The tambolâ and the warriors' shouts are a distinctly coercive summons: villagers cannot help hearing the noise and music that announces a shift in communal tenor and practice. Getting caught up in or going along with the "official" moods of the community—moods brought about and legitimated by ritual—puts one in political alignment with the dominant trajectories of social thought and action. Not to yield to the enlivening mirth and noise of mappurondo headhunting festivities is to place oneself outside the polity. A refusal to allow oneself to be lightened by the ritual is an act of resistance, a failure to find solidarity with one's community. In this sense, someone's personal sentiments are always politicized by the discursive work of pangngae.

Emotions and emotional discourse aside, pangngae cannot fail to take place, or to effect a discursive and situational move, unless the mappurondo community in a given settlement has become moribund. In cases where epidemic or famine plunge an entire community into mourning (effectively preventing any male from going on the headhunt), a summons will go out to another village (usually Rantepalado, in its capacity as the Indona Bambang) to send someone with a tambolâ to "open the hamlets." Even death

cannot bring a halt to pangngae once the ceremonial fires have been lit—
that is, once the first chicken or pig has been sacrificed to welcome the headhunters. In the event that someone dies in the village while pangngae is under way, the village will ordinarily divide itself in half. One half will follow
pangngae, the other will observe funerary rites with the hamlet of the deceased. Those stained by grief will bear the emblems of mourning until the
next postharvest headhunt, a year later.[31]

From Vow to Violence

So far I have argued that the resolution of communal mourn-
ing and the structuring of political affect are more significant than individual sentiment and personal catharsis in shaping the discourse of pangngae.
There is no question that personal emotions are caught up in the ritual, but
they do relatively little in molding the pragmatic contours of the rite. In
contrast to Ilongot practices, the community, not the individual, is the central concern of mappurondo headhunting ritual. Bereaved individuals do
not rely on personal acts of violence to rid themselves of a turbulent sense
of loss. As we have seen, villagers may not carry their anguish onto the trails
in search of a hapless scapegoat. Instead, the bereaved rely on others to se-
cure them solace. What leads these others to assume the role of headhunter?
   Renato Rosaldo has argued that turbulent emotions propel the Ilongot
headhunter to seek a victim.[32] He explains that an

. . . account of youthful anger and older men's rage born of devastating loss lends
greater human plausibility to the notion that headhunters can find their cultural
practices compelling. Because the discipline correctly refuses to say that by nature
headhunters are bloodthirsty, it must construct convincing explanations of how
headhunters create an intense desire within themselves to cut off human heads.
(1984:191–192)

Rosaldo, however, gives us relatively little in his corpus of work to suggest
how the Ilongot sustain their emotions in such high pitch. That is to say,
anger, rage, and desire appear sharp and without fluctuation and rhythm. In
particular, Rosaldo portrays Ilongot grief as virtually all rage; the torpor and
weight of personal loss are missing from this picture. At the same time, the
emphasis on inner experience runs the risk of missing the ways in which
forces external to the feeling-self may lead someone to kill. As should be
clear, the mappurondo case poses real difficulties for an approach that teth-

ers the project of violence to personal distress. The mappurondo headhunter is in some ways selfless—he "kills" for the sake of another. What, then, motivates the mappurondo headhunter if the driving force of grief is sequestered? What stirs him to journey seaward?

I think the answer lies in the pledge, the oath, or the vow, or what in Bambang is called *samaja*. Put in the most general terms, it is the illocutionary entailments of a speech act that motivate the topangngae, not unmediated desire or rage. The binding power of the oath commits the headhunter to violence. Furthermore, the illocutionary force of making a vow, in my view, not only introduces factors of personal will, intention, and hope, but potentially serves as a way of acknowledging and coping with strong currents of desire, want, or anger. In particular, the vow may work to direct, constrain, and display strong personal emotions by linking them to the communal project of headhunting.[33]

Vows of the sort I have in mind are not absent in the Rosaldos' work. Renato Rosaldo (1984:191) tells us that "older men often vow to punish themselves until they participate in a successful headhunting raid." Michelle Rosaldo offered still more detail:

Some Ilongot men in youthful "clouds" have taken oaths (*binatan*), like those occasionally pronounced by mourners, who—to heighten their own *liget* and notify their fellows of an intention to take a life—forswear the use of certain foods or weapons, or even, in extreme cases, carry whips that they have friends and neighbors use to beat them on entering any but familiar homes. (1980:140)

The authors make very clear that making a vow displays or signals a person's emotional intensity.[34] In that sense, the discursive act of making a vow bears an indexical relationship to turbulent rage or desire: the smoke of an oath signals the fires of feeling.

But the promissory oath is also a pledge to act. In the Ilongot examples, an oath connects intense feelings of anguish, rage, and envy to displays of sincerity and personal willpower, and to a course of action. In the context of a vow, emotional intensity can convey personal sincerity, purposefulness, and strength of will. At the same time, the pledge to act offers reciprocal measure of one's heightened emotional state. *Yet turbulent emotion obliges no one to act; the utterance does.* Once the oath has been made, failure to see it through throws one's sincerity, will, and depth of emotion into doubt. Just as important, the vow brings time into the picture: the oath leashes the impulse to act and defers action until the appropriate moment. Until then, the vow holds the oathmaker in its grasp, an entangling or burdensome state of self-imposed obligation.

It is not unusual for mappurondo men and youths to make oaths that commit them to join in the headhunters' cohort. What differentiates them from the Ilongot male is that their vows are made in silence and withheld from public awareness. And nowhere does anguish provide an emotional foundation for the headhunter's pledge. Rather, personal interests, status concerns, and the envy of other men lie at the root of mappurondo headhunting vows. As in the Ilongot case, young men and boys envy those who have been honored as topangngae. In these instances, mimetic desire (to borrow a phrase from Girard [1977]) motivates the pledge to act. Elders, too, make pledges, and these reveal a diverse range of motivations. For example, a ToSalu man has the prerogative of holding the settlement's annual ritual at his home in order to make good on a personal vow to the spirits. Typical are vows in which a man promises to lead or join up with the topangngae in return for providential favors. Vows connected to the restoration of personal health culminate in a version of pangngae called *undantai kalena* ("striking [making a thudding noise on] one's image"). Those made in order to seek the strength and resources to build a new house or rice terrace end in *ulleppa'i samajanna* ("releasing the vow"). But it is also possible for a man to combine sacred vows with a desire for personal aggrandizement. One way is to stage *umpokasalle kalena* ("enlarging one's image"; also called *malampa sali-sali,* or "making and loading the offering rack"), a ToSalu version of pangngae in which one displays one's good fortune, devout moral character, and stature in the community by giving substantial offerings to the debata. The most elaborate of such "signature" (or personally sponsored) versions of pangngae is *ma'patuhu'i botto* ("having the hamlets follow"). Here a villager makes a vow of unusual breadth or sincerity; in return for providential blessings he pledges to lead able-bodied men and youths out of the village on a headhunt and to then host an enormous feast in their honor.

When the time to hold pangngae approaches, men and youths will approach the babalako or topuppu and make their pledges known. One virtue of the secrecy surrounding such pledges is that the oathmaker can put off his commitments for another time. Several of my friends volunteered that from time to time men will use the cover of silence and secrecy to back away from their solemn commitments. But they added that for a man to do this would invite possible reprisal from the debata. The same custom also allows someone to fake a sincere pact with the spirits. Ambe Teppu, for example, told me the story of a To Salu man who happened upon a cohort of headhunters returning to his village. Announcing that he, too, carried a vow to take part in pangngae, the man joined in with the others on their way back into village lands and shared in the honor heaped upon them. The man's wife, however, was not to be fooled. "What vow?" she complainingly asked. Convinced that her husband was interested only in food and public praise, she refused to take part in singings and put out only meager portions of rice and meat for her husband.

It should be clear, then, that the mappurondo headhunter carries a vow, rather than turbulent feelings of anguish, onto the trails leading downriver. I should refrain from suggesting that the vow has replaced the originary rage of headhunters past, even if such a replacement would be consistent with the current of historical forces in the mountain region. More reasonable is the claim that the oath—born from complex, heterogeneous, and uncertain wants and interests—may not (or may no longer) include grief as one of its wellsprings. I think there can be no question that the oath is a discursive incarnation of "emotion-work," and I would hazard that the samaja (or oath) has long been a basic mediating form between intense feeling and the headhunter's violent act. Making a vow can be a way for an individual to cope with strong emotions, giving him or her purpose—and thus virtue—while according that individual a measure of control over the flux and intensity of emotion. Furthermore, the vow shows a person's strength of will and character in working and living with intense feeling. If the samaja serves as a discursive restraint on feeling and action, making good on a vow may afford the headhunter not only a sense of accomplishment, but a sense of release as well.[35] And I would suggest, too, that the exercise of will implicit in the headhunter's vow demonstrates to the bereaved that people can master their temporal existence. In this sense, the vow is both a demonstration that one can get on with life and a gesture of confidence and faith in the community's fate.

The political dimensions of the vow are no less important for understanding the discursive construction of pangngae. It is by way of the vow that the private wants and interests of males are harnessed to communal ends. For men young and old, the "individual" and the "communal," the "private" and the "public," are not opposed spheres of action and understanding, but rather mutually shaping ones where personal wants and concerns gain intelligibility and consequence, and communal tasks open paths for personal pursuits. By the same token, the samaja vows of men grant them the capacity to act and make tactical choices quite unlike that available to women . . . or to the bereaved, who are in a sense feminized by their exclusion from the imagined arenas of ritual violence.

In bringing this chapter to a close, I am too aware of what I cannot know directly—the course of anguish in a villager's life, the words of a solemn oath murmured in solitude, the secret tasks and adventures of the journeying topangngae. The lyrics of ritual song, the burst of noise at a'dasan, and the cautious remarks of friends made so as not to divulge too much are what I have by which to fathom the experiential currents of mappurondo headhunting. I console myself with a remark Gananath Obeyesekere (1990: 55) makes about dreams: "The dream for all of us was not the dream that was dreamt but the dream that was reported." There is no "other" side to which I can cross in search of the lived experiences of mappurondo headhunters as they suffer anguish and envy, or commit themselves to a journey I will never see.

But lived experience is not my quarry in this study. Rather, I am trying to discern the thematic tenor and pragmatic workings of ritual discourse in pangngae. As a starting-off point, I have emphasized that pangngae is staged to bring an end to communal mourning, a process related to, but incommensurate with, the passing of personal anguish or grief. Nevertheless, the ritual provides a discursive space in which participants can work at overcoming feelings of loss. In a very important sense the ritual maps out an "emotion-scape" in which violence, anguish, pity, and solace, along with allusions to heaviness and lightness, take on a political character. Refiguring individual sentiment in collective terms as political affect, ritual discourse exacts a transcoding of social hierarchy and social solidarity. In this context, the demonizing and debasing of a downstream rival together have the potential to distract participants from the crises of mourning. "Looking down" on a subaltern rival from the past through the lenses of pity and disgust potentially confers upon the seeing/feeling subject a reflexive sense of exalted and superordinate being. Put very simply, to be lightened and relieved of the burdens of mourning is to be heightened vis-à-vis a political rival. Yet the discourse of solace also suggests a polity of sentiment constructed around the community's official moods and trajectories of action. Finding solace and giving in to mirth and festivity become expressive signs of social solidarity.

I am sure that catharsis from time to time has had a significant place in the politicized terrain of mappurondo headhunting ritual. But as a product of social history, cathartic violence is susceptible to changing political conditions. In the case of the mappurondo communities, it has been shelved to keep it from disturbing (and bringing reprisal from) regional and state orders. Yet, it is recalled in the negative sanctions of tabu and in ritual song. The current suppression of cathartic violence persuades me that turbulent emotions are not—and perhaps have never been—the driving force for local headhunting practices. Catharsis and cathartic theories of emotion may play a part in local ethnopsychology and ritual practice, but they do not legitimate or provide a rationale for the institution of headhunting. The catharsis that may come with violence does not lend social, political, or historical intelligibility to pangngae.

The headhunters' violence, I have been at pains to point out, is not the outcome of powerful emotions, but of powerful obligations made in discourse. Making vows is central to the trajectories of action and violence in pangngae, and to linking the personal interests of men to communal ends. Indeed, violence and vow-making appear to be the prerogative of men in this ritual. The will to act overshadows emotion as a pivotal dimension of mappurondo headhunting. From the vantage point of emotion, mourning and oathmaking involve intense feeling. Yet, from the vantage point of human will, mourning and oathmaking underscore different capacities to act. In mourning, mappurondo villagers are helpless, and subject themselves to burdensome and immobilizing tabus. In oathmaking, the young man or elder leashes himself to action and proves himself master of his own existence.

The sudden return of music and sound signals a situational move within the community, and makes coincident the trajectories of mourning and the oath. The durative aspects of bereavement and being held by a vow are constituted and measured by the noise of the headhunters and their tambolâ flutes. More than just marking an end to mourning and the vow, a'dasan brings them to an end in a musical simulacrum of violence. Made possible in the shared (or coerced) apprehension of musical noise, releasing a vow and shedding the public emblems of grief help mappurondo villagers remake the world, allowing the community to resume its ways (cf. Good 1994:130–131).

More remains to be said, however, about the themes and projects of pangngae. In this chapter I have tried to clarify the way in which the problems and crises of mourning are worked upon by demonizing an other within the ritual frame. Intermingled with the ceremonial representations of violence and solace are themes of envy and adornment. But in contrast to the political affects described thus far, the themes of envy and adornment have less to do with mourning and the hierarchical relations linking mountain and coast than they do with the mimetic desires of men and women, a topic to which I now turn.

5

Envy, Adornment, and Words That Make the Floor Shake

Pangngae and the Rhetoric of Manhood

Pua' Soja, my friends said, was already a village leader in Minanga when Dutch expeditionary patrols crossed into the Salu Mambi valley for the first time. That was in 1906. Sitting with him in 1984, reticent with wonder and disbelief, I tried to imagine what someone would have seen, heard, and endured in living through the hundred or more years since the internecine collapse of Pitu Ulunna Salu. I pitied Pua' Soja his aches, his clouded eyes and swollen joints, his being plain worn out by nothing except having to live another day. But weariness of body had yet to defeat his courage and dignity, especially during the season of pangngae and other *pa'bisuan* rituals when he would put on headcloth and ceremonial gear, and struggle the climb in and out of houses and up and down the village paths, to take his place with the other senior men gathered at the rites.

Among my mappurondo acquaintances, no one had firsthand experience of the precolonial order, save for a few who would have been very young children in 1906. Elder women were reluctant to say much about the past. Although their recollections of local events and family histories were every bit as sharp as men's, women left "official" history to the men. As for elder men, most discussed the ancestral past—the time prior to the fall of Pitu Ulunna Salu in 1870—as a turbulent golden age. Ambe Tibo, a grandson of Pua' Soja, was not alone, for example, in claiming that before misfortune fell upon the headwaters, village men were tall and big-boned and always lived to be 100, their bodies evidencing a greatness now gone. He himself had

Fig. 8. *Pua' Soja, 1983.*

been in another village one time when someone unearthed a huge bone, said to be part of a human leg. "A span this long or more," he said, making a cutting gesture on the upper part of his extended arm. "Back then, the people here were powerful and rich. But look at what we have become." Others would give a more mixed picture of the past. Ambe Assi', the tomatua-tonda' at Minanga, was proud of headwater history and mappurondo tradition. But I painfully recall a remark he made one day as he listened to several of us speaking about the corrosive effects of the Dutch colonial period. "Listen up," he said curtly. "Before the Dutch came we weren't human yet. We didn't even know how to talk."

The prospect of speaking at length with Pua' Soja about the close of the nineteenth century promised both a less gilded and a less demoralized account of local history. That was never to happen. My conversations with the old man were brief and few, and were always distracted by the company of others. He remained a remote figure. Seeing him again during the pang-ngae celebrations of 1985, I gently pressed Pua' Soja about the headhunting rites of the past. His fleeting remarks never made it clear whether or not heads were taken during his lifetime. In contrast, his answer to my question about the ritual's central theme was unambiguous: pangngae was all about *kelondongan* (the daring and audaciousness of a cockerel; cockiness), and *kemuanean* (manhood).

Putting manhood into action and on display in pangngae calls attention to a social poetics (Herzfeld 1985) or a social aesthetics (Brenneis 1987) in which villagers summon a select vocabulary and image of masculine conduct and being. I share with Herzfeld and Brenneis their interest in performance as the means through which sense-making, self-making, and experience coalesce as a strategized and consequential event. But because the ceremonial formulation (or evocation) of manhood in pangngae is so partial and select, and because it so animates the communal body, its basic rhetorical character deserves emphasis. Like the Glendiot idioms described by Herzfeld (1985: 16), the rhetoric of manhood in mappurondo headhunting rites involves "being good at being a man." Yet I would argue that recourse to a Jakobsonian concept of poeticity—"the set (*Einstellung*) toward the *message* as such, focus on the message for its own sake" (Jakobson 1960:356)—does not take us very far. "Being good at being a man" in the arena of mappurondo ceremony is a way to set specific social and political projects into motion. For that reason, the "set (*Einstellung*) toward the message as such" is not enough. The deployment (*Ausstellung*) of the message, and its effective expression in performance (*Darstellungsgabe*) are basic to the rhetoric of manhood in the mappurondo community, and must play a part in any considered analysis of pangngae.

In previous chapters, I have tried to throw light on ritual violence from the vantage points of political history, mourning, and vowmaking. Pua' Soja's remarks, however, compel a reading of the headhunters' violence in light of ideas about manhood. Exploring the ritual discourse of manhood should also help us to understand why the demonization of the rival "other" and the cessation of mourning take place in a setting that underscores the social hierarchies predicated on seniority and gender. In the course of this chapter, I will argue that a ceremonial politics of envy and emulation animate both hierarchies. That is to say, the headhunting rites of pangngae are a turbine of social difference and mimetic desire. The rhetoric of manhood in pangngae thrives on these political currents. But as I want to show, that rhetoric is also the discursive mode for conjuring envy and emulation.

It is worth repeating that pangngae takes place under the authority of men and is considered both a village concern and a male spiritual pursuit. In a conventional sense, pangngae is not a rite of passage for males; it does not bring about a permanent change in social status. But youths must follow the trails to the sea, so to speak, if they wish to join the company of mature men. And as we have seen, those already in the ranks of men may undertake the journey for personal ends. Women of course play a fundamental if circumscribed role in the ceremonial activities associated with the headhunt. Yet taken as a group, women are not fully subject to the ritual's focal transformative operations. To use Bourdieu's (1991) terminology, pangngae is a rite of consecration and institution. That is, pangngae separates

> those who have undergone it, not from those who have not yet undergone it, but from those who will not undergo it in any sense, and thereby [institutes] a lasting difference between those to whom the rite pertains and those to whom it does not pertain. . . . By treating men and women differently, the rite *consecrates* the difference, institutes it, while instituting man as man . . . and woman as woman. (Bourdieu 1991:117–118)

Mappurondo headhunting rites thus bring gender differences into being and impose them upon participants as their social destiny. At the same time, the ritual makes hierarchical distinctions within a community of males, distinguishing those "seniors" who have been honored as topangngae, and those who have not. The rhetoric of manhood, I would argue, takes up this double business and ties it to the project of ritual violence.

Though it is possible and perhaps necessary to describe these hierarchies in terms of "structural" differences, I think it is important to capture something of the anxiety, want, and restlessness common to the ongoing foment of social categories. Contemporary mappurondo communities are relatively egalitarian, neither producing nor tolerating dramatic differences in prestige or power.[1] That said, differences having to do with gender and seniority are basic to local thought and conduct; they help to motivate social life and to make it intelligible. The rhetoric of pangngae, in my view, summons and plays with these differences, juxtaposing them in such a way as to spark social movement.

Although villagers show a deep practical and ideological regard for human sameness, the simple fact is that in mappurondo ritual life, not everyone can be a headhunter. That women are excluded from becoming the central actors and focal subjects of pangngae fractures human sociality and marks part of the faultline that distinguishes manhood and womanhood. Yet because the rituals of *pa'bisuam baine* put women centerstage, I caution against a rushed analysis that would see pangngae as an occasion for men to gain a position of lasting dominance and privilege vis-à-vis women. By instituting and consecrating a difference between men and women, pangngae declares a limit to human sameness. But it does not relax or suspend the egalitarian ideal. In fact, I would argue that the social distinctions delimited in the ritual rest upon or are carved into the bedrock of sameness. Stated more strongly still, ritual discourse puts ideas about gender difference and human sameness into productive tension and conflict. As a result, the will to sameness, confronting difference, experiences envy and a desire to emulate. The will to differ, confronting sameness, strives for excess and the "talismans of supremacy" (to borrow a phrase from René Girard 1977). Girard (1977, 1987) would argue that the tension between sameness and difference is a source of generative violence, a violence so terrible and contagious that it must be directed out of the community. And he would likely see mappurondo headhunting ritual as an attempt to solve the problem of rebounding violence (cf. Bloch 1992). I seriously doubt that mimetic desire plays such a decided part in the political violence of pangngae. Yet it is far from absent in this ritual. For the purposes of the present discussion, I merely wish to identify mimetic desire as one of the principal rhetorical strains in pangngae and to call attention to its relevance to local ideas about manhood and womanhood.

In the rhetoric of headhunting ritual, men strive for excess and superiority, and women look on with envy (a situation that is reversed in the grand rites of pa'bisuam baine). I should stress that women's envy does not derive from lack or absence, but from a wish for still more. That "still more" is denied to women, withheld from them as the defining secret of manhood. Here it is worth noting that the tasks deemed most significant for making men men—slaying a victim, making a tambolâ—happen outside the village and out of the gaze and earshot of women. The excess that belongs to men is discovered on seaward trails and in the forest during the headhunters' journey downriver. Surrounding these tasks, too, are a set of tabus that put a woman at risk should she happen upon men in their secret work. Violating these tabus is no less than a transgression of the boundaries marking male and female. Thus, the breach of category erupts into somatic symbolism as physical dissolution and death. Seeing men make their tambolâ flutes, for example, is said to bring illness or death to a woman. By concealing some of their practices the way they do, mappurondo men essentially hide themselves, and something of themselves, from public view. It should be evident, then, that masculinity and femininity depend upon differences made and kept in secret as much as upon differences made visible and audible in the domains of ritual and everyday life.[2] For this reason, women cannot slake their envy during pangngae through emulation. It must remain hungry and restless until the rites of pa'bisuam baine, when women can discover excess in their own secret sources. At the same time, women are complicit—indeed, instrumental—in heaping praise and admiration upon the topangngae. Once more, then, we see the work of others as crucial to the management and representation of self. Just as the bereaved cannot remove the burdens and emblems of grief through self-effort, neither can the headhunter acquire an excess of manhood, a superabundance of being, without the help of women and the collective at large. To sum up, it falls to women to witness, to gaze at, to envy, and to desire the headhunter.

The discursive force of envy and emulation also colors the hierarchy of senior and junior males, of men and not-yet-men. Once again, the desire for difference becomes entangled with the desire for sameness. Young males see presented to them an opportunity to join the ranks of adult men, and in this sense are very much unlike women, who are precluded from achieving sameness with men through the headhunt. The figure of the headhunter is, of course, the model image of the adult male. If the mappurondo youth is to achieve peership in the company of men, and thereby make his passage into adulthood, he must make the headhunting journey of pangngae. Yet there is no need to drag the young across the threshold of maturity. The mimetic aspirations of the young are clear: they want their chance to wear the headhunter's amulets, to have their names celebrated in chant and song, to be honored with gifts of rice and meat, and to sound their tambolâ and deliver a skilled and impassioned oration to the ritual gathering. "It was great," a ToSalu friend recalled, thinking back to his first time among the topangngae in the 1950s, "Everyone was looking at me and my chest was just bursting. I was important. Besides that, I had never seen so much rice, and it was all for me."

Once a youth has proved himself a peer in the company of adult men, there are no further statuses to be pursued. The game becomes one of flexing and holding onto one's status as an adult man by marrying, raising a family, and taking part in village affairs. Yet the sameness of peership, linked as it may be to ideas of harmony and social accord, shows real instability. For example, in the sphere of a domestic politics grounded in uxorilocality, a young husband is said to "live beneath the ends of the floorbeams" of his wife's natal home. As such, a husband must subordinate himself to his parents-in-law. Trysts with married women bring shame to cuckolded husbands and threaten to steal from them both spouse and home. And a man's desire for greater wealth, influence, and reputation—the desire to be a *to-makaka'* (the prosperous one, who is "like an elder sibling")—also stirs beneath or behind the politics of peership. Whether to defend himself against a loss of esteem or to enlarge his reputation and influence, a man will often return to the ceremonies of pangngae as a headhunter and once more assert his manhood and difference. These accomplished ones who seek to "enlarge their self-image" (*umpokasalle kalena*) in turn can lead novices into the mystery of the headhunt.

What I describe for the mappurondo communities—tensions between ideas about social difference and ideas about sameness, tensions theorized and animated by envy and emulation—bear a decided resemblance to the social dynamics informing Ilongot headhunting (M. Rosaldo 1980, 1983; R. Rosaldo 1980, 1984, 1987). Among Ilongot youth, there is a strong desire to emulate the violent feats of their "fathers" (M. Rosaldo 1980:139), and to wear the coveted red hornbill earrings that will mark them as accomplished men (R. Rosaldo 1980, 1984, 1986). Especially striking is the intensity of the youth's envy. Ilongot youth "coming of age undergo a protracted period of personal turmoil during which they desire nothing so much as to take a head. . . . Young men weep, sing, and burst out in anger because of their intense, fierce desire to take a head" (R. Rosaldo 1984: 191). This adolescent turmoil involves a "tremendous sense of envy or rivalry," a deep "want to become like older men" (R. Rosaldo 1987:242). The emotional intensity of Ilongot men also distinguishes them from their wives and sisters. The hearts of men, according to the Ilongot, are "higher" than women's, and "exceed" them in the intensity of anger, passion, and "knowing" (M. Rosaldo 1980). But curiously, women's envy of the headhunter is missing or muted. As suggested by my discussion of grief and violence in the preceding chapter, the intensity of emotional expression among the Ilongot throws into relief the emotional restraint of the mappurondo villager. As with anguish, so too with want. Envy and desire may not burn as brightly in the hearts of mappurondo youth as they do in the Ilongot, but their presence is immanent in the discourse of pangngae.

My immediate purpose in this chapter on manhood, then, is to explore the discourse of headhunting ritual for signs of envy and desire, and to say something about their rhetorical force and formulation. As a first step, let me turn to everyday terms for these forms of wanting. Perhaps the most common word meaning to want, like, or wish for something is *maelo*, which derives from the root *elo* and the stative verb prefix *ma-*. It implies a willful state of desiring something. Envy, like grief, is rendered as something that happens to a person without their being able to foresee it or control it: *kaindai* (from the root *inda*, the prefix *ka-*, and the transitive verb suffix *-i*). Falling somewhere between the most negative form of wanting (kaindai) and the more positively valued expressions of want (like maelo), there is the term *kailui* (from the root *ilu*), "loving" or "coveting" something. These terms, as such, do not enter the ritual discourse of pangngae as the most prevalent expression of want and envy. But they offer a vantage point from which to understand the celebration of manhood.

The Week of Adornment

A'dasan ends with the light of dawn and the cohort's noisy entrance into the hamlets. As the topangngae move from house to house letting out their shouts and blowing their tambolâ, drumming erupts throughout the village, following the warriors as they release home after home from the prohibitions of mourning. Drums (*ganda*, also *gânda*) have long been cinched up to the rafters of any homestead that owns one, silent since the pa'bisuan ceremonies of the previous year, or since the death of an important villager. Men and youths now lower the drums, and in teams of two or three find the correct beat for the distinctive, stirring rhythms of *pabuno* (literally "one that kills with a spear"), the percussive emblem of headhunting ceremony. As pabuno swells through the hamlets, males break out with loud whoops, laughter, and the *mua'da'* shouts of "lelelele." The drumming erupts throughout the day at the whim of the village males, and it is very clear that most youths take real pleasure and pride in beating out the rhythms of pabuno with exuberance and finesse. It is only with the onset of evening and night-long tabus that the drums fall silent.

Fig. 9. *As the sun rises each morning during* pangngae, *village men lower drums from the rafters of their households and unleash the exuberant rhythms of* pabuno, *"one who kills with a spear."* 1984.

The hamlets now belong to men, so to speak, and above all to the head-hunters, who are referred to as *tobarani*, "the courageous," in recognition of their warriorlike bravery and feats. The tobarani carefully hang their tambolâ on the door frames or interior houseposts of their home. For the next seven days the instruments remain silent and on display, transposed into eye-catching icons of a warrior's knowledge and power. Although men and women may from time to time sing sumengo in praise of the tobarani, the drumming of pabuno dominates the musical "space" of the village, its mas-culine signature holding the hamlets in its grip. Indeed, in a significant sense the drumming is an enacting sign of masculine power, of irresistible social control: *no one* can *not* listen to the drumming. It is everywhere and thus consolidates the community through the senses as a listening polity, legiti-mating its order under masculine authority. Kept by pemali tabus from handling or playing the drums, women are constrained from subjecting themselves and others to these compelling and enlivening rhythms; women cannot find political authority over the senses through drumming. In this light, drumming is part of that masculine "excess" that provokes the envy and desire of women.

The severed head, cloaked in a rice pouch, rests in the home of the tomatuatonda' or the babalako (or topuppu). The headhunters are now free to relax at home or wander about the hamlets during the day. Throughout the community, villagers honor, even spoil, the tobarani, inviting them to share a meal or to take a gift of tobacco and betel. For the time being, the headhunters are forbidden to undertake any kind of labor, and may eat only rice, meat, fish, and eggs, the point being to avoid the "feminine" greens from women's gardens. Evenings are spent relaxing in mirthful gatherings. Youths—and especially the unmarried topangngae—find opportunities in these gatherings to flirt a bit with unmarried girls. At night, however, it is customary for the tobarani to sleep at the household of the tomatuatonda' or at the house of the cohort leader rather than at their own homes. Seven days and six nights pass in this fashion, during which time villagers ready the hamlets in anticipation of the grand closing festivities of pangngae.

A new set of objects, signs, and gestures is brought out of safekeeping. So far, the trophy head and the tambolâ have been the principal working objects of pangngae, signifying its violent destruction of mourning and the "other" downstream. Villagers now bring out rings, bracelets, beaded neck-laces and sashes, headcloths, shining lime and betel-quid containers, and fine clothes. These adornments (*belo-belo*) figure importantly in the principal dis-cursive project of the ritual until its closing: glorifying the tobarani and, more generally, exalting the image of men and manhood. In spite of their

Fig. 10. *The jewelry of the headhunt, and the basket in which it is kept. The to-barani—the courageous ones who went on the headhunting journey—wear rings and bracelets like those to the left. Women wear necklaces similar to the one on the right. Headhunters will sport a different kind of necklace, one usually made of silver. 1985.*

superfluousness, or rather, because of it, the adornments of the topangngae are crucial in projecting the headhunters' "excess," their possession of "something more." Worn on and around the contours and features of the body, adornment opens up a radiant and stylized surface where the strivings of self and community become fused. No mere aesthetic frill, adornment is key to the politics of envy and emulation.

The penetrating remarks of Georg Simmel's (1950:338–344) essay, "Note on Adornment," require mention here, and most of what follows below reflects his brilliant understanding of the politics of ornamentation.[3] Adornments are worn to catch and please the eye. It is by way of that pleasing that a person "desires to *distinguish* himself before others," seeking their envy (338). "Pleasing may thus become a means of the will to power: some . . . need those above whom they elevate themselves by life and deed, for they build their own self-feeling upon the subordinates' realization that they *are* subordinate" (338). Thus adornment is both self-interested and altruistic, singling out the wearer with objects designed for the pleasure of others, but signifying, too, the wearer's paradoxical dependence on those he wishes to surpass. The style and radiance of bodily ornamentation absorb the person's individuality, enlarge it. They sensuously announce the wearer's social power and draw the gaze of others. If adornment creates a space for envy ("I have something which you do not have" [342]), it also foments desire by saying "I am here for you . . . take me." As Simmel writes, "adornment creates a highly specific synthesis of the great convergent and divergent forces of the individual and society, namely, the elevation of the ego through existing for others, and the elevation of existing for others through the emphasis and extension of the ego" (344).

I have already introduced key terms for the project of adornment in the mappurondo headhunting rites: *umpokasalle kalena,* "enlarging the self." Some further comments may be helpful, however. *Kale* denotes neither an interior self (which is usually rendered as *penaba,* or breath), nor a person per se, but rather the *image* of the self, the surfaces, features, and reputation a person presents to the world. Adornments and being adorned, meanwhile, are rendered, respectively, as *belo-belo* and *dibeloi* (from the root *belo*). In local tongue one could speak of decorating the self-image by using the phrase *dibeloi kalena,* a grammatical form that puts focus on the self-image and as-signs agency to someone other than the wearer. This construction captures nicely the political dynamics Simmel so carefully ascribes to adornment.

Like the red hornbill earrings coveted by the Ilongot (M. Rosaldo 1980; R. Rosaldo 1984, 1986), the white beaded bracelets of the tobarani indi-cate that the wearer has been on a headhunt. In this sense, the bracelets are also the amulets of someone who knows the "secret" of a man's journey to other regions. The tobarani thus are doubly adorned, for the secret also serves as an adornment. As Simmel (1950:337) explains, "what recedes before the consciousness of others and is hidden from them, is to be em-phasized in their consciousness; . . . one should appear as a particularly noteworthy person precisely through what one conceals." Further still, the bracelets and finery of the tobarani mark them as persons who have under-taken a heroic task for the collective good. Their deed, a flashing ornament itself, is both altruistic and self-interested.

The week between a'dasan and the closing ceremonies of pangngae finds the tobarani decorating their tambolâ with cascades of plaited streamers made from palm leaves of pale green and gold. On the seventh day after a'dasan, guests arrive from other villages, and hearths become heavy with smoke and noisy talk as people prepare for the evening's ceremonial song-fest, called *umpaningoi ulunna,* "playing with the head" (in the dual sense of putting it on display and teasing it). All during the week, men have been busy preparing the house that will host the gathering. Needing room for

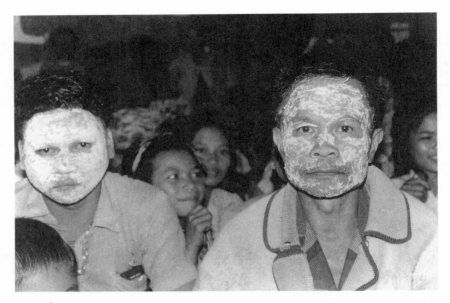

Fig. 11. *Two* tobarani, *their faces caked with rice paste, their bangs trimmed back. They are being honored with an evening of song during the ceremony known as* umpaningoi ulunna, *"playing with the head." 1984.*

roughly 250 to 400 people, they have added floor supports, moved walls, made makeshift porches, and put in place extra ladders. Having enlarged the house, they put in final supplies of firewood, rice, and coffee. As the afternoon passes, the drumming of pabuno grows more fervent and continues without break. Sporting their bracelets and necklaces, the tobarani have their bangs cut by their mothers or sisters, and cake their faces with rice paste in order to lighten and refine their complexion (see Figure 11).

With the setting sun, people throng to the site of the ritual. As the crowd swells, women and girls from the village pack themselves in between the hearth and the downriver side of the house centerpost, which protrudes up through the floor. The beaded and white-faced headhunters begin to arrive, and after hanging their tambolâ in display, find places to sit on the floor upriver from the centerpost. Once it is dark, the drumming comes to an abrupt halt and the entourage of village elders—all men—climb up into the house and solemnly take seats beside the centerpost.

Choruses of men or women begin singing sumengo as the elders help themselves to ample amounts of betel and tobacco from plates being passed around. Some verses extol the radiance of the tobarani:

Inde lako toidandan	These there the ones all in a line
toipasampei belo	the ones adorned with finery
naindo allo mangngura	lit up by rays from a young sun
Tosisarim belo	The ones wearing bracelets and beads
naindo allo mangngura	lit up by rays of the young sun
napomarampia-pia	making them more and more handsome

Another set of metaphoric lyrics likens the tobarani to a kind of sugarcane known for its colorful striping. As the cane ripens and matures, its splendor grows:

Ta'bu sure' mane dadi	Striped colored cane just coming up
mane lulangam allona	just starting to reach for the sun
paneteanna kaloe'	the parrots' dance along the branch

The lyrics portray women and girls as parrots—songbirds, I should note—that "dance" back and forth along their perch straining to see the growing sugarcane.

Songs like these not only extol the radiant virtues of the tobarani but also confirm the admiring gaze of others, a gaze that looks up to the headhunters. At the same time, the song performances function as adornments in and of themselves. In a significant way, these lyrics of praise gild the headhunter's image and magnify his presence. Songs can also glorify the name of the elder who led the headhunters on their journey and made it possible for the village to hold the ritual:

Mennara ampunna londong	Who's the master of that cockerel
tourampa' sali-sali	the one making the level rack
napolenta pemalian	he who cut loose the offering
Takubai-bai	I did not imagine
ladengkam ma'kada senga'	we'd have a chance to speak grand words
kela da Ambena ____	if it were not for Ambe (name)

The splendor of the topangngae and the praise lavished on them can stir envy among the men and youths who for one reason or another did not join the headhunters on the trek downstream. Some of this envy finds its way into song, and thus to the ears of the headhunters:

Edede talinna london	E-de-de the cockerel's headcloth
saputanganna muane	the handkerchiefs of the men there
kikailu-kailui	we really ache for them ourselves

Londom buri' di tanete	Speckled cockerel on the mountain
kiula' kiperombei	we chase it, take tufts of feathers
kipebulu kalandoi	we are taking its long plumed tail

Coveting the headhunters' heroic glory, other men and youths vow to travel the seaward trails. The time and place are uncertain, but they will be the to-barani's equal:

Nakeallo-keallopa	Later under another sun
na bulam umba-umbapa	and under a moon somewhere else
anna kesulle pasuka'	it will be replaced in measure

The turbulent longing for self-distinction, for being above all others, must be tempered with selfless aspiration to help (or subordinate oneself) to a community of others. If a man thirsts with envy, his heirloom knife (connoting moral tradition) must ache with purposeful desire:

Mamali'mi kondo bulo	The blade of layered iron aches
melo' lamabalinono	wanting to soon come roaring down
battu umba sia ngei	who knows, another time and place

As for who will be fated to make good on their pledge and then "bathe" in communal adulation:

Battu menna maki' mai	Hard to say who among us here
to pole mendio' minna'	is to come back and bathe in oils
anta dambara ummoni	so that our sound can carry afar

As these examples show, the songs of pangngae celebrate and foster an envy that is productive, rather than destructive, of social order.[4] An emulative rivalry lies at the heart of male peership and animates it, constantly cycling men through alternating positions of "the gazing" and "the gazed upon." This rebounding mimetic thrives on the bracelets and beads and the songs of praise, adornments that become the focus and incarnating objects of desire.

Women, too, may covet the headhunters' glory, but are denied it under the exclusionary tabus of pangngae. Lyric variations in two sumengo performances I recorded on separate occasions (and in different villages) suggest that women experience a mixture of anxiety and envy during the ritual; or perhaps they reveal an episodic shift in women's experience, a shift in which envy supplants anxiety as the ritual unfolds:

Sama siam malallengki	Not only our worried thinking
sama kainda-indaki	but our restless envy as well
tempomu messubum bamba	when you had left the village lands
Susi siam malallengki	Not only our worried thinking
susi kainda-indaki	but our restless envy as well
ditetangan sulim bulo	gold bamboo flutes carried in hand

Forestalled from taking part in the mimetic rivalries that conjoin men and youths, women look ahead to the emulative politics that separate and distinguish them from males and the masculine order. Women, too, will have their measure, vowing that *no one* (no grain of rice) shall be excluded from the community (metaphorized as a cup made from a coconut shell):

Battu umba sia ngei	Who knows, another time and place
anna kesulle pasuka'	it will be replaced in measure
barra' sisangkararoan	the grains of rice all in one shell

Songs such as these refer in particular to the women's ritual known as *malangngi'*. Difficult to conduct and seldom held, malangngi' not only has a significant place in local ideas about womanhood but also figures as an oppositional or inverting complement to men's headhunting rites. I never had an opportunity to witness malangngi', but in describing the ritual to me, an elder volunteered, "Malangngi', it's the women's pangngae." With a little probing from me he continued, "In pangngae we exalt men. In malangngi' we exalt women." Others, particularly women, were careful to point out that pangngae concerns the village, whereas malangngi' concerns the home and offspring. The ritual promises such real and obvious relevance to the social relationships and practices I am trying to explore that a quick sketch would seem appropriate here.

I am told that malangngi' is set in motion when a group of women and girls gather together in secret under darkness and slip out of the hamlets, moving in an *upstream* direction.[5] At the edge of the village lands, they climb up next to a banyan tree and onto a platform built especially for this ritual. While beside the tree, they become possessed by debata. Said to turn into birds as they dance, the women utter the sound of female sumanga', and issue a laughing *wit-wit-wit-wit*. Panicked by the absence of their wives, sisters, and daughters, village men launch a search and discover them around the banyan. A few men are sent to fetch drums. Upon their return, ritual specialists play set dance rhythms for the possessed women and, after a time, "drum them down" from the banyan. Climbing onto the backs of their husbands or fathers, the women ride back into the village and ascend into a house where they dance and display amulets and curatives obtained "up in the sky" (the meaning of the word *malangngi'*). A ceremony extolling the women, the debata, and the prosperity of the household lasts into the afternoon of the following day.

Little wonder, then, that women seek to journey to the sources of their own order so as to momentarily subordinate village males. As one song puts it, men will know the weight of women:

Masetopa kami' duka'	There is a moment for us too
kalundara-daraangki	we will still find our own chance
lunde' tanete kiola	the peaks on which we journey will sag

So that there is no mistaking malangngi' (and other rituals of pa'bisuam baine) for a fleeting and insignificant inversion of social hierarchy, I note that during the course of pangngae men express their envy of women. For example, there is a song in which the headhunters see women as more accomplished than themselves. As expressed in the lyrics, women come into their own (metaphorized as the task of weaving a blanket) long before men do; the headhunt is a man's first crawling effort to come into manhood:

Marre' untannunna bela	Done the wife completes her weaving
padangki' dipangngidengam	together we were in the womb
mane rumambokangkami'	we're just crawling on hands and knees

If these songs are any indication, mappurondo social order thrives on reciprocal envy within and across gender categories. The desire to distinguish oneself, to surpass others, is something relevant to the experience and interests of both men and women. The power to attract the gaze of others, to stir envy within them, then, is perhaps the most sought-for talisman of superiority and excess being. Yet the exhilaration of being powerful and desired also gets tangled up in ideas of sexual potency. An adoring lover or wife can become a talisman of the headhunter's power. That is, from the vantage point of male peerage and its internal rivalries, women and women's adoration undergo alchemical change to become gilded signs and amulets of the headhunter's elevation above others.

There is no question in my mind that the return of the headhunters marks a festive renewal of erotic discourse, something very much welcome after the long period dominated by the projects of mourning and field labor. Both men and women take part in the mirthful sexual banter. Youths come back from the headhunt feeling their most attractive—vigorous, mas-

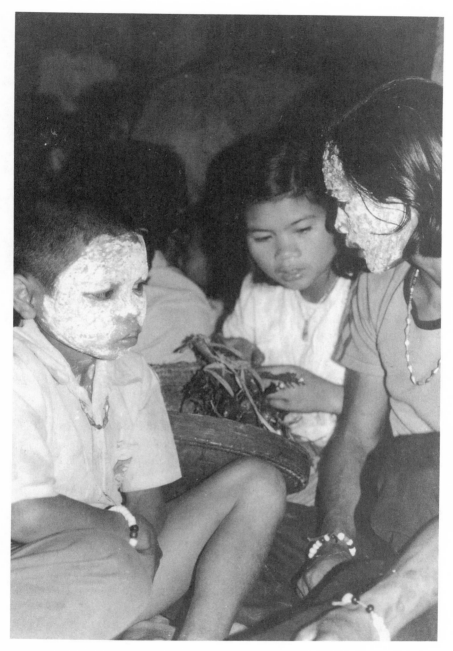

Fig. 12. *A young woman about to give betel and areca to two* tobarani *during the evening ceremony of "playing with the head." 1984.*

culine, and socially important—and are ready to impress and seduce young women. A young woman, too, may show a flirtatious interest in someone, perhaps making attempts to catch the eye of her favorite tobarani. Meanwhile, it is not unusual for older men to boast of their continued potency.[6] Explicit or demonstrative expressions of sexual interest toward specific persons, however, are out of place. Accordingly, villagers resort to covert or indirect gestures to signal their interest in one another. Indeed, the songs are a safe place to voice their interest in one another.

Consider, then, the cleverness of a song such as the following. On one hand, it is about the shy flirtations that might go on during ceremonies. On the other hand, it can be directed toward someone in particular; sung while giving a revealing glance to someone in the crowd turns the performance itself into a flirtation.

Diassiangki' tematin	There is just us among them all
sipasisi' sipasillan	we both let on both glance away
sipasalendoi mata	both of us flirting with our eyes

By way of contrast, some lyrics can be fairly graphic in the way they depict lovemaking. For example, one song I heard sung by women captures the sweat and tangle of sex, and makes a rather obvious pun about the singing cockerel, metaphor for both headhunter and penis:

Mane belue' sitambem	Hair just beginning to tangle
mane appu' silolonni	sweat begins trickling together
anna ummoniram manu'	then the cockerel must be singing

Like the previous example, the song can be performed in such a way as to serve as a come-on to a favorite lover sitting in the crowd.

Seduction and courtship can require stealth on the man's part and, in that sense, are seen as activities that have something in common with headhunting. A lover must be lured toward a man with flattery and sweet-talk (*ussinggi'*), not unlike the way the headhunter may lure a victim with magical incantations or baited charms.[7] Songs like the two that follow candidly depict the whispered sweet-talk of a man who has gone to his lover's house under the cover of darkness in order to sleep with her.

Petindoan ana' dara	The young woman's place for sleeping
disullu' bassi ba'bana	her door is barred shut with iron
umbam pellullabeanna	where'bouts is her shuttered window

Umba tambim muongei	Where is the room in which you rest
umbam pellullabeammu	where'bouts is your shuttered window
onimmu mandang kurangngi	I can hear nothing but your voice

Metaphoric associations that connect headhunting and courtship also prompt different "readings" of sumengo lyrics. For example, both can be likened to the felling of a tree, as in the following sumengo:

Iko barane'-barane'	You, you banyan trees over there
keditambako dilellen	if you are called to be cut down
loe maiko bambaki	fall here into our village lands

From the vantage point of intercultural relations, the song is about felling a Mandar victim. It expresses hope that the victim's head will "fall into the village" and bring prosperity to the upland community. But several ToSalu friends—all men—also suggested that these lyrics alluded to a marriage pro-posal. In their view, a woman does not pass into full maturity until she is "felled" by a marriage proposal. A tree that falls into the village becomes timber; a woman who falls into the village becomes a wife.

Other song-flirtations suggest a masculine anxiety that needs to be soothed with a woman's expression of desire. In an exchange of ToIssilita' songs I recorded at Saludengen, men sang the following to a chorus of women:

Menna' lamuala	Which do you want to take
kandean tadiampalla'	the coarse unpolished wooden dish
anna pindam pebajoan	or the porcelain reflecting bowl

The lyrics pose a choice of objects, a wooden dish from the mountains, or a porcelain bowl from the coast. As icons of upland poverty and coastal wealth, the dish and the bowl are also metaphoric displacements of rival masculinities. The chorus of women responded, reassuring their husbands and lovers that they like things that come from the mountains, from "home:"

Arabopinea	Better that I just keep
kandean tadiampalla'	the coarse unpolished wooden dish
anna pindam pebajoan	than the porcelain reflecting bowl

Moments later, the men and women exchanged another question and reply:

Menna' lamuala	Which do you want to take
labuju pettanetean	the wild cockerel from the mountains
anna londom belo tondo'	or the hamlet's fancy rooster

Arabopinea	Better that I just keep
labuju pettanetean	the wild cockerel from the mountains
anna londom belo tondo'	than the hamlet's fancy rooster

In these sumengo, the men probe the feelings and attitudes of village women with the purpose of adorning themselves with words of flattery and reassurance. As one might expect in a ritual that celebrates and enlarges the image of mountain men, the choices of the women reveal a preference for things and persons less prestigious, and a faith in virtues hidden beneath humble appearances.

The oscillating rivalry between men and women is mirrored, too, in the agonistic and antiphonal play of songs and song riddles.[8] Part of the challenge can be to defeat other choruses simply by outsinging them. Some of the challenge also has to do with knowing an appropriate sequel or rejoinder to the preceding song. For example, a chorus may pose enigmatic questions and riddles in their sumengo, as when men ask:

Diattomokoka' iko	Have you ever woven something
sumau' tadikala'i	with a warp but no thread for weft
marra' tadisumallai	when done it was all of one piece

Women respond with a conventionally spare answer that conceals more than it reveals:

Diattomakantekami'	Yes, we too have woven something
sumau' tadikala'i	with a warp but no thread for weft
marra' tadisumallai	when done it was all of one piece

The same holds true of the following sumengo-exchange, again between men and women:

Diattomokoka' iko	You, have you ever played at it
mogasin tandiulanni	making tops spin but without string
muondo pitu bulanna	they whir and hum for seven moons
Diattomakantekami'	Yes we also have played at it
mogasin tandiulanni	making tops spin but without string
muondo pitu bulanna	they whir and hum for seven moons

The women are not being evasive in these examples. By concealing or withholding answers to the riddles, the women are able to possess something secret and thereby confer upon themselves a radiant noteworthiness. Although they do not divulge it, they know that the first song refers to a braid, and that the stringless top in the second song is a headhunter. (Just as a top may spin away for a moment and then return to hover in front of the person who cast it in motion, the headhunter goes off from the village and then comes back to celebrate for the seven nights of ceremony that make up pangngae.) Sumengo exchanges such as these make up a game of knowledge. But the game of knowledge is also a game of power: to pose questions is to exact a hold on another, and to give answers is to escape that grasp (Canetti 1978:284–290). Seen in this light, men and women are playing for power and control over one another during sumengo performance. Yet neither achieves dominance except for a few moments. The conventions of sumengo performance are such that men and women strike a balance with one another within the game of question and answer, image and counterimage, secret and countersecret.

What is perhaps already obvious is that the song-fest of umpaningoi ulunna conjures an image of women as men would like them to be, an image that obscures (and possibly denies) possibilities for a woman's own subjective presence in the social order. These are women who desire a headhunter and envy his excess of being, who offer reassuring words to their husbands, and who like playful sexual banter. If sumengo performance throws the yoke of complementarity upon men and women, it nonetheless appropriates the feminine so as to exalt and construct a manhood reflecting the prestige anxieties of men. In short, a woman's songs still trace the reach of masculine discourse during pangngae. Her voice does not speak with the free authority of her own experience but, rather, with the purpose of turning man's gaze back upon himself. In no small sense, it is man's self-absorbed gaze, displaced and mirrored back to him through women, that adorns him with such radiant effect.

Yet everyone's gaze must turn, too, to the trophy head, the troubled sign of the tobarani's astonishing violence. Led by the elders, the gathering takes part in a liturgical performance that unites the social and moral hierarchies of the headhunt. The topuppu and the entourage of men sitting beside the centerpost take up the sacred strains of the *sumengo tomatua*, the "sumengo of the elders":

Iamo tolena	That's it, that is just what
naporaena debata	the spirits favor and expect
kema'patemboki' tole	when we do it again, that's it

The topuppu then calls out to the leader of the *tobisu* ("the ones of quickened spirit"), as the warriors are now called, for the head to be brought. One of the tobisu fetches the head and presents it, still wrapped in a rice pouch, to the topuppu as the gathering shouts "It stinks! It stinks!" He puts the shrouded head on the centerpost and places a headcloth on it. Calls for betel and tobacco go up, and gifts of the same go to the topuppu, the entourage of village elders, and the head. As more betel and tobacco pass through the crowd, men cry out Sanda! Sanda! ("Enough! Enough!"), in a stylized plaint of communal overindulgence and excess: the abundant hospitality (an index of hamlets' and homesteads' material prosperity) has sated and overwhelmed any desire to consume.

The gathering then quiets as the topuppu speaks to the head in ritual address (*mualu' ulu*). Soothing the victim with gifts of tobacco and betel, the topuppu explains the headhunters' act of beneficial violence:

Talakupotere' debata	I do not want to act wrongly toward the debata
anna talakupobusungam	and I do not want to fall dead and bloated
Lamualu' pada sappa'ku	I want to celebrate with my being
anna laumpatadongkom pada lesoku	and want to put it in place with my body
Aka iko inde ampona Daeng Maressa	For you this grandchild of Daeng Maressa
todipatadongkon dio ba'bana minanga	the one who is seated below at the rivermouth
Aka umbai' talatikkedu'ko anna talatirambam	So that you will not be frightened nor troubled in sleep
Aka lamengke'de' todiulunnasalu	For the ones at the headwaters stand up
turun dokko di ba'bana minanga	and go down to the rivermouth
Aka lanabattako mebengngi' tamalea lindo lanabattako karubem talaborro pa'todingan	For they want to cut you at sunrise, don't be red of face they want to cut you at sundown, don't ooze blood from your throat
Aka lanababako kende' todiulunnasalu lanapatodongkom lanapasandangko alu' anna lanapagannasan sangka'	For they want to carry you up the ones at the headwaters they set you down they want to honor you with ceremony and they want to receive you with custom

Aka lanapokende'i todiulunnasalu	For they want to make the ones at the headwaters rise up
lanapobakka'i todi-ba'banaminanga	they want to make the ones at the rivermouth flourish
Sapo lanapokende'i lamu-lamungan	They even want to make the plants rise up
anna lanapobakka'i ma'rupatau	and they want to make people flourish
Anna mupanganni inde panganmu	So then savor your betel
malute lindo	with a relaxed look
umpa'sambako'i inde sambako'mu	smoke your tobacco
sende i naba	with contented breath
Latinanda lako ongeam bulabammu	Soon you will arrive there at your place of gold
Anna lanapokende'i todi-ba'banaminanga	And the debata will make the ones at the rivermouth rise
lanapobakka'i todiulun-nasalu	and they will make the ones at the headwaters flourish
Anna tanapotikannai inde toungke'desanni	And they will not change these [tobisu] who stand
Anna ladenni to takulambi'na	And if there is one I did not get
dempi to takuissanna	and still again one that I do not know
Anna lamesako debata bisu	Then together you debata that quicken the spirit
laumpasitontonganna' batta kadangku	will make my words fitting and complete

The topuppu and his entourage then erupt with the mua'da' shout and are answered by the men in the crowd. Once more, the elders lead the gathering in singing the sumengo tomatua:

Iamo tolena	That's it, that is just what
naporaena debata	the spirits favor and expect
kema'patemboki' tole	when we do it again, that's it

As soon as this very solemn song comes to a close, the topuppu and the elders begin the antiphonal ma'denna, taunting the head, but naming, too, each tobisu who journeyed downstream:

Denna le'	Denna le'
ulu petambako sau'	head, start calling downriver
le' ma'adendem ma'denna le'	le' ma'adendem ma'denna le'
Denna le'	Denna le'
tambai baligau'mu	call your *Baligau'*
le' ma'adendem ma'denna le'	le' ma'adendem ma'denna le'
Denna le'	Denna le'
pasitammu ____	have him meet [name of the cohort leader]
le' ma'adendem ma'denna le'	le' ma'adendem ma'denna le'
Denna le'	Denna le'
nakulle eai naeba	he is able and ready to fight
le' ma'adendem ma'denna le'	le' ma'adendem ma'denna le'
Denna le'	Denna le'
natendanni pa'pelamba'	he bridges danger by rising steps
le' ma'adendem ma'denna le'	le' ma'adendem ma'denna le'
Denna le'	Denna le'
ulu petambako sau'	head, start calling downriver
le' ma'adendem ma'denna le'	le' ma'adendem ma'denna le'
Denna le'	Denna le'
tambai pa'bitarammu	call your *Pa'bitara*
le' ma'adendem ma'denna le'	le' ma'adendem ma'denna le'
Denna le'	Denna le'
pasitammu ia	have him meet [name of the younger leader]
le' ma'adendem ma'denna le'	le' ma'adendem ma'denna le'
Denna le'	Denna le'
nakulle ai naeba	he is able and ready to fight
le' ma'adendem ma'denna le'	le' ma'adendem ma'denna le'
Denna le'	Denna le'
natendanni kaloloam	he bridges danger by the straight path
le' ma'adendem ma'denna le'	le' ma'adendem ma'denna le'
Denna le'	Denna le'
ulu petambako sau'	head, start calling downriver
le' ma'adendem ma'denna le'	le' ma'adendem ma'denna le'

Denna le'	Denna le'
tambai pangngulu tau	call your *Pangngulu tau*
le' ma'adendem ma'denna le'	le' ma'adendem ma'denna le'
Denna le'	Denna le'
pasitammu i ____	have him meet [name of the headhunter]
le' ma'adendem ma'denna le'	le' ma'adendem ma'denna le'
Denna le'	Denna le'
nakulle ai naeba	he is able and ready to fight
le' ma'adendem ma'denna le'	le' ma'adendem ma'denna le'
Denna le'	Denna le'
natendanni piso lambe'	he bridges danger by the long blade
le' ma'adendem ma'denna le'	le' ma'adendem ma'denna le'

(A complete example of the ma'denna is given in Chapter 3.)

In mocking the head that sits dumb and nameless on the centerpost, the ma'denna dissects and counterposes the male political bodies from upstream and downstream regions. Lyric blows of the ma'denna dismember Mandar political anatomy, while celebrating the names (not the titles) of village men. As the elders and the gathered throng sing out the names of the tobisu, they also connect their names to metaphors of moral virtue. The name of Ta'bu, for example, may be sung out in association with "the straight path"—a metaphor for dedication; that of Sa'du, with "thick iron"—the symbol of endurance. Thus the song also articulates a moral anatomy specific to the men's political order in the village.

If the ma'denna distinguishes the tobisu as virtuous individuals, spreading their names and placing them above others, the ensuing *kelonoson* celebrates them as a distinguished group. Once again, the entourage of elders leads a mua'da' shout and the sumengo tomatua. Then the kelonoson begins, a performance that combines song and dance to chronicle the assault on the community downriver.[9] As they sing each verse, the elders sitting beside the head move their hands and arms in a dancing gesture. After each verse, the headhunters stand up around the elders, and while repeating the verse, perform the dance of warriors (slowly skipping, and waving their arms from side to side). One performance at Salutabang went as follows:

E-e rimunni alenta	E-e gather ourselves up
rimunni alenta	gather ourselves up
pasanggatai angganna	give everyone weapons
E-e narimuntoi	E-e he is joining up too
narimuntoi	he is joining up too
allena tomakkejoa'	the one with followers

E-e maua' marese	E-e go with a purpose
maua' marese	go with a purpose
baba toa pira tama	take along a few to join in
E-e talao	E-e we journey
talao	we journey
tapamesa naba-naba	our breaths as one
E-e marelappa bela	E-e let us confer my friend
marelappa bela	let us confer my friend
ammuita tomaelo'	to see who wants to do it
E-e tuppuppari batu	E-e unbroken stone
tuppuppari batu	unbroken stone
pasieso naba-naba	our hearts merge as one
E-e olai sebali	E-e go over on that side
olai sebali	go over on that side
angki olai sebali	and we will take this side
E-e sala' mennanta	E-e who among us
sala' mennanta	who among us
natandean debatanta	is marked by our debata
E-e totoi	E-e cut it off
totoi	cut it off
ammu laja tarra' daum	so that you have protruding fronds
E-e pettilinduanna	E-e the hiding place
pettilinduanna	the hiding place
tomarea' mentiroma	of the one frightened to follow
E-e karabai dai'	E-e charge upward
karabai dai'	charge upward
bettenna allo debata	at the fated stronghold
E-e apa i namala	E-e what does he want
apa i namala	what does he want
dikarabai dai' bettem	the stronghold is attacked
E-e salamandibao	E-e it is the same below
salamandibao	it is the same below
tedom mandudu kananna	the carabao drinks at the sulfur spring
E-e apa torillau'	E-e what person is downriver
apa torillau'	what person is downriver
malea di tangnga galung	red amid the grazing ground

E-e batu sinapa	E-e bullets
batu sinapa	bullets
mebaju-baju sangkalla'	shirted in black and red stripes
E-e joa' pira sola	E-e followers of [our] few friends
joa' pira sola	followers of [our] few friends
joa' pambulle sinapa	they carry firearms
E-e joa' kangkami	E-e our followers
joa' kangkami	our followers
joa' pakkabole-bole	carefully carry the rest
E-e ia marea'	E-e he who is afraid
ia marea'	he who is afraid
ia ala bainena	his wife will be taken
E-e ia barani	E-e he who is brave
ia barani	he who is brave
ia sapulo ka'dinna	will have ten lovers
E-e barani kangkami'	E-e we are brave
barani kangkami'	we are brave
sapulo ka'dingki'	we will have ten lovers

The kelonoson portrays the bravery, comradery, and cooperation of men. But the final three verses are especially revealing of the ways in which the violent adventures downriver prefigure a game of dominance in the peer politics of village males. The closing lyrics of the kelonoson entwine threat with unsurpassed sexual bravado. Wife-stealing is a dreaded and explosive issue, for the theft of a spouse undermines a man's prestige and status as a male peer. The lyrics remind those males who did not journey on the headhunt that the sexual license and stealth of the tobarani comes at the expense of other men. At the same time, the cultish and self-admiring boasts of the headhunters persuade them that their irresistible will to dominate can awaken desire in women.

Dipandebarani: The Feast for the Valorous

The sumengo-fest of umpaningoi ulunna can last well past midnight. So long as voices remain strong and plates of betel and tobacco keep circulating, singers are happy to stay up and sing praises to the tobarani. As people drift off to their homes, the topuppu makes his rounds of

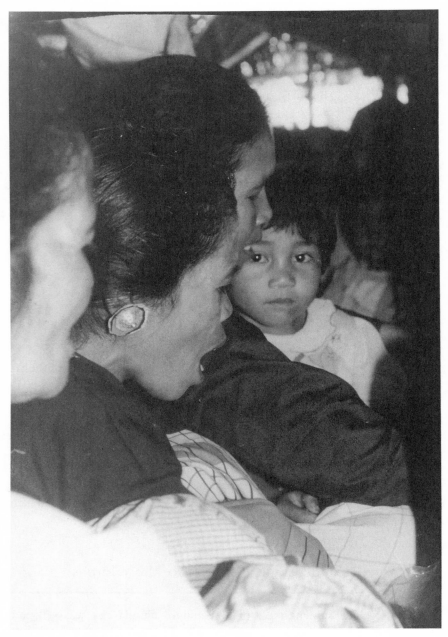

Fig. 13. *A small chorus of women singing the somengo during* dipandebarani, *"feasting the valorous."* 1984.

the hamlets, stopping at the home of each headhunter to make offerings to the *debata bisu muane*—the spirits who quicken the hearts of men. Standing in the firelight of each household's hearth, the topuppu softly chants over the gift of a chicken and seeks providential blessings for those fulfilling their vows:

Takupotere' debata	I do not act wrongly toward the debata
Takupobusungan	I do not fall dead and bloated
Lamulombum pudu'na tomatua	I want to join the mouths of the elders
Lamuumpu' lengko lilana	I want to thread the moving tongues of grandparents to
nene todiponene	those who are made grandparents
Iko to inde ampona	You here grandchild
bukku' bati'na belloa	dove of black descent
toma'bulu tinggi	one with red-spotted feathers
toma'bembe sarita	one with white ribbon
tomuhingngi hedena allo	one who hears the sun boil
tomulatta' tanda masia	one who understands signs of day
Umbai tasumpu dadi mupitia	Probably not yet old enough
Taende' gahagammu	Your deeds have not yet risen up
Aka lamengkalaoko illan ulunna salu	For you want to go inside the headwaters
ombo' di tipahiti'na uai	up to the springs
Lalanunnako ma'hupatau	You want to go along
salli'nako ma'tanda tolino	with people of this world
Anna iko inde mane mapia bulu	And you here chicken with fine feathers
ladikattu bata bahoko	will have a neck broken
latida' lalam penabammu	will have a windpipe snapped
lato'do' haha datummu	will drip blood of your lord
tise'bo' haha ma'dikammu	will scatter blood of your regent
Sapo talamalin illam penabammu	Still you will not be dazed in your heart
Aka lakende'ko langan debata bisu	For you rise up to the debata that quicken spirits
Aka Ambe ____ to inde lao ulleppa'i samajanna	For Ambe ____, this one who goes to release his vow
lannanna napadadi	That's the reason he offers
inde mane' mapia bulu	this chicken with fine feathers

Aka lanatilalla'iam langan debata bisu	For he wants to fill his vow to the debata that quicken spirits
Anna handanni lanapomasakke	And they bring him cooling health as a river bank follows the river
Anna bihi lanapomangngu-hindim	And bless him as the horizon encircles all
Anna tanapengkabuku'i	And they won't work him to the bone
Anna tanapengkatohoi	And they won't draw off his vigor
Anna dondommi	And surely blessings fall
nee' lisu pala'na toba	down into the palm
nee' taluttu' tahunona	down onto the fingers of an outstretched hand
allo sangngallo makkesulle	blessings equal in measure
ampasan daunna	to the unfurled leaf

With this sacrificial gift, the headhunter not only makes good on his oath, but exceeds it. Returning sacrificial meats and rice to the debata is a sign of the abundance that flows to and adorns the virtuous man.

At dawn, the rhythms of pabuno once more awaken the hamlets. Morning will see the mappurondo villagers gather for the final ceremony of pangngae, *dipandebarani* ("feeding the valorous"), the rite that honors the headhunters. Celebration reaches its peak in dipandebarani: drumming and song are at their loudest and most exuberant; decorations and finery are at their most elaborate; and food and drink are at their most abundant. Getting ready to appear before the village, the tobarani rub off the last flecks of paste from their faces, leaving a fine powder on their skin. Garbed in their finest shirts and headcloths, and adorned with bracelets, ceremonial knives, and beaded bandoliers, they take up their tambolâ and go to the ceremonial house.

If the harvest has been a good one, the gathering is sure to put up a tremendous clamor of song, drumming, talk, and laughter. The swirling sound of choruses and drums delights and overwhelms the senses. But as Plessner (1970:68) reminds us "We must not forget that sound includes the power of self-verification: one hears oneself." In this sense, the swirl of sound is an icon of the community in its vanity, exhibiting itself in unceasing festivity. Noise and music are adornments, simultaneously enlarging and engulfing the crowd that wishes to hear itself:

Ma'palisu inde tondo'	This hamlet swirls round and around
ma'batu lampa' banua	the dwelling's signs are cut in stone
tamonda disapukoi	unbroken unfallen spirit

Fig. 14. *Radiant in his finery, the head of the cohort listens as villagers celebrate his name and deeds in song. 1984.*

Fig. 15. *Women and girls cluster near the sons, brothers, and husbands who have gone on the headhunt. The young headhunter pictured here has adorned himself with headcloth, necklace, bracelets, beaded sash, and his best shirt. 1984.*

Nakua oninna gandang	It is said the voice of the drum
pebalinna sulim bulo	the echo of the golden flute
angki tamonda iponi	that we play are never broken
Tanete aka sambali'	What peak lies over on that side
buntu aka tosanganna	what mountain is it people call
tanete diboro mani'	the peak dressed with beaded necklace
Tanete diboro mani'	The peak dressed with beaded necklace
buntu ditete bulawan	the mountain that's gilded in gold
pangandaranna burio	the place spotted carabao dance

The music and noise only subside when the topuppu and the entourage of elders begin to conduct the liturgical acts intended to sacralize the headhunters as tobisu and to present the debata with the head and gifts of meat and rice. The liturgical sequence for dipandebarani repeats much of that performed during a'dasan and the previous night: the sumengo tomatua, the ma'denna, and the kelonoson. To these is added *mararra topangngae anna tambolâ* ("anointing the headhunters and the tambolâ") and the *ma'pai-sun* (when the babalako or topuppu presents the surrogate head to the de-

Fig. 16. *A villager brings a gift for one of the* tobarani: *a bundle of rice, fish, and meat, decorated with betel leaves, clove-scented cigarettes, and small packs of sugar cookies. 1984.*

bata; see Chapter 3 and below). To start the marrara, the tomatuatonda', in his role as the political head of the community, will chant words to the bird or pig to be sacrificed:

Inde tolanaokko'i	This is what will be put in place:
lakuraraan inde tambolâ	I will put blood on these tambolâ
lakupasirara topangngae	I will put the same blood on the topangngae
Anna narandanni kamasakkeam	So that health follows them like a bank to a river
nabirim kamangngurindingan	prosperity encircles them like a horizon
tiambu' tatibissi'	not a seed scattered or thrown
Dempito takuissam	If there is one I don't know
takutula' takulambi'	that I don't mention, that I don't remember
tolakupokada	while speaking
Ma'ganna lakupasola	That's why I give
inde tombongan rumpâ	this pile of refuse too
Aka lamulombunni takulambi'na	For you to complete what I forget
umpondi'i takuissanna	to lessen what I don't know
Aka iko toumpa'tulakanni	For you that speak for them
iko tosibaba ada'	you who together carry adat
tosipassan isanga kabiasaam	you who haul what is called custom

The tomatuatonda', assisted by the topuppu or babalako, then moves among the tobisu and their tambolâ, dabbing them with sacrificial blood. In contrast to the dismembering textual blows of the ma'paisun (see Chapter 3 and below), the gestural discourse of the marrara conjoins, underscoring anatomical movement and strength as the tomatuatonda' anoints each warrior on the ankle, knee, palm, elbow, throat, jaw, and forehead.

Not long after the marrara, the elders ready themselves to present the head and sacrificial foods to the debata through the liturgical act called ma'-paisun ("making an offering"). The topuppu or babalako places the head, packets of meat and rice, and a bamboo vessel filled with water in the loft that faces the headwaters of the river and the rising sun, and then begins his chant to the debata:

E pun debata	E pun debata
debata i diisunni	debata being seated

debata i itongkonni	debata given place to dwell
debata i itananni samba'	debata by the planted beam
debata i diosokki andiri	debata by the planted pillar
debata i ipa'banuai	debata given a house
debata i umpadadi lino	debata making the world
debata i unnampa' rante	debata flattening the field
debata umballa' lino	debata unrolling the world
debata ussare tuka	debata curving the pass
debata umbokkom buntu	debata rounding the mountain
debata ullemo tanete	debata making peaks round as oranges
debata umpaturun uai	debata bringing down water
debata i laipalangngan	debata who will be raised up
debata i laipakende'	debata who will be placed above
debata i tangnganna langi'	debata in the middle of the sky
debata iabo lisunna batara	debata above in the firmament's whirl
debata i bisu muane	debata quickening spirits of men
debata i laipaturun	debata who will be brought down
debata i laipatirandu'	debata who will be placed below
debata i laipatirassa	debata who will be slammed down
debata i popa'dandan	debata who will be put in rows
debata i laipopa'tere-tere	debata who will be put in line
debata i lanamammasan	debata that he will seek in sleep
debata i napa'tindoan	debata that he will wait for in dreams
debata i lanapembangonni	debata as he will awaken
debata i lanake'desan	debata as he will stand
debata i lanapetakingan	debata as he fastens his blade
debata i lanaturungan lita'	debata as he climbs down to the ground
debata i napessubungam bamba	debata as he crosses out of the bamba
debata i ladipalamban	debata who is brought across
debata i ladipatekka	debata who is made to step
debata i Lita'malea	debata at Lita'malea
debata i Pongko'	debata at Pongko'
debata i Limbadengen	debata at Limbadengen
debata i Salururu	debata at Salururu
debata i Limbadebata	debata at Limbadebata
debata i Salutumuka'	debata at Salutumuka'
debata i Rante	debata at Rante
debata i Taneteledo	debata at Taneteledo
debata i Salumokanan	debata at Salumokanan
debata i Salusullu'	debata at Salusullu'

debata i Salukadi	debata at Salukadi
debata i Matuju	debata at Matuju
debata i Mehalaan	debata at Mehalaan
debata i Salutuka'	debata at Salutuka'
debata i Salubombam	debata at Salubomban
debata i Salumarante	debata at Salumarante
debata i Botten	debata at Botteng
debata i Passembu'	debata at Passembu'
debata i Dama-dama	debata at Dama'-dama'
debata i Posi'	debata at Posi'
debata i Merahujo	debata at Merahujo
debata i Matangnga	debata at Matangnga
debata i Tabiban	debata at Tabiban
debata i Tapua'	debata at Tapua'
debata i Pangngala Lemarra	debata at Pangngala' Lemarra
debata i Katirandusan Tampa' Galung	debata at Katirandusan Tampa' Galung
debata i Magalunna	debata at Magalunna
debata i Marampa'na	debata at Marampa'na
debata i Mapilli	debata at Mapilli
debata i Andau	debata at Andau'
debata i Umbu'pada	debata at Umbu'pada
debata i Ta'ba'sala	debata at Ta'ba'sala
debata i Tenggelan	debata at Tenggelan
debata ungkela' pangngabungan	debata slipping out of ambush
debata umpollo' pangngabungan	debata coming out from ambush
debata untaleam pangngabungan	debata scattering grass from the ambush
debata mamunga'	debata landing the first blow
debata mamola	debata slashing open the neck
debata mamumbu'	debata wrestling over it
debata ma'tandean	debata lifting it up high
debata ma'peulu	debata taking the head
debata ma'pemata	debata taking the brain
debata ma'peuta'	debata taking the eyes
debata ma'petalinga. . . .	debata taking the ears. . . .

The chant gives way to a violent crescendo of shouts and noise from the crowd. Women and girls let loose a rain of areca nuts, pelting their favorite men, while up in the loft the topuppu flings a rain of sacral water onto the gathering below. With that, the topuppu closes the ma'paisun:

Pembasei inde uai malesomu	Wash clean with these your clear waters
tailambanni ulunna	its headwaters never crossed
anna taditekkai ba'ba minanganna	and the opening of its mouth never stepped over
anna muandei inde bo'bo busammu	And you eat this white rice of yours
sipatompo ate babimmu	with gulps of the liver of your pig
Anna tamukamallei te inde	And you do not become dazed here
Aka Ambe ____ inde mubaba solana	For Ambe ____ [cohort leader] carries your friend [the head]
Dadi ianana napadadim	So that is the reason
inde babi mapia bulu	this pig with fine hair is being done
Aka lanarandang kamasakkeam	So that health will follow him as a bank along a river
nabihim kamangnguhindingam	prosperity will encircle him as the horizon encircles all
Anna dempi to talakuissanna	And if there is still one I do not know
anna makambampi takulambi'na	and still something wide I cannot cross
mesahangko debata bisu	together you debata bisu will
laumpasilolonganganna' batta kadangku	straighten out my words

After the ma'paisun, the village head and the topuppu oversee the division and presentation of the *tarakan,* broad trays heaped with rice, fish, meat, and eggs for the headhunters.[10] These prestige foods alone display the community's esteem for the tobarani, but their presentation also includes a gestural demonstration of excessive regard, an enacted rhetoric of overabundance. As the two elders point out each warrior, a man enlisted to work as a carrier brings forward a large winnowing tray of food hoisted on his shoulder. Acting as if he were struggling with a load of enormous weight, he lets out a mua'da'-like shout ("*yuhuhuhu*"), buckles at the knees and carefully drops the tarakan tray before the headhunter. This grossly exaggerated portrayal of someone straining and collapsing under a heavy load is itself an enlargement, a stylistic icon of overindulgent excess: too much acting in presenting too much food. Whether the harvest has been meager or abundant, the tarakan always occasions this demonstrative excess. Though it never surprises, the tarakan always impresses.

As the warriors get their tarakan, a team of men pass out smaller packets of food to everyone else in the gathering. No one touches his or her food

Fig. 17. *The* tobarani *sound their* tambolâ *for the final time before flinging them up into the loft. 1985.*

until all has been distributed. As the warriors sit solemnly, if a bit wide-eyed, with their trays before them, the village head designates each tarakan by calling out the name of the headhunter to whom it is being given. Referring to all the foods passed out, but calling forth, too, a hierarchy of social difference, he closes with, "This is for the men. This is for the women. This is for the guests." With that, the men in the gathering make a sudden diving leap across the room at the tarakan of the warriors, digging and tearing at the food, and shoveling a gulp or two of rice and meat into their mouths as the tobarani beneficently look on, making no effort to keep the men from their food. This violent gesture of commensality wrests away some of the headhunters' excess: it is a self-conscious and stylized effort to level hierarchical differences among village males. With it, a community of men place themselves on equal footing, all sharing in the headhunters' glory.

After taking a few mouthfuls of meat and rice, headhunters and guests alike bundle up their portions of food. Later, they will take the packets home and eat there. Singing and drumming resume until about noon. As the sun reaches its zenith, the headhunters take their flutes (which have been silent since the closing moments of a'dasan) and gather near the centerpost. Standing below the edge of the loft, they begin *umbua' tambolâ* "raising (or displaying) tambolâ." Urged on by the crowd, the tobarani blow a long note in unison on their instruments for roughly twenty seconds or more (the longer, the better, it is said), and then deliver their mua'da' shout three times: "*Jelelelele huuui!*" Twice more they sound a long blast on the tambolâ and follow it with three shouts. With their last shout, the headhunters heave their tambolâ up into the loft, where a waiting male will stack them next to the head and the paisun offerings. At the same time, drumming begins again and singers launch into the sumengo tomatua.

Words that Make the Floor Shake

As the rhythms of pabuno pour from the drum, the cohort leader, the tobisu, and any other man so moved take turns leaping up to deliver impassioned speeches at the center of the house. Villagers call this speechmaking *mamose* ("stomping in fury"). As a man rises, the drumming comes to an abrupt stop. Stepping forward, the speechmaker brings his foot down with a pronounced thud and then circles the floor counterclockwise as he speaks, his right hand raised and sometimes holding a kerchief-sized cloth (the symbol of the Pitu Ulunna Salu league). Delivery is especially striking at Saludengen, where the headhunter-speechmakers take bounding, floor-shaking jumps to the center of the house, and circle about with hardened faces and fiery eyes as they talk. When a speaker finishes, pabuno bursts from the drum. To the cheers and shouts of the gathering, the speechmaker circles the floor once more (sometimes carried atop the shoulders of men, sometimes simply by leaping about). Another speaker takes his place until all those who wish to give a speech have done so. In principle, any male may speak during mamose. But in practice, it usually falls to but a few elders and a headhunter or two to make these impassioned speeches.

Mamose offers a way for a man to display his political maturity and readiness, and thus his peership with other men: a skilled and daring headhunter, he is willing to risk danger out of dedication to village tradition. Capable of taking a life and defending his own with force, he is also a wise and talented speaker who knows how to stir the hearts of others. A youthful warrior, he is self-effacing and humble. Advancing in age, he is ready to counsel younger men. In my experience, young men look up to those elders who speak with wisdom and passion. In this sense, mamose speeches are coveted verbal forms that inspire others to oratorical heights. With mamose, a man does not just desire to be like other men, but strives to be a leader, a first among equals.

Unlike the agonistic play of sumengo performances, no one tries to outdo the other in delivering a speech.[11] In fact, a good speech requires some gesture of self-effacement, of humbling oneself before others. On the surface of things, such a gesture serves as a way for a speechmaker to disclaim any interest in distinguishing himself or enlarging his reputation and image. But because this rhetorical tactic of self-effacement draws the admiration of listeners, it only increases the speechmaker's radiance and greatness. At the same time, a good speech must convey the speaker's regard for upholding tradition. So in addition to humbling oneself before others, a speaker tries to commit himself to ritual tradition and the common good.

Youthful headhunters who lack experience in speaking before the community are quick to grasp the importance of playing down the self and playing up tradition. In fact, in most cases their speeches do not go beyond well-rehearsed or memorized expressions of humility and self-sacrifice. However sincere, their efforts tend toward the formulaic and the grandiloquent. For instance, one young headhunter leapt onto center floor and opened his speech with two familiar if well-worn allusions to fate:

Umbai' sissi'na tondo'	Maybe it's the mark of the hamlet
batu lampa'na banua	signs cut in stone for the house
Anna takuita tindo	And I did not see it in sleep
takulambam pangngimpi	nor come across it in dream

With these words, the speechmaker tells the gathering that his becoming a headhunter was unplanned. It was his unforeseen fate to take part in the ceremonial journey downstream. But here he is, a mere infant, so to speak, ready to show what manhood is all about:

Turun di langi'	Suddenly from the sky
ânâ' sumusu	the child at the breast
ussangka' bisu muane	measures the spirit of men

If the village elders will hold fast to tradition, he will do his part for the communal good:

Sapo' maka nabela tomatua	So if the elders can make
umpomarosom kada sarandam	the strand of words thrive
illalam botto	in the village

Inde mandi' ânâ'	This mere child can be
salli'na botto	a timber for the village
lilli'na kada sarandam	a layer on the strand of words

The speech is a good one, as first speeches go, for the speaker has shown modesty (to paraphrase: "fate brought me here," "I'm just a child"), and pledged himself to the social and moral order of the community ("I will follow the elders," "I will serve the village and its tradition").

After calling for the attention of the crowd, another young headhunter protested that he did not know very much or have much experience holding forth in speech:

Tanangko talingammu	Plant your ears
anggammu tau kambam	all you in the crowd
Palempeko sulim pa'perangngimmu	Turn your ears
anggammu tosakombongam	all you gathered as one
Matangku taratu	My eyes cannot see that far
penabangku takume'de'	my breath cannot last

He went on to say that it is hard to make the floor shake, that is, to summon enough spirit and purpose to come before others as a headhunter. It is hard, too, to be an orphan—hard to know what to say and do when one's elders pass away.

Mandanta' sali	Pounding the floor
maparri' isanga	is said to be tough
maparri' bium	tough to be an orphan
maparri' taketomatua	tough not having elders

His words may reflect a personal loss in the recent past. They might allude, too, to some of the pain and directionlessness a community may feel at having lost an elder leader. Yet the young speaker has been moved to become a headhunter and to stand before the gathering:

Umbai' palangke-langkena	Maybe it's the celebration
isanga tomatua illalam botto	of those called elders in the hamlet
anna belona londom	and the finery of the cockerel
sangka'na muanean tau	the weave of one's manhood

Perhaps it was the pleasure of celebration and the attention showered on men that drew him forward. Or perhaps it was a moral calling, for the speech ended with an uplifting if clichéd slogan:[12]

Umbai' iandiuaam	Maybe it's that saying
mesa kada dipotuo	"One word leads to life
pantang kada dipomate	A shattered word leads to death"

Combining formulaic expressions of modesty and fate, along with well-worn mottos, some speakers might deliver a more exhortatory speech, like the following:

Taia kabaraniam	Not bravery
taia katomakakaam	not arrogance
Sapo lamuakanniko	But what else can you do?
sissi'na tonda'	it's the mark of the hamlet
batu lampa'na banua	signs cut in stone for the house
Anna nadanta'kia' saratu'	And he startled a hundred of us
nadondikia' napobulo	he shook us like slender bamboo
Sapo' maka' tabela tapeimam	So if we are able to devote ourselves to
isanga mesa kada dipotuo	what is called "One word leads to life
pantang kada dipomate	A shattered word leads to death"
Umbai' mane lamupomalubu pole'	Maybe you just want to redden
salunna Manda'	the Mandar rivers again
umpomalillim	darken
posi' mapattana le'bo'	the lightless whirlpool of the sea
londo-londona tanete	cockerels of the peak
anna londo-londona kampum baru	cockerels of the new village

The speeches of older men tend to be longer, to show more polish, and to be more reflective than the speeches given by the young headhunters. Having less need to prove their dedication to ancestral teachings, older speakers, like the one who gave the following speech, commonly urge their listeners to stay upon the path of mappurondo tradition. Like many other elders, he begins his speech with a self-effacing remark about being crippled or put together wrong:

Tamaoon inde áná' sajo'na	Coming in again this crippled child of
Rantepalado	Rantepalado
Sapo' lamuakanniko	But what else can you do?
aka salli'na	For it's the timber
anna tala-talainna peadasan	and the joy of adat ceremony

Setongan-tonganna	In truth
ma'banna barinni' penabangku	my breath is but a small thread
muita isanga kita	as I look at us who are called
toillan ada' mappurondo	"those in ada' mappurondo"

He shows his modesty and humility, describing himself as a small thread on something greater (i.e. the woven blanket of tradition, ada' mappurondo). He continues with self-effacing comments as he exhorts others to be pious and strong-willed:

Sapo' maka' tabela mengkalao	But if we are strong-willed
di ånå'-ånå' lambisan baine	going from children to women
sule lako padangku	and coming around to me
tomanesubum isamai' urannallo	who was just born yesterday in a rainstorm
Taissam marea' anna ma'siri'	We know awe and humility
Taissam meimallako indota anna ambeta	We know respect for our mothers and fathers

And he closes with words of praise for the radiance of mappurondo ceremonial tradition:

Aka muakatiko	For what else can you do?
aka naillo' pemali appa' randanna	because the pemali appa' randanna flash
anna matanna allo simba'	brighter than the sun
anna lindo'na bulang	brighter than the face of the moon
Pennasai sola	Listen closely, friends

Yet orations like these pale when compared to the improvisatory rhetoric of the most skilled speakers. The following is a mamose speech given by Tasomba (seen in Figure 18), a descendant of Pua' Soja from Minanga. It is mamose rhetoric at its finest and most elegant: Tasomba is self-effacing, inspiring, and very knowing and deft in the way he takes hold of the moment to extol local tradition.

Tangnga'i anna umpokita-kitai ånå'	Look in the middle and let us gather around children
tosaladadenna tau ToMinanga-Loka'	the crippled ones, people of Minanga-Loka'

Fig. 18. *Assuming a traditional oratorical pose, Tasomba struts across the floor and delivers his* mamose *speech extolling* pemali appa' randanna *and* mappurondo *tradition. 1983.*

Maka lakupikki' anna lakupenahaang	If I want to think and reflect
tamalea lindoa'	my face won't be red
tama di alla'na bija Pattola	going among the descendants of Pattola
pa'todingan	I won't be embarrassed
tama di alla'na topadolam	going among the wise ones
Sapo' solana tala-talainna bata anna romboinna	For the sake of a refreshed body and renewed prosperity
disanga sangka' anna kabiasaang nasurung	it is called measure and custom because of that
tamalea lindoa'	my face won't be red
tama di alla'na	going among
angganna indo' todipoindo'	all the mothers made mothers
anna angganna ambe todipoambe'	and all the fathers made fathers
lambi' angganna bija Pattola	and all those descendants of Pattola

Then Tasomba invokes the memory of Ambe Ma'dose, whose recent death not only saddened the community, but also took away one of its most prominent leaders. In this village, his death was a blow to mappurondo tradition itself.

Anna mane kamaduai	And then second
solana sadekem buaku	for I am stirred
aka maka lakupikki' sama allona	when I think of the past
kua rato ada'	I could say adat sank
umbai' lalumme sangka'	maybe tradition flows slowly
matena Ambena Ma'dose	after the death of Ambena Ma'dose
mennapi launtegerangngi	who is going to awaken
sangka' anna kabiasaang	tradition and custom
illalang botto lita'ta.	in our village lands
Sapo' solana moka	But for the sake of
nene' todiponene'	ancestors who are made ancestors
manurunna inde pa'tadong-	founders of this dwelling place
kongang	
poajona tomatua todipomatua	the ghost of elders made elders
Moka talaombo'	It will not wither
ada' simemangangia lita'	the adat of this ground
anna ada' sulibanna inde lita'	and the adat beyond this ground
aka tau dalakona	since long ago
ma'tanda anna ma'tari-tariang	there were signs and decisions
sirrapang napadeengangki	like we were given
gamba' dehata batta	pictures by the debata
diua contoh mala	it is said
diua sadioam rupanna	it is said the ones we rely on
angganna bija Pattola	all the descendants of Pattola
molindo sanda lindona angganna	all of them meeting together face to face

Next, Tasomba began to address my being in Minanga for pangngae. Elders in the past told of a stranger who would come, but who had given it any thought?

Mala kuua kua tatabai-bai	I can say we didn't think
akanna kende'i	how it would happen
nasanga kada tomatua tosuleko'na	according to the words of the elders
manangnga	a person from far away
lasule launtadongkonniki'	would come to be present with us
Lamaala bajam-bajanna battu	Wanting to take the images
diua gambaranna sangka'	or pictures of the weaving
simemanganna ada'	that measures adat

anna ada' sirettenna pa'tadong-kongan	and the adat that always adorns our dwelling place

As Tasomba saw it, I was drawn to Minanga and ada' mappurondo by the ghosts of their ancestors. My being there was also reason to be glad and to hold fast to tradition:

Mane dengngi takubai-bai	And so I did not think about it
anna takuita tindo	and I didn't see in dreams
lanarenden bombona nene'	pulled by the ghosts of the ancestors
sule ânâ' banuanta	comes a child belonging to our house
mala kua mesa sule	I can only say one came
ampo kusanga la'bi sasa'bu	but I consider him more than a thousand
Aka mui anna diua	Although it is said
manangngako rupa tau kemokapi	some persons worry that it doesn't accord with
manurunna lita'	the founders of the land
manurunna ada'	the founders of adat
manurunna todiponene'	the founders who are made ancestor
launtibeki' sambu'na lita'	we will spread out the blanket of the land
anna bajunna pa'tadongkongang moka talakende'	and will hold up the shirts of the village

Tasomba now reached the point where he would urge the gathering to hold firm to the virtues of manhood and womanhood and to tradition itself.

Ampo maka tabela takambi	So if we are strong-willed enough
baine lasanda manuru'	to lead women to truly
untokei memanna ada'	hold firm with the ways of adat
untobe manda' kabaineang	hold firm with the honor of woman-hood
muane launtokei memanna kemuaneang	men holding firm with the honor of manhood
Talamupadondo kada nuku-nuku	Don't put down words that cause restlessness
talaumpakende' kada bissa'	and don't bring up false words
illalandi pa'tadongkongang	inside the village
muakatiko	for that reason

natapaela'i mengkara naua tomatua	work slowly, said the elders
naua taia pasarra'na	they said not to rush
kekato'longangki di ada'	if we have blessings from adat
kato'longangki di lita' tadongkongang	we will have blessings in the land of our village

Ready to close his speech, Tasomba says that his are not the words of some-one who is past his prime, but rather, of someone who is still young and vir-ile, of someone who is still a man:

Aka moi kao ade' lamangnguraa'	Because after all I am still young
sule ke nabelai baine nakamasaeia'	if a woman comes and is sweet toward me
kao duka' ta' naua saladadi	she won't say I'm put together wrong
Tangnga'tangnga'i anna mupokita-kitai	Look in the middle and let us gather around

As may be clear from the speeches of Tasomba and the others, the prin-cipal idea behind mamose is to animate the community such that it will fol-low the moral path of mappurondo tradition. Put somewhat differently, the speechmakers not only call for moral and ideological solidarity on the part of the gathering, but try to spark emulative action as well. Those making speeches thus put themselves forward as moral actors who are to be emu-lated, as daring and audacious headhunters, as self-effacing speechmakers, but above all, as ones who are animated by tradition. But being animated by tradition is to have given oneself over to the mimetic interests of reenact-ment. In bringing himself before the gathering, the speechmaker presents the image of someone who follows the village ancestors and elders, who ac-cepts their authority and their authoritative understanding of tradition, and who is ready to perform once more the sacred acts and ceremonies of ada' mappurondo.

The rhetoric of manhood, then, includes a portrayal of man *as a rhetori-cian*. That is to say, being good at being a man requires both the valor and violence of the headhunter and the virtuosity and authority of a mamose or-ator. With respect to pangngae, the violent and the verbal mark the extremes of ceremonial performance, to be reckoned not only as polarities of mascu-line discourse but as the beginning and end of the ritual's drama as well. In light of these extremes, the rite may be seen as a ceremonial transfiguration of manhood in which speech displaces violence. Successive modulations of vocal sound trace a path across the social and moral boundaries that distinguish upstream and downstream regions. From the noise of violent ambush downriver, and up through the mua'da' shout at hamlet's edge, emerges a stirring and eloquent speaker. Yet the displacement of violence is never complete. Virtuosity in taking a victim and in giving a speech is likened to felling a tree—a task that falls to men. Cut correctly, the tree "falls into the village" (*loe tama ri bamba*) and so can be used and enjoyed. Cut incorrectly, the tree "falls into the river" (*loe tama ri uai*) and is washed away. Within the metaphoric discourse of masculine virtuosity, felling a speech and felling a victim are potential transformations and transcodings of one another, and recalling the sumengo performances that connect headtaking and courtship, so too is felling a wife.

Women's Coda

When the last of the mamose speeches comes to an end, drummers beat out the rhythms of pabuno for a final time. As the drum plays, a chorus of women may begin to sing the sumengo tomatua, a song that throughout pangngae has belonged to choruses headed by men. At this time, it is common for a married woman to go into trance possession and begin a lively but silent dance under the influence of the *debata bisu baine*—the quickening spirit of women. Her brief dance marks the close of pangngae and the onset of a different ritual order, pa'bisuam baine, an order dominated by possessed women and entrancing spirits. In a sense, the currents of envy in pangngae culminate here in the counter-emulative discourse of women. Under the consecrating exclusions of pangngae, women desired to be like the tobisu muane—the enraptured warrior-speakers—but were prevented from sharing their splendor. With the end of pangngae behind them, women are free to seek splendor and to explore the boundaries of otherness on their own terms. They will not be like men; they will be like themselves.

The head and the tambolâ already rest in the attic loft. Men now hoist up the ceremonial drum, cinching it to the rafters. With that, the festivity of pangngae is put away. In the discourse of song, the sense of ending brings with it sadness and regret. For example, women might have sung the following sumengo a little bit earlier in the day:

Fig. 19. *A woman's coda to* pangngae: *a lively but silent dance under the influence of* debata bisu baine—*the quickening spirit of women. 1983.*

Mara'mo kami' sengoki	Oh it's too bad for us our song
dipasampe langal loko	put up above in the rice barn
dianna tama talukun	put away inside the rice bin

The song looks ahead to the ritual's closing, when women will put aside their festivity, their songs put away for safekeeping in places associated with mothers, daughters, and sisters. Equally bittersweet is the song exchange of male and female choruses facing the close of headhunting festivities:

Aka latakua	What will all of us say
kekipasampe langammi	when we men put it up above
tipandal lolom maroa'	the mirth and noise put back in place
Uai mata mandaram	A ring of tears just that alone
ma'lisu-lisu di ampa'	swirling round on the woven mat
tipurirri' di allongam	whirling about on the pillow

And so, the coda to pangngae belongs to women—perhaps it is more accurate to say that the coda offers an image or verbal icon of women—who give themselves over to weeping and trance, their crying and dancing a so-matic capitulation to unanswerable forces.

Felling a coastal rival from the past and shouting away grief are projects that give moral warrant to celebrations of manhood and the ceremonial politics of envy and emulation. Yet in my view, it is the rhetoric of manhood and the interplay of envy and emulation, rather than a will to violence and catharsis, that do the most to motivate mappurondo men and youths to pledge them-selves to the headhunt. In this fairly egalitarian community of men, pang-ngae serves as a ladder by which youths ascend upward toward male adult-hood. By no local account did anyone have to take a head if they wished to marry or to hold forth in deliberations with other men. But pangngae is a time for youthful males and elders alike to put their manhood on display and to assert ceremonially their peership with other men. In no small sense, then, being on display, being the focus for the envied gaze of others, is a part of what mappurondo manhood is all about.

In local thinking, *ukusam muane* (the rites of men) are synonymous with *ukusam botto* (the rites of the village). The liturgical chants of pangngae oc-casion the exercise of male authority over collective interests; they are au-thorized performances in which men hold a monopoly on the establishment of community and the maintenance of communal prosperity. But the au-thority of men, and the authoritativeness of the elders' liturgical speech (es-pecially that of the topuppu and the tomatuatonda'), in part are grounded in and indeed surrounded by the aggrandizing discourse of praise and song. It is within this exuberant singing that the collaborative assent of the com-munity, including its women, is manifest and recognized.

I do not know if Pua' Soja was ever a "real" headhunter. Maybe he, too, was a weaponless youth when lionized as warrior and orator. The idealized images of manhood that the songs of pangngae conjure up perhaps belong less to the present than to a time Pua' Soja glimpsed in adolescence. Un-earthed from memory each year, the sumengo are the remnant bones of men who are remembered as powerful and large, who continue to stir awe, but whose memory stirs nostalgia as well. Although mappurondo under-standings of masculinity and tradition still hinge on these images, anxiety and uncertainty color ceremonial practice. The civil order in Sulawesi today holds no place for mappurondo practice, and Christians and administrators more often than not show a lack of sympathy, and even contempt, for ancestral religion. As increasing numbers are lured away from the sacred path of the ancestors, the mappurondo community faces the grave problem of sustaining itself and the practices it claims as tradition. In the past, there were no doubt fewer and less powerful ideological challenges to the mappurondo community. Still, I have little sense of the impassioned eloquence of mamose speeches from the precolonial past—a past, it will be remembered, that Ambe Assi' once despondently described as not fully human and intelligible. Yet listening to the exhortations of contemporary speeches, I cannot help hearing speakers trying to keep others from abandoning the mappurondo fold, from giving up on mappurondo tradition altogether.

6

From Violence to Memory

Singing about Singing as a
Headhunt Ends in Song

Pangngae, one might say, begins in violence and ends in commemorative representation.[1] The realities of the headhunters' predatory journey are, and long have been, obscure and in flux. They happen downriver and over the horizon. It is a violence that is absent, something kept out of the community and away from the senses. That violence returns home, and is made present and known, only in the idealized representations of ritual discourse. In the present order of things, the headhunters' violence is doubly distant. After all, the purported victims are the figures of a bygone political order. The headhunters' violence is always marked by its absence and anteriority relative to its commemorative retelling in ritual chant and lyric.

The predations of the mappurondo headhunters can be storied in several ways. Thus far, I have raised the apparition of violence in exploring the polemics of domination and subordination that have colored regional history; in mentioning the untranslatable anguish of the bereaved; and in discussing the celebrated figure of masculinity. I do not consider these reflections to be wrong, but, rather, to be partial. They do not tell the whole story. In the pages that follow, I offer yet another perspective on the violence of pangngae, seeing it instead as an artifact of commemorative discourse itself. I will suggest that the violent subjection of a rival downstream is key to a kind of remembering that keeps the mappurondo polity in each village from passing

186

into oblivion. Villagers represent the scene of violence again and again, not so much for its mythic value, but to occasion the sociality and activity of remembering. Along with Eugene Vance (1979:383), then, I will argue that violent events can be both subject of, and generative force for, their reenactment in ritual chant and lyric. In short, the discursive practices of pangngae stage themselves around violence. Seen in this light, the commemorative work of pangngae keeps an act of exemplary violence moving through time (cf. Yengoyan 1985:171–172). But it should be remarked, too, that this very act of exemplary violence keeps *collective memory* moving through time.

I turn now to the problem of commemoration, and the construction of commemorated violence, because the difficulties facing the mappurondo community today have less to do with a crisis in meaning than they do with a crisis in remembering. Powerful social groups and institutions are asking villagers to forget or forgo mappurondo practices, to forsake what was already put in place by ancestral tradition. Yet I would venture that remembering and mimetic enactments long have been central to the reproduction of the mappurondo social order. "All beginnings," writes Paul Connerton (1989:6), "contain an element of recollection." The effort to renew and animate the community demanded a mimetic gesture of some kind that would recollect a privileged event from the past. Commemoration was a political end in its own right, and in the moment of its activity summoned or brought into being its own subjects and objects.

There are several aspects of reenactment that will concern me in this chapter. Viewed as practice, mimetic enactments include the expressive and instrumental dimensions we associate with representation and performativity. Yet ritual commemoration is also a mode of sociality, a means of shaping social hierarchy and social experience. As previous chapters clearly show, commemoration can serve other spheres of human concern, but it can also recruit such projects for its own ends. These projects have a great deal to do with shaping the social horizon within which the commemorative rite is staged, and for that reason may be an important source of variability or instability in commemorative activity. Over and against that variability, commemoration reveals yet another aspect, that of imitating its prior incarnations. In a sense, it is the purpose of commemorative tradition to produce a kind of simulacrum, "a copy of a copy for which there is no original" (Rosenau 1992:xiv). But at another level altogether, we can discover commemoration becoming a key theme in its representational surface (cf. Vance 1979). Commemoration will displace violence, and the community will sing about singing as the headhunt ends in song.

Commemoration as Adornment

In the last chapter, I introduced the theme of adornment in exploring the discourse of masculinity. I do so again, but now with the purpose of understanding commemorative song and commemorative tradition. I begin by reminding readers that the mappurondo ritual tradition called *pemali appa' randanna* evokes the image of a four-stranded beaded necklace. Villagers thus portray local ritual practice as an adorning object, a source of radiance that enlarges the community, elevating it and exalting it. The festive music and singing of headhunting ritual, in particular, adorns the village, the hamlet, and the homestead. The choruses sing about their commemorative festivity:

Umbai' sissi'na tondo'	Guess it's the mark of the hamlet
batu lampa'na banua	signs cut in stone for the dwelling
tamonda disapukoi	unbroken unfallen spirit
Rua e'de' inde bojan	True stand the lines of this homestead
rua sollo' kulakka'na	true run the lines of its floorbeams
tamonda disapukoi	unbroken unfallen spirit
Ma'palisu inde tondo'	This hamlet swirls round and around
ma'batu lampa' banua	the dwelling's signs are cut in stone
tamonda disapukoi	unbroken unfallen spirit
Nakua oninna gandang	It is said the voice of the drum
pebalinna sulim bulo	the echo of the golden flute
angki tamonda iponi	that we play are never broken
Tanete aka sambali'	What peak lies over on that side
buntu aka tosanganna	what mountain is it people call
tanete diboro mani'	the peak dressed with beaded necklace
Tanete diboro mani'	The peak dressed with beaded necklace
buntu ditete bulawan	the mountain that's gilded in gold
pangandaranna burio	the place spotted carabao dance

As the sumengo suggest, this radiant festivity is a mark of prosperity and virtue. In the mappurondo scheme of things there is virtue in the vanity of celebratory extravagance.

After months of labor, sorrow, and musical silence, the chance to sing brings villagers pleasure and affords them a way, momentarily, to divert their attention from the poverty, pain, and ephemerality of mountain life. Singing for them is an exuberant human act, one to be seized. One song of longing, usually sung late at night after pangngae has come to a close, expresses this sentiment well:

Dako patindo sararearn	Don't fall asleep resting together
inggammu matin dako patindo	all you there don't fall asleep resting
sararearn	together
Dako patindo sararearn	Don't fall asleep resting together
bue'o dai' tala-talai turunatta	wake up, rise, and liven up our place of descent
Tala-talai turunatta	Liven up our place of descent
lino taindam dunia' taparapi	we borrow the earth, we get only a bit of the world
Belo-belo!	Gild it, gild it!

Yet commemorative song also offers the chance to express magnificent and inspiring ideas and attitudes. Within the language of pangngae, the sumengo are an opportunity for villagers to *ma'kada senga'*, to "speak in another way," that is, to speak in a sublime manner. The urgency with which the community rushes against time to announce and extol itself in celebration comes across in a favorite ToSalu song:

Talomba-lomba sumengo	We race ahead with the singing
baju tapa'kada senga'	the chance to voice our sublime words
bassa' simateki' tau	even as we all pass away

"Speaking in another way" is also foretold by the language of prophetic dream-signs:

Tamballe-balle tindoku	My dream sign is not off the mark
tamasselom pangngimpingku	my dreaming does not slip away
ladengkam ma'kada senga	we'll be here speaking sublime words

The otherness of sublime speech has to do not only with its exalted themes and sentiments, but with its formal features as well. The language of ritual speech and song is itself marked and adorned.[2] Relative to everyday language, the liturgical speech and ritual songs of pangngae are richly metaphoric, subject to metrical constraints, and full of syllabic play. Many features we find in other oral poetries—the use of conceits and epithets, parallelisms, repetitions—figure prominently in the sumengo.[3] The idea of adorning or adorned speech, and its otherness, no doubt relates to poetic and rhetorical markedness, and to the figures, tropes, and patterns that constitute such marking. At the same time, speech that is other and adorned (*ma'kada senga'* and *kada-kada dibeloi*) potentially masks the situatedness and contingency of its production. Its very markedness helps objectify adorned speech as a seemingly autonomous and authoritative remembered text.[4]

Thus the themes and metaphors of adornment not only play a significant role in the ceremonial politics of envy and manhood, but also enter into the metalanguage and ideology of commemorative discourse. Language, tradition, community, and the "courageous ones" of the headhunt are all radiant and enlarged in the festivity of pangngae.

The Sociality of Commemorative Song

Singing, in pangngae, is an act of memory, a recollection of lyrics and singings from the past (cf. Halbwachs 1980, Schutz 1977 [1951]). Here, however, the project of recollection is not so much the work of the individual as it is the work of the community. Virtually all the songs of pangngae are choral, and so, before all else, the songs are the commentary of choruses that make up the community. There is, for example, the ma'denna, in which antiphonal exchanges take place between the entourage of male elders and the gathering at large, exchanges that effectively corroborate and communalize the representations of the ma'denna lyrics. Apart from the something remembered, then, there is in the act of recollection a sociality of remembering. From one vantage point, the sociality of the chorus may approximate the mutual tuning-in relationship discussed by Alfred Schutz (1977): a face-to-face relationship grounded in the experience and immediacy of performance.[5] Yet the ritual chorus—its ephemerality notwithstanding—may also make up a significant if idealized form of social hierarchy (cf. Nagy 1990). By taking a look at sumengo performances, I want to suggest that the fleeting social organization of the sumengo chorus resembles, or is grounded in, the organization of the community at large.

Sumengo are performed by groups of men or women, with each chorus guided by a songleader called a *tomantokko*. Although men and women occasionally come together to form a chorus, the predominating form is a group consisting solely of men or solely of women. As a rule, the groups are quite informal, and lack sharp boundaries between singers and listeners. People routinely drop in and out of the groups during ceremonies. Those songleaders with a strong voice, a sharp memory for lyrics, and a practiced feel for sumengo melody understandably draw more singers and hold them to-gether as a group.

As I noted in chapter 1, the sumengo lyric commonly consists of three octosyllabic phrases, sung to a set tune. The tomantokko is usually the one who recalls different sumengo lyrics, and in any event is the singer who de-livers the opening solo phrase. The following two phrases are choral, sung by both the chorus and the tomantokko. In principle, anyone can become a songleader; in practice, it is usually older persons who assume this role. When a tomantokko grows tired, his or her chorus may fall quiet for a while. Or the tomantokko may let someone else assume leadership of the chorus, though perhaps not without some resistance.

It should be obvious that the sumengo choruses are social bodies orga-nized around, and instantiating, gender difference. In ceremonial gatherings most everyone takes part in the singing. This means that the celebrating community is divided and constituted largely by choruses and by the gender differences that shape the organization of singing groups. More precisely, the community divides itself around groups consisting of wives, mothers, sis-ters, and daughters and countergroups made up of husbands, fathers, broth-ers, and sons. Although the social makeup of the chorus can raise problems in the interpretation of lyrics, it is commonly the case that the "subject's voice" residing in the song text is consistent with the gendered identity of the chorus. Groups of women usually sing songs that represent certain points of view, and men sing lyrics that reveal a different outlook. Though there are some suggestive or playful exceptions to this pattern, they strike me as being quite limited in terms of tactical or social consequence. At root, then, the song choruses communalize the lyric representations of the head-hunt, and ground them in gender difference.

In light of these differences, it is worth observing that the commemora-tive practices of pangngae include women as political actors and subjects. Normally excluded from everyday participation in public political discourse, women here have a voice. Central as they are to mappurondo social life and to the reproduction of mappurondo political order, the ceremonies of pangngae make up the most important platform for women's involvement in village politics. Thus women's participation in village politics takes place under ritual constraints.[6] In this sense, women are not free subjects but are subjected by the masculine discourse of pangngae: women appear as cele-brants and singers who glorify their husbands, sons, lovers, and brothers. Men, of course, appear as celebrants themselves. Yet they also enter into the ritual as the celebrated and the commemorated, and as those who exercise liturgical authority, roles (i.e. subject positions) not available to women.

Like all ritual crowds, these choral and liturgical gatherings are ephemeral social bodies. Yet even in their transitoriness we can catch a glimpse of the community's enduring forms of organization. The sumengo choruses in particular embody an idealized view of the community. Emergent in ceremony, they form an egalitarian aggregate, a body that thrives on agonistic exchanges between the choruses that divide and constitute it. No single chorus dominates the aggregate. The individual choral groups, however, require a degree of hierarchy. The tomantokko exercise leadership, authority, and privilege over their supporting singers. Younger and less experienced singers subordinate themselves to those who have spent more time in, or have gained more expertise in, remembering and leading songs. Age and experience define the terms by which an individual emerges from the egalitarianism of the whole to assume the status of tomantokko in a constituent chorus hierarchy (cf. Nagy 1990:411), only to relinquish that leadership and drop back into the group. Like the tobarani who enjoys his moment in the sun, the tomantokko sits before others as one to be followed and imitated. As villagers themselves explain it, one fells a victim, and another fells a song (George 1990).

Violence and Commemoration

At the beginning of this chapter, I suggested that for the mappurondo communities of Bambang, commemorative ritual has been a political end in its own right. This is unquestionably the case in the present order of things. In light of the region's religious pluralism and the state's civil policies, ritual tradition is the very basis of mappurondo identity. That is to say, the mappurondo communities are able to assert their autonomy and difference only by keeping ancestral tradition as their practical and ideological focus. Ritual performance, and commemorative rites in particular, are arguably the most crucial political acts the mappurondo communities can undertake, especially in their effort to retain ideological control of the past (cf. Hoskins 1987). Being mappurondo entails a commitment not only to an ancestral past but to ritual performance as such. Ritual performance, in this light, is the only way to reproduce the community.

Yet any tradition of commemorative ritual necessarily has reenactment as its central principle and problem. We know that traditions can be thoroughly reworked, invented, and reinvented; for that reason we see commemorative reenactment as a fundamental means for conjuring the past, for establishing authentic or authoritative links with the past, and for regulating its debatability (Appadurai 1981; Handler and Linnekin 1984; Hobsbawm and Ranger 1983; Hymes 1981). Commemorative tradition can in this way provide a community with a comforting sense of its own continuity and place in the world.[7] But it also fosters a sense of obligation: reenactment is one of its moral entailments. Ritual performance puts the ongoingness of tradition, however illusory, on show.

At the same time, reenactment works back upon tradition, not only in the obvious sense of reproducing it (however imperfectly), but in organizing its discourse. If a tradition of commemorative ritual entails reenactment, then ceremonial discourse must be edited, so to speak, in such a way that it can be effectively remembered, reenacted, and commemorated (cf. Havelock 1963, 1986; Lord 1960; Ong 1977; Yates 1966). Such discourse must awaken memory and celebrate it. Further, the scene of commemorative reenactment can be shown to occupy a place in the narrative and lyric configurations of ritual discourse (cf. Vance 1979). With these issues in mind, I want to take a brief look at how the commemorative discourse and sociality of pangngae constitute themselves through violence and song. Indeed, the ritual itself is a narrative construction that traces a movement from violence to commemoration and the regeneration of the performing community.

Pangngae, we have seen, constructs the world around polarities of Us and Them, so to speak. The self-defining and self-fashioning festivity of pangngae, I would argue, must conjure a demonized figure whose subjection and mortification are essential to the manufacture and hierarchical ordering of social difference. My point is that the commemorative discourse of pangngae requires a demonic other whose function is to help bring into being a textual or representational code suitable for reproducing the mappurondo polity (cf. Folena 1989). The taxonomic violence of creating social others is intrinsic to the commemorative process at issue here. Taking an enemy head or its surrogate, in my view, is an enacted allegory of this representational violence. This physical violence provides a palpability that discursive violence cannot achieve, yet it does so at the cost of concealing its origins. Heads and coconuts are iconic deformations and displacements of an originary and unacknowledgeable representational violence.

McKinley (1976), of course, does not see it this way. In his analysis, the headhunters' violence is the solution, or rather a resolution of existential contradictions emanating from the structures of social life. The "Other" is a problem, a threat to human order, a reminder of the group's social limits. Subjection and incorporation of the Other erase the social difference McKinley believes to be so troubling. In the scheme I am proposing, the headhunters' social order thrives on the *production* of difference, not its obliteration. Bringing the trophied remnant of violence back into the settlement does not strike me as an effort to make enemies friendly. To the contrary, it appears to be a way to cast enmity in terms favorable to the headhunters' community.

Pangngae, as I have noted, appears to have had but circumstantial connections to feuding and warfare. The predatory violence of headhunting is not a consequence of historical realpolitik. Rather, political realities form the theater in which ritual headhunting takes place. Those realities have left a trace on pangngae, to be sure. And I think that there can be no question that ritual headhunting made its mark in the practical relations between upland and lowland communities. Yet given its ritual and commemorative form, the violence of pangngae is violence of another order, something driven by and constituted through its own ideals and functions.

The taking of heads, I should emphasize once more, was not a solution to regional political dilemmas. The purpose of bringing a trophy head back to the community was to astonish and awe, to mark the violence as exemplary and ritually significant. This dread relic, this grotesque, did more than fascinate and trouble. Rather, it served as a mnemonic object and privileged icon for the commemorative work of communal self-representation. The violence of headhunting could be storied . . . storied in such a way that its commemorative retelling or reenactment led to the reproduction of the communal body. Headhunting was and is a form of memorable violence that can be recollected and narrated with regenerative effect.

I do not mean to suggest that the violence of headhunting works as a mnemonic device or technique in the conventional sense of these terms. It is not an antidote to forgetfulness. It is not equivalent to the formulary devices used by rhapsodists and rhetoricians in oral cultures (Ong 1977, but cf. Finnegan 1988). What I do think the violence of headhunting has offered is a place to begin. Taking a head has been a good way to start up a story of difference and domination. Showing the grotesque trophies from these astonishing, violent events downriver, calling forth a gathering to see heads and hear tales about them, is a way to convene the community and affirm its ongoing presence. In this sense, violence serves, in the words of Eugene Vance (1979:383), as a "generative force in the production of its own discourse."

The ritualized ambush and beheading of a victim downstream, I want to suggest, is already an act of commemoration. It does not take place outside of the commemorative frame. Taking the head of someone downriver within the context of pangngae is an act of memory. There is no need to resort to ideas about bi-presence or consubstantiation, as I once did, to grasp that reenactment confers a kind of legitimacy on both the past and the present. Mimetic stagings of the headhunt display the ongoingness of the community and its moral tradition. Reenactments of pangngae convey a sense of collective survivorship, and with it, a sense of power, especially in striking down an adversary. As Canetti (1978:227) remarks, "There is nothing that can be compared with it, and there is no moment which demands more repetition."

Scenes and images of physical violence are at the heart of this commemorative rite. They are there as a transcoding of representational violence, as precondition to festive and triumphant sociality, and as a display of the community's enduring presence. But this violence, as I noted earlier in this book, has a shifting and ambiguous relationship to regional history. Why headhunt in the political terrain of the past? Perhaps it is to claim and control an autonomous history in an effort to evade or resist the contemporary order. Perhaps the discourse of Indonesian citizenship allows the mappurondo communities no way to overcome grief, no entry into manhood. Ideas about communal regeneration—objectified in the facts and metaphors of fertility, growth, and abundance, and of diurnal and nocturnal cycles—no doubt provide a partial rationale for ritual violence. If the commemorative act is the principal means of regenerating communal sociality and presence, then the community must look to the local past to find an event suitable for recollection and reenactment. It is one of the ironies of pangngae that the mimetic passion for sameness threatens to aggravate the incongruities between ideology and circumstance, between the past and the here-and-now. One wonders whether the rites of pangngae afford any means of working with this incongruity.

As the ritual action moves back to the village and toward a close, mimesis and memory displace violence. If pangngae begins in violence and ends in commemoration, choruses must sing of the ceremony's commemorative purpose and its ephemerality. The commemorative functions of pangngae find clearest expression in the sumengo tomatua, which frames every liturgical act and series of song exchange:

Iamo tolena	That's it, that is just what
naporaena debata	the spirits favor and expect
kema'patemboki' tole	when we do it again, that's it

The idea of pleasing the spirits sacralizes commemoration and disguises the political and social interests that are advanced by the narrative of the headhunt. By appealing to these transcendant forces, the song authorizes the ma'denna and kelonoson, the ma'paisun chant, and the sumengo exchanges, and in so doing legitimates their representational and illocutionary dimensions. In short, all choral and liturgical genres are reenactments, whereas mamose speeches are not. However formulaic they may be, the latter are indices and examples of spontaneity and contingency, and need not be repeated or memorized in subsequent rituals. (In fact, it would be wrong to do so.)

As we have seen already, violence yields to festivity. Celebratory excess emerges as a key theme in pangngae, and the choruses sing about singing as the headhunt ends in song:

Ma'palisu inde tondo'	This hamlet swirls round and around
ma'batu lampa' banua	the dwelling's signs are cut in stone
tamonda disapukoi	unbroken unfallen spirit
Nakua oninna gandang	It is said the voice of the drum
pebalinna sulim bulo	the echo of the golden flute
angki tamonda iponi	that we play are never broken
Mara'mo kami' sengoki	Oh it's too bad for us our song
dipasampe langal loko	put up above in the rice barn
dianna tama talukun	put away inside the rice bin

Mimesis and the regeneration of community, in this rite, involves a restitution of the voice silenced by labor and grief. In celebrating an absent violence, the community hears its own voice, its presence filling the void of the present.

Yet such commemorative festivity, vibrant with song and laughter, can stir up eddies of nostalgia and loneliness, a sharpened sense of longing, loss, and absence. Such feelings, called *rio-rio,* are customarily felt by older singers and spectators. Commemorative song may remind them of the rituals of their youth, rituals peopled by friends now dead. For persons such as these, one senses that the community's enduring presence, fostered by commemorative ritual, creates rather aching reflections on their place in the world. Others may find that the ceremonies allow them to recapture their youth, and still others to live up to the desires and accomplishments of their elders. My point is that the participants in commemorative rites are positioned in different ways to the project of regenerating the community through violence and song.

To move on, then, let me summarily remark that commemoration obliges us to consider both its subjects and its objects, the commemorating and the commemorated. Commemoration cannot be dissociated from the sociality of remembering, nor can it be dissociated from the events that it recollects and reenacts. The stability or instability of commemorative tradition, and its stabilizing or destabilizing effects are largely empirical issues. What I should underscore in the case of pangngae is that the discourse of this ritual leads to the narrative and liturgical genesis of the mappurondo polity in each village.

Commemoration and Other Ritual Themes

The community's practical commitment to ancestral tradition rests on the principle and problem of reenactment. Failure to hold pangngae would disrupt the moral coherence of the mappurondo polities and threaten to prevent the communities from convening and reproducing themselves as social and ideological bodies. But the obligation to hold the ritual brings the mappurondo communities up against desa officers, police, and school administrators, authorities who usually sanction such events with great reluctance. Meeting doubt and censure from such figures can only remind the mappurondo communities of the autonomy they no longer have, a lost autonomy that pangngae paradoxically celebrates. Still, the mappurondo settlements see their fate tied up in this ritual, just as it is tied up in the encompassing state order.

Because the ritual headhunt mediates "official" order and disorder in the mappurondo communities, we will do well to examine how the commemorative surfaces of pangngae refract a range of communal themes and interests. Like other rituals, pangngae is a theater in which the drama of prestige politics can be played out: villagers exchange gifts of meat and other foodstuffs, swap valuables for praise, and make sacrificial exchanges with the spirit-world—all opportunities for advancing the status of the individual or the household, all arenas for contest, discord, and conciliation. Yet headhunting ritual has special significance as the discursive means for the communal management of mourning, masculinity, and communal prosperity. Altogether, then, it is a crossroads for several distinct social projects (cf. R. Rosaldo 1984).

The work of the Rosaldos has left me convinced that their Ilongot acquaintances found the celebratory discourse following a headhunter's assault more significant than the act of violence per se. They found strength, vitality, and a sense of well-being in commemorative speech and song. The songs called *buayat,* in particular, were the most basic source of *liget* (anger and passion) and, in most instances, were instrumental in casting off grief and distress (M. Rosaldo 1980:54–57; R. Rosaldo 1980:163 and 1984:190). The celebratory song and oratory of the Ilongot are obvious rhetorical acts used to manage emotions, social relations, and violence, and the commemorative discourse of pangngae, in this sense, has much in common with Ilongot headhunting celebrations. Yet one key difference is clear: in the current social order, the discourse of pangngae does not incite physical violence. Unlike the buayat, the songs of pangngae do not stir up turbulent feelings. Rather, they amount to an aesthetic reformulation of dynamics now suppressed in current ritual practice. The commemorative lyrics of the sumengo, for example, constitute a running commentary on what should take place in pangngae, but cannot. In short, the mappurondo villagers show themselves to be contemplative lyricists and playwrights of ritual violence. Their ritual has the shape and feel of Brechtian epic theater, where the goal is to force disjuncture and open up reflexive space between representation and reality.

As previous discussion has shown, pangngae no longer sparks the cathartic violence that might allow someone to vent anguish over recently deceased friends and kin. Rage, of course, is not the only way people experience grief. A sense of heaviness or passivity, and feelings of sorrow, make up a burden that lingers on long after anguished rage has run its course. Laden with familiar memories and meanings, and calling forth an enlivening kind of sociality, the commemorative songs have a real potential to provoke feelings of relief. Singing, laughing, feasting, and speechmaking can go a long way in taking people's minds off their sorrows and in helping them get on with life. At the same time, the themes and topics of commemorative celebrations run counter to the moods, sentiments, and conceptions associated with death and grief. The celebration of pangngae also demonstrates the capacity of communal tradition to endure, to prevail when those who have wielded it pass away. The death of an elder, for example, not only stirs an emotional crisis among the bereaved, but marks a potential loss of knowledge and a loosening of authoritative ties to the past. Every death in the village's adult population threatens to orphan the community and cause its moral foundation to diminish. It is a wound to the social body and a wound to ada' mappurondo itself. The reenactment of pangngae requires village men to pledge themselves to communal tradition and to prove their readiness as ones who know and can guard ada' mappurondo. By demonstrating the surviving power and continued well-being of village tradition, mappurondo headhunting ritual fosters a sense of moral and cultural continuity, and socially vests it in the ranks of men and the ideology of manhood.

By the same token, the ritual is an outcome and index of village prosperity. Reciprocal exchange with the spirits, mediated through ceremonial sacrifices of rice and meat, and through the headhunters' oaths, helps propel the fertility and well-being of the village. But understood as a gesture of providential favor, prosperity is contingent, nonetheless, on the commemorative work of pangngae:

Iamo tolena	That's it, that is just what
naporaena debata	the spirits favor and expect
kema'patemboki' tole	when we do it again, that's it

Further still, cosmographic idioms and the polemics of upstream-downstream encounters give the discourse of prosperity a political dimension that stretches beyond the village. The commemorative violence of pangngae, in this light, is simultaneously a display and a bid for divine favor in a threatening and unstable world. Reenacting pangngae, very broadly, links social and ideological reproduction together with the fertility and abundance of the settlement. The commemorative project, then, not only provides a means for surmounting grief and death, but legitimates and brings into being the continuity of the community (cf. Bloch and Parry 1982; Hertz 1960).

Although pangngae figures significantly in the experience of men and youths, it is not, strictly speaking, a rite of passage for males. The ritual does not bring about an irrevocable change in a person's social status. It is not obligatory for a male to take part in pangngae as a tobarani for him to become an adult. Nor is a man's participation as a headhunter a precondition to seeking a wife. Rather, the ritual produces and celebrates an exemplary image of masculinity that can help a man understand and recognize his place in the world. As he moves from childhood, through adolescence, and on to adulthood, his unfolding sense of self and his claim to knowledge and experience will find measure in the headhunt (cf. Crapanzano 1992; R. Rosaldo 1980). The commemorative discourse of the ritual, then, evokes and ratifies a notion of manhood, and connects it to the reproduction of the mappurondo polity in each village. The commemorative sociality of the ritual, with its implicit forms of hierarchy (manifest not only in songs and singing but also in the way the community gazes upon the headhunter), becomes a coveted experience, the object of men's envy. Thus the commemorative discourse of the ritual carefully elicits and constrains a form of envy that in other contexts might be quite threatening to social order. Women, as well, are subject to the commemorative scene, where they are figured as singers and adulators. The biographical path of women, then, necessarily takes them through moments where they celebrate manhood for the sake of regenerating the polity.

What I hope is clear in the preceding pages is that the headhunt is plotted in such a way that commemoration displaces violence. The commemorative discourse of pangngae creates a sense of closure—however illusory and infirm—confirming its plot, its structure, its purpose, and its themes, even as it exposes them to the contingencies and political interests of the moment. Closure, as Barbara Herrnstein Smith (1968:2) reminds us, "is not always a matter of endings." The headhunt does not merely stop or come to an end, but finds possibilities for completion and coherence in the ongoing work of commemoration. Following Smith's speculations on closure, we can perhaps say that the discourse of pangngae situates violence and memory within a structure of gratification. Posed against the indeterminant, the contingent, the incoherent, and the open-ended, the ritual forms an enclosure where procedure and will can produce designed effects, as for example in the tension and resolution of mourning and the vow. And although we may associate commemoration with recollection and looking backward, it is also prospective—it offers a structure of anticipation. Memory—as a form of sociality and as a form of something remembered—is kept in motion.

Violence animates commemoration; commemoration animates violence. The twin-faced structure is also essential to mappurondo social and political order, in the sense that it legitimates ritually remembered violence as a source for the community's anxious claims to autonomy. Yet mimetic efforts to reproduce this remembered violence and its social effects take for their model not a scene of primordial violence, but, rather, prior reenactments. The commemorative rite becomes subject to emulation. Within this context, villagers exploit discursive ambiguities and transcodings for individual and communal ends. Played off of ever-changing social and historical circumstances, stagings of pangngae edit as well as perpetuate the collective memory of the headhunt.[8] Every headhunting rite is a select and open-ended version of itself, motivated by and placed in relation to the immediate goals of the community and its members. In short, every ritual performance is situated. For this reason, I now turn to the matter of the variability, instability, and open-endedness of pangngae, with the hope of discovering how the discourse of ritual violence is produced and reproduced in a climate of censure, doubt, and social difference.

7

The Songs of the ToSalu and the ToIssilita'

The Horizons of Textuality and Interpretation, 1983–85

The commemorative discourse of pangngae, the way it narrativizes and immortalizes violence while reconstituting the community, is not invariant. For many anthropologists, such as Roy Rappaport (1979), the most obvious aspects of ritual have been its invariability, formality, and liturgical order. Yet in my two years of work on headhunting ritual, I invariably encountered difference, variation, and change in ceremonial performance and discourse. As I moved from settlement to settlement, and then returned to them in the following year, I began to grasp how ritual speech and song are deeply circumstanced. The instability and variability of ritual forms, it seems to me, are symptoms of the immediate social purposes and interests of different groups living in different times and places, a reminder that the projects and themes of ritual discourse are always situated. As a result, thinking about ritual language and tradition as idealized and invariant structures seems less useful than examining the ways communities make and authorize "ritual texts" for *ongoing* projects of interpretive and pragmatic work.

Not surprisingly, one of the most basic lines of social difference in Bambang found reprise in the headhunt: that between the ToSalu and ToIssilita'. Friends in the mappurondo communities were quick to point out several liturgical or musical differences that distinguished ToIssilita' performances from ToSalu ones. They acknowledged, for example, that the sumengo melodies sung by one of the two groups differed from those sung by the other.

And as regards liturgical action, it happens that the ToIssilita' rites always included the anointing of the headhunters by the tomatuatonda', whereas the ToSalu had dispensed with this gesture. Acknowledging these distinctive ways of conducting the ritual served both ToSalu and ToIssilita' in the work of mutual definition. Cultural differences served to mark long-standing social differences. Thus the headhunting rites of pangngae did nothing to bridge the mistrust between "the people of the ground" (ToIssilita') and "the people of the river" (ToSalu), a mistrust that stretched back over a century to the first ToSalu raids on Bambang.

Christians and the sole Muslim household in Bambang, I should remind readers, do not observe pangngae, and their local strength and influence has much to do with the waning of pangngae. For example, the ToSalu villages of Limba, Masoso, and Rantelemo are predominantly Christian communities. Pangngae last took place in Limba in 1953, and in Masoso in 1969. By 1984, only one hamlet in Rantelemo still ran pangngae, and then, only sporadically; the handful of mappurondo households there preferred to join in celebrations in the neighboring village of Karakean. Mappurondo ritual traditions in these settlements are moribund.

The scale and enthusiasm with which people conduct pangngae elsewhere in Bambang directly reflect the results of the rice harvest. For instance, the rice crop planted in August 1983 and harvested in January 1984 was a failure throughout the watershed. Devastating losses to rats and disease created an unusually severe subsistence shortfall. That year, the headhunting ceremonies in the ToIssilita' settlements of Minanga and Rantepalado were muted by disappointment and worry. The mappurondo community at Salutabang responded to the same crisis not by holding maringngangi, as did Minanga and Rantepalado, but by staging *mahhaha banne,* literally, "putting blood on the seed." Involving a greater sacrifice of meat than does maringngangi (minimally, a pig), this version of pangngae seeks to solicit blessings from the debata for the yet unplanted rice crop. By way of contrast to the crop failures of 1984, the 1985 harvest was an abundant one, for both ToSalu and ToIssilita' communities. The headhunting rites that followed the harvest that year were exuberant events, marked by large numbers of youths taking part as topangngae and by hosting guests from other villages. Indeed, the good fortune of the mappurondo communities in Minanga, Rantepalado, Saludengen, and Salutabang was especially striking that year: no one died.[1]

That must have come as a relief, for there were other disturbing circumstances and events that were on peoples' minds around this time. The murder of a villager caught up in a family dispute in Minanga in 1981 had repercussions throughout Bambang. No one had come forward to admit to the wrongdoing, and no one had made an effort to calm the debata for this startling crime. Minanga was a community on edge and under suspicion. Pua' Kallang, the Indona Bambang, died in Rantepalado during June 1983. Some whispered that his death and the crop failures of 1984 had been brought on by the crime that had shaken Bambang and that had so seriously breached the juridical tradition of adat tuo (discussed in Chapter 2). During the pangngae celebrations of 1984 and 1985 in Rantepalado, Pua' Kallang's son Dessibulo would speak, for the first time, as the probable successor to this traditional office.

Upriver, the rains of March and April 1984 brought about more than a dozen landslides. The worst of these occurred in May just below Salutabang, when a mountainside slipped into the river, burying scores of terraces and coffee gardens and flooding still others beneath the lake of water that then formed behind the fallen earth and rock. Searching for some cause behind their misfortune, villagers in Salutabang uncovered two cases of incest within the Christian community, and sent one of the wrongdoers away from the settlement with a formal curse:

Wrapped in thorns and burnt
Wrapped in thorns and washed away
Banished to places where there is no adat

Debate over the incest cases reopened wounds between kin-based social factions and between the mappurondo and Christian camps.

Government initiatives persuaded those in Minanga to plant two rice crops in 1983, in April and November.[2] Both crops were failures, but the mappurondo community at Minanga felt obliged to run pangngae after each harvest, in October 1983 and June 1984. The agricultural initiative thus had the effect of accelerating the timing of social and ceremonial events pursued by the mappurondo households. Many were apprehensive about the decision to hold pangngae that often. Yet, the experiment was tried once again in 1985, with the mappurondo community in Rantepalado taking part, too. Crop losses that time ran between 40 and 80 percent of the normal yield.[3] Along with this particular initiative, the government encouraged farmers to experiment with new rice strains, expensive fertilizers, and new cash crops, like chocolate. In short, the 1983–85 period found the mappurondo communities—especially those in ToIssilita' settlements—testing the limits and effects of economic rationalization.

The same period saw the civil administration launch programs to spur compliance with tax laws, to distribute ID cards, and to regulate the coffee trade. Over and against these desa-wide programs, there were events and developments that sustained the long-standing tensions between the ToSalu and ToIssilita' districts. The person appointed as the new Kepala Desa (desa head) in 1984 was a ToIssilita' man from Rantepalado. Replacing an officer of ToSalu descent, the new Kepala Desa brought the political leadership of Bambang back home to Rantepalado, much to the delight of the ToIssilita'. Not long after, the settlement won project funding for the construction of a small bridge. A few kilometers away, the ToIssilita' settlement of Saludengen was selected as the site of an agricultural survey sponsored by the Provincial Governor's Office. Each participating household would receive a small stipend. The ToSalu, for their part, did not see much in the way of favors, nor did they realize significant assistance in the wake of the landslides that caused burdensome agricultural losses in Salutabang and Masoso. The ToSalu consoled themselves with the expansion and improvement of the marketplace at Rantelemo, right in the heart of ToSalu territory—a project initiated under the former desa administration. The market bred new interests and new strategies among the ToSalu, and began to draw them away, if only slightly, from the market activity in Mambi. The ToIssilita', meanwhile, continued their trade principally in Mambi.

The social and political differences between the ToIssilita' and the ToSalu led to no violent disputes but did sustain the mutual wariness, dissatisfactions, and grudges of past decades. Desa administration and the organization of the local Geraja Toraja Mamasa—divided into the ToIssilita' synod called *Bambang Hilir* (Bambang Downstream) and the ToSalu one, *Bambang Hulu* (Bambang Upstream)—provided new institutional contexts for the expression of these social and historical tensions. At the same time, the ToSalu and ToIssilita' each had their own internal strains and interests. The ToIssilita' settlements in Minanga and Rantepalado, for example, had locked horns in a land dispute, a dispute that seemed to aggravate competing claims to political ascendancy in Bambang's history. The fine harvest of 1985 allowed Minanga to host an entourage of mappurondo leaders from Rantepalado during pangngae. But this gesture toward seeking a resolution of the dispute failed. Saludengen remained isolated and closed during these years, hosting no one during pangngae. Nonetheless, Saludengen sent a chorus of singers to Minanga, at the request of the latter, to help enliven the pangngae ceremonies there in 1985 (see below). Upstream in the ToSalu area, villagers from Salutabang provoked comment as they continued to expand their land ownership outside of the settlement, obtaining terraces and gardens in Masoso, Rantelemo, Limba, and as far away as Rantebulahan. Like their ToIssilita' counterparts downstream, Salutabang hosted ToSalu guests from Ulumambi and Salubulo during pangngae ceremonies of 1985, with an interest in promoting or activating alliances between distant friends and kin.

Although not all of these tensions and concerns found direct expression in local headhunting ritual, they certainly offered an ambient sense of whether Bambang was doing well or not, and in 1984 it was not. Mappurondo villagers in most instances read misfortune and conflict in their particular locales, and in Bambang more generally, as the outcome of a crisis in ancestral traditions. The state of ritual tradition was on people's minds, all the more so with an ethnographer trying to fathom their concerns.

The ToIssilita' of Minanga and Rantepalado

Villagers throughout Bambang acknowledge the ToIssilita' settlement of Minanga as the place where ritual speech and song have their origin. The name Minanga itself means "rivermouth." Used metaphorically it connotes the mouth of tradition. Whether by virtue of historical fact or a wish to vest songs with the authority of tradition, ToSalu and ToIssilita' all agreed that Minanga was the birthplace for the songs and liturgies of pangngae. In support of this claim, the ToSalu point to the language of their own ceremonies: all the songs and liturgies of pangngae are in ToIssilita' dialect, a dialect the ToSalu consider noble and refined. But when it comes to headhunting ritual, Minanga, ironically, has lost its voice. Having dwindled to a community of less than 35 households, the mappurondo collective has lost many of its knowledgeable singers and ritual leaders to the church. Singers are few, and the repertoire of sumengo is quite small (less than half of what may be encountered elsewhere), oriented now to themes of adornment, envy, and celebration and lacking signs of violence. Indeed, Minanga celebrated pangngae in 1983 and 1984 with just tambolâ and drums—there was no head.

The first time I ever took part in pangngae was at Minanga in 1983. In response to my interest in the songs of pangngae, an elderly woman explained to me that she and other villagers had forgotten the tune to the ToIssilita' sumengo, a tune remembered only in Saludengen. Claiming to recall *lyrics* from their past, the singers instead follow the ToSalu sumengo *melody* (see Figures A and B, Appendix III). In fact, the most prominent singers among the four or five tomantokko at Minanga are an aging mother and a 40-year-old son of ToSalu birth and upbringing. They are not excellent

singers as such, but they do have a knack for remembering lyrics and leading a song. In a sense, the sumengo tradition at Minanga has coalesced
around this pair of singers.

The melody and lyric play of the sumengo together form a site where
cultural difference, loss, and domination find articulation. Have the ToIssilita'
at Minanga appropriated ToSalu songs for their own ends? Or have ToSalu
songs appropriated the ToIssilita' memory? There is some truth in each perspective. What is clear to me is that people of ToIssilita' descent at Minanga
find irony in the fact that their village, which holds the authority to forge
sacred speech and song, has become forgetful and stammering, and obliged
to borrow the traditions of the ToSalu. Relations between the ToIssilita'
and ToSalu are not so antagonistic that the "cultural exchange" of the sort
I am describing cannot go on. After all, the ToSalu themselves say that the
songs that they sing in pangngae have roots in ToIssilita' tradition. In comparing lyric repertoires from the different villages, I found that Minanga
showed vastly greater overlap with ToSalu communities than with other
ToIssilita' settlements.[4] In this light, it seems that singers at Minanga were
not so much putting ToIssilita' lyrics to a ToSalu tune, as refiguring ToIssilita'
lyric tradition and the ToIssilita' past through ToSalu texts-in-performance.

The sumengo performances at Minanga tended to be faltering and spirit-
less. Songs fell apart, voices cracked or went astray, and seldom did more
than two or three people form a chorus. Through 1984 I had the impression that the polity celebrated in pangngae had withered to the point where
there were few singers and little to sing about, and the situation was not
much different at Rantepalado, where the mappurondo community had de-
clined to just 30 households. Tobarani returned to the village with tambolâ
only; the celebration took place without a trophy head, and villagers did not
bother to perform the ma'denna or kelonoson, the songs that celebrated
the violent feats of the topangngae. The community as a whole no longer
provided foodstuffs for dipandebarani, leaving it to the families of the topangngae to obtain sufficient rice and meat to honor their husbands, sons,
or brothers. The repertoire of choral songs in Rantepalado was exceedingly
spare, and it usually fell to men and guests from other villages to perform
them. The key songleader was none other than the ToSalu man who figured
so prominently in Minanga's celebrations. Not surprisingly, the songs owed
far more to ToSalu traditions than to ToIssilita' ones.

For mappurondo communities in ebb and disarray, holding pangngae
runs the risk of further demoralizing the polity by exposing weakened communal bonds. In celebration of the reassuring harvest of 1985, people at
Minanga made a gesture toward revitalizing and reclaiming village tradi-

tion. In a calculated effort to retrieve the forgotten melody of the ToIssilita' sumengo, Ambe Assi' and the other mappurondo leaders asked elders in Saludengen to send a chorus of singers to take part in festivities. Six young Saludengen men took part in Minanga's ritual, lending their voices to an exuberant evening of song. Just as striking was the effort of Ambe Dido, the young babalako, in writing down lyrics, not to the communal sumengo, but to the kelonoson and ma'denna, two songs that he wished, or was expected, to lead. As we shall see, this was not the first time someone had decided to write down the ritual speech and song in the mappurondo communities. At Minanga, however, this effort to resist forgetfulness, to salvage an autochthonous tradition and authority, was—in light of the murder just four years earlier—a nervous acknowledgment of regenerative violence. Just as in Rantepalado, the kelonoson and ma'denna had not been performed in Minanga during 1983 and 1984, a further sign of the erasure of violence from the idealized representations of pangngae in these two communities. Consulting elder men in his village, Ambe Dido began a project of reclamation that conjured once more the violent acts of the topangngae.

The ToSalu at Salutabang

In contrast to Minanga and Rantepalado, Salutabang is something of a "frontier" settlement. Once the site of a ToIssilita' village, the area fell into the hands of the ToSalu around 1870. In the view of contemporary ToSalu, village history dates back to those first settlers—five or six generations back, roughly speaking. Thus, the community is historically and genealogically shallower than the ToIssilita' settlements downstream. In 1984, just under 60 percent of the villagers professed to be Christian, leaving 54 homesteads oriented to ada' mappurondo. As in most every village, tensions between Christians and the mappurondo community arise from time to time. When relations are calm, villagers say the settlement is *kalebu tellu*, "round like an egg" (that is, characterized by external and internal unity); when they are strained, the village is *kalebu lemo*, "round like an orange" (characterized by a surface unity masking internal divisiveness).

Political and ritual authority in Salutabang are seriously eroded. During the past 75 years, the position of tomatuatonda' has often been in dispute, and in 1985 at least four ritual offices went vacant. Many local specialists have converted to Christianity without passing on their knowledge of various household rites or their authority to stage them. In fact, for rituals other

Fig. 20. *Ambe Dido, a young babalako, looks on during* pangngae *celebrations in 1985, a notebook of lyrics by his feet.*

than pangngae, the mappurondo community at Salutabang often has to "borrow" ritual specialists from other ToSalu villages. Even then, some mappurondo households are reluctant to host the more elaborate women's ceremonies for fear of making liturgical errors thàt would invite the wrath of the debata.

History has left the bonds of communal tradition and polity at Salutabang discernibly loose, a situation sometimes requiring the personal ends and narrow initiatives of individuals to serve broader collective interests. Pursuing his vow made earlier in the year, Ambe Tasi' sponsored *ma'pa-tuhu'i botto*, "having the hamlets follow," in 1985. The extensive feasting connected with this particular headhunt did much to advance Ambe Tasi's status in the community. At the same time, the ritual kept the community in motion with respect to its ceremonial obligations. Yet missing in this celebration was any effort to make a mamose speech with the purpose of publicly dedicating oneself to the village and mappurondo tradition. Interest in speechmaking was little stronger than it had been the year before. That year, there was but one, rather inchoate speech: assuming the enraged look befitting a tobarani, the man rushed his opening words, got tongue-tied, clenched the handle of his machete for a moment, and then abruptly sat down.

I have already hinted that writing and reading are becoming significant features in mappurondo ritual life, and, of course, the current demoralization of the mappurondo communities derives in part from ideas about written texts. Lacking a book of sacred scripture, mappurondo villagers cannot claim to be inheritors to a legitimate religious tradition as defined by Christians and Muslims. Although sacred texts and textual practices have provided a stick with which to beat local ancestral tradition, a few people in the mappurondo community have determined that writing may afford them rescue. This response stands in real contrast to attitudes and tabus that lingered into the 1970s, views that prohibited the use of writing, kerosene lamps, radios, or tape recorders at ceremonial occasions.[5] Several elders, for example, were eager for me to write a comprehensive account of their ritual practices, turn it into a book, and thereby legitimate their religion. Others, most of them under 35 years of age, take a different interest in writing: they have begun to write down materials so as to be able to memorize them and perform them. That is to say, villagers write and read materials with oral performance in mind (cf. Fabian 1992).

No one in Salutabang, for example, uses writing with the idea of preserving or storing ritual texts. In fact, writing in no way guarantees the accumulation and safeguard of traditional materials. One of my greatest disappointments was discovering that a young Christian woman, Indo Kenias, had compiled several notebooks of ritual song and speech during her school years, only to have used the paper later to make house decorations. Relaxing in her home one day I gazed up at the ribbons of paper-cuttings that festooned the rafters. Looking more closely at these doily-like decorations, I recognized the remnant inscriptions strewn through them. That day I muttered something about loss. Looking back, I note that it was but another case in which ritual speech was rendered as adornment.

Some persons have memorized written liturgical texts and then discarded them later. Take the case of Ambe Sope, a man about 30 years of age who had just inherited his father's role as topuppu, the specialist who oversees headhunting ritual in Salutabang. I happened to be there the first time Ambe Sope presided over the ceremonies, in 1984. Throughout the rite he kept looking down at a note pad to his left. Toward the climax of the ritual, he put aside his notes, took an offering up into the loft, and began chanting the ma'paisun to roughly 75 debata, all in the proper sequence. Later that day Ambe Sope said to me, "When I was up in the loft, I could see the names of the debata written in front of my eyes." Although I have no way of being sure, I think his comment is telling evidence that a written text had played a crucial part in his rehearsing and memorizing the performance sometime beforehand. A year later, during his second headhunting ceremony, Ambe Sope worked without a written text of any kind. He was able to recompose the liturgy from memory. Whether he still "saw" the names of the debata before him on that later occasion, I do not know.

Not all ritual specialists learn their materials this way. On another occasion, in another village, I watched a young babalako in his debut, so to speak. This one worked without written notes. An elder sat at his side throughout the ceremonies and prompted him through key performances. When it came time to chant the ma'paisun, for example, the elder was right there, quietly running off the proper names of the debata from memory into the waiting ear of the young babalako. The babalako merely called out each name as it was given to him.

For Ambe Sope, writing played a key part in delivering a sound, smooth, liturgical performance. As the authority in whom liturgical conduct had recently been vested, it was important for him to appear knowing and skilled. It is especially significant, too, that he and other villagers used writing for mastering performances that are considered invariant from one context to the next. But writing did not make these kinds of chants, songs, and speeches invariant. To the contrary, it was their perceived invariance that made them especially suitable for being put into writing. Writing did not provide these genres with a fixity or authority that had been lacking. Rather, writing inhabited seemingly stable and authoritative forms of the "already said."

In Salutabang, no one has bothered to write down the sumengo. The songs remain in oral tradition and are learned, rehearsed, recollected, and improvised in ritual performance. Villagers build up their repertoire of songs simply by listening to the tomantokko and the choruses and singing along. Sumengo performance at Salutabang usually takes the form of a ludic and oftentimes agonistic polylogue between small choruses made up of men or women. (On occasion, a choral group will include both men and women.) The choruses try to outperform one another in what might be termed song duels. The idea is to get the better of another chorus by coming up with a lyric rejoinder, sung loudly and in a manner that "chases" or "steps on" an ongoing performance. Thus, it is not unusual to hear two or three sumengo being performed simultaneously. When several choruses join in, an exuberant, swirling overlay of song fills the ceremonial house. The songs pulse like the buzzing of cicadas, and it is just such moments that bring villagers delight.

In the song play between men and women, no effort is made to sing the songs in any particular order. With the exception of the sumengo tomatua (which figures into the ritual's liturgical sequence), song choice is wholly up to the tomantokko, who use their skills and memories in the tactics of play. The songs do not follow a set narrative line, nor are they performed in set thematic or topical clusters. For instance, I once listened to a chorus of Salutabang men sing about the anguish caused by the headhunters' raid:

Sambanuami tobalu	One homestead the place of widows
satondo'mi ana' bium	one hamlet the place of orphans
santanetemi u'bu'na	one mountain the place of the graves

Meanwhile, a chorus of women sang in praise of the headhunters:

Ta'bu sure' mane dadi	Striped colored cane just coming up
mane lulangam allona	just starting to reach for the sun
paneteanna kaloe'	the parrots' dance along the branch

Before these singers had finished, yet another group of women started up with a song about the felling of a victim:

Indu' ajangan di rante	Black sugar palm on the wide plain
lao natotoi london	its fronds hewn by the cockerel
nababa ma'kulu-kulu	carried by the kulu-kulu [an omen bird]

And while that song continued, the chorus of men performed a flattering rejoinder to the first group of women. Picking up the reference to parrots, the men invited the women to keep singing:

Kaloe' sambali' Manda'	Parrots over there on the Manda'
pentia' lambe'ko mai	fly long and far on the way here
lakiperapi onimmu	we're going to take up your song

Perhaps these songs remain unwritten at Salutabang because they offer the antithesis of that which is desired in liturgical speech. Although the sumengo appear to form a body of stable and easily recalled lyric sets, they are performed in improvisatory play. They are caught up in the disjunctiveness of the game, and are aimed at producing difference and inequality between choruses (cf. de Certeau 1984; Lévi-Strauss 1966:32). They thrive in the din of voices and drums. The liturgical chants and songs conjoin the officiating entourage of men (led by the topuppu and the tomatuatonda') with the collectivity—as in the antiphonal repetitions of the ma'denna—or effect communion between the human and spirit worlds—as in the ma'paisun. Liturgy demands silence: drums may not sound, sumengo may not be sung, and the throng must remain quiet unless joining in antiphonal response to the entourage of elders.

When it comes to sumengo performance, it is play, not writing, that sustains the individual and communal memory. Remembering becomes a mode of play and tactical maneuver, as singers try to gain advantage over one another. The immediacies of song-play, meanwhile, gather up and deploy remembered scenes from the headhunt. Apprenticeship and leadership in choral struggle count as important poles of experience and sociality. Yet the fundamental tension in song exchange lies between men and women. In its most common (or stereotypic) form, the agonistic play of memory and voice pits groups of husbands and groups of wives against one another. Following de Certeau (1984:22-24), we can perhaps look to sumengo exchanges for schemes and repertoires of action that are useful precisely because they are detached from the complexities that entangle men and women in everyday life. They "teach the tactics possible within a given (social) system" (de Certeau 1984:23). There are strong signs here that the tactics of song play are the tactics of gender play. And this leads us to see that in Salutabang, it is gender play that sustains the communal memory. Commemorative representations of the headhunt issue from the fleeting struggles and inequalities of husbands and wives locked in contest.

The song exchange can sometimes have an edge to it. For example, it is not uncommon to hear insults, teasing, bragging, and parody when the ToSalu sing the sumengo. These songs are invariably done in solo style, that is, without a chorus. Here a tomantokko calls another a coward:

Kemalallem-malallengko	If you're worried about something
turu' lelenni boko'na	always follow behind a back
tindo'i pessailena	keep looking over your shoulder

Another song cautions the listener against conceit and arrogance:

Kamma'ko tasibarinni	Take it easy, we are both small
tasiunu' tasikapa'	each has spinners, each has cotton
tasitannum baju-baju	both of us are weaving some shirts

Pushed too far, a singer might improvise an insult:

Mattangko kubeta tula'	Quiet down, I won at talking
mattangko kutalo kada	quiet down, I won at speaking
umpateka' langngam rindim	I'll make the lizard climb the walls
upande sassa bosi	and feed you gecko shit

It was only in Salutabang that I heard such aggressive lyrics, and it was there, too, that I heard sumengo parodies. The common way to parodize the songs (and the ritual itself) is to make a grotesque of sumengo vocal style by exaggerating pitch and vibrato. Singers will even, occasionally, have some fun by asking for water or coffee to the tune of the sumengo's solo line.

In my experience, it was usually women who delivered aggressive, parodic, or humorous verses. Certainly some of their humor was made in innocent fun, yet at other times one had the sense that the singer was disparaging the entire event. Although I never got to the bottom of it, this seemed to be the case during the 1985 pangngae ceremonies. While taking part in a'dasan, Indo Gahu, the most prominent *sando baine* (or, specialist in women's ritual) in the village, sang in a manner that was as wild and mocking as it was deliberate. Later that week, her singing brought her censure. As the evening of umpaningoi ulunna ("playing with the head") drew to a close, a houseful of villagers and guests gathered at Indo Gahu's home to sing and eat. Indo Gahu resumed her parody of headhunting song. Not much time had gone by when a guest from Ulumambi, who herself was a sando baine, was "taken by the debata" (*diala debata*) into trance. After dancing for a few moments the woman collapsed in a swoon and began to say something (see Figure 21). People crowded close around her, fanning her face and listening intently to the strange words coming from her mouth. Whispers of "Mandar! She's speaking Mandar!" swept through the room.[6] A man listening to the entranced woman conveyed the spirits' critique: the debata were angry with those belonging to the house; they had shown little respect for the ritual taking place. Shamed and warned by the words of the woman in trance, Indo Gahu ceased her efforts to amuse and mock throughout the remaining ceremonies of pangngae.

Of the four villages in which I had a chance to witness pangngae, Salutabang presented the largest and most diverse body of sumengo. The rites of 1984 ("putting blood on the seed") and 1985 ("having the hamlets follow") differed in purpose and scale, but showed thematic consistency when it came to the sumengo and the liturgical songs of the elders. Signs and themes of violence were easily discerned: the trophy head, the ma'denna, ma'paisun, and kelonoson, and nearly a score of sumengo conjured a scene of death and dismemberment. Yet the tropes of violence did not emanate from a powerful narrative order. Rather, they took form as the lyric blows of an agonistic poetry, a poetry that entailed a "virtuosity in handling the familiar" (Ong 1977:225). Their rhetoric was forged from an alloy of representational and performative violence.

The ToIssilita' at Saludengen

On the face of it, the mappurondo community in the village of Saludengen should be an ideal shelter for ritual tradition. For one, the community is determinedly endogamous, admitting no males from other villages as sons-in-law, and letting no daughter move off in wedlock. The community has also sequestered itself topographically: after several years of bitter dispute with Christian residents of the village regarding ritual and ritualized planting practices, the community exchanged terraces with the churchgoers and moved upstream along the banks of the Salu Dengen, leaving the Christians to occupy contiguous sites downstream—a tactic not unlike the one used to check the advance of Islam during the last century (see Chapter 2). Historically, the community has been a center of resistance to exogenous forces that threatened mappurondo tradition. For example, it refused to accommodate Dutch-sanctioned leadership in the district (Smit 1937), and it served as headquarters of local resistance during the rebellions

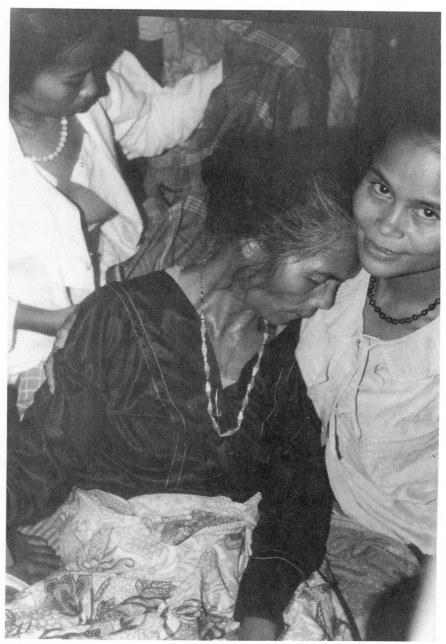

Fig. 21. *"Mandar! She's speaking Mandar!"* 1985.

of the late-1950s. With respect to internal politics, succession to the position of tomatuatonda' has been undisputed since the beginning of the century. The village also has a full complement of ritual specialists. Saludengen, then, is the most striking case in which a mappurondo community has resisted social and ideological admixture from without.

The piety and resolve of this community are acknowledged by ToIssilita' and ToSalu throughout Bambang. For those in Minanga and Rantepalado, ToIssilita' tradition resides in Saludengen in authentic and practical form. Emblematic of its authenticity is the ToIssilita' sumengo melody, now lost in Minanga and Rantepalado. The ToIssilita' melody and its accompanying textual structure (see Figures C and D, Appendix III) are quite distinct when compared to the ToSalu sumengo, differing especially in terms of choral patterning.[7] In contrast to the closure of the ToSalu sumengo, ToIssilita' song structure creates the illusion of an "unfinished" or "interrupted" text. Performing a song, a chorus will go through its lyrics from beginning to end. They then begin to repeat the third lyric phrase or line (see musical lines VII–IX, Music Figure C, Appendix III). But the repetition of that phrase goes "unfinished," for the chorus always stops singing upon reaching the sixth syllable. For example:

Malallengko toibirin	Watch out you on the horizon
tomatilampe bambana	you low on the foot of the land
lembum matil langkam borin	the blackened hawk is heading there
lembum matil langkam . . .	the hawk is heading there . . .

Usually, the close to the song does not fall so neatly on a word break:

Sala' lellen di barane'	A wavering fell at the banyan
sala' patompo ri lamba'	off the mark in the lamba' tree
loe tama ri uai	it falls off into the water
loe tama ri u . . .	falls off into the wa . . .

As soon as the singers come to a halt, a different tomantokko and chorus take up another song. The performance consequently gives the illusion of one chorus interrupting the other (specifically, males interrupting females and females interrupting males, as I shall explain below). In my view, the alternating interruptions of male and female choruses are an artful representation of ludic dialogue between husbands and wives. The very structure of the performed text anticipates the conventionalized "interruption" from another chorus. Agonistic song exchanges—which make up the performative milieux for the ToSalu sumengo—are incorporated as a formal internal feature of the ToIssilita' genre.

By March 1985 I had yet to witness ritual life in Saludengen. In fact I knew very little about the village, having visited there but once, and then in the context of running a household survey, during the planting season of 1984. A chance to take part in pangngae there following the 1985 harvest was one I did not want to miss. Given the rhetoric of authenticity that I had encountered when discussing Saludengen with other ToIssilita', I looked forward to going to the village and working with a sacred oral tradition unsullied by writing. My romantic and utopian views set me up for a real surprise: since 1980, the villagers of Saludengen have put down sumengo lyrics in writing and have forged them into a song cycle. The cycle posed a fresh set of problems and mysteries with respect to representations of violence and to the character of mappurondo ritual tradition. My time in Saludengen was limited to just a few days, but nonetheless I hope I can convey some of the complexity that the cycle poses for the understanding of local headhunting ritual.

THE SUMENGO CYCLE AT SALUDENGEN

Villagers at Saludengen reserve the evening before the concluding ceremonies of dipandebarani to perform the sumengo cycle. Replacing what is elsewhere called umpaningoi ulunna, the song cycle consists of 67 sumengo that depict a headhunt from start to finish. The community repeats the whole cycle three times through the course of the night—an effort that takes about eight hours. When performing the cycle, villagers divide into two large semi-choruses, one throng exclusively male, the other exclusively female. The two groups do not intermingle but sit on opposite sides of the house centerpost. In performance the semi-choruses take turns, and the sumengo cycle thus unfolds as an alternating dialogue between men and women.

The cycle has no plot in the conventional sense of the word. A well-knit plot is replaced by a series of tableaux, images, scenes, or "stations" that capture particular moments or episodes in pangngae. There is no development of character, no foreshadowing of events, no moral conflict. The cycle instead presents a sequence of themes and events, and in this sense has the cast and tenor of epic theater. At the same time, the community of singers also imposes a dialogic counterstructure on the cycle's narrative. The narrative moves forward through the alternating voices of husbands and wives. For that reason, specific songs assume a gendered voice and perspective. As will become clear below, a song dialogue between men and women not only provides a performative context for the cycle, but enters into its very constitution as a narrated scene of encounter. Representation and performance fuse as one: the dialogue that narrates and quotes is also a dialogue that is narrated and quoted.

The narrative cycle begins with a liturgical invocation to the debata, and in the course of the next two songs makes a problematic and ambiguous statement about the fate of the community and the topangngae. The 25 songs that follow recount the headhunters' departure, the felling of a victim, the headhunters' trek homeward, and their sudden arrival at the village. Thereafter, the sumengo portray a long conversation between the headhunters and their wives, consisting of questions and answers (including riddles). The remaining songs depict the ritual celebration that follows a headhunt, and close with a melancholy coda.

It falls to men to begin the narrative by singing the first three sumengo. When choruses repeat the cycle later in the night, women will sing the second song:

Sumengo 1   (men)

Iamo tolena	That's it, that is just what
naporaena debata	debata favor and expect
kema'patemboki' tole	when we do it once more, that's it

Sumengo 2   (men or women)

Ketuo-tuoi tau	Should the people come to prosper
taru' kasimpoi sali	runners wind from the slatted floor
malallengko toibirin	watch out you on the horizon

Sumengo 3   (men)

Naposarokam Bugi'	Made workers for the Bugis
natenakan ToMinanga	we're fed handouts by the Mandar
Ioe tama ri uai	it falls off into the water

The lyrics to the second song, readers will recall, hold out hope for the measure of prosperity that will let the uplanders assert their power over the coast. The third sumengo shatters the illusion of hoped-for prosperity and power. The realities of power bring the uplanders humiliation and failure.

The cycle next moves on to songs about the departure of the headhunters:

Sumengo 4   (women)

Malallengko toibirin	Watch out you on the horizon
tomatilampe bambana	you low on the foot of our land
lembum matil langkam borin	the blackened hawk is heading there

Sumengo 5   (men)

Langkam borim panuntungan	The hawk blackened with mortar stain
lao mengkaroi bonde'	goes to scratch circles on the coast
malepom pengkaroanna	the talon marks spiral and coil

Sumengo 6   (women)

Samboaki' tole	Do not shroud us like that
langkam borim panuntungan	the hawk blackened with mortar stain
lao mengkaroi bonde'	goes to scratch circles on the coast

Sumengo 7   (men)

Dikalleirika londong	Is the cockerel lone and hurt
lembun tama pangngabungan	slipping into the hiding place
tisoja' ula-ulanna	his tail feathers droop to the ground

Sumengo 8   (women)

Mapianna mane' londong	Fine and daring that cockerel bird
lembun tama pangngabungan	hiding in a place of ambush
tisoja' ula-ulanna	his tail feathers cascading down

Sumengo 9   (men)

Salokko' di rante	A cage on the wide plain
sau' nata'dulal londan	downriver is thrashed by the cock
nababa ma'kulu-kulu	carried by the kulu-kulu

Sumengo 10   (women)

Andulenna buntu	The mountain's areca
telo-telona tanete	the telo-telo of the peaks
sau' nasimpajo tasi'	off downriver crossing the seas[8]

Sumengo 11   (men)

Salunna Manamba	Where Salu Manamba
sitappana Mangngolia	and Mangngolia mix waters
napambaratoi londan	cockerels make it the cutting place

Sumengo 12   (women)

Malullu' paku randangan	Trampled ferns on the river bank
naola londom maningo	stepped on by the cockerel at play
untandeam pamunga'na	lifting it up to show first cut

Sumengo 13   (men)

Barane' rumape	Wide and low-boughed banyan
umbalumbunni minanga	whose shade darkens the rivermouth
sau' natotoi london	felled down there by the cockerel

Sumengo 14   (women)

Indu' ajangan di rante	Black sugar palm on the wide plain
sau' natotoi london	downstream fronds hewn by the cockerel
nababa ma'kulu-kulu	carried by the kulu-kulu

The cycle now moves to the headhunters' journey home. The men first sing about preparing their tambolâ:

Sumengo 15   (men)

Battangki' tallan	We hack at the bamboo
timpanangki' daun ube	we lop off all the rattan leaves
tapobungas sumarendu	we make sumarendu flowers

Sumengo 16   (women)

Totiane'-ane'	Those shaking in panic
totian di lolo' ube	forest mice on the rattan tips
murangngi battana tallan	hear the cutting of the bamboo

The next two sumengo are in the form of direct address, with the singers speaking to the returning headhunters:

Sumengo 17   (men)

Ende'o buntu	You reach the mountaintop
saladangko kabalean	you cross through the upper passes
naola rembu andulan	traveled by blades of andulan[9]

Sumengo 18   (women)

Tiondoko buntu	You're swayed by the mountain
tiamballu'ko tanete	tickled and grazed by rising peaks
naola rembu andulan	traveled by blades of andulan

The headhunters now approach their homelands, which are still darkened by mourning:

Sumengo 19   (men)

Malillimmi buntu	Dark indeed the mountains
saleburammi tanete	the peaks are lost beneath a cloud
allo pambukkai boko'	the sun opens from behind them

Sumengo 20   (women)

Andulenna bela	The mate's andulen shirt
lempan napopealloi	he stops here to have it sunned
aka a'bungas sigali	because it is so foul with mold[10]

The moment of a'dasan comes at last. The headhunters stop near the village and let loose their first blasts on the tambolâ flutes:

Sumengo 21   (men)

Ia tole anna guntu	That moment when there is thunder
anna bumbu kaliane	and the rumble of dread places
pa'kuritannamo london	it's the sign of the cockerel's deed

Sumengo 22   (women)

Kabalarribao	The same here up above
katiro rambu rojana	looking everywhere into haze
tengka talataolai	as if we'd never pass through it

The portrayal of a'dasan continues in the next six songs. The headhunters pose three questions to their wives. Their wives answer in turn, always in the affirmative.

Sumengo 23   (men)

Muitaka' tole	You see it, don't you, right?
barri'ki di kabalean	our line at the mountain passes
angkilentem batu api	when we roll 'long the stone of fire

Sumengo 24   (women)

Kiitami tole	We see it just that way
barrimu di kabaleam	your line at the mountain passes
pura malalle iallo	daylight is already beaming

Sumengo 25   (men)

Muitaka' tole	You see it, don't you, right?
banga kisamboi solem	the palm we covered up with leaves
umbai' tangkariammi	it's probably powder and dust

Sumengo 26   (women)

Kiitami tole	We see it just that way
banga disamboi solem	the palm covered over with leaves
umbai' tiamberrem watinna	probably gnawed by swarming grubs

Sumengo 27   (men)

Muitaka' tole	You see it, don't you, right?
bintoen turun di langi	stars suddenly fall from the sky
titale messubum bamba	scattering out from the hamlet[11]

Sumengo 28   (women)

Kiitami tole	We see it just like that
bintoen turun di langi'	stars suddenly fall from the sky
naangkarang kulu-kulu	raised up by the kulu-kulu

Here the cycle comes to a momentary halt, as singers rest their voices for a minute or two. The pause in singing is coincident with a shift in scene. Up to this point, the songs have dealt with episodes from the headhunters' journey. Subsequently, the scene shifts to the village, where celebratory events take place. The pattern of alternating choruses would ordinarily call for men to perform the next song, but it is the women's semi-chorus that resumes the cycle. (Suspending the normal order of chorus turns also helps formally mark the change in scene and action.) The cycle now takes the form of a face-to-face dialogue between the reunited husbands and wives. The wives first speak to the head that has been carried back to the village by their husbands, asking about its parentage:

Sumengo 29   (women)

Mennako keane'	Who are you, child to another?
mennako kekamasean	who are you, loved and looked after
natiampanni balida	you who were struck by the batten[12]

In reply, the men identify the origin of the victim:

Sumengo 30   (men)

Ane'na ToAbo	The child of ToAbo
kamaseanna Tenggelan	the one beloved by Tenggelan
natiampanni balida	was the one struck by the batten

The dialogue moves on to details of the ambush:

Sumengo 31   (women)

Aka' mutampean	What did you set as bait
mutu'biran di bambana	you placed a lure at the hamlet
anna messubum ampunna	and then its keeper came outside

Sumengo 32   (men)

Sambako' ramba'na bela'	Tobacco reaped from the garden
kitu'biran di bambana	we placed as lures near the hamlet
anna loe kaju amba	and then the amba tree fell down

Sumengo 33   (women)

Makanna allo	What was the sun like
lamusullu'i bambana	you're 'bout to enter the village
anna messubunna puana	and then its master comes outside

Sumengo 34   (men)

Katenanna allo	The sun was much like now
kamala susimo too	yes almost like the sun is now
anna lenta' pemalian	and then the offering was cut loose

As a coda to their questions, the women admit the worry and concern they felt while their husbands were off headhunting. They also confess their envy for the adventure and glory that only men may savor:

Sumengo 35   (women)

Sama siam malallengki	Not only our worried thinking
sama kainda-indaki	but our restless envy as well
tempomu messubum bamba	when you had left the village lands

Now it is the men's turn to query their wives. They look for flattery and reassurance.

Sumengo 36   (men)

Menna' lamuala	Which do you want to take
kandean tadiampalla'	the coarse unpolished wooden dish
anna pindam pebajoan	or the porcelain reflecting bowl

Sumengo 37   (women)

Arabopinea	Better that I just keep
kandean tiampalla'	the coarse unpolished wooden dish
anna pindam pebajoan	than the porcelain reflecting bowl

Sumengo 38   (men)

Menna' lamuala	Which do you want to take
labuju pettanetean	the wild cockerel from the mountains
anna londom belo tondo'	or the hamlet's fancy rooster

Sumengo 39   (women)

Arabopinea	Better that I just keep
labuju pettanetean	the wild cockerel from the mountains
anna londom belo tondo'	than the hamlet's fancy rooster

Sumengo 40   (men)

Menna' lamuala	Which do you want to take
sirope londom mangngura	the beads from a young cockerel
anna londo saranea	or those from an old reddened cock

Sumengo 41   (women)

Arabopinea	Better that I just keep
sirope londom mangngura	the beads from a young cockerel
anna londo saranea	than those from an old reddened cock

Sumengo 42   (men)

Menna' lamuala	Which do you want to take
tosumambi' bainena	the one whose wife walks in the hills
anna tolantoi tasi'	or one whose wife floats on the sea

Sumengo 43   (women)

Arabopinea	Better that I just keep
tosumambi' bainena	the one whose wife walks in the hills
anna tolantoi tasi'	than one whose wife floats on the sea

Next, the chorus of men sing out riddles to the women. The riddles and their minimalist answers go:

Sumengo 44   (men)

Diattomokoka' iko	Have you ever woven something
sumau' tadikala'i	with a warp but no thread for weft
marra' tadisumallai	and when done it lacked any parts

Sumengo 45   (women)

Diattomakantekami'	Yes, we too have woven something
sumau' tadikala'i	with a warp but no thread for weft
marra' tadisumallai	and when done it lacked any parts

Sumengo 46   (men)

Diattomokoka' iko	You, have you ever played at it
mogasin tandiulanni	making tops spin but without string
muondo pitu bulanna	they whir and hum for seven moons

Sumengo 47   (women)

Diattomakantekami'	Yes we also have played at it
mogasin tandiulanni	making tops spin but without string
muondo pitu bulanna	they whir and hum for seven moons

Sumengo 48   (men)

Diattomokoka' iko	Have you ever gone to use it
manumpi' tadikumba'i	a blowgun whose darts have no tails
mulosa pitu tanete	but which pierce through seven mountains

Sumengo 49   (women)

Diattomakantekami'	Yes we too have made use of it
manumpi' tadikumba'i	a blowgun whose darts have no tails
mulosa pitu tanete	but which pierce through seven mountains

Following the exchange of riddles and answers, singers reflect on the virtue and good fortune of the upland village.

Sumengo 50   (men)

Sau' lambe' di Da'ala	The long blanket at Da'ala
ditandajan di Takapak	staked to begin at Takapak
marre' di Rantetarima	finished at Rantetarima[13]

The message of the song: the headhunters act at the coast, but the outcome of their deed is felt in the uplands. The women follow with a song about the severed head:

Sumengo 51   (women)

Batu tandinna tasi'	The pillar stone of the sea
melenten illau' mai	rolling around from there to here
natimam pande manari	the clever one he catches it

Like the men's previous song, the next sumengo is tinged with irony. The Mandar light incense during their invocations and prayers to the debata, but the smoke (i.e. providential gifts of well-being and prosperity) sweetens the uplands, not the coast. Note the contrast of swirling images: the sinking whirlpool downriver, and the smoke that spirals upward through the mountains—the former dropping in the direction of death and the afterworld, the latter rising in the direction of the debata.

Sumengo 52   (men)

Illau' mandalal lisu	Down there deep in the whirlpool's eye
tountunnu tagarinna	the one who burns the incense grass
inderi rambu apinna	here the fragrant smoke of its fire

Now come songs in praise of the hamlets, the singers, and the fate of the village and its headhunters.

Sumengo 53   (women)

Sissi'na tondo'	Mark of the hamlet
batu lampa'na banua	signs cut in stone for the dwelling
tamonda disapukoi	unbroken unfallen spirit

Sumengo 54   (men)

Mapia pepairanna	Strong and fast her abidingness
kaloe Rantetarima	parrot of Rantetarima
dibaballolom maroa'	always carrying mirth and noise

Sumengo 55   (women)

Taballe-balle tindoku	My dream sign is not off the mark
tamasserom pangngimpingku	my dreaming does not slip away
ditetangan sulim bulo	gold bamboo flutes carried in hand

Sumengo 56   (men)

Sala' lellen di barane'   A wavering fell at the banyan
sala' patompo ri lamba'   off the mark up in the lamba'
loe tama ri uai   it falls off into the water

Sumengo 57   (women)

Rua' lellen di barane'   A straight true fell at the banyan
rua patompo ri lamba'   on the mark up in the lamba'
loe tama ri banua   it falls right into the dwelling

Sumengo 58   (men)

Maka'to pajummi allo   When a rainbow ringing the sun
sipangngana'mo bittoen   makes stars appear as its children
pa'kuritannamo london   sure sign of the cockerel's deed

Sumengo 59   (women)

Anna maesora betten   And why is the fort in ruins
anna rondom bala kala'   and the fence collapsed into piles
pangngilanna bonga sure'   the scraping of carabao horns

The final eight songs of the sumengo cycle deal with the ceremony of dipandebarani:

Sumengo 60   (men)

Marra' untannunna bela   Done the wife completes her weaving
padaki' dipangngidengam   together we were in the womb
mane rumabakangkami'   but for us we're just now crawling

Sumengo 61   (women)

Masetopa kami' duka'   There is a moment for us too
laundara-daraangki   we will still find our own chance
lumbu' tanete kiola   the peaks on which we journey will sag

Sumengo 62   (men)

Kesaeki' bamba   When we come back to the village
tatetangki' bua-bua   we carry betel in our hands
anta pabeloi tondo'   and we pretty up the hamlet

Sumengo 63   (women)

Ballaranni lante Daba	Go spread out the mat from Java
topole mendio' minna'	the ones that come are bathed in oil
napomarampia-pia	they are already glistening

Sumengo 64   (men)

Paulemo' mai	Come give it over here
tadu diparada minna'	the limeholder polished with oil
disallu' tintim ba'bana	the one with the gilded lid-chain

Sumengo 65   (women)

Lakumi matin tadummu	You there come take your limeholder
tadu diparada minna'	the limeholder polished with oil
disallu' tintim ba'bana	the one with the gilded lid-chain

The cycle ends with a pair of sumengo that lament the close of dipande-barani:

Sumengo 66   (men)

Aka latakua	What will all of us say
kekipasampe langammi	when we men put it up above
tipandal lolom maroa'	the mirth and noise put back in place

Sumengo 67   (women)

Uai mata mandaram	A ring of tears just that alone
ma'lisu-lisu di ampa'	swirling round on the woven mat
tipurirri' di allongam	whirling about on the pillow

Organizing the sumengo into this coherent narrative, dialogic, and cyclic structure has also led the community to put aside a special time for these songs. During my brief visit to Saludengen, there was but one occasion when I heard someone—an old woman working in her houseyard—sing a few of the lyric strains from this genre. In the ritual gathering of dipandebarani, sumengo performance is next to absent, except when a chorus of male elders and the topangngae sing the first three sumengo as a prelude or coda to liturgical acts. In short, the written cycle has become a canonical text, the reoralization of which has resulted in (or more precisely, been constructed as) a communal liturgical act. Communal song, in this village, is a scene of collaborative reading, not a site of improvised, agonistic play.

THE PROJECT OF WRITING AND
READING THE SUMENGO CYCLE

Elders at Saludengen told me that the main reason for writing down sumengo lyrics was simply to keep them intact for a community that was increasingly literate. As one explained, "The ancestors remembered well, but these children like to read." Some youths had already begun writing down sumengo lyrics, so as to be able to sing along with older performers, and around 1980, elders in the community decided to help the younger singers shape a collection of lyrics in notebook form. I have no way of being sure, but Christian hymnals and choirs may have provided the models for this collocation of song lyrics. In any event, no effort was or has been made to inscribe sumengo melody; the tune itself remains in oral tradition. The presence of writing notwithstanding, the very sign of an authentic ToIssilita' tradition is thus a tune known by heart, an embodied memory of rhythms and tonal movement never traced in ink and recaptured only in performance.

In the context of passing on sumengo lyrics, songleaders began to craft a song cycle within and outside of performance contexts. Although song performance remained both a reference point and the ultimate end of the effort to preserve lyrics, skilled singers had to step outside of performance to contemplate and discuss the songs. From the start, then, there emerged a dialectic between oral performance and the work of inscription.[14] In my brief time in this village, I was unable to learn precisely how the villagers set about selecting the lyrics and organizing them into a narrative whole. Judging from the sumengo traditions elsewhere in Bambang, singers rarely did more than couple lyric triads into song pairs. Yet I think it is safe to say that the songleaders at Saludengen were conscious of a narrative waiting to be put together. Thus, writing did not bring about a narrative or narrative logic previously missing. Instead, it facilitated the work of reclamation. The entire project of dictating, copying, comparing, and recomposing lyrics provided a context in which collaboration could retrieve a narrative scattered through the separate memories of individual songleaders. As one might expect, the ludic or agonistic song exchanges so typical elsewhere are wholly missing in performances at Saludengen. There is no impulse to challenge and outperform. In fact, playful behavior seems antithetical to the smooth completion of the cycle narrative. What the project of writing has done is produce an authorized text that has since supplanted the memories and competitive interests of songleaders. Ironically, the making of the sumengo canon led the tomantokko to drop those songs that would not fit into the cycle. Far from preserving all remembered song, the project of sumengo inscription has led to the narrowing of the genre.

The cycle text typically appears in small, paper-covered notebooks—much like the blue books used for exams in American college classrooms. In the several manuscripts I was able to examine, writers invariably put down each set of lyrics as a sentence of prose, unmarked for meter, pauses, or vocal part. It *was* customary, however, for writers to arrange the songs in the order of their performance in the cycle, and a few people went so far as to number them. It was also common to find each song marked so as to indicate who was to sing it—men or women. Greater numbers of books were in the hands of children or teens. Of the three tomantokko in the village, only a lone male and a young female counterpart kept a notebook of sumengo lyrics close at hand during performance, and one senior female songleader did without. The organization of the singers into two semi-choruses strikes me as a good way to take advantage of this proliferation of song scripts. Indeed, the proliferation of scripts opened the way for young singers to swell the ranks of the chorus. The scripts also made it possible for larger numbers of singers to perform together smoothly and cohesively. In particular, the scripts brought the tomantokko and chorus into greater concert.

But the cycle text has also changed the role of the tomantokko. The songleaders still have an important role to play in leading off each song and driving the melody, but the sequence of songs is completely out of their hands, dictated instead by the authority of the cycle text. Indeed, the memory and performance of the songleader are subordinate to a "correcting" and determining written text. While visiting Saludengen, I witnessed a moment when the tomantokko leading the men's semi-chorus skipped songs, despite the notebook of lyrics beside him. The sumengo "fell into the water," as they say. When the chorus did not join in, the tomantokko broke off his singing. After a moment of muted conversation with some of the men beside him, the tomantokko took up the opening strains of the correct song.

Without question, the villagers in Saludengen used writing and reading-in-performances as a way to make recall of the sumengo easier. Aside from this consciously pragmatic effort, younger singers had already begun to trust and favor writing as a way to "handle" song. After all, in the context of their schoolwork, writing (or print) appeared as the authoritative and outward mark of critical knowledge. In that light, writing down sumengo lyrics formed a strategy for turning the songs into a genre of "critical knowledge," or, to put it somewhat differently, for incorporating the sumengo into a body of inscribed "critical knowledge." That strategy of cultural reproduction is wholly consistent with the village ethos at Saludengen, an ethos aimed at recovering and strengthening local mappurondo tradition.

This project of inscription did not free villagers from habits and views shaped by orality, but came to their service in a more detailed and thoroughgoing organization of song performance than the economy of an endangered oral tradition allowed. Those who shaped the cycle had to take into account singers and songleaders who could not read. Indeed, I would argue that the narrative and dialogic structures in the cycle have more to do with the traditional arts of storytelling and ludic song exchange than they do with an innovative "logic of writing." Writing and reading catered to the desire to get performance right, to fell the sumengo so that they dropped "into the village." Putting a check to lyric variation was one way to coordinate song performance. But it was not the intrinsic function of writing to bring a stop to variation. Rather, villagers had to oversee the writing, standardization, and distribution of lyrics. In short, the authority of the written cycle text was not an intrinsic one, but one ascribed by the performers themselves.

DIALOGUE, NARRATIVE, AND REPRESENTATION

As I have already suggested, writing down the sumengo was not simply an effort to put song into a (relatively) fixed textual form, but was, as well, part of the project of narrativizing the communal memory of headhunting. The cycle is a work of reclamation and rationalization. Following the narrative path of the cycle is much like walking the Stations of the Cross, except that it begins rather than ends in violence and death. With each song, the community is witness to the heroic feats of the topangngae and to the celebrations that erupt upon their return home. Once the text is entered and engaged, the community obliges itself to travel the narrative trail to its end, in accordance with its chronologies and thematic emphases. On the way, the reading and performing community discovers itself present in the cycle text.

Read a certain way, the cycle narrative is very caught up in what Johannes Fabian calls "the agitations of voice" (1992:84), not only in its re-oralization, but in its constituent narrative moves. The cycle is about the headhunters' violence, to be sure, but it is also about ritual performance. It provides a scriptural *and* reoralized representation of commemorative orality and exchange. The song cycle recreates ritual performance at the level of narrative representations (that is, at the level of the narrated). Simultaneously, it re-embodies ritual performance in its narrating activity. It is a revisiting of ritual tradition, and a filling up of the present with commemorative and thus regenerative work.

The cycle offers a scene of ritual exchange and orality, a scene conjured as sung dialogue between husbands and wives. The ludic and agonistic exchanges so typical of sumengo performance elsewhere here appear in the narrated rather than the narrating dimensions of song. As I have noted, agonistic song play potentially threatens narrative closure. It also introduces inequality between the male and female semi-choruses: one group wins and the other loses. Eliminated in performance, agonistic song exchange is recollected, nonetheless, in the narrative itself. The song-dialogues, of course, make up a lyric counterstructure to the story of heroic deeds and spectacle. It is in that dialogue that one grasps the positioned outlook of husbands and wives. But the dialogue represented in the cycle is not the speech and song of unruly and unconstrained subjects: in the alternating songs and interrogations portrayed by the cycle, there can be no refusal to answer. There are no improvisatory subversions, no parodies, no failures, no uncertain outcomes. The narrative has exiled chance and the tactics of play. The cycle has thus turned into ritual—it produces conjunction, not disjunction. So in contrast to performances in Salutabang, where the song play of husbands and wives is the context and site for commemorative work, the sumengo cycle at Saludengen is a commemorative representation and textualization of gendered, dialogical play.

The song-dialogue is perhaps less "about" ritual violence than it is about two political paradigms affecting the fate of the community: the heroic and the incorporative. The headhunter-husband inhabits the narrative as its principal heroic figure. Yet judging from many of the songs, he is an uncertain hero, even in his boasting. He repeatedly turns to his wife, whose desire and approbation prevent his being politically diminished. It is curious, too, that the cycle contains little sign of the envy young inexperienced men might feel toward the headhunter. After all, the headhunter is a figure for emulation, and in the context of the mappurondo communities, envy and emulation are important motivating forces in the reproduction of social and moral order. The narrative thus tends to flatten the hierarchy of males. Women, meanwhile, appear as figures of incorporation. They worry over the headhunter and reassure him. They represent what the hero desperately needs— recognition from a community of subjects whose own accomplishments are occluded.

Interpreting a Song: Reading with the Polity

It strikes me that Saludengen's effort to forge (or reclaim) a headhunting narrative reflects a strategy of cultural reproduction wholly consistent with the community's self-conscious hold on identity and polity.

Secluding themselves socially, spatially, and ideologically, people in the mappurondo fold here have shaped a powerful, deeply rooted communal identity. Their ethos is one of control, and it extends not only to people and material resources, but to the past as well. The ritualized and inscribed narrative of headhunting helps moor the community morally and ideologically, for it provides a coherent vision of the past—while eliminating the uncertainty of the agonistic exchanges linking husbands and wives.

The evening after dipandebarani came to a close in Saludengen, I had a chance to discuss the song-cycle with my host, Ambe Siama', and a few of his friends and household. One song in particular had captured my interest, because it was so different in tone from the songs I had heard previously in Salutabang, Minanga, and Rantepalado. It was the song that expressed the humiliation and failure of the mappurondo headhunters:

Naposarokam Bugi'	Made workers for the Bugis
natenatkan ToMinanga	we're fed handouts by the Mandar
loe tama ri uai	it falls down into the water

For Ambe Siama' and the others, the song recalled a history of subordination to coastal patrons and voiced resignation to the humbling realities of regional exchange. The lyrics acknowledged that headhunting could end in disappointment, that the upland headhunters might fail in striking back at exogenous powers. For me, this unique and arrestingly frank appraisal of the upland past demanded a rethinking of my views on local headhunting tradition. Indeed, the theme of failure never emerged in the songs from other villages, nor, in fact, did any of the women's sumengo performed in Saludengen carry a hint of a headhunter's shame. Of course, the inclusion of the song in the sumengo cycle may have been a way to narrativize the present demoralization of the mappurondo community, an effort to deflect the current political tensions into the past. Whatever the facts, this song suggests to me that the prevailing vision of local history and tradition at Saludengen now includes strains of heroic violence *and* demoralizing loss.

Some days later, I made my way upriver to Salutabang, so as to join in pangngae festivities there. I settled into the home of Ambe Teppu, the man who had chided his nephew not to treat mappurondo religion as culture. One evening I pulled out the tape cassettes that I had recorded at Saludengen and played them for Ambe Teppu. The skilled voices of the tomantokko and the narrative arrangement of the songs pleased him very much: "Straight and in place," he said. "I think our ancestors once sang [the sumengo] just that way." Ambe Teppu began to tell me about the headhunting rites of his youth, celebrations that were peopled by fine singers whose very songs were an index to the well-being of the highland villages. Going on, he remarked about how disappointing the contemporary rituals were by comparison. As I listened to him I realized that the tape had reminded him of loss and disorder in the oral tradition of agonistic song exchanges at Salutabang. Ambe Teppu longed for the ordered past that he heard in the cycle. Paradoxically, his demoralized views were a response to a "past" that was conjured from a recent effort to salvage and reconstruct traditional materials through writing.

Like me, Ambe Teppu was not familiar with the song about headhunters getting handouts from their coastal rivals and partners. He called to Indo Teppu to listen to the tape, and she, too, could not recall having heard the song before. I ventured that the song was about the failed headhunts of the past, but Ambe Teppu disagreed: "That song is about husbands and their wives." As he saw it, the Bugis and Mandar mentioned in the song were wives to whom husbands devoted their labor. "We [men] work for them and we get a little bit of rice, maybe some fish. But we are poor, there is so little. What can we give back?"

The differences between the accounts of Ambe Siama' and Ambe Teppu were intriguing. Why would a person from one village give the song a seemingly straightforward historical interpretation while another, from a different village, insists on an allegorical reading? My first instinct was to privilege the "historical" at the expense of the allegorical, a move that favored the seeming straightforwardness (or literalness) of Ambe Siama's reading. That same outlook also privileged the lyrics' singers and authors as interpretive authorities at the expense of Ambe Teppu, who was encountering the song for the first time.[15] Since then I have come to feel that both interpretations— the historical and the allegorical—exist as countermovements that operate in each other's shadows.

Looking back to the moment when I asked Ambe Siama' to reflect on the sumengo, I see that he was reading the lyrics in keeping with local political experience. Although no doubt skilled at weaving allegory from the threads of song lyric, Ambe Siama' was inclined to remain within the orbit of history and the story of upland vs. coast, of an ethnic "us" vs. "them." By the same token, his interpretation followed the path of cultural reproduction at Saludengen. Pangngae provides a ritual mechanism allowing the mappurondo community at Saludengen to internalize—and momentarily overcome—its subordination to exogenous forces, one of the central tensions in local political life.

I would argue, too, that for villagers at Saludengen, "reading with the village polity" through the narrative cycle precludes, or makes unlikely, any metaphoric connections between coastal rivals and wives. Reading with the polity at Saludengen means reading with the written narrative cycle, not against it or away from it. Equally, it means reading with the experience of a homogeneous community that is fearful of exogenous forces and consumed with promoting its own social cohesiveness. The narrative cycle itself mediates and enhances the production of social homogeneity and solidarity, and stands out as an explicit effort to hold on to village tradition as a basis of communal identity.

Ambe Teppu shaped his interpretation of the sumengo with a different set of textual constraints and emphases and a different understanding of political experience. Reading with the polity at Salutabang means seeing all sumengo as weapons in a ludic contest between choruses of husbands and wives. Ambe Teppu was not alone in interpreting songs as metaphorical or allegorical commentaries on the relations between husbands and wives. A song about the felling of a banyan tree offers a case in point:

Iko barane'-barane'	You, you banyan trees over there
keditambako dilellen	if you are called to be cut down
loe maiko bambaki	fall here into our village lands

From a perspective that looks toward the intercultural relations between mountain and coast, the song is about felling a Mandar victim. But several of my male friends at Salutabang felt that the lyrics of this song alluded to a courtship and marriage proposal (in which a woman is "felled"). In contrast to Saludengen, then, the mappurondo community at Salutabang is inclined to emphasize sexual or domestic tensions rather than intercultural ones alone. To use a musical metaphor, Ambe Teppu transposed tension, conflict, and rivalry from the key of historical intercultural politics to the key of gender relations. The headhunters' fleeting subordination of a social and historical "other" is, in Ambe Teppu's reckoning, analogous to a confrontation with a domestic other—a wife.

Still, such a view must acknowledge or recognize a historical understanding of the upland-lowland tensions and political-economic patterns that obtained in the past. In other words, the allegorical supplement, precisely because it is allegory and supplement, depends upon a straightforward historical reading that exists as an "other"—as a figure of difference (cf. Chambers 1991:237–238, 251–252). Because the literal and the figurative are mutually entangled as negative determinants of each other, there are perhaps villagers who would treat a song that is ostensibly about husbands and wives as a figured representation of intercultural tensions. But metaphorical displacements, as Stallybrass and White (1986:196) remind us, are saturated with social history and are always sensitive to a hierarchy of provenance. In my time in Bambang, I met no singer or listener who would use song lyrics that are ostensibly about local sexual politics to discover and understand the conditions of the uplands' historical subordination to exogenous forces.[16] Within the discourse of pangngae, alien figures from the past may be a transcoding of wives, but wives are never a transcoding of the headhunters' victims downstream.

The communities at Saludengen and Salutabang are basically similar in their organizational tensions and logic. They differ in the way those tensions and logics are played out, and in the villagers' strategic use of tradition (that is, the historical processes of reinterpretation) for making sense of their sociohistorical circumstances.[17] The sexual politics so prominent in Salutabang is hardly absent in Saludengen, nor is the coherent historical vision that typifies Saludengen wholly lacking in Salutabang. The different emphases placed on sexual politics and communal history issue from the sociohistorical trajectories of the two villages, and in the arena of headhunting ritual, these themes undergo constant change as the communities adjust to exogenous pressures and the stresses of communal reproduction.

The sumengo, as constitutive of ritual practice and a broader field of village discourse, modulate changes of understanding in local tradition. Singer, listener, song performance, and postperformance reflection assume a place amid local circumstances and historical contingencies (cf. Fish 1980, 1989; Said 1979). How people interpret the singing is both constrained and motivated by this web of circumstances and ongoing projects. When I visited with Ambe Siama' and Ambe Teppu, a historical stance appeared to be a stable and fitting hermeneutic strategy for one, while an allegoristic stance proved to be a key tactic for the other. The inscribed narrativity and textual fundamentalism of sumengo practice at Saludengen compelled Ambe Siama' to read with communal memory and history. The song duels and textual play at Salutabang, on the other hand, coaxed Ambe Teppu to read away from history to discover allusions to local sexual politics. The lesson that Ambe Teppu gave me in interpreting the sumengo shows that a history of intercultural relations can render metaphorically the sexual politics so basic to village order. If anything, his interpretation suggests that the central political tensions at Salutabang have shifted inward, that the fate of mappurondo tradition there has already been conceded to encroaching ideologies and the heat of individual interests. Ambe Siama' has provided a different picture with his historical understanding of song lyrics: at Saludengen, having an autonomous history at all is a way to resist the modern order and requires no allegorical supplement. To put it somewhat differently, the present struggle to maintain mappurondo identity and ideology at Saludengen, although inevitably fought *in* history, is also fought *with* history.

Journeying up and down the Salu Mambi to see how the discourse of pangngae has been situated and circumstanced is, for me, a way to scan the performative and interpretive horizons for this ritual. The staging of pangngae is undertaken in particular villages as a local response to concrete and ever-changing conditions. If the themes and projects of pangngae appear to us to have a transcendant or enduring character, we should not forget that the actual workings of the ritual are ephemeral and contingent. Holding pangngae necessarily places villagers in a historical relation to tradition and in a pragmatic relation to the immediate conditions, purposes, and goals emerging in village life. At stake in pangngae is the forging of social relations and social meanings. Staging the headhunt, in this sense, is a confrontation and a coming to terms with the pressures and asymmetries of mountain life.

    There are few materials that can help us grasp long-term historical change in mappurondo headhunting rites. But a look at four practicing communities reveals some basic differences in the way pangngae is produced and reproduced in a climate of censure and doubt. Villagers recognize and talk about those differences in a variety of ways. But to say this or that song is ToSalu or ToIssilita', to make claims about authenticity and loss, or to look for allegories in the lyrics of others, are all ways to make sense of, and to take measure of, a threatened ritual order. The mappurondo headhunter does not inhabit a timeless preliterate paradise, nor should we suppose that he has fallen from preliterate grace. He inhabits the projects of violence and memory as writer and reader. But he writes and reads in order to sustain the agitations of voice. Yet we have seen, too, that the agonistic exchanges between men and women are themselves "agitations" that animate commemorative tradition. In the end, no matter what their tactical moves, no matter what their instabilities, violence, memory, and voice are caught up in the struggle for meaning and a place in the flow of time.

8

The Spectacle of Dancing Men

Pangngae in the Culture
of Indonesian Modernity

Before bringing this book to a close, I think it important to make clear that it is not just the mappurondo communities who are successors to the upland past, for so, too, are the Muslims and Christians, who today make up the majority of those living in the headwater region. They, too, make interested claims to the past, not only in the course of everyday life, but also—and most strikingly—in their self-conscious possession of what they call culture, history, and tradition. Irrespective of their religious or ideological outlook, the people of the headwaters all have a past in which pangngae once played a part. How headhunting ritual is remembered, or is driven from memory, comprises a socially situated reading of ancestral practice. That Muslims and Christians are busy remembering or forgetting pangngae places them in direct contest with the mappurondo communities for ideological control of the past.

Remembering and forgetting ancestral practice are projects that take form around *adat* (Ind. custom, tradition) and *agama* (Ind. religion), terms promulgated by Indonesian state discourse. Historied with different origins and cultural encounters, adat and agama serve as two of the principal terms through which Indonesian citizens can articulate and objectify their beliefs and culture.[1] Delimited to a few select strains of monotheism, the term *agama* has sparked debate over what constitutes religion and the religious, leading for example to the rationalization and "internal conversion" of

Balinese worship (Geertz 1973) or to the construction of minority religions like that emerging among the Wana in Central Sulawesi (Atkinson 1983). By the same token, adat, as Kipp and Rodgers (1987) point out, is a fluid and "exquisitely contemporary" discourse that both sustains and creates local custom. Citizens have to sort out for themselves, though by no means freely, what is to count as agama and what is to count as adat. Meanwhile, Indonesian discourse has also introduced powerful concepts such as *sejarah* (history), *tradisi* (tradition), *kepercayaan* (belief),[2] *kebudayaan* (culture [in the sense of civilization]), and *seni budaya* (cultural arts). Like adat and agama, these ideologically freighted terms are alien to the areal tongues of upland Sulawesi. But they have become lodged in local conversations and debate, and have already brought about categorical distinctions unlike ones encountered in the past.

The ongoing invention of religion and tradition does not happen in isolation but takes place in the encounter between dominant and subordinate groups or institutions. For example, in the Wana case mentioned above, the emergence of a local minority religion is in no small way an artifact of interethnic exchange with powerful neighboring societies made up of Christians and Muslims (Atkinson 1983). The self-fashioning of religion, tradition, and culture, especially in the communities of upland Sulawesi, most certainly includes what Nicholas Thomas (1992) would describe as "reactive objectification"—a process in which groups not only reify aspects of themselves and others but, in so doing, come to reject practices that may be called local or traditional. People put aside some of the things and practices associated with their own place and take up that which might be considered foreign or different. In this way, a process of "oppositional collaboration"—a term that in my view more accurately captures the social dynamics described by Thomas—leads people to ask questions about themselves (and others) as they fabricate the meaning and form of social conduct and identity. Emergent as such in the history of encounters between groups, oppositional collaboration can thus come into play in fomenting social and ideological instability.[3]

What the people of the headwaters wish to do with their past, and in particular what they wish to do about pangngae in fashioning their own cultural traditions, show how complicated the process of oppositional collaboration (or reactive objectification) can be. First and foremost, the discourse of Indonesian citizenship calls for an identity that encompasses and transcends local, regional, and religious differences. Next, there are the discourses of agama that allow (or compel) Christians, Muslims, and mappurondo followers to establish themselves as distinct groups. Religious differentiation, meanwhile, is not dissociable from efforts of the headwater communities to declare an ethnic identity distinct from that of the Mandar, the Mamasa and Sa'dan Toraja, and, more distantly, the Bugis. At the same time, the adat and administrative territories of Bambang and Mambi have sustained a social divide bridged by a long history of cooperation and rivalry. And within Bambang, as we have seen, largely endogamous villages or groupings of ToSalu and ToIssilita' preserve important lines of social difference. Within the whirlpool of headwater cultural politics, people may reject or forget pangngae altogether. Others may choose to remember it uneasily as an aspect of local history. Some, like those in the mappurondo community, look upon pangngae as a critical and emblematic religious activity. Still others may see it as a source of cultural arts. In short, pangngae may be venerated or held at bay as history, as religion, as tradition, as art, or as animist spectacle.

For many in the headwater region, pemali appa' randanna is what counts as culture, most especially in presenting themselves and their region to outsiders. The mappurondo communities shroud themselves with it as a matter of religious tradition, but not without increasing difficulty or doubt. Christians, on the other hand, reject pemali appa' randanna for its religious dimensions, but are active in acknowledging it as part of local history and enshrining it as spectacle. Keeping ritual violence in the past, and staging "dances" based on pangngae are ways for Christians to assert their progress and modernity as Indonesian citizens, as ones who have left "backward" customs behind. At the same time, that maneuver still leaves them in control of something that could be called local tradition. Muslims, meanwhile, have begun to look elsewhere for what will count as local culture.

My remarks so far have suggested some of the basic strains in the way the people of the headwaters remember the violence and festivity of pangngae. In the pages that follow, I offer a final set of texts of pangngae, texts that, not unlike mine, look to the ritual headhunt for a recognizable and intelligible image of tradition.

Muslim Representations

Social distance and difference complicate Muslim recollections of pangngae. These distinctions are not just a matter of belonging to different ideological precincts, but also reflect the different political and moral histories of the upland adat territories, more recently refigured as desa (see Chapter 2). As of 1985 there was only one Muslim household in all of Bambang, headed by a young convert. So we must turn downstream to Mambi to learn of the Muslim community's attitude toward pangngae. Though many of the Muslim hamlets of Mambi are within earshot of the drumming upriver, seldom do the rhythms of pabuno elicit much in the way of curiosity or explicit censure. For most villagers and townspeople in Mambi, the staging of pangngae, if they are even aware of it, is something that concerns Bambang alone. For them, it is just another sign of those "inside the headwaters" who refuse to divorce themselves from the kafir practices of their ancestors.

The ritual, however, is well within the memory of many older Muslims in and around Mambi. In the village of Mambi proper, for example, pangngae last took place sometime between 1936 and 1942. It lingered in the district's outlying settlements until 1970, but as little more than a postharvest ceremonial meal followed by some singing.[4] There were no heads, no flutes, and no playing of drums. Older Muslims, in my experience, have tended to be forthright in acknowledging a headhunting past, though with varying degrees of distaste, approval, or understanding. Younger Muslims, on the other hand, and nearly all Muslim youths, have virtually no memory or understanding of pangngae.

I got a revealing look at the incommensurable memories of the young and old one morning in 1985 while working in Mama Amang's kitchen, a place I called home during my two years in the Salu Mambi area. I was sitting at the table checking transcriptions and scribbled notes for a set of cassette tapes I had made during pangngae festivities in Bambang several weeks before.[5] As I followed along listening to a cassette of sumengo performances, Amang and Usri, aged eight and five, wandered in from school recess and sat down with me. Amang and Usri had never heard sumengo before and gave me puzzled looks. The songs could only have seemed odd to them: a tune unlike those taught in school or heard on pop-music cassettes; lyrics in *basa Bambang,* the language of Bambang. The songs had no place in their young memories. A few minutes later, Papa' Amang walked in, and found me listening to the sumengo with his sons. A college-trained civil officer for the *kecamatan* then in his forties, and a scion of the last Indona Mambi, Papa' Amang had on more than a few occasions dealt with the mappurondo communities in Bambang and understood well the political traditions of the past. But he had little interest in these songs, and in a gesture typical of his outlook toward the *tomallilin,* "the ones in darkness," he began to poke fun at the songs, parodying the straining voices of the song-leader and chorus. Succeeding in raising a smile from us, Papa' Amang gave a laugh, made a disparaging comment ("What do you think? Those songs are kuno ["primitive"], ey?") and went about finding a glass in which to make coffee.

Papa' Amang joined me and his sons at the table and lit a cigarette. I kept at the tapes. Moments later, in came Papa' Suri, Papa' Amang's uncle. A young 60 or so, Papa Suri' could be counted on for his cheerful enthusiasms and inquisitiveness. No sooner than he asked, "What are you listening to?" did he give a chuckle of recognition. "Hey, I remember them. The elders would always sing them. Is that what you were doing up in there? Going to pangngae?"

I remarked that I had not known he had seen pangngae when he was young. Of course he had, he replied. "I used to go watch them sing and then they'd dance around with cloths." Papa Suri' looked around and grabbed a towel by the concrete washing slab. "Here, like this." He leapt across the kitchen, landing in the pose of mamose speechmaker, his face fixed with an enraged glare. Holding the towel aloft, he bounded back and forth on the washing slab, head arched high in replica of the best mamose performers. Papa' Amang glanced over his shoulder for a moment at Papa' Suri's leaps and thrusts, and then turned back to his cigarette and coffee, a near scowl on his face. I think Papa' Suri' sensed Papa' Amang's displeasure, for he brought an abrupt halt to his very convincing act. "Oh yes," he chuckled, putting the towel down, "but they didn't know shalat [Ind. Muslim prayers], right? We have to know how to pray to God."

Thinking back to that morning, I am struck by the way in which these Muslims presented one another (and me) with different memories and commentaries on pangngae. The traditional songs must have been unintelligible to young Amang and Usri. Their memories, if they look back on that morning at all, will probably recognize in it a moment of play, a time when their father and his uncle made fun of some strange things I happened to record. Papa' Suri's ebullient recollections, ones that awakened memories in his limbs, suggested the nostalgic pleasures of looking back on youth. For Papa' Amang, the sumengo meant something quite different: a jinn-ridden godlessness that should be forgotten or heckled out of memory.

It is significant that the parody and mimetic gestures put on parade that morning attach not in an arbitrary way to ceremonial practice, but to genres of ritual conduct that can be grasped as aesthetic forms, as modes of spectacle. In his spot performance, Papa' Suri' recalled the speeches of mamose not as oratory, but as dance, and so largely stripped of their rhetorical and

ideological force vis-à-vis the dynamics of manhood and mappurondo tradition. There was no recognition of the violence that the "dance" in other
circumstances might imply. Papa' Amang, by way of comparison, parodied
a singing style rather than lyrics per se. His unflattering caricature of the
sumengo rendered mappurondo song as *dissonance,* as *noise,* and thus outside the socialized space of civil musics.[6] Mappurondo "arts" are held in
such poor regard that with few exceptions little effort is expended in the
Muslim community to cultivate pride in pemali appa' randanna. Rather, *ada'*
tuo, the moral and juridical tradition that distinguishes the mountains from
the coast (see Chapter 2), serves as their means of ideological continuity
and entry into the region's past. The Muslims of the headwaters are thus
free to dissociate themselves from the kafir beliefs and *animisme* of ancestral
tradition and to assert solidarity with the Muslim citizenry of Sulawesi. At
the same time, it affords them a virtuous past of their own. The ongoing
tradition of ada' tuo becomes a monument to an undominated moral order
and to a heritage of ethnic difference.

By and large, the Muslims in the Salu Mambi region are eager to promote and take part in Islamic arts: Koranic recitations, *kasidah* performances,
and so on. Yet so that there is no mistake, let me emphasize that the Muslim community has not dispensed with all ritual forms from the local past.
Weddings and funerals, for example, still preserve a good deal of the symbolic and performative edifice of local ritual tradition, even if Islamic authorities keep the events in line with strictures set down by the *Koran* or
Hadits. In short, local Muslims are not hostile to adat so long as agama is
not compromised. In fact, Muslims take an interest in exploring adat in the
name of *da'wah* (Ind. Islamic evangelical mission and outreach), even while
policing the limits of religious tolerance.

Such interests captured the attention of a young Muslim scholar from
the area named Fachruddin. Born in the village of Loka, a small Muslim settlement that looks across the river at Mambi, Fachruddin was schooled in
the city. At the time he entered the State Islamic Institute (*IAIN, Institut
Agama Islam Negeri*), he had virtually no experience with local ritual tradition in the headwaters. He undertook a *skripsi* (Ind. thesis or scholarly paper) project on da'wah and adat in the Mambi area, which he based on
interviews with relatives living high up on the mountain behind Loka, in
Salukepopo'. Pangngae earns just a paragraph in that skripsi (Fachruddin
1983:31), and I include a translation of his remarks for what they can tell
us about representations of local headhunting tradition. The passage begins
with the subtitle, "Pangngae [Gembira]," the bracketed Indonesian term
provided as a gloss for the word "pangngae":

Pangngae [Happy]

Pangngae is a traditional custom for which people feel great fondness, especially those who are already on in years, because in it one can experience many events that are very gladdening.

It needs to be said that in the past this ceremony always involved a few youths going off to a specific place with the task of taking a human head, and after succeeding, they would come back to gather at the adat house, and then those who had succeeded in carrying off the human head were given the title "Tobarani," meaning "brave ones."

Yet a situation like this no longer happens among the dark [i.e., *mappurondo*] community nowadays. Instead this part of pangngae has been replaced by a group of youths who go off in a certain direction, accompanied by loud shouts, by sounds from a bamboo instrument called tambola, and after they reach a certain distance, they come back to the starting point.

Fachruddin's portrayal is interesting for what it tactically admits or conceals, and for what it inadvertently misconstrues. Although he misses the way in which the ritual summons forth diverse themes, he nonetheless strikes a familiar chord with his peculiar translation of the term "pangngae." To have translated the term as "happy" suggests that the writer has learned something of the tenor of the ritual. But his effort reminds us about the basic tactical and political character of translation. To have chosen "happy" as a gloss for "pangngae" is to have evaded a different one: "headhunting." In Fachruddin's representation of the ritual, the invigorating sentiments of pangngae occlude the acts of violence that roil ceremonial discourse. Yet the passage goes on to admit a primordial violence, albeit one now displaced by noise and music. In a sense, Fachruddin raises the troubling specter of pagan violence, and then exorcises it by driving it into the past.

I feel some sympathy for Fachruddin. After all, my own analyses of the headhunt locate its violence back in the past, where it can safely be remembered, explained, and held in check. Fachruddin, too, is making an effort to acknowledge a significant historical change in ritual conduct. Yet his narrative of surrogation calls for the replacement of the head with the sound of shouts and the tambolâ. I note, meanwhile, that he is careful to skirt the matter of where the tobarani took heads: As he euphemistically puts it, they go off "to a specific place" to find their trophies. Even when he discusses flutes and shouts, he is careful to avoid saying that the youths go off from the settlement in a downstream direction. We must of course allow for confusion or lack of awareness on Fachruddin's part, but it seems odd that one would find it necessary to mention the headtaking of the past only to balk at asking about or revealing the identity of the victim. Here, let me suggest that Fachruddin may have been too aware that the quarry in pangngae was someone from the coast, a figure who can be reckoned today only as a Muslim. To have said as much in his brief account would have portrayed upland adat as inimical to Muslim interests.

What about grief and mourning? What about fertility? What about manhood? Fachruddin's silence on these issues hints that the specter of a now-absent ritual violence may have forestalled his exploration of the ritual's purposes and rationale. In any event, his brief mention of pangngae in the skripsi suggests not only Fachruddin's understandable ambivalence toward headhunting, but a difficulty fitting it into his conception of *pa'bisuan* as *seni budaya,* or "cultural arts" (Fachruddin 1983:30), a form of adat tradition that can be tolerated by the religious institutions associated with Islam, and that can be made intelligible to a readership of religious scholars and bureaucrats.

Christian Representations

While Muslims in the Salu Mambi area show a general lack of interest in indigenous ritual practice, Christians often look upon pemali appa' randanna as a basis for local culture and the cultural arts. For those Christians in Bambang, part of this interest stems from the territory's historical role as *Su'buan Ada',* the watchpost of adat. In joining the church, villagers feel no obligation to relinquish their guardianship of adat, or their privilege and authority in speaking about tradition. But conversion to Christianity has forced them to rethink the meaning of local ritual practice and the ways it should be tolerated, erased, or enshrined. It has also brought them into conflict with their mappurondo neighbors and kin.

Let me remind readers that most adults in the church between the years 1983 and 1985 were not born into Christian families, but converted to this world religion only after 1970.[7] This means that the majority of Christian adults had had some experience as participants in mappurondo ritual, including at least half a dozen who at one time had held ritual office in the mappurondo community. Adults who *were* born into Christian families typically claimed descent from ritual specialists who were said to have joined the church in the early 1930s. The upshot of all this is that Christians in Bambang can be rather dismissive of those remaining in the mappurondo community when it comes to knowing about pemali appa' randanna. They commonly claim—by virtue of descent or from having once held ritual office—that they themselves are the authorities on ceremonial knowledge, and that contemporary mappurondo villagers are inclined to mistakes and mis-understandings in their practices. In short, having relinquished their author-ity as *practitioners,* Christians in Bambang nonetheless insist on their au-thority as *interpreters* (and thus, representatives) of pemali appa' randanna.

This is not to say that Christians intrude upon mappurondo practices, or that Christian and mappurondo camps feud incessantly over ritual perfor-mance and meaning. In fact, conflict between the two groups happens more commonly over slights and hurtful remarks in daily encounters; the appro-priate time for planting terraces or playing music; or land or inheritance dis-putes involving people from mappurondo and Christian households. Rather, Christians put themselves in a position to speak to the world that lies be-yond the horizon. They are more adept than those "covered by the dark shroud" in adjusting to the discourse of Indonesian citizenship. Within that state-sanctioned discourse, Christians are more often than not *the* local au-thorities on what counts as religion, as adat tradition, and as history in Bambang and in much of the headwater region beyond.

Although the national government encourages its citizens to explore their past for the roots of local and regional tradition, it is careful to stress that traditions worth preserving and commemorating should fit with *Pan-casila,* the "Five-Point" state ideology.[8] By sifting through their local tradi-tions for signs and relics of Pancasila, people and communities throughout the archipelago discover that they have always been what they already are: Indonesian citizens. At the same time, the state, as much as any religious body, insists on distinguishing adat and agama. In light of these distinctions and pressures, Christians are inclined to set aside the pragmatic or purpose-ful dimensions of mappurondo ceremony in favor of the symbolic, allegori-cal, and aesthetic features of ritual life that fit with Pancasila morality. Just such an effort culminated in a skripsi, now lost, written by the Head of the Department of Education and Culture (formerly *P dan K,* now *Depdik-bud*), Kecamatan Mambi. A man of ToSalu birth, this civil servant felt that the "Four Points" of pemali appa' randanna were basically compatible with the "Five Points" of Pancasila.

Many Christians in Bambang are convinced that pemali appa' randanna has an acceptable moral foundation. More than a few openly expressed the view that if those holding to ada' mappurondo would just forsake making sacrifices to false gods, then everyone in Bambang could take part in the rites and ceremonies of pemali appa' randanna. In the most sophisticated treatment of ada' mappurondo available in Indonesian, Makatonan (1985), a clergyman born in the headwater region, argues that the rituals are mor-ally compatible with Christianity in most respects. In fact, he argues that pemali appa' randanna *already* expresses the Christian faith or creed and goes on to correlate mappurondo practices with Christian rites, concepts, liturgy, and scripture (Makatonan 1985:145–147). Not surprisingly, he uses a metonymic sleight of hand to reductively equate all of pangngae with dipandebarani, and then finds its Christian parallel in the Eucharist.

In contrast to Christians who describe pangngae as "a kind of harvest festival," the clergyman readily acknowledges that ritual violence plays a basic part in pangngae (Makatonan 1985:105–106). He begins on an ambivalent note, for the ritual does not quite fit his earlier description of pa'bisuan ceremonies as rites of passage:

Pangngae

Even though pangngae really no longer has a place in the [ritual] series of "*libana ma'rupatau*" (rites of passage on the path of a person's life), since it seems this ritual stands alone, it in fact still forms a special rite for raising/heightening the status of men, insofar as in the regional language pangngae is called "*tende-tendena pettomuanean*," meaning holding up the prestige of men. "Pangngae" is a kind of ceremonial headhunt.

Because there is nothing in the present that justifies the headhunters' violence, Makatonan turns to the past to find some reasonable grounds for taking heads. A story of treachery and resubordination, not unlike the one I discussed earlier in this book, offers a legitimating narrative for the commemorative violence of pangngae:

There are two sorts of background to the rites of pangngae, and they are as follows:

- It is told that in the past there was a slave family that poisoned their lord and then fled to the coast, where they hid in a place called Tenggelam. After a while they settled in a place called Abo' and prospered there. But because the community and family of the lord who died from poisoning were angry, every year courageous ones would go down to the coast in order to kill someone from Abo' in Tengkelam [Tenggelam] and as proof they had to carry a head back to their village. They were met with great joy and treated as heroes who had returned from the battlefield.

The commemorative violence of the headhunter is thus a heroic act that restores moral advantage to the uplands. It is violence that is good for everyone, including the coastal communities that Makatonan finds to be self-interested, complicit, and in any event, given over to human sacrifice:

- People on the coast also agreed with this practice. On the contrary, if people from Pitu Ulunna Salu did not come down to the coast again, they became worried that their prosperousness would be held back (failure of the rice crop, principally). So if they came down, then people on the coast would help them find a human head, especially if by coincidence those on the coast were running *"morara tau"* (a ritual that included human sacrifice, usually of an old slave), in which case the sacrificed head was turned over to the warriors who had gone down to the coast.

Then begins the narrative of surrogation and displacement. The violence that was the seal of regional sociality, prosperity, and accord absents itself, leaving coconuts and pretense its only trace. As "good" violence receded, so too did the gift economy that linked mountain and coast:

But in time, especially after Dutch administration, headhunts like these were forbidden. Because of that, the ritual regularly was run in a symbolic and commemorative way only. For example, the human head was replaced by a coconut shell. People on the coast only gave belongings instead of a head, and then in time these things were no longer given away, but bought or exchanged for other things.

Like Fachruddin, Makatonan gives no hint that the headhunt may have something to do with the work of grief and mourning; anguish remains untranslatable. Nor does he mention its connection with the recent harvest. Rather, the ritual simply brings the village together in communion:

The staging of pangngae goes like this:

- A person becomes the sponsor or principal who readies everything to hold pangngae (food, meat, and so on).

- After the preparations were completed, the sponsor along with a few other men would leave the village for as long as three days with the pretense, for example: of wanting to go get rattan or to go to the coast to buy fish and salt, or other reasons.

- After three days and three nights, they suddenly appear in the village in the middle of the night blowing bamboo called "tambola" (the form is almost the same as that used for bamboo music), but the tambola is decorated with palm or coconut leaves. They yell with an earsplitting voice until people in the village are startled awake. The shout is called mu'ada' [sic]. They are met by the head of the hadat [i.e. the tomatuatonda'] along with the people of the village.

- The next day at dawn they are received at the adat house. During midday they may return home, but at night they must stay at the adat house.

- Three days later, all the people in the village and their guests gather at the adat house. A rooster (it has to be a rooster, the symbol of the special qualities of men and cockerels) is for a sacrifice to God. Then everyone eats together. After eating, the ritual of pangngae is considered finished.

As I have noted, Makatonan was interested in demonstrating the way in which the moral foundations of ada' mappurondo fit with Christianity. To the extent that he succeeds, he opens a pathway between adat and agama:

Christians should not fear the celebration of local tradition, and mappurondo followers should not hesitate to enter Christianity. Yet another reading of these passages finds the author, too, absorbed in theological reflection on the symbolism of the Holy Communion, an effort couched in the allegorical narrative of headhunting. Surrogations and displacements of the headhunters' originary violence (from "literal" killing to "symbolic" killing) coalesce in a cultural narrative not unlike the one that ties bread and wine to the flesh and blood of Christ. In Makatonan's account, not only are the moral foundations of Christianity prefigured in ada' mappurondo, but both rely on shared logics of originary sacrifice and consumption.

Other strains in upland cultural politics complicate the way in which Christians picture the headhunt. Since as far back as the last years of Dutch colonial administration, there has been an effort on the part of those in the Christliche Gereformeerd Kerk and the Gereja Toraja Mamasa (GTM) to define a distinct upland social and cultural area that would contrast with lowland Muslim regions and with the Sa'dan Toraja (who had their own Protestant mission and church). Called *Kondo Sapata'* ("The Wide Rice Terrace"), this cultural and political project conjures a phantasmal social and historical order with Mamasa as its center.[9] It has yet to make its way into mappurondo ritual discourse. It in fact marks the cultural and political ascendancy of Mamasa in the late colonial and national periods. Yet its greatest influence is perhaps within the GTM, where it shapes church politics and presentations of the church's identity to the national community of Indonesian Christians.

Makatonan's treatment of ada' mappurondo—and, perforce, that of pangngae—may be read as an effort to subvert Mamasa's privileged position within Kondo Sapata' while retaining the rubric as the cultural bulwark for denominational identity. With his tract, a son of Pitu Ulunna Salu declares that his ancestral traditions are key to the past in Kondo Sapata'. Yet Christians from Mamasa have for some time been culture-poaching on the other side of the mountains, and in doing so, have had to grapple with headhunting. For example, the following text about pangngae is from an undergraduate thesis by Elisa Tamausa (1974:38–39). His work draws heavily on data from the Mamasa area, the place of his birth, and on information from his father, a Christian schoolteacher assigned to Salukepopo', the same village from which Fachruddin obtained his accounts of pangngae. Tamausa writes:

In order to rise to the "golden stake" [the highest social rank at Mamasa], a man must "pangngae" and a woman must do "bisu."

Etymologically, pangngae means to go fight a war. When the troop comes home from fighting the war, usually they are greeted in festive fashion by the whole village, dancing and singing mainly in praise of God for his protection, in praise of the heroes who are handsome and brave, and in praise of their weapons. In order to honor the victory obtained by the soldiers, a huge ceremony is held.

Pangngae, in the sense of a ritual for men who want to rise to the golden stake, is conducted only in a symbolic way. Before the ceremony is held, [some] people leave the village for three days. This is likened to pangngae or going to war, and on the third day, they come back to the village as if they were done fighting a war and carrying their spoils of victory. At that time the ritual is run in a ceremonial atmosphere that is joyful and festive. This rite of pangngae is conducted by sacrificing at least one water buffalo or forty pigs.

The point of pangngae is to plant a heroic and brave soul in the person who goes through it. Only when it is compared to the situation of the present does pangngae and its sacrifice of livestock become a matter that is fitting to be left behind. The goal of pangngae to plant the soul of heroism is good, even if the ceremony is excessive.

Like Makatonan, Tamausa emphasizes themes of manhood and heroic virtue.[10] But like Fachruddin, he has offered a peculiar etymology or meaning for the word "pangngae." It seems to me that Tamausa's ambivalence about ritual violence has led him to translate away the focal object and pursuit of pangngae: there is no headhunting here. In the alchemy of his account, the base violence of the headhunter turns into a bright and virtuous kind of masculine combat: celebratory warfare, that is, warfare with no enemies and no victims. Still, I suspect that Tamausa knows that pangngae is a commemorative headhunt. Not only does he point out that the ritual is "only run in a symbolic way," but he also finds himself censuring the sacrificial excess, so to speak, of the rite.

Dancing Men

So far, I have looked into the ways young scholars have represented the ritual headhunt in their analyses of local tradition. In preparing their skripsi or articles, they wrote for a fairly narrow readership of Indonesian speakers, and often with the purpose of obtaining credentials of some kind—a degree, a teaching certificate, or whatever. A potentially more influential group of commentators is to be found in tourguides, figures who have increasingly become key interpreters of upland traditions in Sulawesi (cf. Adams 1984; Volkman 1985, 1990). By and large, these tourguides come from the ranks of those who see ritual tradition as a source of cultural arts and values, a view encouraged by government efforts to revive and promote folk arts and tourism. They join other Christians in the region—usually those with schooling, positions in educational or administrative bureaucracies, and ties to Mamasa—in viewing pangngae as if it were a kind of song-and-dance spectacle.

This "ritual-as-art" interpretation comes across clearly in an English-language tourist pamphlet written by a Mamasa tourguide, Arianus Manda-dung, with the help of several Christians of ToSalu descent. The précis of pangngae in the pamphlet (Mandadung 1977:10–16) presents the ritual as a performance that symbolizes a man's overcoming the difficulties associated with rice cultivation. Trying to appeal to an audience that would no doubt look upon signs of ritual violence with deep worry, Mandadung's transla-tions of songs and other texts contain no references to headhunting.[11] In-stead, the tourist is treated to a comprehensive list of events, gestures, props, instruments, and key meanings (I retain the English of the original):[12]

MAN DANCE OF ADA' MAPPURONDO BELIEVING

I. The name of dance: "KAPANGNGAEAN DANCE" (Victory).

This dance is a part of the Pemali Appa' Randanna Principles of Ada' Mappurondo Believing. It's a ceremony separating Pa'totiboyongan Ceremony and Pa'bisuan Ceremony.

This dance is a symbol of Winning in a war. According to Ada' Mappurondo Believing that Pa'totiboyongan period is a difficult period. They must cultivate their ricefield with many difficulties to be successful, it means all the rice-field working is finished, they are winning like heroes retruning [returning] from a war. So, they hold the dance as a thanks ceremony to God. . . .

As mention above, the kapangngaean dance is a victory dance. They succeed in har-vest time and get a satisfactory yield. Kapangngaean Dance is held at the beginning of Pealloan (after harvest). Willing the success of harvest in the next year.

II. *THE MEANING OF EACH ACTION.*

There are 7 actions as below:

1. *Ma'tambola.* (They blow bamboo flute) Ma'tambola is symbolic of victory in a war.

They come to blow bamboo flute in order for the community to hear and testify as trough [though] they return from a war victriously [victoriously], blow the bamboo flutes to symbolize victory.

2. *Kelong Osong.* (Co-operation Song).

When they start for the war, they keep something secret. They perform cooperatvly [cooperatively] untill [until] they get Victory.

3. *Denna.* (The main victory song)

They perform as evidence that they are winners in war. They ara [are] far from evil and they are faithful to Pemali Appa' Randanna (Four Principles).

4. *Sengo.* (Worship song to the heroes).

The followers of the ceremony and heroes sing together as thanks to God and Heroes celebrate their winning.

5. *Sibatta.* (War action using knife).

They perform to show that war is not an easy thing, but a difficult thing.

6. *Sirussung-russung.* (Orderly).

Performance that they cooperate in war. Not won by someone but their compact to oppose enemy.

7. *Sarabandang.* (Variation).

This actin [action] is a variation of the Pa'bisuan Dance.

III. *THE LEADERS OF DANCE AND EQUIPMENT*

1.a. *Pangngae dance,* led by Topuppu (a man as leader in a war command). . . .

2.a. *The equipment of Pangngae Dance*

—Tambolang.   —Unta'.
—Knife for war.   —Drum.
—Spear.   —Etc. . . .

IV. *THE MEANING OF WORDS SONG (sung) BY THE DANCERS*

1. *Kelong Osong.*

Rimuanni alenta passanggatai angganna, talao-talao tapamesa naba-naba, olai sibali angki olai sibali, karabai dai bottenna lasi balinta

The meaning:

Let's assemble to get supplies. Strategy will demolish the fortress of our enemy.

2. *Denna.*

Mattangko-mattangko tau, anta tanan talingai alukna bisu muane.

The meaning:

Let's be quiet and follow the program in this ceremony.

3. *Sengo.*

Kulu-kulu sae bongi saraso sae nannari sae umbungka' bambata.

The meaning:

The heroes compared with kulu-kulu (a kind of bird). Kulu-kulu is a kind of bird, like a cock's crow, always wakes up a person.

4. *Sirussung-russung komai.*

Pomakambanni boko'ki, indanna tandaan usukki, tandaan maka boko'ki.

The meaning:

Let's follow the ceremony, in hoping all the programs end successful without obstacles.

VI. *THE LITERARY WORDS BY THE LEADER AND MEMBERS.*

The dalogue [dialogue] between the leader and members.

Leader: Toaka koa'?
        Who are you?

Member: Tountungka'i botto.
        Who will open the harvest.

Leader: Menna mamunga'?
        Who is the first planner?

Member: To mention a first planner.

Leader: Menna ma'peulu?
        Who is the first working?

Member: To mention the first worker.

Leader: Menna ma'tandean?
        Who is the follower?

Member: Topatalo!
        The winner.

Leader: Masakke-sakke koka'?
        Are you well?

Member: Masakkekan!
        Yes we are.

Leader: malesoka?

        [deletion]

Member: Maleso. Malepon anna bulan.
        Yes, we are. Right like moon round.

Penassa'i lesola, pomakita-kita'i, tala kabaranian, katomakakaan, sapo mesa-mesanna simemanganna Botto anna katonanna peadasan.

The meaning:

To let know, they aren't base or brave, wealthy, deviant, but all of them are demand of Pemali Appa' Randanna.

Thus, the short explanation of Men Dance of Ada' Mappurondo Believing.

Mandadung's pamphlet anticipates, and in a sense promises, an encounter in which the foreign tourist will have an opportunity to look upon and listen to mappurondo ritual. Through 1985, chances remained slim: After all, most pa'bisuan rituals take place sometime between mid-March and mid-May, and even then they proceed under pemali restraints that prevent much in the way of advance notice. Tourism, meanwhile, has hardly put down roots in the Salu Mambi watershed. Between 1982 and 1985 five foreign tourists passed through Mambi, two of whom trekked through Bambang, and there were no tourists of Indonesian nationality. In short, the area had been more or less neglected, eclipsed by the spectacle of Tana Toraja, a place known for elaborate funerary rites, carved effigies of the dead, and the ornate, eye-catching facades of the traditional-style houses called *tongkonan*.

Mandadung, it should be recalled, is himself an outsider when it comes to headwater culture. Basa Bambang is not his native language, nor has he spent much time in the mappurondo communities. In preparing the pamphlet he relied on ToSalu Christians who were interested in organizing and promoting their own team of dancers and drummers, a group that consciously styled itself as traditional. Never a stable group, as such, and made up of siblings and cousins under the leadership of Petrus Dadeko (a local entrepreneur) it would come together *outside of Bambang* to rehearse for *pameran budaya* (cultural exhibitions) sponsored by the GTM, the Kecamatan, or the Kabupaten. The intent of the "Man Dance" text, then, is to represent not only the mappurondo rite that a tourist or outsider might encounter in Bambang, but also the performances of a revivalist dance-and-drum team that would be putting on a show in Mamasa, Polewali, or Ujung Pandang.

The vocabulary of Mandadung's text presents both headhunting ritual and revival performance as culture, as worthy of exhibition and translation to an audience of outsiders. It is a vocabulary familiar to the arts: the ceremony comprises dances and dancers, and songs and gestures. There are "literary words" by the topuppu and the dancers. The neat survey of genres and their meaning reflects an effort to put the ritual in order, so to speak. But I note, too, that the pamphlet also reads like a program for a stage performance, and in that sense is no guide to the actualities of ritual drama.

Like Tamausa, Mandadung and his collaborators recognize strains of

deadly fury in pangngae. And like Tamausa, they render it as symbolic violence—as violence that is absent except in the commemorative form of a
victory dance. At first glance, no one appears to fall victim to this cloaked
violence. Rather, the subsistence farmer is now the warrior; it is rice that has
been felled. But it is precisely here that an act of textual violence occurs, for
it is women, not men, who are the principal planters and harvesters of the
rice crop. In this way, the "Man Dance" tourist pamphlet elides and subordinates the figure of women.

Mandadung is not the first uplander from Sulawesi to equate headhunting with harvesting. In fact, the commentaries of Downs (1955) and Adriani and Kruyt (1950) on the central highlands would support Mandadung.[13]
The interest in establishing pangngae as a *pesta panen,* a harvest festival,
leads Mandadung and his coauthors to erase or write-over violence in translating "The Literary Words by the Leader and Members," substituting a
scene of harvest for a scene of violence (and within the scene of harvest,
substituting men for women). My own translation of "the literary words"
would not feature rice harvesters, but would go as follows:

Leader:	Who are you?
Member:	The one who opens the village.
Leader:	Who landed the first blow?
Member:	[name]
Leader:	Who took the head?
Member:	[name]
Leader:	Who held it up?
Member:	The victor.
Leader:	Are you well?
Member:	We are well.
Leader:	Is it clear?
Member:	It's clear. Rounder than the moon.

Listen up, okay, my friends, and gather round. It isn't bravery or arrogance but only
for village tradition and the principles of adat.

The "Literary Words by the Leader and Members" contain the only signs
of harvest to be transcribed into the pamphlet. Although this section of the
pamphlet may have accurately rendered a memorized exchange between
dancers, the text has its genealogy in the shifting and unstable memories of
past *a'dasan* ("the shouting"; see Chapter 4). Several ToSalu acquaintances
remembered Mandadung's visit to their headwater village, and the effort of

Christians there to help him compile the text that would become "literary words." Mandadung did not tape-record a'dasan during his visit. Had he done so, he might have recorded something like the following, transcribed and translated from the a'dasan ceremonies of 1985, ceremonies that took place in the very village where Mandadung sought his materials:

Topuppu:	*Too'na [Cohort Leader]:*
Oe what are you?	Oe ones from Tenggelan!
Oe what are you?	Oe ones from Tenggelan!
Oe you there what are you?	Aei ones from Tenggelan!
Who landed the first blow?	Oe [name of too'na]!
Who slashed open the neck?	E [name of lolona]!
Who lifted up the victim?	E [name of headhunter]!
Who took his things?	E [name of headhunter]!
E are all of you all right?	E listen closely friend and look at us, isn't it clear?
Is it clear?	It's clear, eight heads are carried as seven limbs go swinging!

The differences between Mandadung's text, the a'dasan greetings of 1985, and the memories of villagers were significant enough to spark concerned discussion over ritual speech and its presumed fixity. Like others in Bambang, Mandadung and his collaborators chose to inscribe genres of speech that they perceived or thought to be invariant (George 1990). Instead of instantiating the fixity of ritual speech, the "Man Dance" text exposes its ephemerality and flux.

For many, changes in ritual speech, examined in memory and from different religious precincts, signaled a culture in disarray. One friend recalled for me the way a'dasan was done in Salutabang in the 1940s and 1950s:

Topuppu:	*Topangngae:*
E who is it?	[silence]
E who is it?	[silence]
E who is it?	E someone from Tenggelan!
Who took the first blow?	E [name of too'na]!
Who raised the victim?	E [name of lolona]!
Who took the head?	E [name of eldest topangngae]!

Who grabbed loot?	E [name of next eldest]!
Who slashed open the neck?	E [name of next eldest]!
Yalelelele yuhuhu!	Listen closely, friend!
	Not bravery not arrogance
	but only village tradition
	the abundance of pemali appa' randanna

Another, recollecting his first experience as a topangngae in the early 1970s, remembered the a'dasan exchange somewhat differently, insisting that it should go like the following:

Topuppu:	*Topangngae:*
E who is it?	[silence]
E who is it?	[silence]
E who is it??	[depending on version of pangngae to take place]:
	E the one who opens the village! [or]
	E the one who puts blood on the seedlings! [or]
	E the one who strikes his self! [or]
	E the one who sets loose his vow! [or]
Are all of you all right?	We are well!
Who took the first blow?	E [name of too'na]!
Who raised the victim?	E [name of Iolona]!
Who took the head?	E [name of eldest topangngae]!
Who grabbed loot?	E [name of next eldest]!
Who [witnessed this?]?	E [name of next eldest]!
Yalelelele yuhuhu!	Listen closely, friend!
	Not bravery not arrogance
	but only village tradition
	the principles of adat!

The changes in the way the headhunters announce themselves in a'dasan (1940s: as ones from afar; 1970s: as ones from home) or make mention of adat—however slightly—caused my friends to worry. Yet their concern had less to do with which version was authentic or right, but rather with what appeared to be a crisis in memory. Memory had failed to fix these forms; there was slippage. And it was lapses like these that Christians could and would seize upon in their effort to attack or erode the authority of those remaining in the mappurondo communities.

Ambivalence, Nostalgia, and Scepticism

Resistance to exogenous forces is a key theme in pangngae and, indeed, holding pangngae at all is, for the mappurondo communities of Bambang, a gambit in the asymmetrical play of conflicting social and cultural spheres. After all, the effort to maintain cultural continuity with the past through the rites of pangngae may itself be a form of resistance to the contemporary order. Yet from time to time the pressures bearing on the mappurondo communities have sparked a confrontational response. In 1958, a time of islandwide rebellion, a cohort of headhunters from an upland village ambushed a rebel military patrol near Mambi and took a head. Twenty-seven years later, singers from another village took on a parade of oppositional figures conjured from both the past and the present. Taunting the head to call downstream for help, the babalako and the chorus summoned opponents from the ranks of the dominant polities of the last 200 years:

call the baligau
call the kingdom
call the kepala desa [head of village district]
call the tuan landschap [Dutch controlleur]
call the police
call the kepala daerah [head of regional district]

Daring words. But, then, to have challenged these forces in song is to have made concession once more to the political realities that have forestalled more direct resistance to a threatening world.

Over and against such outbursts of fear, resentment, or opposition, the headhunters of today are usually quite eager to prove themselves good citizens. The exhortations of mamose speakers from Rantepalado by 1985 could include calls to compliance with government programs:

Whenever he who is strong-willed
starts off for below
enough children follow. . . .
And he will follow . . .

the government agent's orders
work and work
pay taxes pay taxes. . . .

Because alu' mappurondo is brighter than the sun
clearer than the face of the moon.
If we are strong-willed
we will bring it about again
we will grasp firmly
what was said by the elders.
They said:
It is golden, pemali appa' randanna
It is golden, the government
Listen closely, friend

Going downstream need not be a gesture of violent resistance to the contemporary political order. As the speech suggests, committing oneself to
pangngae and, more broadly, to mappurondo tradition could be an exercise
in citizenship.

For more than a century the mappurondo communities of Bambang have
relied on a tradition of concealment as a practical means of defending themselves and their ritual practices against encroaching ideologies and social
formations. As I have argued elsewhere (George 1993a), that culture of
concealment was not just the work of the mappurondo enclave but rather
a phenomenon that emerged in, and served both sides of, the mutual encounter between Islam and local ancestral practice. In short, the culture
of secrecy took shape as the collaborative work of opposed groups. But
from the vantage point of the present regime, the practicalities of enclavement look more like the gestures of the backward, the subversive, and the
wrongheaded.

This dilemma was enough to prompt Ambe Deppa', a ToIssilita' man
from Rantepalado, to campaign for official recognition of ada' mappurondo
under the auspices of Parisada Hindu Dharma. Given the insularity of the
mappurondo communities in each village, it is not surprising that Ambe
Deppa' got at best only lukewarm support from people elsewhere in Bambang. Although most were eager to have their ritual tradition recognized as
agama, they were deeply worried about the practical consequences of being
named a branch of Hinduism. Would they have to be subordinate to the
Hindu and Aluk To Dolo leadership in Bali and Tana Toraja? Would they
have to host guests from those regions? Could they afford to? Still, Ambe
Deppa' went ahead with his idea and asked for my company and support in

a visit to the Hindu representatives in the provincial capital. Received very graciously and with sincere interest, Ambe Deppa' nonetheless met disappointment: Parisada Hindu Dharma could not arrange or extend recognition unless the mappurondo community could set up fixed sites for ritual gatherings and, most problematically, establish administrative offices, or formal representation, at the Desa, Kecamatan, and Kabupaten levels. For a minority religious community with no followers outside of a few desa in a single kecamatan, the bureaucratic obstacles to gaining recognition far exceed ideological ones. The mappurondo community is too small to matter.[14]

As of 1985, recognition of ada' mappurondo was not forthcoming, and practicing communities continued to erode. Although the rites of pangngae resonate with the strains of resistance, it seems doubtful that they will be the means for a thorough revival or revitalization of mappurondo practices. For now, the ritual is a place for pride and parody, for faith and irony, for order, nostalgia, and disarray, a place to question the community, its horizons, and one's commitment to it. In Rantepalado, Ambe Deppa' was trying to get the whole community to give, once again, shares of rice for dipandebarani, rather than let the burden fall just upon the parents of the tobarani and the tomatuatonda'. Across the river in Minanga, Ambe Assi' and Ambe Dido exercised their prerogative in coining new practices and hosted a version of pangngae that they called *ma'kainda-indai,* "always envying it" or "always longing for it," an innovation that guests from Rantepalado greeted with derision: "What is this ma'kainda-indai? That's nothing any of our elders did."

Farther upstream in Salutabang, Ambe Teppu—the man who taught me about the raw, the religious, the cooked, and the cultural—was showing signs of doubt. Or perhaps I should say he was showing a change of heart. A man of his wealth, some complained, should host a pa'bisuan ceremony for his household and the community. Once again he would disappoint them, reserving his rice and pigs for the wedding planned between his daughter, now converted to the church, and a Christian schoolteacher from the Salu Mokanan. In fact, his household and family reflected the strains and tensions evident throughout Bambang. Though he had the wealth and prestige of a *tomakaka'* ("the prosperous one"), Ambe Teppu showed a reluctance to sacrifice resources for acts of hospitality in ritual. Schooled for brief periods by the Dutch, he could improvise a prayer and on one occasion even passed himself off for a Christian, on a journey we took together to a remote village in another watershed. His brother, a retired civil servant, lived in Mambi and was devoted to games of chess. The two did not get along and easily slighted one another (a few short weeks before I left the headwaters, they were in a heated inheritance dispute). Ambe Teppu's wife, Indona Teppu, was a *sando baine*—a key specialist in mappurondo household rites— but she was experiencing pains and flashes. Something had happened to her in the rice granary, and it left her unable to stand erect for a week or more. It was a sign, and Ambe Teppu wanted her to turn over her ritual authority and obligations to someone else.

His oldest son and another two daughters held firm to ada' mappurondo. But Paulus, Ambe Teppu's youngest son, had entered the church several years before and had married the pastor's daughter, Ina. Bright, cheerful, and devoted to his wife, Paulus for a while had moved his household to Mambi, where he kept a team of ponies to work the trade of goods in and out of the watershed. He and Ina had done well, and had moved back upstream to Salutabang to work the weekly market at Rantelemo. Ambe Teppu voiced real pride in Paulus, and bragged how his son once had gone to the provincial capital with Petrus Dadeko's dance team to represent the people of the headwaters.

Several weeks before the pangngae celebrations of 1985, Ina passed away. She had given birth to their first child, but her placenta failed to descend. Paulus and her family waited six days, hopeful about her recovery, unsure what to do as she lay writhing with fever. Afraid of a predatory spirit that is said to linger beside trails in order to attack women weakened from giving birth, Paulus and the others decided not to carry her out of the safety of the village to the clinic, 14 kilometers downstream. She died in a moment of stillness, exhausted from the pain within her.

Arriving two days ahead of a'dasan ceremonies in Salutabang, I made my usual stop at Ambe Teppu's. Paulus was grieving there and would not leave the house or yard. His father turned to me, making sure he spoke loud enough for Paulus to hear, "What about this? Won't leave the house at all." While his father kept up the bluff that he hoped would stir his son, Paulus would not look at me. "For me," Ambe Teppu said, "one day after my wife dies, I'll go look for another." For most of the morning Paulus sat below the rice barn or paced restlessly over the packed dirt of the yard. Ascending once more into the house when his mother put out some food, Paulus slumped over to cry. Breaking into loud shaking sobs, he gasped out words that seemed to look for blame and some answer to Ina's death and his suffering. Paulus started to thrash his head and his father barked at him to stop. Paulus leaned over, crying for me to pity him, and as I stroked his shoulder, I looked up at Ambe Teppu only to find him staring out the window lost in what was probably his own bitterness. By now, Ambe Oma was at our side, and he too was taken by the atmosphere of grief and remorse. Like Ambe Teppu, he tried to ease the disconsolate man beside me. "When Mama Oma died we were married just four years. But I said, 'This isn't my business. It's God's.' So I started looking for a new wife."

That Sunday, Ina's father barely managed to take part in worship services, and Paulus himself was absent. A few evenings later, after a'dasan had already taken place, Paulus showed up at a pangngae songfest looking drained and lost. The exuberant singing did little to lift his spirits and he soon stepped back out into the dark. He was a Christian, after all. No tambolâ had sounded below his door, he was not up to singing, the church frowned on such things, and nothing was going to bring back his wife. Paulus would have to find his own way of putting the world back together after Ina's death. Yet his few minutes at the ritual songfest continue to impress me as the searching, hopeful gesture of someone looking to a ceremonial gathering that promised some measure of comfort.

Ambe Teppu did not take part in pangngae ceremonies either, that year (these were the ceremonies I described in Chapter 7). He, too, stayed close to home. Over meals he would tell me that all the debata summoned in the topuppu's presentation of the head were manifestations of Debata Tometampa, "The Shaper," and I wondered to myself if his explanation did not show the influence of Christian thinking and Pancasila ideology. He looked back, too, to the time before his waning years, comparing himself to the youths that would parade themselves in dipandebarani the next day. "These guys think they are real roosters, and know all about women. When I was young, I was like this all the time." He put two fingers together and held them erect. "If I wanted a woman I was with her."

I pestered the man about why he had decided not to take part in pangngae. "The singing's no good now. Listen to it. When I was younger, the gathering was smaller, everything was in place." His complaints, it seemed to me, were signs of someone readying himself for a change, the small tremors that may alert us to a major shift in thinking. Doubt, grief, disillusionment, and calculation all may have played a part in his reluctance to attend pangngae that year. After leaving the Salu Mambi valley in 1985 I had little way of knowing whether his doubts had led him to abandon ada' mappurondo. News did come once: I quote a short passage from the only letter I have from him. Dated in June 1991 and composed with the help of a Christian writer, the passage reads, translated,

The dances of pa'bisuan are still going on at Salutabang, and please pass that along to friends in America so that they will make a visit to Salutabang. Tourists already have come once to see the dances of pa'bisuan. Please try, so that the dances can get promoted in other lands.

Reading Ambe Teppu's letter, I could only be apprehensive about changes that might have taken place in the headwaters. After all, beans do get roasted for coffee. Grain does get hulled and cooked. And in light of Indonesian modernities, it should not surprise us if someone in a remote highland village decided to forsake local religion for state culture, and put away the relics of a headhunter's violence in the attic of memory.

9

Epilogue

The Headwaters, 1994

Headhunting rumors and scares are a persistent and troubling facet of social life in many parts of Indonesia. In most instances, people fear a kind of headhunter who is rather different from the ones I have written about in this book. These days the more common predator is a "government headhunter" (Tsing 1993, forth.) or a similarly violent figure associated with development projects, international corporations, and some of the other dangerous forces that have been unleashed in the postcolonial era (Drake 1989, Erb 1991, Hoskins forth. [a], Pannell 1992). In places accustomed to coercion and state violence, a sense of dread understandably overtakes people when they learn of a construction project, of plans for oil or logging ventures, or of new bridges, roads, and hotels that will bring outsiders closer to their communities. In their panic, people worry that powerful strangers will have to find human heads for the official ceremonies that will ratify and strengthen these public works. Though it seems unlikely that planners, police, engineers, military figures, foreign consultants, or civil servants actually do engage in this particular kind of violence, the persistence of headhunting rumors is a telling expression of people's anxiety and vulnerability in coping with the Indonesian state order, an order whose leadership frequently relies on coercion and terror to exercise its authority and promote its vision of economic development.

Ethnographic interest has in fact begun to quicken around the figure of the government headhunter. I suspect some of this interest stems from the pleasure felt in watching a small community upset the demonologies of Indonesian modernity. Many Indonesian "moderns" think of the unruly and marginal uplanders of Sulawesi, Kalimantan, and Eastern Indonesia as headhunters and primitive relics. But in not a few upcountry locales, it is the "moderns" who are the violent and the feared. Taking our cue from these fearful upland outcasts, we might try to relocate the headhunter in the civil order, and so expose the state's exercise of official power and violence. Yet this effort finds us retaining or reinstalling—in very problematic ways—the image of the savage (cf. Trouillot 1991).

Although they may be destined for a struggle over the ideas and emblems that will define civility and modernity, today's marginal communities are not so much concerned with the savage as absorbed with flows of official power. Headhunting traditions of the sort described in this book typically represent acts of legitimate or legitimating violence. Headhunting rumors and panics, by contrast, usually signal a small community's loss of political autonomy. Commenting respectively on the Dayak and Mayawo, societies that once had headtaking practices of their own in the precolonial era, Drake (1989) and Pannell (1992) have argued that colonial suppression of headhunting rituals proved to be instrumental in the collapse of local political power. Contemporary headhunting scares in these two societies reflect ongoing anxieties over the loss of autonomy to colonial and postcolonial forces.

In a more complex and nuanced analysis of such panics, Tsing (1993, forth.) finds that stories of government headhunters circulating among the Meratus of southeast Kalimantan contribute to the maintenance of peripheral vulnerability, a situation that plays right into the hands of the Indonesian state. Yet she is at pains to point out that the Meratus' current intimidation is consonant with a long regional history of headhunting, a history in which they were usually victims rather than predators. Furthermore, the terrain of terror and vulnerability has formed "leadership landscapes" in which shamans and other local leaders make tactical use of fearfulness to promote their own authority. Leaders use stories of violence to remind others of their common vulnerability. But through "fierce eyewitnessing" these leaders assert their bravery and their ability to transcend, appease, recruit, elude, or survive the violence emanating from afar. Although their communities are encompassed by the state, Meratus leaders do not concede defeat in the face of postcolonial order and violence. Rather, they come up with new ways and new stories to manage fear and power. Here, local autonomy is not so much lost as continually refigured.

Rumors about government headhunters and predatory project engineers are not lacking in Sulawesi. I myself heard some from urban acquaintances, having to do mostly with the construction of bridges and cement factories in the Bugis lowlands. But the mappurondo communities of Bambang, I should emphasize, were free of such panics or rumors during my time there. It would have been quite odd, in fact, for those who performed pangngae on an annual basis to worry about losing their own heads to strangers. Neither did mappurondo headhunters cause alarm downstream in Mambi, or in Mandar settlements. They pass through these places unnoted, their violence long stilled.

Seclusion and a tradition of ritualized headhunting practices have helped the mappurondo communities to cope with the rise and expansion of the postcolonial order. Enclavement in an isolated highland valley—a place consistently overlooked for development, welfare, or resettlement projects—has hidden them from view and for the most part has kept them out of the violent plans and fears of administrative officers and state agencies. Pangngae, meanwhile, has been a way for the communities to reclaim political autonomy—however fleetingly and problematically.

Well rooted in tradition and place, the mappurondo communities nevertheless have suffered social and cultural dislocation. Enclavement has kept them from keeping up with other communities in the national sphere, and pangngae largely alludes to a vanished political terrain. Generally speaking, the headhunters of the mid-1980s were more than willing to join the ranks of Indonesian citizens, but on terms that allowed them to carry on with pangngae, the central political event of their communities. The choice posed was not an easy one: give up the headhunt and, with it, mappurondo history and polity, or remain headhunters and suffer the epithets *yang terbelakang, yang terasing, orang kafir, tomalillin*—"the backward," "the remote," "the godless," "persons of the dark"—all euphemisms for those suspected of resisting the dominant order. What was and is at stake in pangngae, then, is the making of social relations and social meanings, both within the community and without. Staging the ritual headhunt, in this light, is a hunt for meaning and some measure of autonomy in the asymmetrical play of conflicting social and cultural spheres.

Contrary to the workings of violence and the grotesque in carnival and other rites of inversion, the exaggerated and anatomizing violence of pangngae is central to mappurondo political order: it is the official violence of a small ideological enclave. As we have seen, this discourse of violence, this ritualized gesture of autonomy, includes elements of both resistance and acquiescence to powerful exogenous forces. It preserves a language for articulating the enclave's dependence upon and vulnerability to a social world lying just over the horizon. One may plausibly read pangngae as an allegory of struggle against the modern Indonesian order. But a ceremonial reversion to precolonial times—and thus a momentary return to a period when enmity was harnessed to indices of prosperity—suggests that pangngae is not so much an allegorical discourse of struggle against the contemporary order as a practical discourse of retreat into the past. Denied the ideological or institutional legitimacy enjoyed by Christians and Muslims, it seems realistic for this minority religious community to make predatory raids in the social terrain of a bygone era, not only for the purpose of seeking legitimacy in the past but with the task of sustaining commemorative control of its historical foundations as well.

Rarely do we see the mappurondo communities trying to defy the Indonesian government. On the contrary, pangngae already includes efforts to accommodate or comply with the state's program for good citizenship. But the violence at the heart of pangngae is stubborn proof that the discourse of Indonesian citizenship has failed to reach deeply into mappurondo sociality. The mappurondo communities still evince a desire to govern their own remembering, their own mourning, and their own images of manhood and womanhood, through the idiom of violence.

Walking upriver from Mambi into Bambang in June 1994, Papa Ati and I stopped at the home of Ambe Deppa' at Rantepalado. Things were different. Behind us in Mambi, a paved road led out of the mountains to the coast, carrying a light, but steady, back-and-forth traffic of goods and people. Chocolate, the new cash crop, had proven extremely profitable. Bugis-backed trading ventures seemed to have been a success as well. Several households now had televisions and satellite dishes, and most townspeople spent their evenings in prayer and watching programs originating from Jakarta, Malaysia, Singapore, Australia, and the United States.

It looked like Ambe Deppa' was doing all right, too. In place of a home with earthen floor, thatched roof, and woven bamboo walls, stood a two-story house made of boards and zinc roofing. Sitting on the veranda, I asked about the floods of 1987 that devastated the valley floor at Mambi and some of the neighboring watersheds. Ambe Deppa' was more eager to talk about the United States' display of power in taking on a Muslim adversary in the Gulf War of 1991. Yet that topic proved to be a way of getting around to a more immediate worry: there had been fights at the border between Bambang and Mambi. Growing suspicion and smoldering resentments between Muslims and Christians had sparked the encounters, and just weeks before my visit there had been an effort on the part of the district administration at Mambi to annex land from Bambang. The proposed annexation brought the mappurondo and Christian communities of Bambang together in mutual interest. As Ambe Deppa' and Papa Ati saw it, Mambi's attempt to appropriate land from Bambang did not differ that much from Iraq's absorption of Kuwait. The annexation, in their view, was illicit, and served the interests of an aggressive Muslim neighbor.

But in a sense, Bambang no longer existed. Divided into two desa in the late 1980s to reflect ToSalu and ToIssilita' spheres of interest, the former adat territory of Bambang was reorganized yet again in 1993 and now comprises five rather underpeopled desa. It is too early to know what impact the administrative partitioning of Bambang will have on local political life. Individual settlements may enjoy a greater degree of autonomy, but the autonomy thus won may erode a sense of the shared interests and shared history of the ToBambang. Then, too, the partitioning of Bambang evidences the steady, bureaucratic advance of the Indonesian state into the headwater communities. Yet although an expanded government presence will surely alter the political terrain of Bambang with respect to state interests, it nonetheless may create new opportunities and tactical choices for furthering individual or community agenda.

By Ambe Deppa's account, the mappurondo communities were holding their own. The community at Rantepalado still held pangngae every year, and Ambe Deppa' had heard that a household in the village was planning to run *melambe,* one of the more important rites directed by women. But Ambe Deppa' had special news for me. Nine years earlier, he and I had gone to Ujung Pandang together in the hope of finding support for ada' mappurondo from Parisada Hindu Dharma. Opening a locked drawer, Ambe Deppa' took out a set of documents prepared and signed in the provincial capital a few short months before. The provincial offices of the Department of Education and Culture (Depdikbud) had recognized ada' mappurondo as a government-sanctioned "sect" or "stream of belief" (Ind. *aliran kepercayaan*) under provisions set down by laws passed in 1986. Years of effort had finally started to pay off. With these documents, Ambe Deppa' could begin to bring pressure on Kabupaten and Kecamatan offices to shield rather than censure mappurondo practices. Although ada' mappurondo did not enjoy the status of state-recognized religions, at least steps could be taken to help it persist as a cultural tradition.

Reading the documents, I of course felt surprise and delight, but I also harbored some worries. Official recognition of ada' mappurondo brought with it some troubling terms and possibilities. Followers were obliged to swear allegiance to Pancasila (the Indonesian state ideology), profess faith in a supreme god, declare themselves clean of communist leanings, and commit themselves to national development. Perhaps more burdensome than these ideological gestures—which were required of all Indonesian citizens—were organizational demands. Under the terms of the documents, the mappurondo communities were obliged to let any Indonesian citizen participate in adat celebrations and to establish a leadership at desa and kecamatan levels consisting of secretarial and administrative officers. These boards of officers would oversee and police group interests and report on all activities to concerned government agencies. Official recognition thus demanded that the mappurondo enclave reformulate its social horizons and open itself to the gaze of Indonesia's state apparatus.

We have seen that political autonomy, for the mappurondo communities, involves not only reasserting and managing their claims to ritual tradition, but also keeping a rein on a communal economy of mourning. No matter what ideological precinct the upland villagers choose to inhabit, they will have to confront crises of grief and loss. For those in the mappurondo communities, pangngae offers a discursive means for overcoming personal anguish. Yet the violence of the headhunt also quiets collective anxieties that occur in the wake of someone's death, especially that of an elder, whose passing is experienced communally as a wound to the social body. Finding solace in ceremonial violence is a way to surmount such problems in communal reproduction. Violence, vows, song, and oratory, we have seen, set up trajectories for sentiment and will within the polity, and effectively relieve the community of the burdensome sense of darkness, weight, and immobility it associates with loss.

Across the river in Minanga, Ambe Assi' and Ambe Dido told me that Pua' Soja, the last living witness to the earliest Dutch patrols in the headwater region, was dead. I was not surprised, and ventured that the old man was missed. I was far less prepared to learn that Tasomba, the gifted orator whose mamose speech welcomed me to Minanga in 1983, had died as well. I told Ambe Assi' and Ambe Dido how much I would have enjoyed speaking with Tasomba again, and how keenly I remembered his speechmaking, storytelling, and flute playing. Tasomba's mamose speeches about being strong-willed and firm in support of ada' mappurondo obviously had fallen on listening ears. Pangngae continued to take place every year, and the *peal-loan* season that had just passed brought to five or six the number of elaborate women's rites that had taken place since 1985. The despair I had felt for several years over the fate of the mappurondo communities now seemed prejudiced and premature. The mappurondo community at Minanga had grown by several households, a rebound brought about in part by three young men who—born and raised as Christians—abandoned the church in order to take mappurondo wives.

Political autonomy in the mappurondo enclave also entails some control over ideas about manhood and womanhood, and over the structures of envy that animate village life. The rites of pangngae are a means for creating an exemplary figure of manhood: headhunter and rhetorician. Valorous and violent as headhunters, men also try to prove their virtuosity and authority as speechmakers. Although the ritual excludes women from its focal work, it nonetheless epitomizes women as adulatory singers whose desire and flattery sustain the masculine will to power. Local social hierarchies relating men to men and men to women rest in this discursive field. Envy, emulative desire, and a striving for excess—an edgy mix of the will to sameness and the will to differ—have their generative source in pangngae. Put into motion, they not only play into the reproduction of mappurondo social order but also go a long way toward setting the tenor of contemporary village life.

The images of men and women portrayed in the discourse of pangngae have continued relevance for those who remain committed to ada' mappurondo. But this may be true, too, for some of those who have left the mappurondo community for the church. Reunited with friends in Salutabang, I had a chance to speak with Mikael, a young man who directed the musical group in his church. I had previously known Mikael by another name when he was a young teen and had been honored as a mappurondo headhunter. A photo of him from that time can be found on p. 166 (Figure 15). Taller, married, and Christian, he seemed now to have the respect of the men and women around him, and his position as a figure in the local church hierarchy no doubt contributed to his prestige. But like many other Christian men who had been born to mappurondo families, Mikael had waited until he had been honored in pangngae before embracing the church. Having accomplished himself as a valorous tobarani (though not as an orator, as I recall), he had achieved equality with other men, and fulfilled the masculine ideal. He had not run away from the challenges of pangngae; rather, he had exhausted them and then opted for a privileged involvement in the church.

The headwater settlements in Bambang seemed on the whole more prosperous in 1994 than they had been when I left them nine years earlier. Like their Muslim neighbors downstream, mappurondo households have done quite well with chocolate (introduced just as I was leaving in 1985) and with new varieties of coffee. The increasing flow of cash into the mappurondo communities has had the effect of reviving local interest in the household-prosperity ceremonies associated with women, and promises renewed and expanded involvement of women in managing mappurondo traditions. Although other factors have no doubt contributed to a climate of confidence and sufficiency, it is very clear to me that pangngae is no longer fated to be the sole exercise of ancestral ritual tradition or the sole celebration of prosperity. The commemoration of pangngae remains, of course, a political necessity and an end in its own right, but the ceremonial apprehension of the ancestral past has been returned in part to women.

The commemorative work surrounding the violence of pangngae has been crucial for animating and reproducing mappurondo social order. In this sense, mappurondo headhunting ritual in the late twentieth century is neither a relict form of primitive violence nor an obsolete discourse on the social horizons of a remote upland enclave. Rather, it is an enduring and central event for a minority religious community trying to shape its own history and its fate. The themes of pangngae certainly throw light on the mappurondo social world. But in this book I have tried to go beyond an analysis of the "represented" to show that ritual or commemorative modes of speaking and singing are themselves modes of social action and relationship. The projects of pangngae—a mingling of political definition and resistance, griefwork, gender discourse, and festive commemoration of the past—shape the social and historical world of the mappurondo communities. Differences in ritual discourse issue from the situated character of ceremonial practice. Indeed, we find telling changes or shifts of emphasis in the themes and projects of pangngae as the communities adjust to exogenous pressures and the stresses of communal reproduction in a circumstanced world.

The discourse of headhunting ritual, with its imagery of violence, manhood, and valor, its explicit concern for tradition, history, and polity, its entanglement with mourning and memory, and its gestures of resistance and acquiescence, is produced and ruptured within social relations that are—to use the words of Hans Medick (1987:98)—"asymmetrically structured, laden with contradictions, and in every case complex." At the same time, this discourse of ritual violence delimits a cultural sphere in which these uneven and often ambiguous social relations come into being. In 1994, followers of ada' mappurondo continue to look upon pangngae as an act of communal self-definition, one that sustains mappurondo identity and practice and their privileged role in guarding the traditions of pemali appa' randanna. It sets them apart, though not without some anxiety and confusion about what being set apart by ritual violence might mean in the Indonesian order. What Christians and Muslims choose to exploit as cultural art or condemn as backward of course falls largely beyond the control of the mappurondo communities, and official recognition of ada' mappurondo by the Department of

Education and Culture will no doubt complicate the debates and struggles of these ideological camps over the character and necessity of pemali appa' randanna and its strains of ceremonial violence.

Sitting once again with Ambe and Indo Teppu in their home in Saluta-bang, I looked and listened for signs of their allegiance to a Christian or mappurondo world, wondering what choices they had made since 1985. No tambolâ rested in the loft, and no drum hung cinched up to the rafters. But neither were there church calendars on the walls, or prayers of thanks-giving spoken over plates of rice. Paulus had married again—this time to a Christian schoolteacher from Rantelemo—and had assumed the administra-tive office of *Kepala Dusun,* head of the hamlet. His older brother remained firmly within the mappurondo community.

I let two nights pass before bringing up the issue. Laughing with surprise and looking at me as if I should know better, Ambe Teppu answered, "Map-purondo!" I confessed the apprehensiveness I had felt over the intervening years. No, I need not have worried, he told me. Indo Teppu was still a sando, and they were even considering holding the elaborate women's rite of *melambe* for their household. And besides, he went on, there is no need to make problems over religion. Pointing to his stomach, Ambe Teppu said, "I have God inside of me. I am Muslim. I am Protestant. I am Catholic. I am Hindu. This is Pancasila. I have Pancasila inside of me. What is wrong if I am mappu-rondo, too?"

Appendix I

Linguistic and Orthographic Notes

Appendix I

Linguistic and Orthographic Notes

Orthography and Pronunciation

The following list provides orthography, phonetic categories, and approximate pronunciations for vocal sounds used in the ToSalu and ToIssilita' dialects of Bambang:

p	(voiceless bilabial stop)	As in *p*oint
t	(voiceless dental/alveolar stop)	As in *t*ake
k	(voiceless velar stop)	As in *k*ill
'	(glottal stop)	As in "Uh'oh!"
b	(voiced bilabial stop)	As in *b*ark
d	(voiced dental/alveolar stop)	As in *d*ark
g	(voiced velar stop)	As in *g*o
j	(voiced alveopalatal affricate)	As in "Woul*dy*a do it?"
s	(voiceless alveolar fricative)	As in *s*oon
m	(voiced bilabial nasal)	As in *m*oon
n	(voiced alveolar nasal)	As in *n*oon
ny	(voiced palato-alveolar nasal)	As in ca*ny*on
ng	(voiced velar nasal)	As in so*ng*
l	(dental/alveolar liquid lateral)	As in *l*ip
r	(alveolar liquid flap)	As in the British ve*r*y
h	(voiceless fricative)	As in *h*elp

i	(high front vowel)	As in f*ee*d
e	(mid/low front vowel)	As in h*a*lo, or b*e*t [see below]
â	(low front vowel)	As in c*a*t
a	(low back vowel)	As in p*o*t
o	(mid back vowel)	As in b*oa*t
u	(high back vowel)	As in b*oo*t

Some comments are in order:

1. As a rule, /e/ is somewhat lowered in closed syllables, and kept slightly raised and fronted in open ones.
2. /h/, which is used in ToSalu dialect only, corresponds to the ToIssilita' /r/.
3. When not conditioned phonologically, nasals in the final position are rendered as /m/ by the ToSalu, and, depending on village, as /n/ or /ng/ by the ToIssilita'.
4. Some ToIssilita' villages pronounce vowels with more spreading and rounding than is indicated in the chart above.
5. /ny/ is decorative and appears only in song.
6. When a consonant is doubled, each should be pronounced (e.g. *parri', appa', botto, malangngi', randanna*).

Grammar

The best work to date on local grammar is that by Philip Campbell (1989). His analysis is grounded in ToSalu dialects. Elsewhere (George 1989), I provide a complete transcription and morpheme-by-morpheme translation of the sumengo that appear in this book; that work, too, provides some insight into local grammar, especially grammars peculiar to the sumengo.

A Linguistic Sketch of Village and Region

The social and geographic distribution of languages and dialects in the uplands of South Sulawesi is quite complex and renders classification difficult. Since 1850, slavery, rebellion, migration, Bugis domination of markets, national or colonial languages and administration, Christianity, Islam, literacy, and the broadcast media have kept speech communities in flux. Meanwhile, however, rugged terrain and the conservative and somewhat closed character of upland villages (or village groupings) have acted to check the dispersal and diffusion of languages. Generally speaking, the different speech communities form dialect chains throughout the highlands— a pattern that reflects the communities' geographic proximity, political and social interaction, migration, and history. It is also my experience that many highlanders—especially men—are adept at (or have a basic familiarity with) several mountain dialects, some Indonesian, some Bugis, and, occasionally, some Mandar.

On the basis of my knowledge of the region, I agree with Strømme (1985) that a Pitu Ulunna Salu linguistic subfamily should be distinguished from Mandar and Sa'dan groupings. Such a classification also accords well with how uplanders from Pitu Ulunna Salu see the situation. As for basic differentiation of the chained dialects with the Pitu Ulunna Salu group, Strømme's provisional findings, based on lexicostatistic surveys (but scant or poorly understood historic and sociolinguistic information), strike me as very sound. He identifies three language groups: Aralle-Tabulahan, with three dialects and 12,000 speakers; Pitu Ulunna Salu, with eight dialects and 22,000 speakers; and Pannei, with two dialects and 9,000 speakers. Eastern dialects show stronger cognate relationships with the Sa'dan subfamily than do the western ones. The western dialects correlate more closely with Mandar than do the eastern dialects.

When talking about the languages of their region, uplanders sometimes speak of Aralle-Tabulahan as the "mother" tongue (*basa indo*) of Pitu Ulunna Salu, and the language of Bambang and the districts to its south as the "father" tongue (*basa ambe*), a classification that has ties to the mythic origins of the upland league. More often, villagers identify their dialect by territory (e.g. *basa Mambi,* or *basa Aralle*). When further distinctions need to be drawn—usually for social or political rather than "scientific" reasons— they mention a village dialect, i.e. one associated with a specific village. The situation in Bambang is somewhat different. Here, villagers speak of *basa Bambang, basa ToIssilita',* and *basa ToSalu,* and then the various *basa lembâ*— or village dialects—taking into account the major social divisions in the watershed.

Of the Pitu Ulunna Salu languages, the ToSalu and ToIssilita' dialects of Bambang are the most important to this study. Grammatically, they are virtually identical. Lexically, the two dialects are quite close, showing a cognate relationship of 90 percent or more (depending on what word lists are used).

Villagers customarily point to phonological differences rather than lexical or grammatical ones when explaining how the dialects relate to one another. Yet it was my experience that ToSalu speakers had difficulty grasping some of the lexical elements in the ritual speech registers of Minanga and Saludengen, both of them ToIssilita' villages.

Current speakers of ToIssilita' dialects live in the villages of Rantepalado, Minanga, Saludengen, Karakean, Masoso, and Ulumambi (and to the north in some areas of Buntumalangka'). Users of ToSalu dialect live in Limba, Rantelemo, Salutabang, Ulumambi, Karakean, and Masoso (and to the north in eastern Aralle and parts of Buntumalangka'). This distribution corresponds to a survey of local views on dialect similarity that I ran in 1984. All of the respondents in that survey, however, including residents of Minanga, identified the Minanga dialect as something of a swing dialect, i.e. being ToIssilita' but sharing a significant number of features with Mambi dialect.

Appendix II

Tables

Table 1 *Profile of villages at Bambang*

Village	Number of households	Number of hamlets	Approx. number of hectares (n.d.a. = no data available)	
			Terraces	Gardens[a]
Minanga	151	20	145[b]	250
Saludengen	120	5	120	40
Rantepalado				
(Rantepalado)	142	10	200[c]	100
(Salubulo)	43	4	n.d.a.	n.d.a.
Karakean	171	11	35[d]	45
Limba	69	7	20[e]	20
Rantelemo				
(Rantelemo)	56	10	10[e]	10
(Salukadi)	51	4	n.d.a.	n.d.a.
Masoso	58	5	5[e]	5
Salutabang	128	8	75[f]	100
Ulumambi	131	12	10	40

SOURCE: Author's survey (1984).

NOTES:

[a] Coffee holdings are not included in these estimates.

[b] Includes about 45 ha. of terraces lying outside of the lembâ, but owned by residents of Minanga.

[c] Includes about 70 ha. of terraces lying outside of the lembâ, but owned by residents of Rantepalado.

[d] Not including terraced land within the lembâ owned by residents of Rantepalado.

[e] Not including terraced land within the lembâ owned by residents of Salutabang.

[f] Includes about 15 ha. of terraces lying outside of the lembâ.

Table 2 *Religious composition of villages at Bambang*

Village	Number of Christian households	Number of mappurondo households	Mappurondo households as percent of total
Minanga	117	34	22.5%
Saludengen	70	50	41.7
Rantepalado			
(Rantepalado)	112	30	21.1
(Salubulo)	5	38	88.4
Karakean	148	23	13.5
Limba	62	7	10.1
Rantelemo			
(Rantelemo)	56	0	0.0
(Salukadi)	41	10	19.6
Masoso	56	2	3.4
Salutabang	74	54	42.2
Ulumambi	60	71	54.2

SOURCE: Author's survey (1984).

Table 3 *Pattern of rice terrace ownership at Bambang, by village*

Village	Average holding (ha.) per household	Maximum holding (ha.) per household[a]	Percent of land controlled by residents[b]
Minanga	1.00	2.00	95%
Saludengen	1.00	1.50	100
Rantepalado	1.00	2.00	95
Karakean	0.25	1.50	75
Limba	0.25	<1.00	80
Rantelemo	0.10	<1.00	65
Masoso	0.10	<0.75	50
Salutabang	0.60	1.50	95
Ulumambi	0.10	<1.00	100

SOURCE: Author's field interviews (1984).

NOTES:
[a] Including land owned outside of lembâ.
[b] Including village-born males residing elsewhere.

Table 4 *Reported coffee holdings for Bambang, 1984, by village*

Village	Average holding (ha.) per household	Maximum holding (ha.) per household	Total hectares in coffee per village
Minanga	1.50	2.60	250
Saludengen	.75	1.75	90
Rantepalado	2.15	2.60	400
Karakean	.25	2.40	40
Limba	1.15	4.75	80
Rantelemo	2.05	2.00	220
Masoso	.01	.25	5
Salutabang	.50	1.75	65
Ulumambi	.40	.70	50

SOURCE: Author's field interviews (1984).

NOTE: Areal estimates are derived from tree counts, using the conversion formula of 100 trees per hectare. Average yield is about 150 kilos of coffee per hectare (i.e. per 100 trees).

Table 5 *Comparisons of village endogamy and exogamy among the mappurondo community at Bambang, 1971–84*

Village	Endogamous marriages	In-marrying males[a]	Out-marrying males[b]
Minanga	7	1	0
Saludengen	14	0	0
Rantepalado			
(Rantepalado)	21	0	1
(Salubulo)	2	2	9
Karakean	7	1	0
Limba	1	0	1
Rantelemo			
(Rantelemo)[c]			
(Salukadi)	1	1	1
Masoso[c]			
Salutabang	14	13	0
Ulumambi	25	0	3

SOURCE: Based on marriage records kept by the *Kantor Desa Bambang* at Rantepalado. Figures include all mappurondo marriages recorded from 1971 to 1984.

NOTES:

[a] Includes two males from Desa Rantebulahan and one male from Desa Mambi.

[b] Does not include males who married out of Desa Bambang, since the registry notes only marriages taking place within the desa. Males marrying out of Bambang during the time period probably number four or less.

[c] No mappurondo marriages took place during the time period. Rantelemo is entirely Christian, and only two mappurondo households remain in Masoso.

Appendix III

Music Figures

Music Figure A. *The common melody for the ToSalu sumengo.*

NOTES FOR MUSICAL FIGURES A AND C:

1. The tempo is free, but the song becomes increasingly rhythmic in the choral phrases. There is no regular underlying meter.

2. A bar line marks the end of a musical phrase.

3. A rest corresponds to a pause of 1–1.5 seconds.

4. It takes roughly two minutes for the singers to perform a song in its entirety. The songleader usually takes 13–14 seconds to deliver the opening solo line. The chorus enters a song as soon as the songleader completes the first eight-syllable lyric phrase.

5. The notes show only relative duration to one another in the context of a musical phrase (e.g. an eighth-note is about half as long as a quarter-note). Blackened notes without stems are grace notes.

Music Figure B. *Textual Structure of the ToSalu Sumengo.*

Musical line	Phrases of text by syllable	Total syllabic count
Tomantokko		
I.	$A_1 + A_2 \ldots A_8$	8
Tomantokko and chorus		
II.	$B_1 + B_2 + B_3$	3
III.	$ny[\,B_3 \text{ vowel}\,] + B_4 + B_5$	3
IV.	$ny[\,B_5 \text{ vowel}\,] + B_6 + B_7 + B_8$	4
V.	$nye + C_1 + C_2 + C_3$	4
VI.	$ny[\,C_3 \text{ vowel}\,] + C_4 \ldots C_8$	6
	Malallengko toibirin	
	tomatilampe bambana	
	lembum mati langkam borin	
Tomantokko		
I.	*Ma-lal-leng-ko to-i-bi-rin*	8
Tomantokko and chorus		
II.	*to + ma + ti*	3
III.	*nyi + lam + pe*	3
IV.	*nye + bam + ba + na*	4
V.	*nye + lem + bum + ma*	4
VI.	*nya + ti + lang + kam + bo + rin*	6

6. Pitches indicated are rough approximations of equivalent pitches in a G clef. The actual choice of pitches appears to follow an equidistant pentatonic scale. By arbitrarily assigning the pitch value of D from the Western diatonic scale to the first pitch of the pentatonic scale, we may correlate the scalar material as follows: 1: D; 2: E, F, F sharp; 3: G; 4: B flat, B; 5: C. Variation on the second and fourth pitches does not appear to be significant, and probably reflects a variety of musical factors at play.

7. Arrows show a deviation from the pitch indicated, as much as a quarter-tone sharp (arrow up) or flat (arrow down).

8. A glissando indicates a slide between two pitches; the microtones in the interval receive articulation. A slur also indicates a slide between two pitches, but the microtones in the interval are not articulated.

Music Figure C. *The common melody for the ToIssilita' sumengo.*

Music Figure D. *Textual Structure of the ToIssilita' Sumengo.*

Musical line	Phrases of text by syllable	Total syllabic count
Tomantokko		
I.	$A_1 + A_2 \ldots A_8$	8
Tomantokko and chorus		
II.	$B_1 + B_2 \ldots B_8$	8
III.	$nye + C_1$	2
IV.	C_1 vowel $+ C_2 + C_3 + C_4$	4
V.	C_4 vowel $+ C_5 + C_6$	3
VI.	$C_4 + C_5 + C_6 + C_7$	4
VII.	C_7 vowel $+ C_8 + C_1$	3
VIII.	C_1 vowel $+ C_2 + C_3 + C_4$	4
IX.	C_4 vowel $+ C_5 + C_6$	3
	Malallengko toibirin *tomatilampe bambana* *lembum mati langkam borin*	
Tomantokko		
I.	*Ma-lal-leng-ko to-i-bi-rin*	8
Tomantokko and chorus		
II.	*to-ma-ti-lam-pe bam-ba-na*	8
III.	*nye + le*	2
IV.	*em + bum + ma + ti*	4
V.	*i + lang + kam*	3
VI.	*ti + lang + kam + bo*	4
VII.	*o + ri + le*	3
VIII.	*em + bum + ma + ti*	4
IX.	*i + lang + kam*	3

Notes

Chapter 1: Relics from Alien Parts

1. I quote from Mary Morris (1993:xv), who attributes the view to the late John Gardner. See also Walter Benjamin's essay "The Storyteller" (Benjamin 1969:84–85).

2. Cf. remarks by Carol Fleisher Feldman (1987:213), and by Michelle Rosaldo (1980:32–34, 54–56).

3. The severed head that *listens* lurks uncannily in Walter Hasenclever's play *Humanity* (1963 [1918]). In this Expressionist drama, a murdered man shows up in a city carrying his head in a sack. He is discovered, brought to court, and branded as his own murderous assailant. Hasenclever's play, I should point out, antedates the listening heads described in this book.

4. The idea is that harmful spirit-beings will try every "open door" in the comb and become exhausted before reaching the door to the house.

5. If any reader is puzzled, I am alluding to *The Raw and the Cooked*, by Claude Lévi-Strauss (1969).

6. For overviews of the critique, and efforts to resume work beyond it, see Dirks, Eley, and Ortner (1994), and R. Fox (1991).

7. Rosaldo's treatment of Ilongot hunting stories (1986) shows a similar regard for the play of memory, history, experience, and circumstance.

8. Jane Atkinson takes the same approach in her work on the art and politics of Wana shamanship (1989:14).

9. Burur's violent feat does not appear to figure into R. Rosaldo's history of Ilongot headhunting (1980). By the reckoning of that work (1980:302), Burur's beheading of a victim would have taken place around the time a covenant of amity was being put into place. The way in which Burur remains problematically beyond

the horizons of R. Rosaldo's study suggests that an unexplored set of difficulties surrounded the case and the celebratory event thereafter.

10. Sherry Ortner's use of "cultural schema" (1989)—when applied to rituals or narratives—strikes me as problematic, and draws our attention away from the very practices she might best illumine. Very simply, Ortner's cultural schema is a synoptic construct (reminiscent of Propp's syntagmatic structuralism) that puts aside a history of specific narrative events and eliminates the role of memory. Ortner then has to struggle to (re)ground the schema in *types* of practice, rather than in events and practices as such. For an important critique bearing on the use of cultural schemas and other basically basic stories, see Barbara Herrnstein Smith (1981).

11. The dominance of formalist, structuralist, and semiotic theories during the 1960s and 1970s drove the concept of theme into exile. Though there are problems with the term in light of contemporary interpretation theory (especially deconstruction), I think it is a concept worth recuperating for the purpose of my analysis. I note that Michelle Rosaldo (1980) used the notion of "theme" to explore Ilongot headhunting.

12. For a brief look at the cultural politics of ethnography in these communities, see George (1993a).

Chapter 2: The Mappurondo Enclave at Bambang

1. The same images have also played a significant and lingering role in nineteenth- and twentieth-century representations of an oppositional human figure (i.e. an "Other") suitable for ethnological study and contemplation. I have already mentioned this problem in Chapter 1, where I touch on headhunters and headhunting in the anthropological construction of the primitive and the exotic.

2. For a discussion of politics and the construction of minority religions in Sulawesi, see Atkinson 1983 and 1989.

3. See Acciaioli (1989:283–284) for a related application of the term among Bugis communities.

4. These recollections amount to a search into the past for a golden age, a process Michael Herzfeld calls "structural nostalgia" (Herzfeld 1990).

5. The membership of the league shifted through time, especially in response to the growth of Mandar principalities and to the advent of Islam. For example, Tabang (a community lying to the east of Mamasa) is often mentioned as a member of the upland league. Accounts that include Tabang usually omit Tu'bi, a community that appears to have been absorbed into the Mandar sphere following its conversion to Islam.

6. Toraja genealogies collected by C. H. M. Nooy-Palm and L. T. Tangdilintin (Nooy-Palm 1979) identify him as Patiang Boro from the Sa'dan settlement at Napo. Genealogies from Rantepalado also trace Pongka Padang's ancestry back to Sa'dan deities.

7. People of Bambang say that these raids brought about the collapse of Pitu Ulunna Salu (cf. Smit 1937). The violent event may have had roots in the political

instability of the lower peninsula and the Dutch attack on Mandar in 1872 (Suther-land 1983a). Also, Bigalke's portrait of upland turmoil (1981) shows the impact of the regional coffee-, slave-, and weapons trade of the late nineteenth century.

8. Their request was granted since the time of my research. The ToSalu settle-ments were grouped to form a single desa, Bambang Hulu, while the ToIssilita' ones comprised Bambang Hilir. This administrative partitioning of Bambang, it should be noted, reflects and follows upon the long-standing organization of Protestant assem-blies in the district. See the Epilogue for subsequent developments.

9. Enang, the last surviving *parengnge* (Dutch-appointed district head) in the area remarked to me that mappurondo rituals persisted in the village of Mambi until 1936.

10. Krüger (1966) identifies Kijftenbelt of the Protestantsche Kerk at Makassar as the figure who oversaw the introduction of Christianity to the region that included Bambang.

11. Thus, the Hindu Dharma bureaucratic apparatus has no means to shelter highly localized religions. There is no provision for setting up offices for the benefit of followers who live in but one desa or kecamatan.

12. The structure of the house has changed radically in the last 80 years. For-merly, the great majority of banua had as many as eight hearths. A nuclear family resided at each hearth, and maintained their own rice barn in the yard. The families were related to one another through sibling or parent-child ties. The first campaigns for single-hearth, single-family dwellings were under the direction of Dutch admin-istrators and missionaries. Indonesian officials and religious institutions renewed these campaigns after independence. The success of their efforts has contributed to the opening of new residential sites within village territory and the appearance of very rudimentary dwellings. Nonetheless, most villages still have several double- or triple-hearth houses, often in which young married couples, or divorced or widowed fe-males make a home with siblings or parents. Further change has taken place with the placement of the house. In keeping with local cosmology, houses once faced upriver into the rising sun, toward the dwelling place of the gods. (When a house had mul-tiple hearths, it was lengthened along an east-west axis, rather than north-south.) This pattern underwent abrupt change in 1980 when civil administrators decided to "beautify" hamlets. Henceforth, houses were to face one another along a central lane or yard.

13. Lacking the human and material resources to act as a practicing ritual com-munity, these households usually take part in ceremonies staged by kin in neighbor-ing settlements.

14. For a discussion of the coffee trade in upland Sulawesi prior to the twentieth century, see Bigalke (1981:29–59).

15. Given the way a "sense of place" enters into local social organization, it would not be off the mark to identify Pitu Ulunna Salu as a "house society" of the kind described by Errington (1987) and Waterson (1986).

16. I was unable to obtain women's viewpoints on polygyny.

17. Incest tabus also apply to classificatory siblings at the parental generation, i.e. first cousins of ego's parents.

18. There is evidence in the ceremony for understanding somba as a swap for a wife: It is presented in thirds, of which the first two are proclaimed, "Not enough!"

Only with the third presentation do the bride's kin announce that a proper amount has been given. In this sense, somba might be best described as bridebarter.

19. Some landless households have appeared in the last twenty years in the villages of Masoso and Rantelemo, two settlements that are almost exclusively Christian.

20. Jane Atkinson (1990) reports that the Wana of eastern Central Sulawesi also use the term *bela* to denote husband and wife. In the Wana case, too, the term is unmarked for gender. In each case, the term implies that the husband-wife relationship shares formal, functional, and moral features with the ties appearing within unisexual cohorts and task groups.

21. For theoretical debate over male/female, public/domestic, and encompassing/encompassed hierarchies, see Ortner (1990); M. Rosaldo (1980); and Yanagisako (1979).

22. If I am correct in my assessment, the mappurondo case weakens any claim that cultural assertions of male dominance are universal.

23. The most recent morara recalled by elder men are, by village: Minanga, 1977; Rantepalado, before 1906; Saludengen, not since c. 1870; Karakean, 1937; Limba, twice before 1906; Rantelemo, before 1906; Ulumambi, 1933 (with Salutabang); Salutabang, 1933 (with Ulumambi); Masoso, before 1906. Knowledge of how to properly stage *morara* has seriously eroded, to the point where one village, Rantepalado, even refuses to hold the ritual for fear of making liturgical errors that will invite the wrath of the spirits.

24. Cf. with Bugis *sumange'*. See Errington 1989.

25. Informants describe morara as an enormous potlatch that demands a month of elaborate preparation. Guests and hosts consume huge surpluses of rice and meat, stage mock battles, and exchange gifts of cloth and other valuables. Excluding preparation time, morara takes about two weeks to perform. Elders explained that the ritual requires that a head be taken, and the few morara song texts that I have been able to get suggest thematic, metaphoric, and generic parallels with those of pangngae.

26. The succession of ceremonies is as follows:

ToSalu	ToIssilita'
metinda'	
ma'kambio	*dikuo*
mekolâ	*mekolâ*

[The rituals listed below belong to the parri' category]

melambe	*melambe*
malangngi'	*malangngi'*
ma'bua'	*ma'bua'*

The sequence is presented in simplified form. ToIssilita' practices include (1) sacrificial variations that call for yet more elaborate terminology in the case of mekolâ and (2) an alternate form of ma'bua' called *ma'bua' tumbâ* (also called *ma'bua' mata*). I am uncertain of the status of medio, a female-domain ritual, common to ToIssilita' and ToMambi communities, that vanished before 1940. It appears not to have been part of the sequence, but may account for why ToIssilita' communities presently lack a counterpart to the ToSalu metinda'. An eyewitness account of medio suggests the elaborateness of a parri' ceremony.

27. The curing rarely involves trance or other shamanic techniques. Shamanism appears to have been in practice among males until about 1950. My language assistant, for example, reported a curing in his natal household during his childhood. In his account, a male shaman from another village treated an uncle. The shaman howled and beat his chest, and then pulled a crab from the uncle's body. I was not able to verify claims that there remain two or three persons versed in shamanic techniques at Ulumambi.

28. I treat this issue at length in "Music-making, Ritual, and Gender in a Southeast Asian Hill Society" (George 1993c).

Chapter 3: Defaced Images from the Past

1. My thanks to Johannes Fabian for pointing this out to me (pers. comm. 1991).

2. It may be helpful to think of the head and surrogate as different editions of the "same" text. (See McGann 1991).

3. For other confrontations with the textuality of history in the archipelago, see: Boon 1977, 1990; Bowen 1991; Siegel 1979; and Steedly 1993.

4. I here include ethnographic studies and surveys, travel accounts, and mission diaries.

5. An investigation of colonial juridical records would probably turn up something to the contrary.

6. In their critique of Freeman's analysis, Davison and Sutlive (1991) point out that Iban discourse offers little support for symbolically associating head with phallus. They argue that the metaphors of Iban ritual comprise a "frugiferous" model of headhunting in which trophy heads are equated both with the fruits of the mythical *ranyai* palm and with the infant offspring of the demon *Nising*. Though Davison and Sutlive show a willingness to explore ritual discourse for an understanding of Iban headhunting practices, they remain certain that in local thinking, seed-laden enemy heads bring about prosperity. For Davison and Sutlive, this is only natural. In their analysis, Iban headhunting has its roots not in psyche and libido, but in the Bornean rain forest. Concerned to swap an ecological determinism for a psychological one, Davison and Sutlive never seriously challenge the logic in which severed heads make fields and communities thrive.

7. Note, too, that the throng turns its heterophonous shouts against the babalako, beheading the chant.

8. I believe this viewpoint is implicit in some of the comments of M. Rosaldo (1977, 1980) and R. Rosaldo (1980, 1984).

9. The headhunters of the mappurondo community are not alone in linking heads and prosperity through the vow. Writing about headhunting practices of the ToMangki (or Galumpang Toraja), a group living to the north and east of the Salu Mambi region, A. C. Kruyt (1942:543) explained that, "One pledged to seek a head

if the rice the following year were successful. If one then had a good harvest, he would make preparations to go."

10. Hospitality, as Michael Herzfeld writes, "signifies the moral and conceptual subordination of the guest to the host" (1987:77). Seen from this perspective, hospitality in pangngae further underscores the subordination of the victim.

11. For comparative materials, see Hoskins (1989), who shows how Sumbanese headhunting practices factored into eras of exchange, alliance, and trade between rival groups.

12. For the southeastern peninsula, see Kennedy (1935), J. Kruyt (1924), and Schuurmans (1934); for the eastern peninsula and central mountain region, see Adriani and Kruyt (1950), Atkinson (1989), Dormeier (1947), Downs (1955), A. C. Kruyt (1930); and for the western and northern mountain regions, see Kennedy (1935) and A. C. Kruyt (1938). Key accounts and commentaries for the so-called "Southern Toraja" region are: Bigalke (1981), Goslings (1924 [rep 1933]), A. C. Kruyt (1923; 1942), Nooy-Palm (1986), Tangdilintin (1980) and Volkman (1985).

13. It should be kept in mind that grief, fertility, and the welfare of the community may have a scope that goes beyond the local, and may in fact articulate regional political strains.

14. Compare: Mambi and Bambang, *pangngae*; Galumpang, *pangaye*; Sa'dan *mangaung*; Bare'e, *menga'e*; Indonesian and Malay, *kayau*. In the Bare'e case, discussed by Downs (1955), some association is made between the term for headhunting (*menga'e*) and the term for harvesting rice (*menggae*). I am skeptical of Downs's claim that the two words are synonyms. Nonetheless, I would allow for Bare'e wordplay and a metaphoric thinking that connects harvesting rice to taking heads. For further notes on cognate terms for headhunting in the Malay world, see Maxwell (forth.).

15. One Mandar *Bupati*, or regent, in my acquaintance was celebrated for having killed his first man over loss of face at the age of ten.

16. Daetta, the fourth Mara'dia of Balanipa, was the first of the region's elite to enter Islam (DepDikBud, n.d.[d]). Islam appears to have prevailed in nominal fashion until the beginning of the twentieth century, at which time reformist Islam began to purify and deepen local belief. For a persuasive discussion of how Islam influenced political life in South Sulawesi, see Andaya (1984).

17. Given what I can reconstruct from oral histories and written sources, the historic exchange system between the uplands and the coast basically conforms to the hypothetical model advanced by Bronson (1977).

18. Hoorweg appears to have been unaware of the ritualized agricultural calendar at Pitu Ulunna Salu.

19. Famines and harvest shortfalls were not unusual in the highlands, and continue to this day. Oral histories suggest that food shortages were common by 1870. Dutch authorities, too, mention this problem in their reports (e.g. anonymous [Militaire Nota] 1924).

20. A comparable situation may have obtained in parts of Borneo. Dr. Peter Kedit of the Sarawak Museum (pers. comm.) claims that Iban headhunting often took place in association with *bejalai*, journeys undertaken for profit or social prestige (cf. Freeman 1970).

21. The ma'paisun chants would lend this claim credibility.

22. *"Masae! Tellu bulam!"* "A long time. Three months!"

23. I write about "the grotesque" in the same manner that some write about "the ludic" or "the carnivalesque." What the grotesque is, or might be, varies from society to society. Its specific aesthetic, rhetorical, and political functions are by no means stable, but are manifest as particular cultural and historical projects. For example, Bakhtin (1984) argues that the Renaissance grotesque differed profoundly from Romantic grotesque. Further, he sees the grotesque as an oppositional mode of language and practice set against official discourse. Below I will argue that the discourse of the grotesque in pangngae is official discourse.

24. Cf. Bakhtin 1984.

25. Cited in Holman (1972:246).

26. My use of the terms "marked" and "unmarked" owes much to discussions in Caton (1987), Nagy (1990), and Waugh (1982).

27. Some commentators on Bornean headhunting practices (Davison and Sutlive 1991; Freeman 1979; and Metcalf 1987) mention the way women will take the trophy skull and dance with it between their knees. For these scholars, such dance-gestures suggest that the head is a symbol of fecundity or birth. I find that gestures like this are intended to mock, humiliate, and subordinate an oppositional other.

28. See Bakhtin (1984) and Canetti (1978) for reflections on laughter, terror, power, and survivorhood.

29. I borrow the term "undominated discourse" from James Scott (1990:175).

30. This resembles a Nietzschean turnabout of cause and effect (Culler 1982: 86–87). As the feeling of pain leads someone to look for a cause and thereby discover an offending pin, so too does the headhunter reflect on his tradition of violence and look for its cause in the past.

31. In the spirit of celebrating the indeterminacy of causes and origins, a claim might be made that the head is a surrogate coconut. Indeed, the rites of the past may have involved any number of symbolic objects that could (1) summon or render the body politic of the "other" and (2) withstand disfiguring abuse. Nonetheless, I think we have to be mindful of *"the gradient and direction of flow of metaphor and symbolic substitution from one domain to another"* (Stallybrass and White 1986: 196, emphasis theirs). Though it is true that that gradient and direction are subject to historical change, I think it unlikely that a severed head would displace the coconut except in a project of restoring a prior sociosymbolic formation.

Chapter 4: Violence, Solace, Vows, Noise, and Song

1. The first term is applied to rites that share the emphases of maringngangi'. The latter term applies to the headhunting rites that follow upon the death of the tomatuatonda'.

2. Some reports from Borneo (see McKinley 1976) suggest that sacrifice of a slave or dependent provided an acceptable alternative to headhunting in some settlements. In contrast, the communities of Pitu Ulunna Salu seem to have drawn

around themselves a social line within which dehumanizing violence was unacceptable. In this light, the human sacrifice at Rantebulahan may be read as headhunting out of place. Note, too, the double out-of-placeness of human sacrifice in the Rantebulahan episode: violence happened during *pa'bisuam baine*, the sphere of domestic rites run under the authority of women, not during the village rituals directed by and toward men.

3. It should be obvious that world religions deliver a similar message. As discussed in Chapter 2, the Indonesian state insists that participation in a monotheistic world religion is the keystone to progress-oriented citizenship.

4. I do not mean to suggest that the "boundaries of the human" were free of instability prior to the advent of Dutch and Indonesian administrations. Yet the transcendant citizenship of the contemporary era opposes and subverts pangngae in ways quite different from the oppositional threat posed by the encroaching lowland societies of the precolonial period.

5. Some societies commemorate sacrifice and the valorous loss of life in ways that still violence. Societies that remember and enshrine their anguish run the risk of becoming spawning grounds for violence. See Feldman (1991) and Girard (1977).

6. The transformation of emotional discourse under different political regimes and crises has been explored in Iran by Good and Good (1988), and in China by Kleinman and Kleinman (1991).

7. As discussed in Chapter 3, McKinley (1976) makes a strong case for the relevance of knowing enemy names.

8. Ghost-souls (*anitu*) of the recently deceased may linger in the village, brooding or playing pranks on the living. Ancestral anitu are also summoned when household rituals get under way. In no instance do the anitu show such suffering and disquiet that they would bring about further deaths in the village.

9. For some key anthropological works and surveys on the politics and social-structural implications of emotion, see: Abu-Lughod 1990; Lutz and Abu-Lughod 1990; Lutz and White 1986; Myers 1986; and M. Rosaldo 1984a.

10. Michelle Rosaldo (1980:138) also writes that, when asked why they take heads, the Ilongot occasionally mention '*uget*,' "bad feelings."

11. Renato Rosaldo's use of the term "piacular" probably derives from Durkheim's discussion of "principal ritual attitudes" in *The Elementary Forms of the Religious Life* (1965 [1915]:434–435). Although the term usually suggests expiation or atonement for wrongdoing, Durkheim applies this term to rites "celebrated by those in a state of uneasiness or sadness" and "whose object is either to meet a calamity, or else merely to commemorate it and deplore it." For him, rituals of mourning are important examples of piacular rites. If I am not incorrect, Rosaldo has called headhunting a "piacular sacrifice" in order to underscore its connection with mourning. In passing, let me note that a recent verbal or transcriptive slip threatens to erase the genealogy of Rosaldo's thinking about Ilongot headhunting: "Their ritual is a kind of *peculiar* [sic] sacrifice. . . . in the ritual attitude, it's probably more like sacrifice than one would imagine at first" (R. Rosaldo 1987:253; italics mine).

12. I find a special set of problems and analytic dangers in efforts that confound violence and catharsis. Construed as catharsis, violence appears "natural" and appro-

priate to the ends and needs of personal emotional balance. Such a perspective cannot grasp violence as a product of history. The problem and some of its consequences are spelled out in Walter Benjamin's "Critique of Violence" (1978). Cathartic violence needs to be interpreted in light of its capacity to shape and be shaped by changing historical conditions.

13. It seems to me that Metcalf (1987; forth.) misreads the Ilongot case and Rosaldo's essay, which takes Metcalf and his co-author R. Huntington to task for conflating death, mourning, and mourning ritual in their monograph *Celebrations of Death* (1979). Metcalf (1987:4; forth.:28) insists that the Ilongot have no headhunting ceremonies even though the Rosaldos' descriptions of the *buayat* and the song-and-boast fests that followed beheadings clearly indicate otherwise. As regards Renato Rosaldo's essay, Metcalf (forth.:26) argues that Rosaldo believes: (1) that the force of emotion is the "principal shaper of human behaviour", and (2) that the Ilongot headhunter's deadly violence is the "natural" outlet of a universal emotion—the rage that comes with grief. Metcalf distorts Rosaldo's more measured claim: that an apprehension of anguished rage can offer us a glimpse of how the Ilongot sometimes turn to violence in coping with painful experience. Rosaldo never reduces Ilongot headhunting practices to pure rage, nor does he argue that sentiment forms the basis for culture and conduct. And although relying on his own sense of loss and grief to fathom Ilongot experience, Rosaldo cautions against thinking about emotions and their cultural formulation in terms of human universals (1984:188–189).

14. I thank a reviewer for reminding me that "from a psychological point of view, a symbol could just as easily trigger a cathartic release as the thing the symbol represents. Whether the symbol actually triggers catharsis would have to be actively investigated."

15. There is a huge literature on ritual transformation. Among recent statements, a few of the more important include: Geertz 1973; Kapferer 1979a, 1979c; Obeyesekere 1990; Ortner 1978; Peacock 1968; Tambiah 1985; and Turner 1969, 1974.

16. See Just (1991) for a discussion of "other-control" in the display and management of emotions on the Indonesian island of Sumbawa.

17. The lyrics hint at the vulnerability of local women. They suggest that upland women may be potential, if very mistaken, targets for a headhunter's violence. See comments in Chapters 5, 6, and 7.

18. Among the village elders of Minanga there is one who holds the office of *toma'gasinna* ([?] "the one who is like a top" [i.e. going out and back]). He is obliged to accompany the cohort and procure the right kind of bamboo for their tambolâ flutes (see following text). For Minanga, it is not unusual for the babalako and toma'gasinna to occupy the roles of *too'na* and *lolona,* respectively.

19. From a structural viewpoint, the ToSalu village holds fast to the topuppu, keeping him among women and weakened, grief-stricken men.

20. For example, special caution is exercised to keep necessary discussion of the ritual out of the earshot of women and girls. On the evening before departure, headhunters customarily refrain from having sex; many husbands find a place of sleep away from their wives. Moreover, the headhunters may not eat from the sheaves of

young rice taken by their wives, sisters, and daughters just before the most recent harvest. Violation of any of these tabus is said to make the headhunter vulnerable and perhaps bring illness upon the women concerned. In principle, a man's wife and close female relatives should not know that he intends to join the cohort of head-hunters. But, of course, women are free to figure things out.

21. In earlier times an inauspicious reading might have led the cohort to post-pone their journey. Presuming that pangngae has always been an obligatory rite, one would conclude that negative signs from the "wrong chicken" would never cause a raid to be canceled altogether.

22. In the past, the headhunters would look and listen carefully for bird omens. Calls heard off to the left, birds seen flying to the left, and hawks trailing the cohort from behind all portended failure or death. Herons flying upstream toward the pack signaled that the victim's territory could soon be reached. In these days of surrogate heads, however, the importance of bird omens has faded.

23. Coconut palms do not thrive in Bambang because of the altitude and climate, and the nuts must be purchased at a local market or requested from villagers in Mambi, a place where the palms do grow.

24. The flutes are roughly a meter long and 3 inches in diameter.

25. See George (1993a, 1993c) for discussions of secrecy, gender ideology, and local musical culture.

26. Women seldom journey beyond local markets or the villages of relatives. From their view, going off on pangngae is to step off into unknown territory. It needs to be kept in mind, too, that many older mappurondo women do recall the not-so-distant past when their menfolk traveled off to the coast. But the years since 1970 have probably been the most tranquil and safe in the last century. Any confidence the headhunters and their wives may have about the journey is likely a very recent phenomenon.

27. Local discourse associates the coals and fires of the hearth with wives and mothers. In local cosmology, the debata of fire is also the debata of gossip. If I am not wrong, the tabu against lending coals to another hearth in the husband's ab-sence puts a metaphorical check to the spread of women's knowledge. If coals can-not pass to another house, neither can knowledge of a husband's absence. Paradoxi-cally, the refusal to lend coals would be a sure tip that some male in the house was away on the headhunt.

28. "Lelelele" is the *name* for male sumanga' (spirit, elan vital) in the sacred lan-guage of women's ritual. It is also the *sound* of a man's sumanga'.

29. My use of the term *illocutionary* derives from the pioneering work of Austin (1962) and Searle (1969) in speech-act theory, and from the work of Tambiah (1985) on a "performative approach" to ritual. Following Tambiah's scheme (1985:135), the shout and the drone comprise a "performative act" subject to "constitutive rules," but with uncertain perlocutionary effects in terms of participants' emotional states.

30. During two years of research I saw no instances of *latah*, the startle-hysteria widely reported throughout the Malay world. At the same time, persons are at pains not to startle others with frightening noises, or with the sudden and painful news of a loved one's death.

31. In 1984 I had the opportunity to catch a glimpse of a crisis of sorts in a

ToSalu village in the Salu Mokanan watershed of Rantebulahan. The fires of pang-ngae were already burning when a villager passed away. Instead of dividing the village in two, the elders put a halt to pangngae and began funerary rites. They even took a chicken dedicated to pangngae by sacrificial prayer, and offered it up in death ritual. What was for some a misappropriation of sacrificial meats became topic of bitter debate. My closest friend was especially disturbed: "They better acknowledge their mistake. If the crops wither away next year or any other misfortune takes place in this village, it is sure that that chicken will be the reason." The mistake appeared to be a compound one—halting pangngae after it was under way, and "confusing" life and death in taking meats dedicated to the enlivening rites of pangngae and consuming them in the mournful ceremony of funerary ritual.

32. So as to leave no confusion, Rosaldo is not saying that volatile emotions caused headhunting to emerge as a cultural practice.

33. Atkinson (1989:27, 1990:68) reports that the Wana of Central Sulawesi link vows to headhunting and duels.

34. See, too, Renato Rosaldo's account of how, in the weeks following the accidental death of his wife Michelle, he vows to return to writing anthropology (1984: 184). Regarding arguments I make elsewhere in this book (see Chapter 6), note that Rosaldo's vow, as a generative force in writing "Grief and a Headhunter's Rage," must surface in that account as subject matter.

35. Although I have yet to come across supporting metaphors or comparisons in mappurondo discourse, it seems to me that being released from the grip of a vow could be likened to being released from the grip of personal anguish. If this happens to be the case, the samaja vow potentially offers a model for grief-work. In any case, I do not find it a matter of accident that this particular illocutionary act should become so entangled in the cathartic scenes of Ilongot and mappurondo ritual life.

Chapter 5: Envy, Adornment, and Words That Make the Floor Shake

1. See Chapter 2 for a general overview of the mappurondo social order. Social hierarchy and egalitarianism are subject to historical forces, and no doubt have changed over time. I have in mind the influence of slavery and debt bondage, forms that were prevalent through the nineteenth century. The communities of the present may in fact be more egalitarian than they were in the past. I should note, too, that several ToSalu described a now-vanished system of social rankings that seem to have been quite similar to those that traditionally informed Sa'dan and Mamasa society. Frankly, I find those remarks suspect, for they were all made by Christians who had enjoyed schooling in the Mamasa district. That is, I think these historical views belong to a decades-old cultural politics aimed at drawing Bambang within the orbit of the Toraja.

2. For a deeper exploration of secrecy in the mappurondo enclave, see George (1993a).

3. The essay itself appeared as an adornment on a larger essay entitled "Secrecy" (Simmel 1950; see the translator's note on p. 338).

4. See Taussig (1987) for an account of envy and its embodiment in a culture of terror and fear.

5. One woman I knew in Salutabang recalled that the last malangngi' to be staged in her village took place around 1950. On that occasion, 40 women took part as dancers in the secret group.

6. A husband's impotence was a common source for complaint among village women of my acquaintance. See, too, the *mamose* speeches described below.

7. See R. Rosaldo (1986) for Ilongot ideas about the parallels between courtship and headhunting.

8. Judging by reports from villagers throughout Bambang, antiphonal riddling and song challenges were far more common during the pangngae ceremonies of the past. Whole hamlets would take part, with choruses in separate households challenging or answering each other in song. Elders reminisced about times when whole mountainsides were swollen with singing, as house after house, hamlet after hamlet, would take part in the antiphonal and agonistic din of voices. The antiphonal contests of today are far briefer and more muted.

9. The term means, roughly, "narrative song." *Kelonoson* (or *kelonnosong, kelong ossong*) crops up as a song term throughout Sulawesi and Borneo. For example, Rubenstein has published a Sarawak *kelon* about headhunting (1985:237). Tammu and van der Veen (1972) list the Sa'dan *kelong* as meaning "song" or "*pantun*," and *osso'* as meaning "to arrange" (as story, history, etc.); cf. *gelong*, a song in the *maro* ritual. Zerner and Volkman (1988) further describe the Sa'dan gelong as an octosyllabic form common to maro ritual. Stokhof (1986:6–8) mentions that the Makassan *kelong* is a quatrain (8-8-5-8 or 8-8-8-8) that deals with themes from daily life, and which traditionally was recited on adat occasions. The Mandar *osong* he describes, following Azis Syah, as a "fighting song."

10. Usually, households throughout the village donate the foodstuffs for the tarakan. In Rantepalado, however, recent practice has been for the immediate families of the tobarani to provide the tarakan foods. An elder from there reports that the village has grown unhappy with this procedure and is planning to return to their former practice of taking food shares from all mappurondo households in the village.

11. Nonetheless, a speaker might feel real satisfaction in having made a speech deemed more eloquent or moving than that of another.

12. The same clichéd slogan is heard in Sa'dan Toraja ritual (Coville 1989:121).

Chapter 6: From Violence to Memory

1. Yet insofar as representation is a form of violence, one might say that a headhunt not only begins in violence but ends in violence as well. At the same time, this chapter should provide grounds for claiming that pangngae begins in representation and ends in representation.

2. For a detailed linguistic and musicological description of these liturgical registers, see George 1989:226–264.

3. A list of key works on oral poetry is impossible here. Some places for the reader to start: Bauman 1977, J. Fox 1988, Hymes 1981, Lord 1960, Ong 1977, and Tedlock 1983. See also the important recent statements by Bauman and Briggs (1990, 1992), which reflect the influence of Roman Jakobson and Michael Silverstein.

4. Bauman and Briggs (1990) call this process of making an autonomous text *entextualization,* a concept applied with great insight by Kuipers (1990) to a body of ritual discourse in eastern Indonesia. The term—which has become a bit of a cult object itself—has its roots in the writings of Roman Jakobson and Paul Ricoeur, and in the unpublished work of Michael Silverstein.

5. The social modalities Schutz has in mind sound much like the social bonds of *communitas* described by Victor Turner (1969, 1974).

6. For a more detailed discussion of this issue, see George 1993c.

7. Commemorative rites and traditions, of course, can be the context or subject of political contest, and may lead to radical rejections of the local and the communal (cf. Thomas 1992). Still, what seems to be at stake in these contests are claims to continuity and a place in the world.

8. Cf. Battaglia 1990:188.

Chapter 7: The Songs of the ToSalu and the ToIssilita'

1. Headhunting rituals subsequently kept, but played down, thematic linkages to mourning.

2. As noted above, the rest of Bambang planted in August 1983.

3. I left the Salu Mambi region in July 1985 and have no firsthand data about the pangngae ceremonies that followed this harvest.

4. Full details of the comparison can be found in George 1989.

5. Wherever one goes in the Salu Mambi and Salu Hau region, one discovers that the mappurondo communities have a long history of anxiety about polluting objects, technologies, and practices that come from afar. At the same time, exogenous objects—severed heads, cloth, porcelain bowls, exotic words—have an important place in ritual practice. This tension between sacred and polluting objects that make their way into the community has suggestive links to geographies of power and conceptions regarding its exogenous sources (cf. Atkinson 1989).

6. The language of entranced women is always an exogenous tongue and, quite often, Mandar. Readers must be curious, as am I, about the significance of Mandar as a woman's trance language in pangngae. Mandar is the language of the ambushed victim, after all. Let me risk a speculative remark. It seems fitting that women in trance would use the language of those who were traditionally the region's dominant political power. Women's trance-critique is thereby authorized by the signs of a dominant power.

7. I note one exception: the melodic structure of the sumengo tomatua at Salutabang is quite similar to that of the ToIssilita' melody heard at Saludengen. For a basic musicological analysis of sumengo melodic structure, see George 1989.

8. In this song, the women praise the mountain communities and their head-hunters. They sing about the andulan (alternate spelling, andulen; see also sumengo 17 and 20 in this group, and note 9, below), which is a variety of areca prized for the yellow leaves and trunk that make the tree stand out in the upland forests, and which is considered emblematic of the mountain region's virtue and glory. The women liken the headhunter to a telo-telo, a swift-flying bird that nests in the mountains but searches for fish in the sea (i.e., it finds prey along the coast, as do the headhunters). Tammu and van der Veen's Toraja dictionary (1972) indicates that telo-telo can also refer to decorative buds, tassels, and leaf tips, though I am un-aware of this usage at Bambang. If it does hold true for Bambang, the sumengo then appears to play with the term's semantic possibilities, alluding both to the tips of the andulen tree and to the bird that flies over the seas.

9. *Rembu andulan* (blades of andulan) are the leaves that the headhunters use to make the streamers that spill from the throat of a tambolâ. The swaying of the tam-bolâ streamers indicates that the warriors are on the move, making their return trip.

10. This song is puzzling to me. I believe it may refer to the mourning shirt worn by women who have been grieving for the dead. Yet my language assistant ar-gued that it was a song of a woman's longing for her husband. He has been gone so long that his shirt is foul with mold; the invitation to take it off is an invitation to lovemaking.

11. The descending stars are the torches carried by villagers who pour down from the hamlets to meet the returning headhunters.

12. The song mentions the *balida,* a batten used in weaving, as the instrument that brought down the victim. Villagers customarily think of tradition and the ongo-ingness of adat as a blanket that is continually being woven. In keeping with this metaphoric logic, the "balida" by which the enemy was slain was a war knife used for the sake of adat.

13. Using, as it does, metaphors having to do with weaving, the first song com-ments on the headhunt and the providential gifts it will bring about. One weaves *sau' lambe',* the cloth for a striped blanket, in lengths of approximately 3 meters. The threads run the length of the cloth, from one end of the loom to the other, and then back again, and are thus quite long. The back-and-forth run of the thread is here a metaphor for the headhunting journey. When making such a blanket, women first lay out a skein of thread between two stakes (*tandajan*) planted in the ground. The blanket in the song has its beginning at Takapak, a Mandar village, and is com-pleted at Rantetarima—the place where uplanders receive (*tarima*) the returning headhunters. The reference to Da'ala seems to point to the name of a Mandar vil-lage. Still, it is worth noting that the term echoes the Muslim expression *Allah ta'ala,* roughly, "Allah the Perfect."

14. See George (1990), Fabian (1992), Street (1984), and Tedlock (1983) for discussions about the theoretical implications of the dialectic between the written and the oral.

15. I leave aside the problem of chronological or temporal privileging. That is, I tended to favor the interpretation I had heard first as being the authoritative and conditioning one.

16. The discourse of contemporary headhunting ritual thus fails to illuminate

the past with the imagery of husband and wife. Interestingly, this is precisely the imagery used in local myth to explain the social and political origins of the highland region (see Chapter 2).

17. In a slightly different version of this chapter subsection (George 1993b), I have argued that differences in song interpretation are symptomatic of the same historical forces that have led one of these two communities to tolerate village exogamy and the other to avoid it.

Chapter 8: The Spectacle of Dancing Men

1. For key discussions and case studies about adat, agama, and local ritual practice, see: Acciaioli 1985; Aragon 1992; Atkinson 1983; Bowen 1991; Geertz 1983; Hefner 1985; and Kipp and Rodgers 1987.

2. I thank Mary Steedly for reminding me about the importance of this term. Kepercayaan corresponds with ritual expression that does not have the status of religious practice (i.e. agama) and shows itself recalcitrant to reformulation as secular custom (i.e. adat). See Steedly (1993:69–70).

3. Beneath a somewhat different rubric, I have elsewhere examined the process of oppositional collaboration as it relates to secrecy and concealment in the mappurondo community (George 1993a). See, also, Chapter 2, and below.

4. In fact, two mappurondo communities still exist in Mambi, and still observe pangngae. One, at Saluassing, consists of eight households; because it is too small to hold pangngae on its own, it joins in festivities at Minanga or Saludengen. The other community is in Salukepopo', a village deeply divided over religious issues; there, mappurondo households make up a little over 40 percent of the total, and are successful at holding pangngae annually. I regret that I had no opportunity to join in the ritual there.

5. I made it a habit to remove myself from the regulated soundscape of mappurondo settlements when working on the musics of pangngae, unless, of course, pangngae was in progress.

6. Papa' Amang's parody of singing style is also a surreptitious dismissal of the song's meaning. The music and meaning of the sumengo are noise and nonsense to the ear of this civil officer.

7. Typical scenarios for conversion to Christianity are: (1) marriage, in which a husband always follows the religion of his wife; (2) entry into middle school, which requires a student to profess a recognized religious faith; and (3) parents "following" their children into Christianity, if all of the latter have converted.

8. Comprising the following principles: (1) the belief in one supreme God; (2) a just and civilized humanitarianism; (3) the unity and integrity of Indonesia; (4) consensual democracy; and (5) social justice for all Indonesians.

9. Both Makatonan (1985) and Tamadjoe (1983) discuss the emergence of Kondo Sapata' at midcentury.

10. I have real suspicions about the references to the "golden stake" (*tana' bulawan*) in Tamusa's account. The term alludes to a former hierarchy of prestige and

social rank that in my researches appears to have been absent or muted in most head-water settlements. I suspect that the ranking system was peculiar to Mamasa, or has been derived (through cultural literature) from the social order of the Sa'dan Toraja around Makale and Rantepao.

11. Subsequently, the same author would prepare a similar outline for the Kabupaten Office of Education and Culture (Samar & Mandadung 1979). In this later Indonesian version he restores references to headhunting with the explanation that "this pangngae dance merely portrays difficulties as if one were fighting an opponent" and constitutes a "former theory/practice" of war (1979:17).

12. For many readers, the English in this pamphlet will seem awkward and strange. I have no wish to make fun of its flaws or its viewpoints, but retaining the original English seemed the best way to convey a sense of textual encounter, and to acknowledge the tactical struggles and choices of authors trying to work in a language not their own.

13. The claims of these scholars rest largely on linguistic evidence. In their findings on the Bare'e Toraja, *menga'e* (headhunting) is synonymous with *menggae* (harvesting). I am suspicious about this, and wonder whether the investigators' interest in cognate word roots might not have sparked the "discovery" of the synonymous relationship between these two words.

14. The mappurondo failure to become "Hindu" contrasts with the successful campaigns of larger, more viable groups in protecting ancestral religion as local variations of Hinduism. See: Boon 1990; Hefner 1985, Kipp and Rodgers 1987, Steedly 1993, and Volkman 1985). Compare, meanwhile, the case of the Meratus Dayak (Tsing 1993:273).

References Cited

Abeyasekere, S.
1983   Slaves in Batavia: Insights from a Slave Register. *In* Slavery, Bondage, and Dependency in Southeast Asia, ed. A. Reid, pp. 286–310. St. Lucia and New York: Queensland University Press.

Abidin, Andi Zainal
1982   Usaha La Ma'dukelleng Arung Singkang untuk Menggelang Persatuan di Sulawesi Selatan pada Abad XVIII Guna Mengusir V.O.C. dari Makassar. *Bingkisan Budaya Sulawesi Selatan* 1982/1983 No. 1:1–26.

1983a   The Emergence of Early Kingdoms in South Sulawesi: A Preliminary Remark on Governmental Contracts from the Thirteenth to the Fifteenth Century. *Tonan Ajia Kenkyu* [*Southeast Asian Studies*] 20(4): 455–491.

1983b   Persepsi Orang Bugis, Makassar tentang Hukum, Negara dan Dunia Luar. Bandung: Penerbit Alumni.

Abu-Lughod, Lila
1990   Shifting Politics in Bedouin Love Poetry. *In* Language and the Politics of Emotion, ed. C. Lutz and L. Abu-Lughod, pp. 24–45. Cambridge: Cambridge University Press.

Acciaioli, Gregory L.
1985   Culture as Art: From Practice to Spectacle in Indonesia. *Canberra Anthropology* 8:148–172.

1989   Searching for Good Fortune: The Making of a Bugis Shore Community at Lake Lindu, Central Sulawesi. Ph.D. thesis, Department of Anthropology, The Australian National University, Canberra.

Adams, Kathleen M.
1984   Come to Tana Toraja, "Land of the Heavenly Kings": Travel Agents as Brokers in Ethnicity. *Annals of Tourism Research* 11(3):469–485.

Adriani, N., and Alb. C. Kruyt
    1950   De Bare'e sprekende Toradja's van Midden Celebes. [2d ed., rev.] Ver-
            handelingen der Koninklijke Nederlandse Akademie van Wetenshappen,
            Afdeling Letterkunde 54–56. [1912]

Amin, Entji'
    1963   Sja'ir Perang Mengkasar, ed. & trans. C. Skinner. Verhandelingen van
            het Koninklijk Instituut van het Taal-, Land-, en Volkenkunde 40.

Andaya, Leonard Y.
    1984   Kingship-Adat Rivalry and the Role of Islam in South Sulawesi. *Journal
            of Southeast Asian Studies* 15(1):22–42.

[anonymous]
    1924   Militaire Nota van het Patrouillegebied te Mamasa. Memorie van Over-
            gave. [March]

Appadurai, Arjun
    1981   The Past as a Scarce Resource. *Man* (n.s.) 16(2):201–219.

Aragon, Lorraine V.
    1992   Revised Rituals in Central Sulawesi: The Maintenance of Traditional
            Cosmological Concepts in the Face of Allegiance to World Religion.
            Anthropological Forum 6(3):371–384.

Armstrong, Nancy, and Leonard Tennenhouse
    1989   Introduction: Representing Violence, or "How the West was Won."
            In The Violence of Representation: Literature and the History of Vio-
            lence, ed. N. Armstrong and L. Tennenhouse, pp. 1–28. New York:
            Routledge.

Atkinson, Jane Monnig
    1983   Religions in Dialogue: The Construction of an Indonesian Minority
            Religion. *American Ethnologist* 10(4):684–696.

    1984   Wrapped Words: Poetry and Politics among the Wana. *In* Danger-
            ous Words: Language and Politics in the Pacific, ed. D. Brenneis and
            F. Myers, pp. 33–68. New York: New York University Press.

    1987   The Effectiveness of Shamans in an Indonesian Ritual. *American An-
            thropologist* 89(2):342–355.

    1989   The Art and Politics of Wana Shamanship. Berkeley: University of Cali-
            fornia Press.

    1990   How Gender Makes a Difference in Wana Society. *In* Power and Dif-
            ference: Gender in Island Southeast Asia, ed. J. M. Atkinson and S. Er-
            rington, pp. 59–94. Stanford, Calif.: Stanford University Press.

Atlas der Protestantsche Kerk in Nederlansch Oost-Indië
    1925   "14. Hulppredikersafdeeling Mamasa," pp. 126–129. Protestantsche
            Kerk.

Austin, J. L.
    1962   How to Do Things with Words. Cambridge, Mass.: Harvard University
            Press.

Bakhtin, Mikhail M.
    1984   Rabelais and His World, trans. H. Iswolsky. Bloomington: Indiana Uni-
            versity Press.

1986   Speech Genres and Other Late Essays, trans. V. McGee. Austin: University of Texas Press.

Battaglia, Debbora

1990   On the Bones of the Serpent: Person, Memory, and Mortality in Sabarl Island Society. Chicago: University of Chicago Press.

Bauman, Richard

1977   Verbal Art as Performance. Prospect Heights, Ill.: Waveland Press.

Bauman, Richard, and Charles L. Briggs

1990   Poetics and Performance as Critical Perspectives on Language and Social Life. *Annual Reviews in Anthropology* 19:59–88.

1992   Genre, Intertextuality, and Social Power. *Journal of Linguistic Anthropology* 2(2):131–172.

Becker, Alton L.

1979   Text-Building, Epistemology, and Aesthetics in Javanese Shadow Theatre. *In* The Imagination of Reality: Essays in Southeast Asian Coherence Systems, ed. A. L. Becker and A. A. Yengoyan, pp. 211–243. Norwood, N.J.: Ablex.

Becker, Alton L., and Aram Yengoyan, eds.

1979   The Imagination of Reality: Essays in Southeast Asian Coherence Systems. Norwood, N.J.: Ablex.

Benjamin, Walter

1969   Illuminations. New York: Schocken.

1978   Critique of Violence. *In* Reflections: Essays, Aphorisms, Autobiographical Writings, trans. E. Jephcott, pp. 227–300. New York: Harcourt, Brace, Jovanovich.

Bigalke, Terance W.

1981   A Social History of Tana Toraja 1870–1965. Ph.D. dissertation, University of Wisconsin–Madison.

Bloch, Maurice

1974   Symbols, Song, Dance, and Features of Articulation: Is Religion an Extreme Form of Traditional Authority? *European Journal of Sociology* 15:55–81.

1992   Prey into Hunter: The Politics of Religious Experience. Cambridge: Cambridge University Press.

Bloch, Maurice, and Jonathan Parry

1982   Introduction: Death and the Regeneration of Life. *In* Death and the Regeneration of Life, ed. M. Bloch and J. Parry, pp. 1–44. Cambridge: Cambridge University Press.

Boon, James A.

1977   The Anthropological Romance of Bali, 1597–1972: Dynamic Perspectives in Marriage and Caste, Politics and Religion. Cambridge: Cambridge University Press.

1990   Affinities and Extremes: Crisscrossing the Bittersweet Ethnology of East Indies History, Hindu-Balinese Culture, and Indo-European Allure. Chicago: University of Chicago Press.

Bourdieu, Pierre
    1991   Language and Symbolic Power, ed. J. B. Thompson, trans. G. Ray-
            mond and M. Adamson. Cambridge, Mass.: Harvard University Press.
Bowen, John
    1991   Sumatran Politics and Poetics: Gayo History, 1900–1989. New Haven,
            Conn.: Yale University Press.
Brenneis, Donald
    1987   Performing Passions: Aesthetics and Politics in an Occasionally Egali-
            tarian Community. *American Ethnologist* 14(2):236–250.
Bronson, Bennet
    1977   Exchange at the Upstream and Downstream Ends: Notes Toward a
            Functional Model of the Coastal State in Southeast Asia. *In* Economic
            Exchange and Social Interaction in Southeast Asia: Perspectives from
            Prehistory, History, and Ethnography, ed. K. Hutterer, pp. 39–54. Mich-
            igan Papers on South and Southeast Asia No. 13. Ann Arbor: Center for
            South and Southeast Asian Studies, University of Michigan.
Bruns, Gerald L.
    1988   The New Philosophy. *In* Columbia Literary History of the United States,
            ed. E. Elliott, M. Banta, and H. A. Baker, pp. 1045–1059. New York:
            Columbia University Press.
Campbell, Philip J.
    1989   Some Aspects of Pitu Ulunna Salu Grammar: A Typological Approach.
            M.A. Thesis, Department of Linguistics, University of Texas at Arlington.
Canetti, Elias
    1978   Crowds and Power, trans. Carol Stewart. New York: Seabury Press.
    [1960]
Caton, Steven C.
    1987   Contributions of Roman Jakobson. *Annual Reviews in Anthropology*
            16:223–260.
Chambers, Ross
    1991   Room for Maneuver: Reading Oppositional Narrative. Chicago: Uni-
            versity of Chicago Press.
Collier, Jane F., and Michelle Z. Rosaldo
    1981   Politics and Gender in Simple Societies. *In* Sexual Meanings: The Cul-
            tural Construction of Gender and Sexuality, ed. S. B. Ortner and
            H. Whitehead, pp. 275–329. Cambridge: Cambridge University Press.
Connerton, Paul
    1989   How Societies Remember. Cambridge: Cambridge University Press.
Coville, Elizabeth
    1989   Centripetal Ritual in a Decentered World: Changing Maro Perfor-
            mances in Tana Toraja. *In* Changing Lives, Changing Rites: Ritual and
            Social Dynamics in Philippine and Indonesian Uplands, ed. S. R. Rus-
            sell and C. E. Cunningham, pp. 103–131. Michigan Studies of South
            and Southeast Asia, No. 1. Ann Arbor: University of Michigan.
Crapanzano, Vincent
    1992   Hermes' Dilemma and Hamlet's Desire: On the Epistemology of Inter-
            pretation. Cambridge, Mass.: Harvard University Press.

Culler, Jonathan
    1982   On Deconstruction: Theory and Criticism after Structuralism. Ithaca, N.Y.: Cornell University Press.
Davison, Julian, and Vinson H. Sutlive, Jr.
    1991   The Children of Nising: Images of Headhunting and Male Sexuality in Iban Ritual and Oral Literature. *In* Female and Male in Borneo: Contributions and Challenges to Gender Studies, ed. V. H. Sutlive, Jr., pp. 153–230. Borneo Research Council Monograph Series, Volume 1. Williamsburg, Va.: Department of Anthropology, College of William and Mary.
de Certeau, Michel
    1984   The Practice of Everyday Life, trans. S. Rendell. Berkeley: University of California Press.
de Jongh, D.
    1923   Eenige gegevens betreffende het Boven-Karamagebied (Celebes). *Tijdschrift Nederlansch Aardrijkskundig Genootschap* (2e serie) 40:462–474.
DepDikBud (Departemen Pendidikan dan Kebudayaan)
    1981   Naskah Hasil Keputusan Seminar Sejarah Mandar (Polmas-Majene-Mamuju) di Tinambung Tahun 1971. (mimeo.) Ujung Pandang: Kanwil DepDikBud, SulSel.
    n.d.[a]   Hikayat Tanah Mandar. (mimeo.) Polewali: DepDikBud Kabupaten Polmas.
    n.d.[b]   Lontara' Mandar, No. 118. (mss.) Ujung Pandang: Kanwil DepDikBud, SulSel.
    n.d.[c]   Sekilas Lintas Kabupaten Polmas. (mimeo.) Polewali: DepDikBud Kabupaten Polmas.
    n.d.[d]   Susunan Arajang Balanipa. (mimeo.) Polewali: DepDikBub Kabupaten Polmas.
Dirks, Nicholas B.
    1994   Ritual and Resistance: Subversion as Social Fact. *In* Culture/Power/History: A Reader in Contemporary Social Theory, ed. N. Dirks, G. Eley, and S. B. Ortner, pp. 483–503. Princeton, N.J.: Princeton University Press.
Dirks, Nicholas B., Geoff Eley, and Sherry B. Ortner
    1994   Introduction. *In* Culture/Power/History: A Reader in Contemporary Social Theory, ed. N. Dirks, G. Eley, and S. B. Ortner, pp. 3–45. Princeton: N.J.: Princeton University Press.
Dormeier, J. J.
    1947   Banggaisch Adatrecht. Verhandelingen van het Koninklijk Instituut voor Taal-, Land- en Volkenkunde 6.
Downs, R. E.
    1955   Headhunting in Indonesia. *Bijdragen tot de Taal-, Land- en Volkenkunde* 111:40–70.
    1956   The Religion of the Bare'e-speaking Toradja of Central Celebes. The Hague: Uitgeverij Excelsior.

Drake, Richard Allen
  1989   Construction Sacrifice and Kidnapping Rumor Panics in Borneo. *Oceania* 59:269–279.
Durkheim, Emile
  1965   The Elementary Forms of the Religious Life. New York: Free Press. [1915]
ENI [Encyclopaedie van Nederlansche-Indie]
  1918   Vol. 2 [H–M], "Koppensnellen," pp. 430–433; "Mandar," pp. 664–665. Leiden: Nijhoff/Brill.
Erb, Maribeth
  1991   Construction Sacrifice, Rumors and Kidnapping Scares in Manggarai: Further Comparative Notes from Flores. *Oceania* 62:114–126.
Errington, Shelly
  1983   Embodied Sumange' in Luwu. *Journal of Asian Studies* 42(3):545–570.
  1987   Incestuous Twins and the House Societies of Insular Southeast Asia. *Cultural Anthropology* 2(4):403–444.
  1989   Meaning and Power in a Southeast Asian Realm. Princeton, N.J.: Princeton University Press.
Fabian, Johannes
  1974   Genres in an Emerging Tradition: An Approach to Religious Communication. *In* Changing Perspectives in the Scientific Study of Religion, ed. A. W. Eister, pp. 249–272. New York: Wiley.
  1983   Time and the Other: How Anthropology Makes Its Object. New York: Columbia University Press.
  1990   Power and Performance: Ethnographic Explorations through Proverbial Wisdom and Theater in Shaba, Zaire. Madison: University of Wisconsin Press.
  1992   Keep Listening: Ethnography and Reading. *In* The Ethnography of Reading, ed. J. Boyarin, pp. 80–97. Berkeley: University of California Press.
Fachruddin
  1983   Da'wah dan Adat Malilling di Kecamatan Mambi Kabupaten Polewali-Mamasa. Draft ms. for *skripsi* (thesis), Fakultas Ushuluddin, IAIN Alauddin, Ujung Pandang.
Feldman, Allen
  1991   Formations of Violence: The Narrative of the Body and Political Terror in Northern Ireland. Chicago: University of Chicago Press.
Feldman, Carol Fleisher
  1987   Remarks at the Symposium on "Literacy, Reading, and Power," Whitney Humanities Center, November 14, 1987. *Yale Journal of Criticism* 2(1):209–214.
Finnegan, Ruth
  1988   Literacy and Orality: Studies in the Technology of Communication. New York: Basil Blackwell.
Fish, Stanley
  1980   Is There a Text in This Class? The Authority of Interpretive Communities. Cambridge, Mass.: Harvard University Press.

1989   Doing What Comes Naturally: Change, Rhetoric, and the Practice of
           Theory in Literary and Legal Studies. Durham, N.C.: Duke University
           Press.

Folena, Lucia
1989   Figures of Violence: Philologists, Witches, and Stalinistas. *In* The Vio-
           lence of Representation: Literature and the History of Violence, ed.
           N. Armstrong and L. Tennenhouse, pp. 219–238. New York: Rout-
           ledge.

Foster, Brian L.
1977   Trade, Social Conflict, and Social Integration: Rethinking Some Old
           Ideas on Exchange. *In* Economic Exchange and Social Interaction in
           Southeast Asia: Perspectives from Prehistory, History, and Ethnography,
           ed. K. Hutterer, pp. 3–22. Michigan Papers on South and Southeast
           Asia No. 13. Ann Arbor: Center for South and Southeast Asian Studies,
           University of Michigan.

Fox, James J.
1988   To Speak in Pairs: Essays on the Ritual Languages of Eastern Indonesia.
           Cambridge: Cambridge University Press.

Fox, Richard G.
1991   Recapturing Anthropology: Working in the Present. Santa Fe, N. Mex.:
           School of American Research.

Freeman, Derek
1970   Report on the Iban. London School of Economics Monographs on So-
           cial Anthropology No. 41. New York: Humanities Press.
1979   Severed Heads That Germinate. *In* Fantasy and Symbol: Studies in An-
           thropological Interpretation, ed. R. H. Hook, pp. 233–246. New York:
           Academic Press.

Galestin, W. A. C.
1936   Nota betreffende het Landschap Tapalang. Memorie van Overgave.
           [March]

Geertz, Clifford
1973   "Internal Conversion" in Contemporary Bali. *In* The Interpretation of
           Cultures, pp. 170–189. New York: Basic Books.
1980   Negara: The Theatre-State in Nineteenth-Century Bali. Princeton, N.J.:
           Princeton University Press.
1983   Local Knowledge: Fact and Law in Comparative Perspective. *In* Local
           Knowledge: Further Essays in Interpretive Anthropology, pp. 167–234.
           New York: Basic Books.

Geertz, Hildred, and Clifford Geertz
1975   Kinship in Bali. Chicago: University of Chicago Press.

George, Kenneth M.
1989   The Singing from the Headwaters: Song and Tradition in the Head-
           hunting Rituals of an Upland Sulawesi Community. Ph.D. dissertation,
           Department of Anthropology, University of Michigan.
1990   Felling a Song with a New Ax: Writing and the Reshaping of Ritual Song
           Performance in Upland Sulawesi. *Journal of American Folklore* 103(407):
           3–23.

1991   Headhunting, History, and Exchange in Upland Sulawesi. *Journal of Asian Studies* 50(3):536–564.

1993a   Dark Trembling: Ethnographic Notes on Secrecy and Concealment in Highland Sulawesi. *Anthropological Quarterly* 66(4):230–239.

1993b   Lyric, History, and Allegory, or the End of Headhunting Ritual in Upland Sulawesi. *American Ethnologist* 20(4):697–717.

1993c   Music-making, Ritual, and Gender in a Southeast Asian Hill Society. *Ethnomusicology* 37(1):1–26.

1995   Violence, Solace, and Ritual: A Case Study from Island Southeast Asia. *Culture, Medicine, and Psychiatry* 19(2): 225–260.

Girard, Rene
1977   Violence and the Sacred, trans. P. Gregory. Baltimore: The Johns Hopkins University Press.

1987   Generative Scapegoating. *In* Violent Origins: Walter Burkert, René Girard, and Jonathan Z. Smith on Ritual Killing and Cultural Formation, ed. R. G. Hammerton-Kelly, pp. 73–148. Stanford, Calif.: Stanford University Press.

Good, Byron J.
1994   Medicine, Rationality, and Experience: An Anthropological Perspective. Cambridge: Cambridge University Press.

Good, Mary-Jo Delvecchio, and Byron J. Good
1988   Ritual, the State, and the Transformation of Emotional Discourse in Iranian Society. *Culture, Medicine, and Psychiatry* 12(1):43–63.

Goslings, J. F. W. L.
1933   De Toradja's van Galoempang. *Kolonial Tijdschrift* 22:53–84. [Originally prepared as "Memorie van het district Galoempang van de afdeeling Mamoedjoe." Memorie van Overgave, 1924.]

Gusdorf, Georges
1965   Speaking, trans. P. T. Brockelman. Evanston, Ill.: Northwestern University Press.

Halbwachs, Maurice
1980   The Collective Memory, trans. F. J. Ditter and V. Y. Ditter. New York: Harper Colophon.

Handler, Richard, and Jocelyn Linnekin
1984   Tradition, Genuine or Spurious. *Journal of American Folklore* 97(385): 273–290.

Hasenclever, Walter
1963   Humanity. *In* An Anthology of German Expressionist Drama: A Prelude to the Absurd, ed. W. H. Sokel, trans. W. Sokel and J. Sokel, pp. 172–201. New York: Anchor Doubleday. [1918]

Havelock, Eric A.
1963   Preface to Plato. Cambridge, Mass.: Belknap Press.

1986   The Muse Learns to Write: Reflections on Orality and Literacy from Antiquity to the Present. New Haven, Conn.: Yale University Press.

Hefner, Robert W.
1985   Hindu Javanese: Tengger Tradition and Islam. Princeton, N.J.: Princeton University Press.

Hertz, Robert
  1960   Death and the Right Hand, trans. R. Needham and C. Needham. London: Cohen and West.
Herzfeld, Michael
  1985   The Poetics of Manhood: Contest and Identity in a Cretan Mountain Village. Princeton, N.J.: Princeton University Press.
  1987   "As in Your Own House:" Hospitality, Ethnography, and the Stereotype of Mediterranean Society. *In* Honor and Shame and the Unity of the Mediterranean, ed. D. Gilmore, pp. 75–89. Special Publication No. 22. Washington, D.C.: American Anthropological Association.
  1990   Pride and Perjury: Time and Oath in the Mountain Villages of Crete. *Man* (n.s.) 25:305–322.
Hobsbawm, Eric, and Terance Ranger
  1983   The Invention of Tradition. Cambridge: Cambridge University Press.
Hollan, Douglas
  1988   Staying "Cool" in Toraja: Informal Strategies for the Management of Anger and Hostility in a Nonviolent Society. *Ethos* 16(1):52–72.
Holman, C. Hugh
  1972   A Handbook to Literature. [Third Edition.] Indianapolis: Odyssey.
Hoorweg
  1911   Nota Bevattende eenige Gegevens Betreffende het Landschap Mamoedjoe. *Tijdschrift voor Indische Taal-, Land- en Volkenkunde* 53:57–154.
Hose, Charles, and William McDougall
  1912   The Pagan Tribes of Borneo. London: Macmillan.
Hoskins, Janet
  1987   The Headhunter as Hero: Local Traditions and Their Reinterpretation in National History. *American Ethnologist* 14(4):605–622.
  1989   On Losing and Getting a Head: Warfare, Exchange, and Alliance in a Changing Sumba, 1888–1988. *American Ethnologist* 16(3):419–440.
  forth. [a] Introduction: Headhunting as Practice and as Trope. In Headhunting and the Social Imagination in Southeast Asia, ed. J. Hoskins. Stanford, Calif.: Stanford University Press.
  forth. [b] The Heritage of Headhunting: History, Ideology and Violence on Sumba, 1890–1990. *In* Headhunting and the Social Imagination in Southeast Asia, ed. J. Hoskins. Stanford, Calif.: Stanford University Press.
Huntington, Richard, and Peter Metcalf
  1979   Celebrations of Death: The Anthropology of Mortuary Ritual. Cambridge: Cambridge University Press.
Hymes, Dell
  1981   "In vain I tried to tell you:" Essays in Native American Ethnopoetics. Philadelphia: University of Pennsylvania Press.
Jakobson, Roman
  1960   Linguistics and Poetics. *In* Style in Language, ed. T. Sebeok, pp. 350–377. Cambridge, Mass.: MIT Press.
Just, Peter
  1991   Going Through the Emotions: Passion, Violence, and "Other-Control" among the Dou Donggo. *Ethos* 19(3):288–312.

Kapferer, Bruce
1979a   Introduction: Ritual Process and the Transformation of Context. *Social Analysis* 1:13–19.
1979b   Entertaining Demons: Comedy, Interaction, and Meaning in a Sinhalese Healing Ritual. *Social Analysis* 1:108–152.
1979c   Emotion and Feeling in Sinhalese Healing Rites. *Social Analysis* 1:153–176.

Keane, Webb
1991   Delegated Voice: Ritual Speech, Risk, and the Making of Marriage Alliances in Anakalang. *American Ethnologist* 18(2):311–330.

Kelly, John D., and Martha Kaplan
1990   History, Structure, and Ritual. *Annual Reviews in Anthropology* 19: 119–150.

Kennedy, Raymond
1935   The Ethnology of the Greater Sunda Islands. Ph.D. dissertation, Yale University.
1942   The Ageless Indies. New York: John Day.

Kipp, Rita Smith, and Susan Rodgers
1987   Introduction: Indonesian Religions in Society. *In* Indonesian Religions in Transition, ed. R. S. Kipp and S. Rodgers, pp. 1–31. Tucson: University of Arizona Press.

Kleinman, Arthur, and Joan Kleinman
1991   Suffering and Its Professional Transformation: Toward an Ethnography of Interpersonal Experience. *Culture, Medicine and Psychiatry* 15(3): 275–301.

Krüger, Th. Müller
1966   Sedjarah Geredja di Indonesia. Jakarta: Badan Penerbit Kristen.

Kruyt, Alb. C.
1906   Het Animisme in den Indischen Archipel. The Hague: Martinus Nijhoff.
1923   De Toraja's van de Sa'dan, Masoepoe en Mamasa-Rivieren. *Tijdschrift Bataviaasch Genootschap van Kunsten en Wetenschappen* LXIII:81–175, 259–401.
1930   De To Loinang van den Oostarm van Celebes. *Bijdragen tot de Taal-, Land- en Volkenkunde* 86:327–536.
1938   De West-Toradja's op Midden Celebes. Verhandelingen der Koninklijke Nederlandse Akademie van Wetenschappen, Afdeling Letterkunde 40.
1942   De Bewoners van het Stroomgebied van de Karama in Midden-Celebes. *Tijdschrift Nederlansch Aardrijkskundig Genootschap* (2e Serie) 59:518–553, 702–741, 879–914.

Kruyt, J.
1924   De Moriërs van Tinompo. *Bijdragen tot de Taal-, Land- en Volkenkunde* 80:33–217.

Kuipers, Joel C.
1986   Talking about Troubles: Gender Differences in Weyéwa Speech Use. *American Ethnologist* 13(3):448–462.

1990   Power in Performance: The Creation of Textual Authority in Weyéwa
          Ritual Speech. Philadelphia: University of Pennsylvania Press.
Langer, Suzanne K.
1951   Philosophy in a New Key. New York: New American Library.
Lévi-Strauss, Claude
1966   The Savage Mind. Chicago: University of Chicago Press.
1969   The Raw and the Cooked: Introduction to a Science of Mythology,
          Volume 1. New York: Harper Colophon.
1982   The Way of the Masks, trans. S. Modelski. Seattle: University of Wash-
          ington Press.
Lord, Albert B.
1960   The Singer of Tales. Cambridge, Mass.: Harvard University Press.
Lutz, Catherine A., and Lila Abu-Lughod
1990   Introduction: Emotion, Discourse, and the Politics of Everyday Life. In
          Language and the Politics of Emotion, ed. C. Lutz and L. Abu-Lughod,
          pp. 1–23. Cambridge: Cambridge University Press.
Lutz, Catherine A., and Geoffrey M. White
1986   The Anthropology of Emotions. Annual Reviews in Anthropology 15:
          405–436.
Macknight, C. C.
1983   The Rise of Agriculture in South Sulawesi Before 1600. Review of In-
          donesian and Malaysian Affairs 17(winter/summer):92–116.
Makatonan, Als.
1985   Ada' Mappurondo. Peninjau XII(1 & 2):61–150.
Mandadung, Arianus
1977   Untitled tourist guide to Mamasa and Pitu Ulunna Salu area. (mimeo.)
Maurenbrecher, L. L. A.
1947   Nota van overdracht van den Assistent-Resident van Mandar, L. L. A.
          Maurenbrecher, periode 13 Januari 1946–2 Juni 1947. Ms. copy at
          Arsip Nasional, Ujung Pandang Branch. Kode 19-1.
Maxwell, Allen R.
forth.   Headtaking and the Consolidation of Political Power in the Early
          Brunei State. In Headhunting and the Social Imagination in Southeast
          Asia, ed. J. Hoskins. Stanford, Calif.: Stanford University Press.
McGann, Jerome J.
1991   The Textual Condition. Princeton, N.J.: Princeton University Press.
McKinley, Robert
1976   Human and Proud of It! A Structural Treatment of Headhunting Rites
          and the Social Definition of Enemies. In Studies in Borneo Societies:
          Social Process and Anthropological Explanation, ed. G. N. Appell, pp.
          92–126. DeKalb, Ill.: Center for Southeast Asian Studies, Northern
          Illinois University.
Medick, Hans
1987   "Missionaries in a Row Boat"? Ethnological Ways of Knowing as a
          Challenge to Social History. Comparative Studies in Society and History
          29(1):76–98.

Metcalf, Peter
    1982   A Borneo Journey into Death: Berawan Eschatology from Its Rituals. Philadelphia: University of Pennsylvania Press.
    1987   Eroticism and Headhunting. Paper given at the Annual Meeting of the American Anthropological Association, 1987. (ms.)
    1989   Where Are You | Spirits: Style and Theme in Berawan Prayer. Washington, D.C.: Smithsonian Institution Press.
    forth. Headhunting in Context. In Headhunting and the Social Imagination in Southeast Asia, ed. J. Hoskins. Stanford, Calif.: Stanford University Press.
Montrose, Louis
    1989   Professing the Renaissance: The Poetics and Politics of Culture. In The New Historicism, ed. H. A. Veeser, pp. 15–36. New York: Routledge.
Morris, Mary
    1993   Preface. In Maiden Voyages: Writings of Women Travelers, ed. M. Morris. New York: Vintage.
Myers, Fred
    1986   Pintupi Country, Pintupi Self: Sentiment, Place, and Politics among Western Desert Aborigines. Washington, D.C.: Smithsonian Institution Press.
Nagy, Gregory
    1990   Pindar's Homer: The Lyric Possession of an Epic Past. Baltimore: The Johns Hopkins University Press.
Natanson, Maurice
    1970   The Journeying Self: A Study in Philosophy and Social Role. Reading, Mass.: Addison-Wesley.
Needham, Rodney
    1976   Skulls and Causality. Man (n.s.) 11(1):71–88.
Nooy-Palm, C. H. M.
    1979   The Sa'dan Toraja: A Study of Their Social Life and Religion, Part I. Verhandelingen van het Koninklijk Instituut van het Taal-, Land- en Volkenkunde 87. The Hague: Martinus Nijhoff.
    1986   The Sa'dan Toraja: A Study of Their Social Life and Religion, Part II, Rituals of the East and West. Dordrecht: Foris Publications.
Obeyesekere, Gananath
    1990   The Work of Culture: Symbolic Transformation in Psychoanalysis and Anthropology. Chicago: University of Chicago Press.
Ong, Walter J.
    1977   Interfaces of the Word: Studies in the Evolution of Consciousness and Culture. Ithaca, N.Y.: Cornell University Press.
Ortner, Sherry B.
    1978   Sherpas Through Their Rituals. Cambridge: Cambridge University Press.
    1981   Gender and Sexuality in Hierarchical Societies: The Case of Polynesia and Some Comparative Implications. In Sexual Meanings: The Cultural Construction of Gender and Sexuality, ed. S. Ortner and H. Whitehead, pp. 359–409. Cambridge: Cambridge University Press.
    1984   Theory in Anthropology since the Sixties. Comparative Studies in Society and History 26(1):126–166.

1989   High Religion: A Cultural and Political History of Sherpa Buddhism. Princeton, N.J.: Princeton University Press.

1990   Gender Hegemonies. *Cultural Critique* 14:35–80.

Pannell, Sandra

1992   Travelling to Other Worlds: Narratives of Headhunting, Appropriation and the Other in the "Eastern Archipelago." *Oceania* 62:162–178.

Patunru, Abd. Razak Daeng

1983   Sejarah Gowa. Ujung Pandang: Yayasan Kebudayaan Sulawesi Selatan.

Peacock, James L.

1968   Rites of Modernization: Symbolic and Social Aspects of Indonesian Proletarian Drama. Chicago: University of Chicago Press.

Plessner, Helmuth

1970   Laughing and Crying: A Study of the Limits of Human Behavior, trans. J. S. Churchill and M. Green. Evanston, Ill.: Northwestern University Press.

Rappaport, Roy A.

1979   The Obvious Aspects of Ritual. *In* Ecology, Meaning, and Religion, ed. Roy A. Rappaport. Richmond, Calif.: North Atlantic Books.

Rauws, Joh.

1930   Overzicht van het Zendingswerk in Ned. Oost- en West- Indië. *Mededeelingen Tijdschrift voor Zendingswetenschap* 74:159.

Reid, Anthony

1983a   'Closed' and 'Open' Slave Systems. *In* Slavery, Bondage, and Dependency in Southeast Asia, ed. A. Reid, pp. 157–181. St. Lucia and New York: Queensland University Press.

1983b   Introduction: Slavery and Bondage in Southeast Asian History. *In* Slavery, Bondage, and Dependency in Southeast Asia, ed. A. Reid, pp. 1–43. St. Lucia and New York: Queensland University Press.

1983c   The Rise of Makassar. *Review of Indonesian and Malaysian Affairs* 17 (winter/summer):117–160.

Rijsdijk, L. C. J.

1935   Nota betreffende het Landschap Pembaoeang. Memorie van Overgave. [January]

Rodgers, Susan

1990   The Symbolic Representation of Women in a Changing Batak Culture. *In* Power and Difference: Gender in Island Southeast Asia, ed. J. Atkinson and S. Errington, pp. 307–344. Stanford, Calif.: Stanford University Press.

Rosaldo, Michelle Z.

1977   Skulls and Causality. *Man* (n.s.) 12(1):168–170.

1980   Knowledge and Passion: Ilongot Notions of Self and Social Life. Cambridge: Cambridge University Press.

1983   The Shame of Headhunters and the Autonomy of Self. *Ethos* 11(3): 135–151.

1984a   Toward an Anthropology of Self and Feeling. *In* Culture Theory: Essays on Mind, Self, and Emotion, ed. R. Shweder and R. LeVine, pp. 137–157. Cambridge: Cambridge University Press.

1984b   Words That Are Moving: Social Meanings of Ilongot Verbal Art. *In* Dangerous Words: Language and Politics in the Pacific, ed. D. Brenneis and F. Myers, pp. 131–160. New York: New York University Press.

Rosaldo, Michelle Z., and Jane Monnig Atkinson
1975   Man the Hunter and Woman: Metaphors for the Sexes in Ilongot Magical Spells. *In* The Interpretation of Symbolism, ed. R. Willis, pp. 43–75. New York: John Wiley and Sons.

Rosaldo, Renato
1978   The Rhetoric of Control: Ilongots Viewed as Natural Bandits and Wild Indians. *In* The Reversible World: Symbolic Inversion in Art and Society, ed. B. Babcock, pp. 240–257. Ithaca, N.Y.: Cornell University Press.

1980   Ilongot Headhunting, 1883–1974: A Study in Society and History. Stanford, Calif.: Stanford University Press.

1984   Grief and a Headhunter's Rage: On the Cultural Force of Emotions. *In* Text, Play, and Story: The Construction and Reconstruction of Self and Society, ed. E. M. Bruner, pp. 178–195. Washington, D.C.: American Ethnological Society.

1986   Red Hornbill Earrings: Ilongot Ideas of Self, Beauty, and Health. *Cultural Anthropology* 1(3):310–316.

1987   Anthropological Commentary. *In* Violent Origins: Walter Burkert, René Girard, and Jonathan Z. Smith on Ritual Killing and Cultural Formation, ed. R. G. Hammerton-Kelly, pp. 239–256. Stanford, Calif.: Stanford University Press.

1988   Death in the Ethnographic Present. *Poetics Today* 9(2):425–434.

Rosenau, Pauline Marie
1992   Post-Modernism and the Social Sciences: Insights, Inroads, and Intrusions. Princeton, N.J.: Princeton University Press.

Rubenstein, Carol
1985   The Honey Tree Song: Poems and Chants of the Sarawak Dyaks. Athens: Ohio University Press.

Said, Edward
1979   The Text, the World, the Critic. *In* Textual Strategies: Perspectives in Post-Structuralist Criticism, ed. J. V. Harari, pp. 161–188. Ithaca, N.Y.: Cornell University Press.

Samar, Abd. Azis, and Arianus Mandadung
1979   Ungkapan Sejarah dan Budaya di Kabupaten Polewali-Mamasa SulSel, Seri A Daerah Kondosapata Mamasa. (mimeo.) Polewali: DepDikBud Kabupaten Polmas.

Scheff, Thomas J.
1977   The Distancing of Emotion in Ritual. *Current Anthropology* 18(3):483–505.

Schutz, Alfred
1977   Making Music Together: A Study in Social Relationship. *In* Symbolic Anthropology: A Reader in the Study of Symbols and Meanings, ed. J. Dogin, D. Kemnitzer, and D. Schneider, pp. 106–119. New York: Columbia University Press. [1951]

Schuurmans, J.
    1934   Het Koppensnellen der To Laki. *Mededeelingen van wege het Neder-landsch Zendelinggenootschap* 78:207–218.
Scott, James
    1990   Domination and the Arts of Resistance: Hidden Transcripts. New Haven, Conn.: Yale University Press.
Searle, John R.
    1969   Speech Acts: An Essay in the Philosophy of Language. Cambridge: Cambridge University Press.
Siegel, James
    1978   Curing Rites, Dreams, and Domestic Politics in a Sumatran Society. *Glyph: Johns Hopkins Textual Studies* 3:18–31.
    1979   Shadow and Sound: The Historical Thought of a Sumatran People. Chicago: University of Chicago Press.
Simmel, Georg
    1950   The Sociology of Georg Simmel, ed. and trans. K. H. Wolff. Glencoe, Ill.: The Free Press.
Sinrang, Andi Syaiful
    n.d.   Mengenal Mandar Sekilas Lintas. Group "Tipalayo" Polemaju (private printing).
Smit, P. C.
    1937   Gegevens over Bambang (1936). Adatrechtbundels XXXIX: Gemengd. The Hague: Martinus Nijhoff.
Smith, Barbara Hernstein
    1968   Poetic Closure: A Study of How Poems End. Chicago: University of Chicago Press.
    1981   Narrative Versions, Narrative Theories. *In* On Narrative, ed. W. J. T. Mitchell, pp. 209–232. Chicago: University of Chicago Press.
Smith, Jonathan Z.
    1978   Map is Not Territory: Studies in the History of Religions. Leiden: E. J. Brill.
    1982   Imagining Religion: From Babylon to Jonestown. Chicago: University of Chicago Press.
Stallybrass, Peter, and Allon White
    1986   The Politics and Poetics of Transgression. Ithaca, N.Y.: Cornell University Press.
Steedly, Mary Margaret
    1993   Hanging without a Rope: Narrative Experience in Colonial and Postcolonial Karoland. Princeton, N.J.: Princeton University Press.
Stokhof, W. A. L.
    1986   The National Convention on Languages and Literatures of East Indonesia (Ujung Pandang, January 1985). *Archipel* 32:3–14.
Street, Brian V.
    1984   Literacy in Theory and Practice. Cambridge: Cambridge University Press.
Strømme, Kåre J.
    1985   UNHAS-SIL Sociolinguistic Survey, Kabupaten Polewali Mamasa, West-Central Section, September 27–October 9, 1984. (ms.)

Sutherland, Heather
    1983a   Power and Politics in South Sulawesi: 1860–1880. *Review of Indonesian and Malaysian Affairs* 17(winter/summer):161–208.
    1983b   Slavery and the Slave Trade in South Sulawesi, 1660s–1800s. *In* Slavery, Bondage, and Dependency in Southeast Asia, ed. A. Reid, pp. 263–285. St. Lucia and New York: Queensland University Press.

Syah, M. T. Azis
    1980   Biografi I Calo Ammana Iwewang Topole Di Balitung Pahlawan Daerah Mandar Sulawesi Selatan. PEMDA TKT I Propinsi Sul-Sel (private printing).

Tamadjoe
    1983   Sejarah Pitu Ulunna Salu oleh Indo Kadanene, Arale 1934. (ms.)

Tamausa
    1974   Tinjauan Tentang Aluk Pemali Appa' Randanna di Pitu Ulunna Salu. Skripsi Sarjana Muda (undergraduate thesis). Fakultas Keguruan Ilmu Sosial, IKIP, Ujung Pandang. 58 pp.

Tambiah, Stanley
    1985   Culture, Thought, and Social Action: An Anthropological Perspective. Cambridge, Mass.: Harvard University Press.

Tammu, J., and H. van der Veen
    1972   Kamus Toradja-Indonesia. Rantepao: Jajasan Perguruan Kristen Toradja.

Tangdilintin, L. T.
    1980   Toraja dan Kebudayaannya. Cetakan IV. Tana Toraja: Yayasan Lepongan Bulan.

Taussig, Michael
    1987   Shamanism, Colonialism, and the Wild Man: A Study in Terror and Healing. Chicago: University of Chicago Press.

Tedlock, Dennis
    1983   The Spoken Word and the Work of Interpretation. Philadelphia: University of Pennsylvania Press.

Thomas, Nicholas
    1992   The Inversion of Tradition. *American Ethnologist* 19(2):213–232.

Traube, Elizabeth G.
    1986   Cosmology and Social Life: Ritual Exchange among the Mambai of East Timor. Chicago: University of Chicago Press.

Trouillot, Michel-Rolph
    1991   Anthropology and the Savage Slot: The Poetics and Politics of Otherness. *In* Recapturing Anthropology, ed. R. Fox, pp. 17–44. Santa Fe, N. Mex.: School of American Research.

Tsing, Anna Lowenhaupt
    1993   In the Realm of the Diamond Queen: Marginality in an Out-of-the-Way Place. Princeton, N.J.: Princeton University Press.
    forth.   Telling Violence in the Meratus Mountains. *In* Headhunting and the Social Imagination in Southeast Asia, ed. J. Hoskins. Stanford, Calif.: Stanford University Press.

Turner, Victor
    1969   The Ritual Process: Structure and Anti-Structure. Chicago: Aldine.

1974 Dramas, Fields, and Metaphors: Symbolic Action in Human Society. Ithaca, N.Y.: Cornell University Press.

Vance, Eugene
1979 Roland and the Poetics of Memory. *In* Textual Strategies: Perspectives in Post-Structuralist Criticism, ed. J. V. Harari, pp. 374–403. Ithaca, N.Y.: Cornell University Press.

van der Kroef, Justus M.
1970 Messianic Movements in Celebes, Sumatra, and Borneo. *In* Millenarian Dreams in Action: Studies in Revolutionary Religious Movements, ed. S. Thrupp, pp. 80–121. New York: Schocken.

van Goor, M. E. A.
1922 Militaire Memorie betreffende de Onderafdeeling Mamoedjoe. Memorie van Overgave. [March]

Vayda, Andrew P.
1969 The Study of the Causes of War, with Special Reference to Head-Hunting Raids in Borneo. *Ethnohistory* 16(3):211–224.

Veen, W. E. C.
1933 Vervolg Memorie van Overgave van het Bestuur van de Afdeeling Mandar. Memorie van Overgave. [March]

Volkman, Toby Alice
1985 Feasts of Honor: Ritual and Change in the Toraja Highlands. Urbana: University of Illinois Press.
1990 Visions and Revisions: Toraja Culture and the Tourist Gaze. *American Ethnologist* 17(1):91–110.

Vološinov, V. N.
1973 Marxism and the Philosophy of Language, trans. L. Matejka and I. R. Titunik. Cambridge, Mass.: Harvard University Press.

Waterson, H. Roxana
1986 The Ideology and Terminology of Kinship among the Sa'dan Toraja. *Bijdragen tot de Taal-, Land- en Volkenkunde* 142:87–112.

Waugh, Linda R.
1982 Marked and Unmarked: A Choice between Unequals in Semiotic Structure. *Semiotica* 38:299–318.

Wellenkamp, Jane C.
1988a Notions of Grief and Catharsis among the Toraja. *American Ethnologist* 15(3):486–500.
1988b Order and Disorder in Toraja Thought and Ritual. *Ethnology* 27(3): 311–326.

White, Hayden
1978 Tropics of Discourse: Essays in Cultural Criticism. Baltimore: The Johns Hopkins University Press.

Williams, Raymond
1977 Marxism and Literature. Oxford: Oxford University Press.

Yanagisako, Sylvia
1979 Family and Household: The Analysis of Domestic Groups. *Annual Reviews in Anthropology* 8:161–205.

Yates, Frances A.
   1966   The Art of Memory. London: Routledge.
Yayasan Kebudayaan Sulawesi Selatan. Ujung Pandang.
   n.d.   Lontara' Balanipa (ms. photocopy).
Yengoyan, Aram A.
   1985   Memory, Myth, and History: Traditional Agriculture and Structure in
            Mandaya Society. *In* Cultural Values and Human Ecology in Southeast
            Asia, ed. K. L. Hutterer, A. T. Rambo, and G. Lovelace, pp. 157–176.
            Michigan Papers on South and Southeast Asia No. 27. Ann Arbor: Cen-
            ter for South and Southeast Asian Studies, University of Michigan.
Zeemansgijd
   n.d.   Zeemansgijd voor den Oost-Indischen Archipel, Vol. 3, Part 2. [3d
            edition; copy at the Yayasan Kebudayaan Sulawesi Selatan, Ujung Pan-
            dang.]
Zerner, Charles, and Toby Alice Volkman
   1988   The Tree of Desire: A Toraja Ritual Poem. *In* To Speak in Pairs: Essays
            on the Ritual Languages of Eastern Indonesia, ed. J. J. Fox, pp. 282–
            305. Cambridge: Cambridge University Press.

Index

Abeyasekere, S., 75
Abidin, Andi Zainal, 73, 74
Abu-Lughod, Lila, 300n.9
Acciaioli, Gregory L., 294n.3, 307n.1
Ada' mappurondo: civic pressures to abandon, 40; concealment of, 35, 259, 266; cultural politics of term, 21–26; disparaging attitudes toward, 25; efforts for official recognition of, 259–260, 268–269, 308n.14; and Indonesian bureaucracy, 260, 269; origin of term, 25, 35; as religion of social enclave, 35; as ritual tradition, 7, 10, 24. *See also Pemali appa' randanna*
Ada' mate, 28
Adams, Kathleen M., 250
A'dasan ("the shouting"): description of, 119–128, 141; "felling grief" (*dirondongi barata*), 125; photo, 121; and political affect, 127; at Rantepalado (1985), 62–64; ritualized greeting in, 83, 255–257; "shouting at grief" (*dia'da'i barata*), 125. *See also Mua'da; Tambolâ*
Adat, 25, 238. *See also* Indonesian state culture
Ada' tuo, 28, 102, 243
Adat vs. *agama*, 40, 238. *See also* Indonesian state culture
Adornment: commemoration as, 188–190; during *pangngae*, 143–145; music as,

164; *pemali appa' randanna* as, 188; and politics of envy, 144; and sublime speech, 189; terms for, 145
Adriani, N., 37, 255, 298n.12
Afdeeling Mandar (Colonial District of Mandar), 39
Agama vs. *adat*, 40, 238. *See also* Indonesian state culture
Age and prestige hierarchy, 31, 49–50
Agriculture and horticulture, 43–45
Allegory, 233–237
Alu', 24, 26
Amang, 241
Ambe Assi', 136, 185, 207, 260, 269
Ambe Deppa', 259–260, 267
Ambe Dido, *babalako* at Minanga, 207, 208 (photo), 260, 269
Ambe Ka'du, 63–64
Ambe Lusa, 6–7
Ambe Ma'dose, 178–179
Ambe Oma, 262
Ambe Siama', 233–236
Ambe Sope, *topuppu* at Salutabang, 95 (photo), 98 (photo), 103, 104, 210
Ambe Tasi', 209
Ambe Teppu, 7–10, 18, 85, 130, 233–236, 260–263, 272
Ambe Tibo, 134
Amin, Entji', 74
Andaya, Leonard Y., 298n.16

Cosmography: and exchange, 77–78; and ideas about death, 56, 105; and identity of headhunters' victim, 68; as idiom of regional political order, 33; as topographic transcoding of political affect, 105–106; and violence, 68–69

Coville, Elizabeth, 304n.12

Crapanzano, Vincent, 199

Culler, Jonathan, 299n.30

Cultural politics: and control of the past, 2, 15, 99–100, 102–104, 134–136, 192, 232–237, 238–263, 267; and the discursive construction of violence, xi–xii; of mourning and catharsis, 102–105, 132; and oppositional collaboration, 239; and reactive objectification, 239; of religious pluralism and conflict, 238–272; of song interpretation, 232–237. *See also* Indonesian state culture; Mappurondo enclave at Bambang

Cultural schema, 14, 294n.10

Dadeko traditional dance troupe, 254

Davison, Julian, 297n.6, 299n.27

Debata (spirits): connection with rituals, 54–58; *debata bisu muane,* 163; *debata bisu baine,* 182; *Debata Tometampa,* 262; *Debata Totibojongan,* 44; guardianship of rice crop, 34, 44; and place, 6; vows and obligations to, 67, 130, 163–164. *See also* *Ma'paisun; Mualu' ulunna;* Trance (*diala debata*)

de Certeau, Michel, 212

de Jongh, D., 71

Dessibulo, 203

Dipandebarani ("feting the valorous"), 161–184

Dipokadai mâne (sacrificial message), 163–164

Dirks, Nicholas B., 10, 16, 293n.16

Dormeier, J. J., 298n.12

Downs, R. E., 63, 105–106, 255, 298nn.12, 14

Drake, Richard Allen, 9, 264, 265

Dress, 111, 143, 164

Drums and drumming: described, 6, 141, 142 (photo); *pabuno* rhythm, 141, 146, 164, 173; and political authority, 143. *See also* Tabus

Durkheim, Emile, 300n.11

Dutch, in colonial period: administration and mission, 36–39; arrival in Bambang, 36–37; historical record about regional headhunting practices, 60–61

Economy and subsistence (in Bambang): coffee, 44–45; decline of hunting and gathering, 43; gardens, 44; general remarks, 43–45; rice harvest and impact on ritual, 44–45

Editions: and interpretation, 2–3; and situatedness of *pangngae,* 15

Eley, Geoff, 16, 293n.6

Emotion and politics, 300nn.6, 9. *See also* *Pangngae* and emotions; Political affect

Emulation and mimetic desire, 138, 139, 140–141, 148, 173–174, 182, 184

Entextualization, 13, 305n.4

Envy: in culture of terror, 304n.4; and mappurondo social hierarchy, 138–141, 145, 147–148, 150, 184; in *pangngae,* 134–185. *See also* *Pangngae* and emotions

Erb, Maribeth, 9, 264

Errington, Shelly, 10, 63, 73, 295n.15, 296n.24

Ethnic groups and ethnicity in Sulawesi, 26–30

Ethnography: cultural politics of, 9, 294n.12; and notes on research in Sulawesi, 18–20; and practice theory, 16; as revisionary task, xi–xii, 18–20; text-centered, 16

Fabian, Johannes, 3, 14, 15, 16, 209, 231, 297n.1, 306n.14

Fachruddin, 243–245

Feldman, Allen, 2, 300n.5

Feldman, Carol Fleisher, 293n.2

Fertility. *See Pangngae* and prosperity

Festivity. *See Pangngae* festivity

Finnegan, Ruth, 194

Fish, Stanley, 15, 236

Flutes. *See Tambolâ*

Folena, Lucia, 193

Foster, Brian L., 78

Fox, James J., 13, 305n.3

Fox, Richard G., 293n.6

Freeman, Derek, 64–65, 297n.6, 298n.20, 299n.27

Galestin, W. A. C., 74

Geertz, Clifford, 9, 12, 46, 239, 301n.5, 307n.1

Dipokadai mane; *Kelonoson*; *Ma'denna*;
Mua'da; *Mualu' ulunna*; *Ma'paisun*;
Marrara topangngae anna tambolâ;
Sumengo cycle at Saludengen; *Sumengo
tomatua*; *Umbua' tambolâ*
Lord, Albert B., 193, 305n.3
Ludruk, 15
Lutz, Catherine A., 300n.9

MacDougall, William, 63
McGann, Jerome J., 14, 15, 17, 20, 297n.2
McKinley, Robert, 13, 63, 68–69, 86, 91,
    105–106, 193, 299n.2, 300n.7
Macknight, C. C., 75
Ma'denna (song taunting the head), 79–82,
    94, 96, 158–159, 166
Mahhaha banne, 202
Ma'kainda-indai, 260
Makassar, 27, 30, 74
Makatonan, Als., 246–250, 307n.9
Malangngi', 102, 149–150, 304n.5
Mama Amang, 241
Mamasa, 27, 37, 39, 71, 72, 249
Mambi, 19, 20, 21, 22 (map), 28–29, 32–
    36, 241–245, 267
Mamose speeches, 126, 173–182, 304n.11;
    and calls for emulation and solidarity,
    180–181; as dance and spectacle, 242;
    about ethnographer and mappurondo
    tradition, 179–180; and Indonesian citi-
    zenship, 258–259; and mappurondo tra-
    dition, 176–181; older speechmakers,
    176–181; photo, 178; young speech-
    makers, 174–176
Mamuju, 37, 71
Mandadung, Arianus, 73, 251–256, 308n.11
Mandar: and *ada' mate*, 28; awareness of
    pangngae, 60, 84–85; ethnic designation,
    27; political history, 70, 73–88, 295n.7;
    precolonial *adat* territories, 29 (map), 30–33;
    and *siri'*, 298n.15; social and political ori-
    gins, 30–33; as trance language, 213–
    215, 305n.6; as victims in *pangngae*, 78–
    85. *See also* Highland-lowland ethnic rela-
    tions; *Pitu Ba'bana Binanga*
Ma'paisun (presenting a sacrificial offering),
    65–66, 67, 83, 92, 93, 166, 168–171,
    298n.21
Ma'patuhu'i botto, 209
Mappurondo communities in Mambi, 307n.4
Mappurondo enclave at Bambang, 21–58; at-

titude toward Mandar, 102; civil adminis-
    tration (1982–85), 42–43; commemora-
    tion, ritual, and polity, 186–200; crisis in
    remembering ritual practices, 187, 257–
    258; cultural autonomy, 9, 10, 15, 258,
    264–272; and cultural politics, xi–xii, 9;
    death of elder as wound to community,
    178, 198; defined, 7; demoralization of,
    136, 185; efforts to cooperate with gov-
    ernment, 267; efforts for formal recogni-
    tion of *ada' mappurondo*, 41, 259–260,
    268–269; egalitarian character, 137, 140;
    epithets for, 25, 265; exogenous sources
    of power, 305n.5; foundational discourse,
    30–33, 306n.16; gender relations, 50–54;
    as guardian of *pemali appa' randanna*
    and *ada' mappurondo*, 271; as "house
    society," 295n.15; and Indonesian state,
    41, 184, 271; key events (1983–85),
    201–205; key events (1985–94), 264–
    272; kinship, 41, 45–47; male peer poli-
    tics, 140, 161; marginality, xi, 266; mar-
    riage, 47–48; political disenfranchisement,
    40; population figures, 43; postharvest ac-
    tivity, 110–111; prosperity in early 1990s,
    270–271; relations with Christians and
    Muslims, 24, 245–246; as a religious mi-
    nority, 24; and secrecy, 259, 302n.25,
    303n.2, 307n.3; settlement pattern, 24,
    42–43; shamanism, 297n.27; social, polit-
    ical, and demographic decline, 40, 234;
    social and economic data by village, 281–
    285; social hierarchy, 49–54, 140, 303n.1,
    307n.10; social life, 41–58; ToIssilita' and
    ToSalu subgroups, 35–36, 41, 201–205.
    See also Mappurondo ritual life; *Pangngae*
Mappurondo ritual life, 54–57; differences
    between ToIssilita' and ToSalu, 55,
    296n.26; display of radical gender differ-
    ences, 57; and historical change, 57;
    minor rites, 56; *morara*, 55, 296nn.23,
    25; *pa'bannetauan*, 54, 56; *pa'bisuam
    baine* and *pa'bisuam muane*, 54–55;
    pangngae, 54–55; *parri'* ceremonies 55,
    296n.26; *patomatea*n, 54; *patotibojongan*,
    54–55; *pealloan*, 54; sexual division of rit-
    ual activities, 55–56, 270–271; *ukusam
    botto* and *ukusam banua*, 54–55. *See also
    Pemali appa' randanna*
Maringngangi', 125
Markets, 36, 45, 39

139, 141, 143, 301n.20, 302n.27, 303n.31, 307n.5

Pangngae, versions of: as "editions," 15–16, 17, 202, 260; change and variability in, 201–237; Christian representations, 238–239, 245–263; *mahhaha banne*, 202; *ma'kainda-indai*, 260; *malampa sali-sali*, 130; *ma'patuhu'i botto*, 130; *maringngangi'*, 125; Muslim representations, 240–245; ToIssilita' practices, 101, 205–207, 214–233, 260, 301nn.18, 19; ToSalu practices, 101, 130, 207–214, 299n.1; *ulleppa'i samajanna*, 130; *umpokasalle kalena*, 130, 140; *undantai kalena*, 130; *untauam bahata*, 101; *untungka'i botto*, 101

Pangngae and commemoration, 16, 17, 186–200

Pangngae and communal mourning, 16, 17, 103–104, 110–128, 133, 269

Pangngae and emotions: catharsis, 17, 104–110, 112, 118; envy and mimetic desire, 17, 137–173, 184, 199; erotic discourse, 150, 152; and nostalgia, 196, 233–234; personal grief, 103–105, 123–128; political affect, 17, 104, 118, 127, 132

Pangngae and gender relations: gender hierarchy, 112, 115, 133–185, 191, 211–212, 217–232, 255, 270; male peer politics, 134–185; rhetoric and exemplary image of manhood, 16, 17, 134–185, 199, 234; sexual potency of men, 161, 181, 304n.6; in *sumengo* interpretation, 234–237, 306n.16; women in, 65, 112, 115–116, 117, 120, 139, 143, 146–155, 162 (photo), 166 (photo), 182–183, 190–191, 211–214, 218–232, 234, 301n.17, 302n.26

Pangngae and headhunters: cohort of headhunters, 112, 114; and headhunters' *sumanga'*, 63–64, 302n.28; headhunting journeys, 103, 114–115, 120, 139; motivations to become headhunter, 128, 139, 197–199; and vows, 17, 67, 128–133, 163–164

Pangnage and prosperity, 64–66, 100, 199

Pangngae and signs of modernity: absence of trophy head, 64, 205; absence of weapons, 90, 103; as aesthetic reformulation of violence, 198; as allegory of represen-

tational violence, 193–194, 195; Christian history of, 247–248; equated with Eucharist, 247; and Indonesian state culture, 102–103, 197, 238–272; ironies and incongruities in, 59, 90, 100, 195, 198; and problem of cathartic violence, 104–110; and writing, 207–211, 217–232, 237

Pangngae and the grotesque, 91–96, 99–100

Pangngae as political gesture: as act of resistance, 70, 88–90, 99–100, 237, 258, 267, 271; as allegory of contemporary struggle, 99, 267; and claims to autonomous history, 60, 69–70, 99, 104, 195, 233, 234, 236, 237; as commemorative reproduction of mappurondo polity, 9, 58, 96–99, 134–185, 186–200; demonization and debasement of victim, 65–66, 91, 116–118, 298n.10; and domination of ethnic rival, 16, 65–100, 231–237; as effort to maintain cultural autonomy and continuity, 15, 258, 264–272; as exemplary violence, 92, 96, 187, 194; and objectification of victim, 92; and official order, 197, 266

Pangngae in historical perspective: absence in mission and civil records, 70–72; history of, 59–100, 102; at Mambi, 241, 295n.9; Mandar complicity in, 84–85, 247–248; masked by trade, 82–84, 89; and partner trade communities, 83; and polemics of pre-colonial regional exchange, 69–91; and politics of history, 60, 69–70, 99, 233, 236, 237; and theft of goods, 83, 88

Pangngae festivity: and adorned speech, 164, 189–190; and adornment, 17, 143–145, 164; and celebration, 141–152, 164–167, 182–184, 188–190; food prestations for headhunters, 167, 171–172; jewelry used in, 143–144

Pannell, Sandra, 9, 264, 265

Papa' Amang, 241–243

Papa Ati, xiv, 19, 90, 267

Papa' Suri', 242

Parisada Hindu Dharma, 41, 259, 295n.11

Parry, Jonathan, 199

Patomatean, 54, 111

Patotibojongan, 54, 110

Patunru, Abd. Razak Daeng, 73, 74

Paulus, 261–262

Peacock, James L., 15, 301n.15

214, 218–232, 234; political role in mappurondo enclave, 31, 52–53, 134, 271
Wona Kaka, 11
Writing and reading in *pangngae,* 207–211,
217–232, 237

Yanagisako, Sylvia, 296n.21
Yates, Francis A., 193
Yengoyan, Aram A., 14, 187
Zerner, Charles, 304n.9

Designer:	UC Press Staff
Compositor:	Prestige Typography
Text:	10/13
Display:	Galliard
Printer:	Edwards Brothers, Inc.
Binder:	Edwards Brothers, Inc.